THE OBSOLETE PARADIGM OF A HISTORICAL JESUS

THE OBSOLETE PARADIGM OF A HISTORICAL JESUS

Richard Carrier, PhD

Pitchstone Publishing
Durham, North Carolina

Pitchstone Publishing
Durham, North Carolina
www.pitchstonebooks.com

Printed in the United States of America

Library of Congress Cataloging-in-Publication Data

Names: Carrier, Richard, 1969- author
Title: The obsolete paradigm of a historical Jesus / Richard Carrier, PhD.
Description: Durham, North Carolina : Pitchstone Publishing, [2025] | Includes bibliographical references and index. | Summary: "Ten years have passed since peer reviewed studies began questioning the historical existence of Jesus. This study surveys what has happened since, and how biblical studies has continued moving toward that conclusion even while attempting to avoid it. By exploring newly published takes on Docetism, the aims and sources of the Gospels, the interpretation of the Epistles, and the logic of historical reasoning, the old paradigm of biblical studies is here argued to be obsolete. Too much work is being built on the assumption that Jesus existed, and that something about him can be recovered, and this is leading them to false conclusions about all those subjects. Historians need to rethink their entire paradigm, and begin studying the Bible anew on the assumption that there was no such Jesus to recover. It is here shown how that approach will produce important new knowledge of early Christian history and the interpretation of the New Testament"— Provided by publisher.
Identifiers: LCCN 2025020481 | ISBN 9781634312820 paperback | ISBN 9781634312837 ebook
Subjects: LCSH: Jesus Christ—Historicity | Jesus Christ—History of doctrines—Early church, ca. 30-600 | Josephus, Flavius | Tacitus, Cornelius | Bible. New Testament—Criticism, interpretation, etc. | Docetism | History—Methodology
Classification: LCC BT303.2 .C363 2025
LC record available at https://lccn.loc.gov/2025020481

Cover image: Head of Christ, *a 1648 oil-on-panel painting by Rembrandt*

To Earl Doherty,
for solving the Jesus Puzzle.

Notice: Except where stated, quotations of Greek texts in this volume are derived from the online Thesaurus Linguae Graecae maintained by the University of California at Irvine (at stephanus.tlg.uci.edu). My gratitude for their achievement and service is beyond words.

Contents

1

Questioning the Historicity of Jesus Ten Years On

It has been ten years since I published the first peer reviewed study in nearly a hundred years on whether Christianity actually began with or without a real historical Jesus.[1] For most of the 20th century and into the 21st many books doubting or defending the historicity of Jesus appeared; mostly inept, and none under peer review. Meanwhile, actual peer-reviewed studies of a historical Jesus generally assumed historicity, at most spending a few pages on why, but never conducting anything like a comprehensive study of the question. The last to have accomplished anything like that was Shirley Jackson Case a century ago.[2] And his results are wholly obsolete now, even by mainstream standards.[3]

The subject had been touched on a few years before me, in Thomas Brodie's (presumably) final memoir (for which he was forced into si-

[1] Richard Carrier, *On the Historicity of Jesus: Why We Might Have Reason for Doubt* (Sheffield-Phoenix, 2014; rev. ed. 2023); I later published a pop-market summary (with a concordance to the formal study) as *Jesus from Outer Space: What the Earliest Christians Really Believed about Christ* (Pitchstone, 2020).

[2] Shirley Jackson Case, *The Historicity of Jesus: A Criticism of the Contention that Jesus Never Lived* (University of Chicago Press, 1912; 2nd ed. 1928).

[3] Carrier, *Historicity*, 52, 592–94.

lenced retirement).[4] But he did not attempt a comprehensive study of the evidence for or against a historical Jesus, nor did he offer any alternative model for how Christianity could have begun without one.[5] By the time Brodie published I was already well into a privately funded postdoc research program on exactly those questions, begun immediately after receiving my PhD in ancient history from Columbia University in 2008.[6] I then released its firstfruits the same year as Brodie, a peer-reviewed study of the methodology required.[7]

Subsequent to then publishing my completed results in *On the Historicity of Jesus* two years later, another peer-reviewed study of the matter was published five years after that, by Raphael Lataster (a PhD graduate in religious studies from the University of Sydney), to examine the competing merits of my results and those of recent popular market attempts to defend the historicity of Jesus (expanding on a prior series of studies).[8] Lataster found large disparities in quality of method and argument, concluding that doubting historicity is the more plausible position. The

[4] Thomas Brodie, *Beyond the Quest for the Historical Jesus: Memoir of a Discovery* (Sheffield-Phoenix, 2012). On his fate: Patrick Counihan, "Irish Priest Disciplined after Claims Jesus Never Existed in Controversial Book," *IrishCentral* (21 January 2013) at tinyurl.com/36duh6fk (on how to use the TinyURL protocol see Bibliography); and Bernard Treacy, "Official Dominican Response to a Controversial Book," *Doctrine & Life* 64.5 (May-June 2014), 2–4.

[5] As noted by his critics, including an entire issue of *Doctrine & Life* 63.6 (July-August 2013) and a review by Jeremy Corley in *Irish Theological Quarterly* 79.2 (2014), 177–94.

[6] For the background to my postdoc research grant and how I came to study this subject, see Carrier, *Historicity*, xi–3.

[7] Richard Carrier, *Proving History: Bayes's Theorem and the Quest for the Historical Jesus* (Prometheus Books, 2012). Prometheus (now an imprint of Rowman & Littlefield) is not an academic press, but I mandated in my contract that this book be subject to peer review before publication, by a professor of mathematics and a professor of biblical studies, chosen by Prometheus.

[8] Raphael Lataster, *Questioning the Historicity of Jesus: Why a Philosophical Analysis Elucidates the Historical Discourse* (Brill, 2019); with a preface by James Crossley. His previous works leading to this: "Book Review: Richard Carrier: *On the Historicity of Jesus*," *Journal of Religious History* 38.4 (2014), 614–16; "The Fourth Quest: A Critical Analysis of the Recent Literature on Jesus' (a)Historicity," *Literature & Aesthetics* 24.1 (June 2014), 1–28; "Questioning the Plausibility of Jesus Ahistoricity Theories—A Brief Pseudo-Bayesian Metacritique of the Sources," *Intermountain West Journal of Religious Studies* 6.1 (2015), 63–96; "Bayesian Reasoning: Criticising the 'Criteria of Authenticity' and Calling for a Review of Biblical Criticism," *Journal of Alternative Perspectives in the Social Sciences* 5.2 (2012), 271–93.

pop-market cases for historicity that Lataster examined, by Bart Ehrman and Maurice Casey, appear not to have been significantly peer reviewed, and were completed and published before my study, and thus could not have responded to it.[9] And still to this day no such response has been published. A handful of critical articles have attempted something of a rebuttal, but they oddly avoid discussing my (or Lataster's) actual evidence and arguments, deploying rhetoric, disinformation, and apologetics instead (as I'll demonstrate in chapter three). Nor do they offer anything like a complete analysis sufficient to settle the matter. Yet there have already been numerous attempts to chastise the field for this state of affairs.[10]

It would seem academia holds no evident interest in actually examining, much less rebutting, our actual findings. Which any objective observer will find disappointing. We have all been hoping for a 'best case' for historicity to appear, one that responded to our findings rather than evaded them. The field of Jesus studies very much needs this. Without that, we have a field where the historicity of its central character has been found dubious by the only comprehensive peer-reviewed studies of the question in a century. Normally, when a new result is multiply corroborated, and no countermanding result produced, a field would shift its consensus to the new result. If scholars of the historical Jesus really want to justify their refusal to accept these new findings, then they need to

[9] Bart Ehrman, *Did Jesus Exist? The Historical Argument for Jesus of Nazareth* (HarperOne, 2012); Maurice Casey, *Jesus: Evidence and Argument or Mythicist Myths?* (T&T Clark, 2014).

[10] For example: Petteri Nieminen, Juuso Loikkanen, Esko Ryökäs, and Anne-Mari Mustonen, "Nature of Evidence in Religion and Natural Science," *Theology and Science* 18.3 (2020), 448–74 (467); Justin Meggitt, "'More Ingenious than Learned'? Examining the Quest for the Non-Historical Jesus," *New Testament Studies* 65.4 (2019), 443–60; Tom Dykstra, "Ehrman and Brodie on Whether Jesus Existed: A Cautionary Tale about the State of Biblical Scholarship," *Journal of the Orthodox Center for the Advancement of Biblical Studies* 8.1 (2015), 1–32; Philip Davies, "Did Jesus Exist?" *The Bible and Interpretation* (August 2012) at bibleinterp.arizona.edu/opeds/dav368029. See also: Fernando Bermejo-Rubio, Richard Carrier, and Franco Tommasi (with a contribution from Robert M. Price), *Jesus: Militant or Nonexistent? Two Views Compared* (Philosophy Press, 2025), which is an updated English edition of the original: *Gesù resistente Gesù inesistente: Due visioni a confronto* (Manni, 2022); and Richard Miller's foreword to John Loftus and Robert Price (eds.), *Varieties of Jesus Mythicism* (Hypatia Press, 2022). See also remarks throughout Fernando Bermejo-Rubio, *La invención de Jesús de Nazaret: Historia, ficción, historiografía* (Akal, 2023).

produce a proper defense of doing that.

Until then, all I can do is keep the field updated on where my and Lataster's results stand. To that end it is crucial for the reader to know that the theory of Christian origins without a real Jesus that has twice now been found to be plausible under peer review does not resemble most of the ideas found on the internet or in amateur conspiracy books. Of those I have long been and remain an unrelenting critic.[11] Lataster and I do not imagine Christianity was a secret fabrication of the Roman government or a Gnostic astrotheological cult hidden by a global Church conspiracy. Our theory involves no conspiracies at all, just the ordinary course of legendary development and propaganda documented for other religions that historicized their myths, and documented extensively for early Christianity even by mainstream scholars. So anyone who claims we are advancing a conspiracy theory is thereby demonstrating that they read neither of our studies, as both explicitly reject any conspiracy model of Christian origins and development—so much so in my case that I even put this fact in my study's index.[12]

In our model, Christianity began with a sincere belief in a historical Jesus—in the same sense as it began with a sincere belief in a historical Satan. Neither man's origin story involved visiting Earth. Satan's rebellion took place in outer space. It was believed to be historical nonetheless. Our proposal is that Christ's reversal of the spiritual and cosmic effects of Satan's rebellion, by becoming mortal and undergoing a self-sacrificial death (Philippians 2:5–11), also took place in outer space (or, perhaps, if on Earth at all, then in some distant realm beyond human civilization, like the Garden of Eden in some versions of Jewish lore at the time). That this had happened was then learned of through revelations (whether dreams or visions, or both; and whether real or pretended, or both) and the finding of hidden messages in scripture (in the manner of a Hebrew pesher), exactly as Paul says in Romans 16:25–26: "my gospel and the preaching of Jesus Christ" is "according to the revelation of the mystery

---

[11] See: Richard Carrier, "Book Review: *Varieties of Jesus Mythicism* Edited by John W. Loftus and Robert M. Price," *Socio-Historical Examination of Religion and Ministry* 4.1 (2022), 171–92, and: Richard Carrier, "The Problem with Varieties of Jesus Mythicism" (8 October 2022) at richardcarrier.info/archives/21352.

[12] Carrier, *Historicity*, 683 ('conspiracy theories'); cf. Lataster, *Questioning*, 4, 91, 179n22, 327, 444.

which was kept secret for long ages but is now disclosed, and through the prophetic writings is made known to all nations" (RSV). It was only a generation later that a historicization of this cosmic hero as a Galilean preacher came into anyone's mind—indeed, that idea likely began with the author of Mark, possibly in response to the existential impact of the Jewish War. The other Gospels were just redactions, embellishments, and rewrites of Mark's contrivance. Within a few generations of that, however, by natural selection or historical happenstance (or both), the original conception was replaced by a more literal adherence to the new one.[13]

Exactly this sequence of events characterized the Melanesian cargo cults of the early twentieth century; likewise, the modern legend of a Roswell flying saucer complete with alien autopsies.[14] The historicization of other heroes and mythic events often followed the same model in antiquity. Many gods and heroes were only celestial or mystical spirits until eventually converted into historical persons complete with biographies and even kin, struggles, and genealogies. One example of this process even appears within Christianity itself: that the 'Risen Jesus' was believed in on a basis of mere revelation and scripture is pretty well agreed by secular historians today; and yet this original version of events was completely eclipsed by absurdist narratives of a Jesus physically rising from and departing his grave (Mark 16, Matthew 28) to then have dinner parties with his 'disciples', for days or even weeks (Luke 24:36–53, Acts 1:1–11, John 20:1–21:25). None of the original narratives survive. They were erased by this instead. All extant narratives are unanimous in supporting that fake history over the real one. Perhaps a fossil of it is preserved under layers of legendary development in Acts' many contradictory accounts of the visitation to Paul.[15] But corresponding accounts for the other apostles are lost to history. Did this require a conspiracy? Or was it just the organic outcome of Christianity's sociopolitical development?

Objective historians today must admit there was no resurrected Jesus—no animated corpse rose from the grave to hang out and have din-

[13] For a description of this process, see Carrier, *Outer Space*, 152–70 (expanding my technical brief in Carrier, *Historicity*, 608–10).

[14] For both examples: Carrier, *Historicity*, 9–11, 159–63, 248–52.

[15] Acts 9:3–9, 22:6–10, 26:12–18; cf. Acts 22:17-21, 23:11.

ner with his followers. That man is not historical.[16] Yet he became so, within a mere generation or two. And the original, *mythical* version of him (who was entirely imaginary, as Paul reveals in Galatians 1:11–16 and 1 Corinthians 15:3–8) was erased. But if a 'historical' Risen Jesus could be invented, and that version narratively erase the original (the one of mere fleeting dreams and visions), then so could a 'historical' Jesus *prior* to that be invented, and that version narratively erase the original. We cannot allow the one sequence of events to have happened (as plainly it did), while denying the other could. The question thus falls to the evidence: does the preponderance of evidence argue more for the traditional account, or this other? Of course the historicity of the *risen* Jesus can be discarded as a matter of science; whereas the historicity of the Jesus prior would be entirely plausible. But other than that, the evidence for them is the same, in every methodologically pertinent respect.

Making that case was entirely the occupation of my original study, and Lataster's evaluation of it. So I won't revisit the entire case here. You can find a complete survey of all the pertinent evidence in our peer-reviewed studies (or, if you prefer to read a simpler brief of it first, begin with my popular summary, *Jesus from Outer Space*, which concludes with a concordance to the formal study).

Here, I will only address where things have landed so far, ten years on. The book you are reading now is in lieu of rewriting (so as to update) *Historicity*. That already well serves as the grounding study, and by covering every necessary subject was already overlong. So it does not need to be lengthened further. Instead, where I would have updated *Historicity* I will make mention here. Then I will expand with more evidence and argument on every subject it introduced, demonstrating why historicity really is an obsolete paradigm now, and that we need to replace it with a different fundamental theory and approach.

I will begin in chapter two with an update on what's changed or developed since I published *Historicity* ten years before now (and Lataster

[16] For the status of that debate see: Carl Stecher, Craig Blomberg, Richard Carrier, and Peter Williams, *Resurrection: Faith or Fact? A Scholars' Debate Between a Skeptic and a Christian* (Pitchstone, 2019), esp. 195–219, with Richard Carrier, "Why the Resurrection is Unbelievable," *The Christian Delusion: Why Faith Fails* (ed. John Loftus; Prometheus, 2010), 291–315, and Jonathan M.S. Pearce, *The Resurrection: A Critical Examination of the Easter Story* (Onus, 2021); which prove unhistorical such faith-driven apologetics as the two volumes of Gary Habermas, *On the Resurrection* (B&H Academic, 2024).

published *Questioning* five years before now), followed by a survey of critical responses to our work in chapter three. Then in chapter four I will survey the most common arguments that continue to be advanced to defend the historicity of Jesus, which were *not* made in response to our findings; and then explain the significance of this to the plausibility of historicity (it doesn't look good). I will follow that in chapter five with a review of Bayesian methodology and why all sound arguments must conform to it, and how to build or critique a Bayesian argument. I will then apply those principles in chapter six, with examples of something I thought would be obvious but evidently was not: why it is that historians are convinced of *other* ancient persons' historicity, and how (and why) the evidence for Jesus does not actually meet that bar.

Then in chapter seven I establish a conclusion I only briefly suggested in my original study: the questionable status of Docetism as really a thing in antiquity, and how this affects the evidence for Jesus. Claiming 'Docetism' is still sometimes used by champions of a terrestrial Jesus to dismiss evidence for a strand of Christianity that seems indeed to have objected to the notion of there actually being such a person. I aver the modern invention of 'Docetism' is thus, like Gnosticism before it, a grave academic mistake that set scholars on completely the wrong trajectory in understanding early Christianity. In fact, the evidence suggests there were entire Christian factions denying the terrestrial historicity of Jesus.

The remainder of this book will address the best arguments attempted in defense of a historical Jesus. These are the three arguments left that at least acknowledge the findings of *Historicity* and *Questioning*, and thus can at least be described as attempts at responding to them. So I will evaluate the responses historicist scholars have attempted in order to rescue these arguments from our original critiques, while presenting new evidence and scholarship bolstering our original conclusions.

To that end, first, in chapter eight, contrary to what many historians maintain, I explain why references to Jesus having been a human being of flesh and blood in general, and the scion of David in particular (as Paul announces in Romans 1:3 and 15:12, for example), cannot argue for a historical Jesus, because Paul is just as expected to say and believe these things even if he had no idea of Jesus ever having been on Earth.[17]

---

[17] Building on Carrier, *Historicity*, 575–77, and Lataster, *Questioning*, 267, 421–24.

Second, in chapter nine, contrary to what many historians maintain, I explain why a single reference to Jesus having been 'born of a woman' (as Paul announces in Galatians 4:4) cannot argue for a historical Jesus because Paul is there engaged in an allegorical argument from start to finish (from Galatians 3 through 4), and outright says the mothers he is referring to are not meant literally (Galatians 4:24). So even if Paul believed Jesus had an ordinary mother (and was then almost certainly a real historical person), Paul is not discussing that fact of him there, and so this remark cannot be used as evidence of it.[18]

Then in chapter ten I address what remains—really—the only argument for a historical Jesus: the claim that Paul knew his biological brothers.[19] Attempts have been made to respond to my and Lataster's arguments regarding this, too, and even though they all ignore what we argue, it warrants renewed treatment, since this remains the only thing close to a 'good' argument historicists have, yet new studies supporting us have now been published. I will demonstrate—again—that it is beyond question that all baptized Christians regarded themselves as Brothers of the Lord, and that numerous mainstream experts now agree with me on that. The earliest Christians believed this to such an extant that this may even have been their name for themselves as a movement before the terms 'Christian' or 'Nazorian' were coined and stuck. But whether that was the case or not, the fact (and it is *a fact*, not a theory) that 'Brothers of the Lord' could mean simply 'Christian' must be seriously taken into account when attempting to argue that Paul's use of the phrase ever meant, instead, biological kin of Jesus. That cannot simply be 'assumed' anymore. It has to be argued. And so far, the arguments made for it are not very good.

Finally, in chapter eleven I survey the aforementioned chapters and conclude with where we need to go from here. I believe the entire field of Jesus studies needs to be reconceived and redirected. We should no longer be exhausting energy, ink, and paper trying to 'get at' the original 'historical' Jesus, but instead we should be pursuing the contexts, experiences, and motives of those first claiming to have 'seen' him, and the

---

[18] Building on Carrier, *Historicity*, 577–82, and Lataster, *Questioning*, 76, 265–70, 423–24.

[19] Building on Carrier, *Historicity*, 582–92, and Lataster, *Questioning*, 75, 100, 309–21, 424–27.

rhetorical and mythical purposes of the tales later told of him, including 'accounts' of what he is supposed to have said. We will never really understand why and how Christianity began, and evolved in the particular ways it did, until we understand that there wasn't any Jesus at the heart of it all, but a kind of shamanic class of 'apostles' with a particular apocalyptic agenda, followed by elite auteurs constructing a mythology for this new superhero and his deeds and teachings for their own particular ends. We should be studying the Jesus myth and cult in the same way we study the myth and cult of any other mythological savior figure of antiquity, from Moses or Michael to Romulus or Dionysus, even Ned Ludd or John Frum.

Which is why this debate matters so fundamentally to the field of Jesus studies.[20] If Jesus did not really exist, if Christianity began and developed anything like Lataster and I suggest, then we have been exhausting immense resources on futile errands. A complete paradigm shift is needed in the goals and projects of our field. Every attempt to reconstruct the 'real' historical Jesus must be abandoned, and all that attention turned instead toward reconstructing what the Gospels' authors intentions were behind every story about him that they invented or altered; as well as what Paul and his epistolary contemporaries were actually talking about, and where their ideas were actually coming from.[21]

If it was visions and dreams or the 'inspired' discovery of hidden meanings in scripture—as Paul actually says—then their subconscious was the wellspring; and that brings cultural, historico-political, and psychological origins back into play as explanations of their thrust and content. And if data about Jesus was coming almost entirely from scripture, rather than recent biographical events, then we need to put our focus on reconstructing the original Christian pesher: where did they find in scripture all the ideas they related (such as, for example, the crucifixion), and how did they weave and connect them together to produce their specific beliefs? Indeed, what books were they even regarding as scrip-

---

[20] Carrier, *Historicity*, 616–18; Lataster, *Questioning*, 448–63.

[21] Regarding Paul's 'epistolary contemporaries', I argue in *Historicity* (as others have) that 1 Clement and Hebrews (and possibly even James, Jude, and 1 Peter) all date prior to the Jewish War and thus from Paul's generation (1 Clement: 308–15; Hebrews: 538–40; James, Jude, and 1 Peter: 528–31). This position has since been strengthened (see next chapter).

ture for this purpose? And what did their manuscripts of them say?[22] But even more than that, for everything then changes. That we must completely reconceive ancient debates about what modern scholars have misconstrued as 'docetism' already by itself shows how a new paradigm completely alters our entire accounting of Christianity's history. And that is just one example. Our understanding of how and why Christianity began, its precedents and inspirations, the problems of its moment that it was hoped to solve, and what drove its early success (insofar as it can be described as successful then), all need to be rethought and explored anew.

The historicity of Jesus therefore can no longer continue as a dogmatic assumption, defended only with weak or dubious apologetics. It cannot just be flippantly maintained by circular appeals to 'the consensus'. To the contrary, it needs to be firmly established or else certainty in it abandoned. And if the former is where we should go, it needs to actually be done. And this book provides the blueprint for doing that. But if the latter is where we should go, then the rest of our field's paradigms and goals must go with it. And this book also provides the blueprint for doing that.[23]

Instead, the field seems to be contriving reasons to avoid the debate altogether. As an example, in a recent volume on the historicity of Jesus, the subject of historicity *never even comes up*, it is simply blindly assumed—except for a single paragraph buried within that insists more attention needs to be paid to this. And yet no one in that entire volume

[22] On re-recognizing the problem of the first Christians regarding a different set of books as scripture than precisely we have, and their texts of the ones we do have saying different things as well, see Carrier, *Historicity*, 88–92, and now Richard Horsley, "Can Study of the Historical Jesus Escape its Typographical Captivity?," *Journal for the Study of the Historical Jesus* 19 (2021), 265–329.

[23] For a more general point similar, a must-read is the brief essay of Lester Grabbe, "The Case of the Corrupting Consensus," in *Between Evidence and Ideology: Essays on the History of Ancient Israel Read at the Joint Meeting of the Society for Old Testament Study and the Oud Testamentisch Werkgezelschap Lincoln, July 2009* (ed. Bob Becking and Lester Grabbe; Brill, 2010), 83–92; likewise, Burton Mack, *A Myth of Innocence: Mark and Christian Origins* (Fortress, 1988), 3–9, which Jacob Neusner considered important enough to republish in Neusner (ed.), *The Christian and Judaic Invention of History* (Oxford University 1990), 19–28. See also the previously cited scholars chastising the field's dogmatism concerning historicity (Meggitt, Davies, et al.).

pays any attention to it—not even the author calling for it![24] Another example is the background to this very book. It was peer-reviewed by an academic press. Indeed that review took six months. And in the end, the reviewers found no specific errors of fact or logic in it (not a single one). They recommended against its publication solely for the strange reasons that it makes no new contributions to the field, is too popular in style, and won't be "interesting for readers within the discipline of biblical studies" (or for even more trivial reasons like that they just 'didn't like' its findings or the order of its chapters). You can now judge for yourself if these objections are relevant or even true. And then ask yourself, "Why are these the excuses being made to discourage their peers from reading it?"

[24] James Crossley and Chris Keith (eds.), *The Next Quest for the Historical Jesus* (Eerdmans, 2024); see: Justin Meggitt, "The Resurrection and Comparative Microhistory," 507–27 (508), who doesn't even mention a single peer-reviewed study of it (neither Carrier nor Lataster).

2

Updates, Developments, Trendline

First I must summarize developments in this subject in the published literature over the last decade, starting with my own, then moving to the contributions of others (and finally critics, in the next chapter). Because any further debate of this subject must take into account what has been published since my original study.

What I've Published

Since releasing *On the Historicity of Jesus* in 2014 I identified an array of typos and minor errors in it. Almost all of them were corrected in an official Revised Edition of 2023, which retained the same pagination (since the changes and corrections were not substantial). A list of corrections or updates still needed is maintained online.[1] My other peer-reviewed publications on this subject are already referenced in the original edition of *Historicity*.[2] Other articles in development I will discuss as they become

[1] See Richard Carrier, "Errata for *On the Historicity of Jesus*" (30 September 2015) at richardcarrier.info/archives/8551, with remaining errata topmost and continually updated; and errata that made it into the 2023 edition recorded below that.

[2] Richard Carrier, *Proving History: Bayes's Theorem and the Quest for the Historical Jesus* (Prometheus Books, 2012), on which see chapter one, and *Hitler Homer Bible Christ: The Historical Papers of Richard Carrier 1995–2013* (Philosophy Press, 2014), which includes

relevant. I also maintain several ongoing projects online that are of use to those who want to keep up with the debate.[3]

I also published a popular-market summary of my formal study's findings as *Jesus from Outer Space: What the Earliest Christians Really Believed about Christ* (Pitchstone, 2020).[4] Though not an academic monograph, *Outer Space* remains important to the debate. While summarizing only the topmost points in *Historicity* (with a full concordance thereto in an appendix), it also added new material expanding arguments originally only briefed. Though that new material is not entirely new (as the concordance there indicates, every issue was treated in *Historicity*), it added examples or explication that can assist in grasping its points. Which includes some material now expanded or summarized in this volume.

Outer Space presents a summary of my theory and why it is plausible that is less cluttered with digressions. But it also includes a more direct comparison with the Hellenistic Osiris cult as a proof-of-concept. We know from Plutarch that Osiris was also publicly preached as a historical earthly 'king' but privately preached to be a celestial whose incarnation, death, and resurrection 'really' occur in outer space just below the moon, at the hands of Egypt's functional equivalent to Satan.[5] There are many incidental differences between the two gods and their stories and the-

---

all my peer-reviewed articles on historicity cited in *Historicity*: "Thallus and the Darkness at Christ's Death," *Journal of Greco-Roman Christianity and Judaism* 8 (2011/2012), 185–91; "Origen, Eusebius, and the Accidental Interpolation in Josephus, *Jewish Antiquities* 20.200," *Journal of Early Christian Studies* 20.4 (2012), 489–514; and "The Prospect of a Christian Interpolation in Tacitus, *Annals* 15.44," *Vigiliae Christianae* 68 (2014), 264–83.

[3] Richard Carrier, "An Ongoing List of Updates to the Arguments and Evidence in *On the Historicity of Jesus*" (10 July 2023) at richardcarrier.info/archives/24341; "List of Responses to Defenders of the Historicity of Jesus" (18 June 2014) at richardcarrier.info/archives/5730; and "List of Historians Who Take Mythicism Seriously" (25 August 2022) at richardcarrier.info/archives/21420. I have also presented results at conferences and in trade magazines, but those merely summarize my cited publications. To keep up with those (and my work in other subjects), I maintain my cv at richardcarrier.info/cv.pdf.

[4] *Outer Space* has since been published in Greek, as *Ιησούς: Τι Πραγματικά Πίστευαν Οι Πρώτοι Χριστιανοί Για Την Ιστορικότητα Του Ναζωραίου* (tr. Achilleas Fakatselis; Thessaloniki, Greece: Daedaleos, 2021), and Polish, as *Jezus z kosmosu. Chrystys w wierze pierwszych chrześcijan* (tr. Magdalena Górska; Katowice: STAPIS, 2023). Editions in other languages are expected. I also helped develop an app for historicity (called CHRESTUS, for Apple and Android), with a Bayesian calculator into which you can input your own premises and observe the results (see www.chrest.us).

[5] *Outer Space*, 35–40, 111–13, 117–19; cf. Carrier, *Historicity*, 181, 186–87.

ologies, of course. But the basic structure might be the same, the only fundamental difference being that, aligning with the expectations of Judaism, Christianity's cosmic murder-and-resurrection drama occurs only once for all time (as explained in Hebrews 9), whereas in Osiris cult it recurred annually.[6] I also more directly explain why 'outer space' is a more accurate description of ancient thought regarding the heavens than the words 'heaven' or 'heavens' (which today imply other planes of existence, not spatial locations contiguous with Earth).[7] And that view of the matter has since been independently confirmed, by Catherine Hezser and Robyn Faith Walsh.[8]

In *Outer Space* I also include a chapter summarizing my debate with Fernando Bermejo-Rubio and Franco Tommasi, who argues a historical Jesus is indeed not plausible—*unless* Jesus was a whitewashed militant. They present the best succinct defense of that conclusion yet in print, and Jesus scholars need to answer their case before rejecting it out of hand—just as they must do for doubting historicity altogether.[9] I responded that their methodology simply replicates the same mistakes as

---

[6] *Outer Space*, 122–27.

[7] *Outer Space*, 7–10.

[8] Catherine Hezser, "Outer Space in Ancient Jewish and Christian Literature," in *Religion and Outer Space* (ed. Eric Michael Mazur and Sarah McFarland Taylor; Routledge, 2023), 9–24; Robyn Faith Walsh, "*Argumentum ad Lunam*: Pauline Discourse, 'Double Death', and Competition on the Moon," *Harvard Theological Review* 117.4 (2024), 720-743. Both cite more recent scholarship on ancient cosmology than I had available to establish the same point. Walsh also adds much more to the evidence I already presented in Carrier, *Historicity*, 178–97, e.g. the first century (BCE) Pseudo-Ocellus Lucanus, *On the Nature of the Universe*, as reported in Stobaeus, *Extracts, Sayings and Precepts* 1.20, who (like most people then) demarcates reality between the Earth, the Atmosphere (capped by the moon), and the Heavens (capped by the stars), as the realms of men, demons, and gods, respectively. On how that divine heaven was moved 'above' the stars only in the Middle Ages and then to 'another plane of existence' only in the modern era, see Stephen Case, "Inventing Heaven," *Aeon* (2 December 2022) at aeon.co/essays/how-heaven-became-a-place-among-the-stars.

[9] See Fernando Bermejo-Rubio, Richard Carrier, and Franco Tommasi (with a contribution from Robert M. Price), *Jesus: Militant or Nonexistent? Two Views Compared* (Philosophy Press, 2025). Which is an updated English edition of the original: *Gesù resistente Gesù inesistente: Due visioni a confronto* (Manni, 2022). Bermejo-Rubio's argument there is built on his prior thesis in *La invención de Jesús de Nazaret: Historia, ficción, historiografía* (Siglo XXI de España Editores, S.A., 2018; now Akal, 2023) and has been perfected in his most recent study, *They Suffered under Pontius Pilate: Jewish Anti-Roman Resistance and the Crosses at Golgotha* (Lexington Books/Fortress Academic, 2023).

the field's methodology generally: their entire approach employs circular argumentation, whereby a hypothesis about what is authentic in a text is then used to rewrite the text, and that rewritten text is then used as evidence for the hypothesis; while competing explanations of that same evidence are not properly considered.[10] One way or another, this is how every version of a 'historical Jesus' gets constructed now. I just used their own effort to illustrate the point. And historicists might start to realize this in themselves through *their own* effort to justify rejecting Bermejo-Rubio's reconstruction of the historical Jesus. Because his case is as good as theirs—or better. But avoiding this circular approach, I aver, gets very different results. So anyone concerned about methodology in the broader historicity debate might want to take a look at that (along with my book *Proving History*). But I revisit this debate here in chapter five and expand one key example from it in chapter six.

Finally, in *Outer Space* I included a chapter fleshing out one plausible pathway by which belief in an earthly (and thus possibly historical) Jesus arose from the foundation of an original belief in a cosmic (and thus *not* possibly historical) Jesus, and then eclipsed it. In *Historicity* I left that question open for further study and only provided a generalized outline of what would be essential to any such model of Christianity's development—and why these essentials would be plausible in context.[11] But if that is too vague or abstract—if you want to hear a more concrete example of how that development could have transpired—that chapter in *Outer Space* will help.

One just need remember that it is not possible for us to know exactly what happened; thus any reconstruction is speculative. All we can discern with any confidence is what *must* have happened, and in only general terms. Consider the analogy I introduced there, and again here in chapter one: we don't know 'exactly how, when, where, why, and by whom' Christian accounts of Jesus's resurrection appearances completely transformed from ephemeral and mystical visions into elaborate narratives of empty tombs and dinner parties, and those fantasies completely

[10] In addition to my contributions to *Jesus: Militant or Nonexistent?*, for a more point-by-point analysis see Richard Carrier, "A Thorough Fisk of the Arguments of Fernando Bermejo-Rubio and Marco Tommasi" (27 March 2025) at richardcarrier.info/archives/26700.

[11] Carrier, *Historicity*, 606–16.

erased whatever the original stories were. We only know for sure *that this happened*, and roughly over what timespan; likewise, historicity altogether. But there are plausible accounts of it. And I propose one there.

New Developments

Since I published *Historicity* a number of academic publications began to reinforce many of its findings—without drawing any line to doubting historicity altogether; yet they increase the warrant for it. So to catch up, the following topics were covered in *Historicity*, and are here updated in no important order.

The Gospels: Literary Art or Collections of Lore?

For example: the traditional dogma of the field regarding the supposed existence of an 'oral lore' concerning a historical Jesus, preserved under layers of literary and legendary embellishment in the Gospels, has come under more concerted attack as not only unevidenced but even implausible. In *Historicity* I made a detailed case for this myself.[12] But now we have the very effective argument of Robyn Faith Walsh.[13] She demonstrates that that dogma never had any evidential foundation—it has always simply been a presumption at worst; a hypothesis at best. And then she shows that when you situate the Gospels in their actual literary context instead (as we ought to have done all along, rather than inventing some special exception for them), we find that we should hold very different assumptions and expectations regarding how and why they were composed. I concur.

Much the same point has since been made, in different ways, by David Trobisch and Markus Vinzent, who each, like Walsh, situate the New Testament in its context not just as literature *but as a publication*.[14] Tro-

---

[12] Carrier, *Historicity*, ch. 10, reinforced by *Proving History*, ch. 5, and supported by abundant contextual evidence across the first seven chapters of *Historicity*.

[13] Robyn Faith Walsh, *The Origins of Early Christian Literature: Contextualizing the New Testament within Greco-Roman Literary Culture* (Cambridge University Press, 2021).

[14] David Trobisch, *On the Origin of Christian Scripture: The Evolution of the New Testament Canon in the Second Century* (Fortress, 2023); Markus Vinzent, *Resetting the Origins of*

bisch shows the role of editing in producing our 'canon'; while Vinzent situates the whole Bible in the corrosive context of a pervasive Christian propaganda war. Their results are not favorable to oral lore theory either. They each show that even in its Christian context the New Testament resembles a plethora of contemporary and subsequent fabricated literature serving the aims of propaganda, not of researched histories or faithfully collected testimony. Like Walsh, Trobisch and Vinzent reorient us toward what we should actually be studying: each author's (and, just as importantly, their editors') motives in producing the statements and stories that they do, and in the form we now have.

Trobisch and Vinzent conclude from this that we have lost access to *any* original text, that our New Testament was either entirely fabricated (Trobisch) or at least hopelessly redacted (Vinzent) in the second century (first by Marcion and then by his detractors). Their studies do not establish that (in each case I find it is merely a fallacious inference); but they do establish the more general point that we need to be actively suspicious of the role of forgery or editing (or both) of every book in the New Testament, first by Marcion and then by a specific anti-Marcionite faction of the late second century—and even insofar as any 'pre-Marcionite' version of these texts can be recovered, we must assign the same suspicions even to them for their *pre*-Marcion agendas.[15] We can no longer gullibly treat any of these texts as faithful records of anything—not even a supposed 'oral lore' their authors received. It was all designed to a purpose. Even the authentic works of Paul were designed by him for winning his own propaganda war. They therefore preserve a fossil of their own distorting context. And this has consequences for how we understand what they include—and what they don't.

Others have now made similar arguments against 'oral lore' theory,

---

Christianity: A New Theory of Sources and Beginnings (Cambridge University Press, 2023).

[15] Though I am not persuaded, anyone exploring Vinzent and Trobisch's more controversial theses must also now consult Nina Livesey, *The Letters of Paul in their Roman Literary Context: Reassessing Apostolic Authorship* (Cambridge University Press, 2024), who argues (similarly) that *all* the letters of Paul are a Marcionite fabrication. Which makes a mainstream trend now. See Richard Carrier, "Was the Entire New Testament Forged in the Second Century?" (26 February 2024) at richardcarrier.info/archives/27161 and "Are Paul and His Letters a Second Century Fabrication? A Critical Review of the Livesey Thesis" at richardcarrier.info/archives/34573.

again indicating a trend.[16] There are of course many works enthusiastically still defending the 'oral lore' theory and applying memory theory to it and the like, but I do not believe they survive these recent critiques.[17] Enthusiasts more typically just ignore them, or flippantly dismiss them with careless apologetics rather than careful examination, and just go on building on an assumption that was never really established in the first place. Hence my point here is that it's not just me now; other scholars are starting to notice that this idea simply has no merit commensurate with the witnessed enthusiasm.[18] As I pointed out in the last chapter, most scholars are on the wrong track, looking for the wrong thing, because they are relying on a poorly established assumption (which just 'happens' to favor the needs of faith-based scholars more than objective historians).

Furthering that same trend, the initially (and needlessly) scandalous suggestion by Dennis MacDonald that the Gospels and Acts are literarily emulating the works of Homer and other classical literature has

---

[16] See, for example, the debate started by Paul Foster, "Memory, Orality, and the Fourth Gospel: Three Dead-Ends in Historical Jesus Research," *Journal for the Study of the Historical Jesus* 10.3 (January 2012), 191–227. His arguments were 'rebutted' only by still not establishing the validity of the assumption he was questioning, which ironically only validated Foster's point: see Eric Eve, "Orality Is No Dead-End," *Journal for the Study of the Historical Jesus* 13.1 (2015), 3–23; and the earlier exchange between Stanley Porter and Hughson Ong, "Memory, Orality, and the Fourth Gospel," *Journal for the Study of the Historical Jesus* 12.1–2 (2014), 143–64, and Paul Foster, "Memory, Orality, and the Fourth Gospel: An Ongoing Conversation with Stan Porter and Hughson T. Ong," *Journal for the Study of the Historical Jesus* 12.1–2 (2014), 165–83.

[17] Examples are surveyed in the sources cited in the preceding and following note.

[18] Besides Walsh, *Origins*, and Trobisch, *Origin*, and Foster's 'Dead-Ends' and 'Conversation', see: Robert Matthew Calhoun, David Moessner, and Tobias Nicklas (eds.), *Modern and Ancient Literary Criticism of the Gospels: Continuing the Debate on Gospel Genre(s)* (Mohr Siebeck, 2020); M. David Litwa, *How the Gospels Became History: Jesus and Mediterranean Myths* (Yale University Press, 2019); Eve-Marie Becker, *The Birth of Christian History: Memory and Time from Mark to Luke-Acts* (Yale University Press, 2017); Eric Eve, "Memory, Orality and the Synoptic Problem," *Early Christianity* 6.3 (2015), 311–33; Zeba Crook, "Matthew, Memory Theory and the New No Quest," *Theological Studies* 70.1 (2014), 1–11; William Sanger Campbell, *The We Passages in the Acts of the Apostles: The Narrator as Narrative Character* (Society of Biblical Literature, 2007); Marianne Palmer Bonz, *The Past as Legacy: Luke-Acts and Ancient Epic* (Fortress, 2000); and also the recent work of Evan Fales, who made good on his promise (Carrier, *Historicity*, xiv) and published *Reading Sacred Texts: Charity, Structure, Gospel* (GCRR Press, 2021).

found considerable published support.[19] I did not rely on this conclusion, but I did summarize it as relevant.[20] Now, I think the case is pretty well established, such that resistance to his thesis is now only dogmatic or desperate.[21] Moreover, by the time *Historicity* was published, MacDonald had already expanded his literary model to demonstrating even more extensively what was already a mainstream conclusion: that the Gospels and Acts emulate *biblical* literature (in the Greek tradition) as well.[22] Which only further secures the 'literary thesis' as a more credible model for understanding Gospel literature altogether. But that this practice was limited to biblical (and apocryphal) source material is no longer plausible. If the Gospels emulate the likes of Deuteronomy, Daniel, Kings, and Chronicles, why should we not expect them to emulate (even to deliberately transvalue and upstage) the analogous 'scriptures' of the Greeks and Romans? The Gospels are written *in Greek* after all. And as all scholars of

[19] This support is overwhelming now: Walsh, *Origins*, 134–36. See: Christopher S. Crawford (ed.), *Greco-Roman and Jewish Tributaries to the New Testament: Festschrift in Honor of Gregory J. Riley* (Claremont Press, 2019); Brad McAdon, *Rhetorical Mimesis and the Mitigation of Early Christian Conflicts: Examining the Influence that Greco-Roman Mimesis May Have in the Composition of Matthew, Luke, and Acts* (Pickwick, 2018); Mark Bilby, Margaret Froelich, and Michael Kochenash (eds.), *Classical Greek Models of the Gospels and Acts: Studies in Mimesis Criticism* (Claremont School of Theology Press, 2018); Austin Busch, "New Testament Narrative and Greco-Roman Literature," in *The Oxford Handbook of Biblical Narrative* (ed. Danna Nolan Fewell; Oxford University Press, 2016), 61–72; Margaret Froelich, Michael Kochenash, Thomas Phillips, and Ilseo Park (eds.), *Christian Origins and the New Testament in the Greco-Roman Context: Essays in Honor of Dennis R. MacDonald* (Claremont School of Theology Press, 2016). See also Bonz, *The Past as Legacy*, 170–72.

[20] Carrier, *Historicity*, 396, 399, 417, 422, 436–42.

[21] After *Historicity* MacDonald published numerous studies shoring up his argument: most importantly, *Mythologizing Jesus: From Jewish Teacher to Epic Hero* (Rowman & Littlefield, 2015), and especially his invaluable *Synopses of Epic, Tragedy, and the Gospels* (Mimesis Press, 2022), wherein all his work is usefully organized, catalogued, and cited. And besides the works I cite in *Historicity*, 643, see now also: Dennis MacDonald, *The Gospels and Homer: Imitations of Greek Epic in Mark and Luke-Acts* (Rowman & Littlefield, 2014); *Luke and Vergil: Imitations of Classical Greek Literature* (Rowman & Littlefield, 2014); *Luke and the Politics of Homeric Imitation: Luke–Acts as Rival to the Aeneid* (Fortress, 2018); and more in following notes. See also the exchange between Dennis MacDonald ("Response to Karl Olav Sandnes," 69–72) and Karl Olav Sandnes ("Mimesis and Criticism," 55–68) in *New Studies in Textual Interplay* (ed. Craig Evans, B.J. Oropeza, and Paul T. Sloan; T&T Clark, 2020).

[22] I cite numerous experts and their results in chapters nine and ten of *Historicity*, and MacDonald has expanded beyond what I there cite in his *Synopses*.

ancient education have noted, it was not possible to achieve such compositional skill as we find in the Gospels without thorough exposure to Greco-Roman classics and training in their emulation.[23] Which remains a problem for anyone intent on recovering historical facts from the Gospel narratives.

Though MacDonald still holds out for some oral-lore background to his own reconstruction of the hypothetical 'Q' source, his own findings actually undermine that hypothesis by demonstrating that 'Q' (or 'Q-Plus' in his parlance) is simply an updated emulation of Deuteronomy and other Jewish literature.[24] MacDonald's arguments regarding the mimetic construction of his hypothetical 'Q-Plus' document are entirely compatible with Matthew being the composer (and Luke, redactor). We thus have no need of it. This is especially obvious when we look at the complex structure of Matthew, which actually explains the origination of all this supposed 'Q' material.[25] Findings of even more structure than I already documented have also been published for Mark and Luke.[26] Similarly, for the Gospel of John, MacDonald has demonstrated that its original layer of redaction was a sequential emulation of Euripides' *Bac-*

[23] Scholarship cited in Carrier, *Historicity*, 166–68 and 397–98. The point is also made throughout Walsh, *Origins*.

[24] See Dennis MacDonald, *Synopses*, and MacDonald, *From the Earliest Gospel (Q+) to the Gospel of Mark: Solving the Synoptic Problem with Mimesis Criticism* (Fortress, 2019). Of course I still do not find any arguments for Q to be successful, including his. Beyond what I already cite on this point in *Historicity*, 269–70 and 470–73, see now: John Poirier and Jeffrey Peterson (eds.), *Marcan Priority Without Q: Explorations in the Farrer Hypothesis* (T&T Clark, 2015); Thomas Mosbo, *Luke the Composer: Exploring the Evangelist's Use of Matthew* (Fortress, 2017); Mogens Müller and Heike Omerzu (eds.), *Gospel Interpretation and the Q-Hypothesis* (T&T Clark, 2018); Eric Eve, *Relating the Gospels: Memory, Imitation and the Farrer Hypothesis* (T&T Clark, 2021); and Mike Duncan, *Rhetoric and the Synoptic Problem* (Fortress, 2022).

[25] To the examples I summarize in Carrier, *Historicity*, 460–69, can be added those of James Patrick, "Matthew's Pesher Gospel Structured around Ten Messianic Citations of Isaiah," *Journal of Theological Studies* 61.1 (2010), 43–81, and M. Eugene Boring, "Structure," in *The New Interpreter's Bible, Volume 8: Matthew – Mark* (ed. Leander Keck; Abingdon, 1995), 110–18. Likewise, adding to my examples of literary structure in Luke-Acts (Carrier, *Historicity*, chs. 9 and 10.6) is now Rob James, *The Spiral Gospel: Intratextuality in Luke's Narrative* (Clarke 2022).

[26] More structure in Luke: previous note; for Mark (Carrier, *Historicity*, ch. 10.4) are now Roland Meynet, "La composition de l'évangile de Marc," *Gregorianum* 96.2 (2015), 231–52, and René Jacob, *L'Évangile de Marc: L'Évangile de la Foi* (L'Harmattan, 2020).

chae.[27] I assume historians are wont to balk, but the evidence he has for this conclusion is quite solid. Even more so than the evidence that one of the redactional layers of John was heavily drawing on Ezekiel as a model, and yet even that is persuasive.[28] Likewise recent studies confirming that the Gospel of John used the Gospel of Mark as a source, and otherwise did not have *any* historical sources, only literary models.[29] These conclusions cannot be dismissed without close examination—even more so

[27] Dennis MacDonald, *The Dionysian Gospel: The Fourth Gospel and Euripides* (Fortress, 2017). This idea was already proposed and defended decades before in Mark Stibbe, *John as Storyteller: Narrative Criticism and the Fourth Gospel* (Cambridge University Press, 1992), 131–47. And it has growing support now. See, for example, Michael Kochenash, "Better Call Paul 'Saul': Literary Models and a Lukan Innovation," *Journal of Biblical Literature* 138.2 (2019), 433–49; Charles Puskas and C. Michael Robbins, *The Conceptual Worlds of the Fourth Gospel* (Cascade, 2021); Jae Hyung Cho, *This Is My Flesh: John's Eucharist and the Dionysus Cult* (Pickwick, 2022). For a summary of opposition (yet also citing growing support): Fergus J. King, "Hit or Myth? Methodological Considerations in Comparing Dionysos with the Johannine Jesus," *Biblical Theology Bulletin* 51.2 (2021), 88–100.

[28] Brian Neil Peterson, *John's Use of Ezekiel: Understanding the Unique Perspective of the Fourth Gospel* (Fortress, 2015). That holds even after agreeing with the corrections offered in Wil Rogan's review in *RBL* (December 2017) at sblcentral.org/home/bookDetails/11199.

[29] Eve-Marie Becker, Helen Bond, and Catrin Williams (eds.), *John's Transformation of Mark* (T&T Clark, 2021) and Mark Goodacre, *The Fourth Synoptic Gospel: John's Knowledge of Matthew, Mark, and Luke* (Eerdmans, 2025), which add to the scholarship I already cited on John's use of the Synoptics as a source (Carrier, *Historicity*, 487–89). Likewise the work of Jörg Frey in *Theology and History in the Fourth Gospel: Tradition and Narration* (Baylor University Press, 2018) and the observations in Harold Attridge, *History, Theology, and Narrative Rhetoric in the Fourth Gospel* (Marquette University Press, 2019) and Trobisch, *Origin*, 82–90, which all undermine efforts to argue any history of Jesus can be recovered from John. Such efforts continue nonetheless, but any objective comparison of the quality of arguments pro and con does not support them: see, for example, the critique of Annette Merz, "Response to the Essays in Part 2," in what I find to be an apologetically desperate collection of essays: *John, Jesus, and History, Volume 3: Glimpses of Jesus through the Johannine Lens* (ed. Paul Anderson, Felix Just, and Tom Thatcher; Atlanta: SBL Press, 2016), 299–317. Notice the frequent recourse across its other chapters to *possibiliter* fallacies (anything 'possible' or 'plausible' becomes 'probable', as if by magic: on the fallacy, see *Proving History*, index) and arguments from assumption (e.g., again the existence of oral lore is assumed rather than treated as a hypothesis in need of evidence; while competing literary-rhetorical explanations of the same evidence are rarely considered). We could already see this in Stibbe's *John as Storyteller*, where he proves John's entire composition to be fiction (and built out of both Greek and Jewish literature) with solid evidence and logic, then tries insisting some minimal oral lore *still* lay behind it, yet with nothing but speculative apologetics. The difference is stark.

than MacDonald's other work on the literary production of the Gospels, which is already far more credible than has been portrayed.[30] Meanwhile, the fact that the Gospels build their stories about Jesus from *Jewish* literature (most particularly the Septuagint) is already mainstream.[31] The recent study of Nathanael Vette, for example, situates Mark's invention of stories for Jesus in the context of other early Jewish literature doing the same for other legendary figures and events.[32] Once you place the Gospels back into their literary context, the notion of their just being collections of oral lore and not deliberate literary creations collapses.

In short, with all this in mind, any justified hope that the historicity of Jesus could yet be secured from the Gospels has *declined* since I published, not improved. The field's cutting edge isn't going that way. There will always be holdouts, particularly among the devoted. Christian apologetics exists to defend the faith from exactly such doubts; not to elucidate their merits, but to obscure them. But when we look at the scholarship coming from those in the field who *aren't* beholden to de-

[30] See previous notes for copious evidence of concurring scholarship. MacDonald himself already adequately dispatches apologetic efforts to remove his theory from the table in his *Synopses* and other recent work.

[31] See the evidence and scholarship I cite in Chapter 10 of *Historicity*, as well as the recent surveys in *The Reception of Jesus in the First Three Centuries, Volume 1: From Paul to Josephus* (ed. Helen Bond; T&T Clark, 2019): Sandra Huebenthal, "Gospel of Mark," 41–72 (especially her survey of frame analysis, 59–69, which very ably supplements my case); Matthias Konradt, "Gospel of Matthew," 107–38 (whose analysis of how Matthew intentionally transforms Mark also supplements my case; although unfortunately Konradt still assumes Q existed and wasn't, in fact, the literary product of Matthew, which blinds him to a fully sound understanding of the text: see my prior note on Q theory); Michal Beth Dinkler, "The Gospel of Luke," 139–64 (whose rhetorical analysis is useful but ignores far too much of the state of the field, including the most important studies I cite in *Historicity*, and all the work I cited in earlier notes here); and Helen Bond, "Gospel of John," 165–85 (likewise). Bond is also behind the curve on another key detail: she still cites the now-dubious dating of the Rylands papyrus of John to 125 A.D. (165); it has been conclusively redated to circa 200: see Brent Nongbri, "The Use and Abuse of P52: Papyrological Pitfalls in the Dating of the Fourth Gospel," *Harvard Theological Review* 98.1 (2005), 23–48 and now "Palaeography, Precision and Publicity: Further Thoughts on *P.Ryl.*iii.457 (P52)," *New Testament Studies* 66.4 (2020), 471–99. For a thorough explication of why such earlier dates have always been unfounded see Nongbri's magnum opus, *God's Library: The Archaeology of the Earliest Christian Manuscripts* (Yale University Press, 2018).

[32] Nathanael Vette, *Writing with Scripture: Scripturalized Narrative in the Gospel of Mark* (T&T Clark, 2022).

fending the faith, the trend is going the other way—and hence, quite poorly for a historical Jesus.

This is not only the case for the Gospels, which were never very good evidence for historicity anyway—they are, rather, exactly what a mythological biography is expected to look like.[33] But it is also the case for some of the remaining domains of evidence. For example, outside Christian apologetics, the historicity of what is related in the book of Acts is coming increasingly into question, even more than it already was when I published.[34] And yet the assumption of historicity still hinders

[33] This is precisely the trendline in the latest work of Richard Burridge and colleagues, as evidenced in Calhoun, Moessner, and Nicklas, *Modern and Ancient*. See the updated commentary in the 25th Anniversary Edition of Richard Burridge, *What Are the Gospels? A Comparison with Graeco-Roman Biography* (Baylor University Press, 2018).

[34] Besides the evidence and scholarship I already cited in my chapter on Acts in *Historicity* (359–86), new examples of finding mythical sources and aims in Acts similar to the Gospels include (but are not limited to): Mark Giacobbe, *Luke the Chronicler: The Narrative Arc of Samuel-Kings and Chronicles in Luke-Acts* (Brill, 2023); Mark Bilby and Anna Lefteratou, "A Dramatic Heist of Epic Proportion: Iphigenia among the Taurians in the Acts of the Apostles," *Harvard Theological Review* 115.4 (2022), 496–518; Eric Clouston, *How Ancient Narratives Persuade: Acts in Its Literary Context* (Fortress, 2020); Nathanael Lüke, *Über die narrative Kohärenz zwischen Apostelgeschichte und Paulusbriefen* (Narr Francke Attempto Verlag, 2019); Alexander Soal and Desmond Henry, "The Reversal of Babel: Questioning the Early Church's Understanding of the Gift of the Holy Spirit in Acts as a Reversal of the Curse of Babel," *Verbum et Ecclesia* 39.1 (2018), 1–10; Zachary Dawson, "The Books of Acts and Jubilees in Dialogue: A Literary-Intertextual Analysis of the Noahide Laws in Acts 15 and 21," *Journal of Greco-Roman Christianity and Judaism* 13 (2017), 9-40; Kochenash, "Better Call Paul 'Saul'"; Dale Allison, "Acts 9:1–9, 22:6–11, 26:12–18: Paul and Ezekiel," *Journal of Biblical Literature* 135.4 (2016), 807–26; Christopher Zeichmann, "Herodian Kings and Their Soldiers in the Acts of the Apostles: A Response to Craig Keener," *Journal of Greco-Roman Christianity and Judaism* 11 (2015), 178–90; Alan Bale, *Genre and Narrative Coherence in the Acts of the Apostles* (T&T Clark, 2015); Samson Uytanlet, *Luke-Acts and Jewish Historiography: A Study on the Theology, Literature, and Ideology of Luke-Acts* (Mohr Siebeck, 2014); Joshua Jipp, *Divine Visitations and Hospitality to Strangers in Luke-Acts: An Interpretation of the Malta Episode in Acts 28:1-10* (Brill, 2013); Coleman Baker, "Peter and Paul in Acts and the Construction of Early Christian Identity: A Review of Historical and Literary Approaches," *Currents in Biblical Research* 11.3 (2013), 349–65; Dennis Smith and Joseph Tyson (eds.), *Acts and Christian Beginnings: The Acts Seminar Report* (Polebridge, 2013); plus various contributions in several of the works of Dennis MacDonald cited earlier (see in particular his *Synopses*) and in McAdon, *Rhetorical Mimesis*, and Froelich and Kochenash, *Classical Greek Models*; and in general in Carl Holladay, *Acts: A Commentary* (Westminster John Knox Press, 2016), in contrast to the many confessionalist commentaries on Acts published since 2014. See my summary of the most prominent evidence in Richard Carrier, "How We Know Acts Is a Fake History" (21 April 2023) at richar-

progress in understanding there. As I already argue in *Historicity*, I believe Acts should now be reinterpreted in light of how my theory entails Christianity actually began, explaining many strange silences in Acts.

So, too, the Epistles. Since I published, two good surveys of attempts to find references in Paul to a historical Jesus have appeared.[35] Neither improves on my analysis of the same passages already in Chapter 11 of *Historicity*. To the contrary, their apologetical nature inadvertently shows how far one must rely on unsupported assumptions, and a perpetual recourse to mere 'possibilities' (rather than probabilities), to extract such information. Which was my original point. Once we read Paul's letters *without* assumptions, all references to an actual (as opposed to imagined) historical Jesus dissolve into fatal ambiguity. The most important examples I will treat in the closing chapters of this volume. But a few other examples warrant discussion later in this chapter.

The flip side of that point is another that I only suggested in *Historicity*, but is now well proved by several studies: that the first Gospel (of which all other Gospels we know are redactions or embellishments) was largely constructed by reifying material in the Epistles of Paul.[36] Many

---

dcarrier.info/archives/23447.

[35] Christine Jacobi, "Pauline Epistles," in *The Reception of Jesus in the First Three Centuries, Volume 1: From Paul to Josephus* (ed. Helen Bond; T&T Clark, 2019), 3–38; and Craig Blomberg, "Quotations, Allusions, and Echoes of Jesus in Paul," in *Studies in the Pauline Epistles: Festschrift for Douglas J. Moo* (ed. Matt Harmon and Jay Smith; Zondervan, 2014), 129–43. To which can be added earlier articles by Gregory Jenks, "What Did Paul Know about Jesus?" *The Fourth R* 12.1 (2000), 1–8, and Dale Allison, "The Pauline Epistles and the Synoptic Gospels: The Pattern of the Parallels," *New Testament Studies* 28.1 (1982), 1–32. These add to Carrier, *Historicity*, 515n9.

[36] Studies that, collectively, more than confirm the point now include: Harm Hollander, "The Words of Jesus: From Oral Traditions to Written Record in Paul and Q," *Novum Testamentum* 42.4 (2000), 340–57 (346); Michael Bird and Joel Willitts, *Paul and the Gospels: Christologies, Conflicts and Convergences* (T&T Clark, 2011); David Oliver Smith, *Matthew, Mark, Luke, and Paul: The Influence of the Epistles on the Synoptic Gospels* (Resource, 2011); Tom Dykstra, *Mark: Canonizer of Paul* (OCABS, 2012); Oda Wischmeyer and David Sim (eds.), *Paul and Mark: Two Authors at the Beginnings of Christianity* (De Gruyter, 2014), especially Michael Theophilos, "The Roman Connection: Paul and Mark," in *Paul and Mark*, 45–71; Bartosz Adamczewski, *The Gospel of Mark: A Hypertextual Commentary* (Peter Lang, 2014); Eve-Marie Becker, Troels Engberg-Pedersen, and Mogens Mueller (eds.), *Mark and Paul: For and Against Pauline Influence on Mark* (De Gruyter, 2014); Thomas Nelligan, *The Quest for Mark's Sources: An Exploration of the Case for Mark's Use of First Corinthians* (Pickwick, 2015); Christine Jacobi, *Jesusüberlieferung bei Paulus? Analogien zwischen den echten Paulusbriefen und den*

sayings and teachings of Jesus in Mark were adapted from what began as the teachings of Paul. And many of the deeds and narratives of Jesus there have been constructed to represent what Paul taught in the form of a story, in which Jesus or other characters instantiate Paul's thoughts in action, a technique of story-invention explicitly taught in ancient schools of the time.[37] The evidence for both is convincing.[38] And it has not been meaningfully rebutted. Scholars arguing the contrary ignore nearly all of this literature, and either fail to engage with the extent of its evidence or merely argue from a contrary *possibility* rather than to a contrary probability.[39] So this should now be added to the evidence in ch. 10 of *Historicity*, further confirming that the Gospels are literary constructs and not collections of oral lore—a general conclusion that, as noted earlier in this chapter, has growing support on other grounds as well. But this also goes to eliminate any argument that the Epistles should be interpreted as referring to stories and details in the Gospels; the sequence of causation appears to have gone the other way. Even a skeptic must admit the contrary can no longer be *established*. So no premise of the kind now survives. Which is particularly relevant to debates over the origin of Paul's Eucharist myth, as will be discussed later in this chapter.[40]

Are Colossians and Ephesians Early Mythicist Texts?

Another example is Colossians. Despite it being an undatable forgery I

synoptischen Evangelien (De Gruyter, 2015); Mar Pérez I. Díaz, *Jesus in the Light of Paul's Theology* (Mohr Siebeck, 2020); John-Christian Eurell, "Paul and the Jesus Tradition: Reconsidering the Relationship Between Paul and the Synoptics," *Journal of Early Christian History* 12.2 (2022), 1–16. For my original hints at this being a possibility: Carrier, *Historicity*, 411, 424n72, 437–38, 440–41, 447, 455–56n137, 558. I would make a more forceful claim now.

[37] Carrier, *Historicity*, 397–98.

[38] For a summary of some examples see: Richard Carrier, "Mark's Use of Paul's Epistles" (25 October 2019) at richardcarrier.info/archives/15934.

[39] This is true even of the few critical pieces in Becker et al., *Mark and Paul*; but likewise Michael J. Kok, "Does Mark Narrate the Pauline Kerygma of 'Christ Crucified'? Challenging an Emerging Consensus on Mark as a Pauline Gospel," *Journal for the Study of the New Testament* 37.2 (2014), 139–60, and *The Gospel on the Margins: The Reception of Mark in the Second Century* (Fortress, 2015).

[40] See Carrier, *Historicity*, 557–63.

included Colossians as (albeit, by itself, weak) evidence of the existence of mythicist Christianity.[41] It is thus telling that Andreas Dettwiler failed to appreciate the significance of his own observation that "references to the death of Christ" in Colossians (e.g. 1:22, 24) "are the *only* link to the existence of the earthly Jesus," such that "the figure of Christ could be theoretically misunderstood" there "as an entirely celestial, mythical figure without any link to human history."[42] Well—would that actually be *mis*-understood? Mythicist Christians *also* believed in the death—indeed, crucifixion—of Jesus. They just didn't locate it on Earth. So could Colossians come from a cosmic-Christ branch of Christianity that had not yet even heard of an earthly version of Jesus? And should the same be said of Ephesians (e.g. 2:13–18), as a redaction of Colossians?[43] By contrast, the Pastorals are clearly aware of the Gospels and substantially post-date them.[44] So the chronology appears to go from mythicism *to* historicity.

This would have more impact as evidence for that conclusion if we could confidently date Colossians (or Ephesians) to before the publication of the first Gospel (as I suspect we now can for 1 Peter—see next). As it is, these could just be later texts presuming acquaintance with the Gospels. But isn't it at least a touch more probable that we would find a text like this, within the first hundred years from the religion's founding (possibly even the first fifty years), if indeed it was produced by a community that didn't hold to an earthly Jesus? At worst, you cannot confidently say we *don't have* such texts, when we do have these.[45] Dettwiler's remark thus illustrates the power of assumptions (really, dogmas) to blind scholars to the possibilities behind what they are actually looking at.

Are Hebrews, 1 Clement, and 1 Peter Early Mythicist Texts?

I had already made the case that Hebrews, 1 Clement, and 1 Peter could

[41] Carrier, *Historicity*, 261–62, 537–38, 552, 606–07.

[42] Andreas Dettwiler, "Colossians," in *The Reception of Jesus in the First Three Centuries, Volume 2: From Thomas to Tertullian* (ed. Jens Schröter and Christine Jabobi; T&T Clark, 2019), 3–9 (7). Italics in the original.

[43] Andreas Dettwiler, "Ephesians," in *From Thomas to Tertullian*, 10–17.

[44] Andreas Dettwiler, "Pastoral Epistles," in *From Thomas to Tertullian*, 19–26.

[45] And it's not alone: Carrier, *Historicity*, 349–56. See discussion in chapter seven.

date to Paul's time and as such would then definitely reflect texts ignorant of any yet-to-be-invented earthly Jesus.[46] In other words, *if* these texts are early, then their omission of any references to or even evident knowledge of a historical Jesus (in our sense) is significantly less probable. As later texts, to some probability they could be operating on an assumption of familiarity with Gospels (canonical or apocryphal), although even that is not entirely expected. Either way, these three letters offer some small evidence against historicity, however weak individually or in aggregate. But that evidence becomes stronger the earlier they date.

Hence it is significant that new cases have been made for their indeed having an earlier date. Philip Church independently made the same argument I did for Hebrews dating to the 60s.[47] And I have since learned of Thomas Herron's persuasive work accomplishing the same for 1 Clement—all of whose arguments go to the same conclusion for Hebrews.[48] Herron has also persuaded Clayton Jefford and (almost) Andrew Gregory.[49] At the same time, recent work by Karen Jobes and Elizabeth Myers has made a case for 1 Peter predating Hebrews.[50] Which brings James and Jude back into play (I'll discuss why in chapter four). Only the Pastoral and Johannine Epistles, along with 2 Peter, remain indubitably post-War forgeries (while, as just noted, there's no

[46] Carrier, *Historicity*, 271–74, 308–15, 356–57 (1 Clement), 262–63, 538–53 (Hebrews), and 263, 528–31 (1 Peter; likewise James and Jude, although they contain much less data of use to the question); see also 265n24.

[47] Philip Church, *Hebrews and the Temple: Attitudes to the Temple in Second Temple Judaism and in Hebrews* (Brill, 2017), 16–17.

[48] Thomas Herron, "The Most Probable Date of the First Epistle of Clement to the Corinthians," *Studia Patristica* 21 (1989), 106–21, and *Clement and the Early Church of Rome: On the Dating of Clement's First Epistle to the Corinthians* (Saint Paul Center for Biblical Theology, 1989; Emmaus Road, 2010).

[49] Clayton Jefford, *Apostolic Fathers and the New Testament* (Baker Academic, 2006), 15–19; Andrew Gregory, "Disturbing Trajectories: 1 Clement, the Shepherd of Hermas and the Development of Early Roman Christianity," in *Rome, the Bible and the Early Church* (ed. Oakes; Paternoster, 2002), 142–66, and "I Clement: An Introduction," *The Expository Times* 117.6 (2006), 223–30.

[50] Karen Jobes, *1 Peter*, 2nd ed. (Baker Academic, 2022) and (more importantly) Elizabeth Myers, *Intertextual Borrowing between 1 Peter and Hebrews: Probability of Literary Dependence and the Most Likely Direction of Borrowing* (Pistos Ktistes, 2020).

certain dating for the Deutero-Paulines).[51]

This creates a real problem for historicity: the silences and ignorances of 1 Clement and Hebrews I already calculate the effect of; but if the very first apostle Peter himself wrote 1 Peter (or indeed *anyone* in Paul's day did), then that entails not only that Peter himself never met Jesus in life, but that everyone then knew that to be the case. Even if still a forgery, its authors did not think to invent any eyewitness testimony to Jesus, but instead cite only *scripture* (and allude to revelation) as Peter's only sources of information.[52]

As a later text this could be somewhat explained. An author fabricating (or renaming, to assign authority to) a letter in a community awash with the Gospels might not have thought of the need to invent a testimony. The authors of 2 Peter did, but they had the specific design of refuting deniers of it (see chapter seven). 1 Peter does not have that evident design. But if it were written between the 30s and 60s, then its complete omission of all personal testimony and eyewitness evidence is nigh inexplicable—certainly coming from Peter himself, but even still from someone pretending to be him when he or other apostles were still alive and the movement had only just begun. In that early context, the author (Peter or not) would have to understand that they, like Paul, didn't know anything about human authorities having killed Jesus (e.g., 1 Peter 2:13–14), and only knew of Jesus ministering to spirits (1 Peter 3:17–22), and yet never to people on Earth (beyond, again, scripture and revelation). This would all but prove Jesus never existed. For if even Peter himself could only call up evidence for Jesus (his deeds, sayings, sufferings) from scripture and revelation, then that had to be the

---

[51] Bart Ehrman, *Forgery and Counterforgery: The Use of Literary Deceit in Early Christian Polemics* (Oxford University Press, 2012), 155–229 (Deutero-Paulines), 368–84 (Pastorals), 418–25 (Johannines); Ehrman also makes the best case for forgery for the others I suspect are authentic (1 Peter: 239–59; James and Jude: 283–305), but does not treat the evidence I and now others have presented (as his publication predates ours). On the invention and date of the Johannine epistles see also Tom Thatcher, "Johannine Epistles," in *The Reception of Jesus in the First Three Centuries, Volume 1: From Paul to Josephus* (ed. Helen Bond; T&T Clark, 2019), 297–307. Likewise: Dettwiler, "Colossians," "Ephesians," and "Pastoral Epistles."

[52] For example: 1 Peter 1:10–11 and 1:20; even 1 Peter 5:1, for *martus* more generally means 'testifier' (cf. Hebrews 3:5), not specifically 'eyewitness'; so that does not signify, even if it is an authentic part of the original letter (which has been questioned).

only evidence there was. This letter would then be the very epitome of mythicism, and its best evidence yet. The only caveat is that the case for it being this early is not strong enough to call it a certainty.

Nevertheless, once again, recent work is bolstering my positions on 1 Clement, Hebrews, and 1 Peter. Which further undermines historicity. One need only decide whether to ignore this, or heed it.

Who Killed Jesus?

The same can be said of who Paul imagines having killed Jesus in 1 Corinthians 2:8 ("None of the rulers of this age [lit. 'archons of this aeon'] understood" God's hidden plan, "for if they had, they would not have crucified the Lord of Glory"). I originally cited the debate over this question between Wesley Carr and Walter Wink in the 1980s, and a few others.[53] Arthur Droge can now be added to their number, arguing, as I did, that this passage refers to a murder in outer space, not on Earth.[54] But another case for this conclusion by Beverly Roberts Gaventa I had previously missed deserves particular attention.[55]

Gaventa favors the position of Wink over Carr (as do I). Wink and Carr both attest a growing number of scholars concluding that Paul had to be referring to celestial murderers rather than earthly. I noted how Carr's attempts to wave them off were too apologetical and convoluted to credit. But Gaventa approaches the question through Paul's remark in Romans 8:32 that it is God (not Judas or any human authority) who 'handed over' Jesus to be killed (*paradidômi*), hence explicating 1 Corinthians 11:23, where Paul mentions Jesus "was handed over in the night," which gets tendentiously translated as "was betrayed" even though all

[53] Carrier, *Historicity*, 189, 563–66.

[54] Arthur Droge, "Whodunnit? Paul's Peculiar Passion and Its Implications," in *Recovering an Undomesticated Apostle: Essays on the Legacy of Paul* (ed. C.B. Zeichmann and J.A. Egger; McGill-Queen's University Press, 2023), 305–33. Droge is driven by this realization to argue this passage must be a post-Pauline interpolation (thus reflecting 'second century' mythicism), but it more evidently reflects secret wisdom related by Paul himself (its peculiar features reflecting the fact that Paul never elsewhere discusses these things in surviving materials—although he may have done so in removed materials).

[55] Beverly Roberts Gaventa, "Interpreting the Death of Jesus Apocalyptically: Reconsidering Romans 8:32," in *Jesus and Paul Reconnected: Fresh Pathways into an Old Debate* (ed. Todd Still; Eerdmans, 2007), 125–45.

evidence indicates Paul had no such notion.[56] Instead, the 'Archons of this Aeon' Jesus was delivered to have to be supernatural entities, because Paul attributes to them not only motives but even a knowledge of the cosmos that no human could possess.[57] Gaventa concurs. As does M. David Litwa ("these rulers are probably daimonic agents").[58]

Of course, like others, Litwa attempts to argue that although Paul does mean demons here, he is nevertheless *referring* to human agents, by a kind of metonymy, the Jews and Romans being the tools the demons *used*. But that is exactly what Paul does not say.[59] Litwa's theory requires a layer of *ad hoc* interpretive assumption; indeed, a rather convoluted one.[60] If Paul understood such to be the case, he would have written this sentence quite differently. But as he actually wrote it, he seems only to know of demons having done the crucifying. At best we cannot claim to *know* he imagined anything else, and so this verse falls away as of no use to defending historicity. It lacks the very details such an employment of it would require. Once again Paul is too vague for historicists to get their surety. Which fact alone is evidence against them—they have to posit that Paul's repeated vagueness about Jesus's earthly life is just (strangely) a multiply repeated coincidence, whereas we only have to take him at what he actually says. On our theory, none of this is strange. It's all ex-

---

[56] Carrier, *Historicity*, 311–12, 453, 560–63, and *Proving History*, 151–55 (with 317–19). As argued there, Paul is more probably just referencing Isaiah 53:6, which uses the exact same word in the LXX (Carrier, *Historicity*, 143); Mark then played on its double meaning to invent a mythologically symbolic 'betrayal' narrative.

[57] Carrier, *Historicity*, 184–93, 564–65.

[58] M. David Litwa, *How the Gospels Became History: Jesus and Mediterranean Myths* (Yale University Press, 2019), 37–39.

[59] As usual I already addressed Litwa's argument before he even thought to make it: Carrier, *Historicity*, 564–66. On the curious trend of critics pretending to their peers that we did not already rebut their arguments, see chapter three.

[60] For example, Litwa's only proposed evidence for his take is his own personal disbelief that demons could be imagined to crucify people, or that words designating 'the world' could include the sky, or that anyone could imagine someone being killable there (he evidently did not read the array of evidence I presented that they certainly could: Carrier, *Historicity*, 194–97; cf. 184–94, and 46, 172, 569–70). For a more hand-wavy version of Litwa's approach, which adds nothing to it, see Daniel Gullotta, "On Richard Carrier's Doubts: A Response to Richard Carrier's *On the Historicity of Jesus: Why We Might Have Reason for Doubt*," *Journal for the Study of the Historical Jesus* 15.2–3 (2017): 310–46 (331–34).

actly what Paul would say.

Gaventa's analysis expands on this with more evidence and argument I had not considered, bolstering my case. For example, if God handed Jesus over, not Judas, then the agents God handed him over to are *more likely* to be supernatural than the ones Judas hands him over to. If God handed Jesus over, that should mean to *God's* enemies, those with whom God was at war—and that simply wasn't humans (the very people it was his object to save), but the rebellious celestial entities responsible for 'death' and 'sin'. Paul's language across his letters strongly suggests it was indeed the 'anti-God powers' (as Gaventa puts it) that Paul often laments—actual beings (demons and fallen angels) to whom we could be spiritually enslaved and with whom we wage a spiritual war, like Satan ("the god of this world," 2 Corinthians 4:4), and his demonic minions (e.g., 1 Corinthians 8:5, 10:20–21, even 15:26 and 54–57; Galatians 4:8; Romans 8:38–39; etc.). So if Jesus was slain and hung on a pole by "the rulers of this aeon," we cannot establish that that really happened any more than we could prove Satan's 'rebellion' really happened—even though these same people believed that that, too, was a historical event (and definitely located it beyond Earth).

Gaventa's argument is not by itself conclusive, but it strengthens the arguments I already presented (and it ranges over more evidence than I just mentioned). And though Gaventa still operates on the assumption of historicity, and thus adopts a 'solution' similar to Litwa's (that somehow the earthly authorities must have been agents of the demons Paul is referring to), she has inadvertently undermined that assumption, and thus exposed it *as* an assumption. Because Gaventa offers none of the inept attempts at defending it that Litwa does.

In her words:

> God brings to an end the 'handing over' of humanity to Sin and Death by means of another handing over, this time of God's Son. The consequences of this act are, of course, the reversal of the captivity so terrifyingly outlined in [Romans 1]; this handing over results in the release of captive humanity and defeat of these powerful foes of God.

Quite so. And her case for this is strong. Yet if this is indeed what Paul means, then why do we need human powers at all? If God can give Jesus a mortal body (Philippians 2:6–8) and hand him over to thus be killed by his cosmic enemies (1 Corinthians 2:8) and then exalt him as an immortal once again (Philippians 2:6, 9–11; 1 Corinthians 15:4, 20–28), why should we *assume* there were yet more epicycles in that plan?

Paul, after all, does not believe any human authorities are the enemies of God, but in fact his agents (the entire point of Romans 13). And no human authorities could have known or believed any of the secret cosmic realities that Paul says would impel Christ's killers to stop the crucifixion (1 Cor. 2:6–10) had they known the cosmic metaphysical plan it served (as outlined in Heb. 9). In fact, defeating mere human puppets of the demonic authors of sin in the sublunar world would be pointless in Paul's scheme, as it would leave those authors undefeated and the crucifixion ineffective (they could just pick up new puppets); the actual authors (God's actual *enemies*) had to be defeated by it, and those simply were not humans. Yet these demons are the enemies Paul says are now "ceasing to exist" or "being rendered powerless" (*katargoumenôn*), which cannot describe even the Judean elite much less the Roman Empire, which was at its absolute height at the time. It can only describe the demonic forces disempowered by the magical effects of Christ's death, as Paul elsewhere implies (Romans 8:37–39; cf. Ephesians 6:10-12), and just as later Christians like Justin saw as evident in the power of Christ's name to drive out demons and disable their influence over human souls.[61]

That Jesus was 'handed over' by God, and crucified by the powers aiming to thwart God's cosmic plan, sounds quite a lot like Osiris becoming mortal and submitting to being killed by *his* enemy in the sky (another "archon of the domain of the air" as Satan is described in Ephesians 2:2) in order to rise again triumphant, his enemy defeated for yet another year.[62] The only difference is that, again, in accordance with the Jewish affinity for linear-apocalyptic time over the common pagan affinity for cyclical time, this plan of Jesus is a one-off (he doesn't have to do it again, a difference Christians peculiarly felt they had to explain: Hebrews 9). But other than that, it sounds like Paul is talking about the very same thing. It therefore requires *evidence*, not assumptions, to argue

---

[61] For examples see Carrier, "On the Historicity of Jesus and the Rhetoric of Justin's *Dialogue with Trypho*" (25 March 2023) at richardcarrier.info/archives/23326.

[62] Carrier, *Outer Space*, 35–39; *Historicity*, 186–88 (see, e.g., Plutarch, *On Isis and Osiris* 27.361e and 30.362e).

that he wasn't.

But the evidence seems to point the other way. Neil Godfrey, for example, has provided a valuable bibliographic essay and series analyzing this debate and the direction in which the evidence points overall.[63] And to that he adds his own observation: calling Christ's killers the rulers "of" this age (rather than "in" it) strongly implies these beings rule *the cosmos*, over thousands of years of time, not just a recent local empire or administrative district.[64] An entirely different and mighty empire—the Persian Empire (then under Parthian rule)—bordered relatively near Judea and cannot be credited with the crucifixion; nor could the distant mighty kingdoms of India and China, which were also then well known. Even the Roman Empire was new (just a couple centuries; before, the Greeks ruled Judea). So Paul's totalizing phrase does not appear to encompass human rulers. It appears to mean cosmic ones. This perfects my previous point that the qualifier "of this aeon" is indeed the feature signaling these archons are celestial and not earthly, a point on which the ancient Christian scholar Origen agreed.[65]

Since I published, even more studies than Droge, Litwa, and Gaventa's have come out reinforcing my background evidence regarding the importance of cosmic and demonic agents in the thought of Paul and other early Jews and Christians.[66] Which further bolster yet another study that confirms my conclusion, by Robert Moses, who provides not only a thorough analysis of the texts and their ancient context regarding this question, but adds a perspective from the anthropology of religion.[67]

---

[63] Neil Godfrey, "Are the 'Rulers of the Age' in 1 Cor. 2:6–8 Human or Spiritual? – The Sea Change," *Vridar* (14 June 2018) at tinyurl.com/2ubm5ufv; and, as well, Godfrey's closing observations (and list of other articles in this series) in "Paul's 'Rulers of this Age'—Conclusion," *Vridar* (23 July 2018) at tinyurl.com/3csunnuw.

[64] In Neil Godfrey, "Who Crucified Jesus – Men or Demons? Continuing Miller's Study of 1 Cor 2:6–8," *Vridar* (20 June 2018) at tinyurl.com/j33xy4my.

[65] Carrier, *Historicity*, 565–66 (citing Origen, *Commentary on 1 Corinthians*, fragment 9.14-25).

[66] Thomas Farrar, "The Intimate and Ultimate Adversary: Satanology in Early Second-Century Christian Literature," *Journal of Early Christian Studies* 26.4 (2018), 517–46; Travis Proctor, *Demonic Bodies and the Dark Ecologies of Early Christian Culture* (Oxford University Press, 2022); and Hector Patmore and Josef Lössl (eds.), *Demons in Early Judaism and Christianity: Characters and Characteristics* (Brill, 2022).

[67] Robert Moses, *Practices of Power: Revisiting the Principalities and Powers in the Pauline*

Moses adds more arguments to mine in reaching the conclusion that 1 Corinthians 2:8 refers to demonic, not human, agents—even against the apologetic 'solution' of imagining it somehow refers to both (a position Moses finds "exegetically unsupportable").[68]

Once again, I am not alone. My conclusions are finding increasing rather than diminishing support in the expert literature. Abundant holdouts remain. But they are on the wrong side of the argument, resorting (like Litwa) to apologetics, rhetoric, and denialism, rather than an objective assessment of the facts as they are. Which is illustrative of the hold that 'historicity' has as a dogma in this field, rather than being a well-reasoned conclusion.

Another case in point…

The Eucharist: Tradition or Revelation?

After publishing my own evidence and arguments for the conclusion that Paul is actually saying in 1 Corinthians 11:23–27 that he learned of the Eucharist directly from the Lord in a vision (and not from any historical tradition handed down to anyone),[69] I was delighted to discover Francis Watson had independently made many of my same points and come to the same conclusion, with another persuasive case that reinforces mine.[70] And now another study, by Afetame Alabi, has thoroughly treated the arguments against such a view and found them as wanting as I did; and he cites over a dozen scholars concurring (including half a dozen in just the last decade).[71]

First, Watson adds an important observation: the fact that Paul says 'I' with an actual pronoun (not just a verb in the first person) indicates that "he wished to emphasize the special link between this tradition and

---

Letters (Fortress, 2014).

[68] Moses, *Practices of Power*, 86–92.

[69] Carrier, *Historicity*, 557–63.

[70] Francis Watson, "'I received from the Lord…': Paul, Jesus, and the Last Supper," in *Jesus and Paul Reconnected: Fresh Pathways into an Old Debate* (ed. Todd Still; Eerdmans, 2007), 103–34.

[71] Afetame Alabi, "'I Received from the Lord': Assessing the Arguments Against a Pauline Claim to Revelation in 1 Corinthians 11:23," *Neotestamentica* 56.1 (2022), 1–31.

his own person" (cf. Gal. 5:2 and 2 Cor. 10:1), which "could indeed mean what he appears to say: that he, Paul, received the Last Supper tradition from the Lord himself and not from any merely human process of transmission."[72] Moreover, the suggestion that Paul means some sort of mediated tradition is contradicted by his own formula: "I transmitted to you what I received from the Lord" entails the Lord is Paul's unique access that the Corinthians would lack *but for* Paul; but if he meant that he, too, only had it from tradents, then he could just as well say *the Corinthians* received it from the Lord, Paul being just one more tradent. In that case "if he receives the tradition as 'from the Lord'," Watson observes, "then so do they."[73] So why would Paul make such a distinction, unless his reception *differed* from theirs?[74] Watson thus agrees with my reading of this text that Paul does not refer to any betrayal by Judas here, but (just as Gaventa concluded) to God's handing over Jesus (per Isaiah 53:12 and Romans 8:32), citing John Dominic Crossan in agreement with this.[75]

Further supporting the point, Watson notes that, by contrast, in 1 Corinthians 15:1–4 Paul does not identify his source. Although I noted that Galatians 1:11–16 implies Paul does mean the Lord there as well (a point on which Alabi agrees, as well as Joshua Garroway and Steve Maso), Watson observes that Paul is being *explicit* about that in 1 Corinthians 11:23.[76] I accumulate many more arguments in *Historicity* to the same conclusion (some also shared by Watson); so the reasons Watson adds, even if weak in themselves, only make my case stronger.[77] As Watson says, we are only taking what Paul says "at face value." It is those who reject that interpretation who are interjecting assumptions and possibil-

---

[72] Watson, "Received," 105. He cites as concurring Hans Lietzmann, *Mass and Lord's Supper: A Study in the History of the Liturgy*, vol. 1 (Brill, 1979), 204–07.

[73] Watson, "Received," 108–10.

[74] Watson, "Received," 106.

[75] Gaventa, "Interpreting the Death"; John Dominic Crossan, *The Birth of Christianity* (Harper, 1998), 439.

[76] Evidence that both verses refer to revelation: Carrier, *Historicity*, 516–17, 536 (cf. 553–54, 557–58). That the creed Paul relates in 1 Cor. 15 was also received by revelation is agreed in: Alabi, "Received from the Lord," 6; Joshua Garroway, *The Beginning of the Gospel: Paul, Philippi and the Origins of Christianity* (Palgrave Macmillan, 2018), 26–29; and Steve Mason, *Josephus, Judea, and Christian Origins* (Hendrickson, 2009), 283–302.

[77] Watson himself has additional arguments, such as an informative comparison between the contents of 1 Cor. 11:23–27 and 2 Cor. 12 ("Received," 110–15).

ities not in evidence in order to get Paul to have said something that he (literally) didn't.

This is unaffected by questions of Paul's honesty in the matter. It's possible this was simply a vision any apostle was expected to have and thus claim (hence Paul's truthfulness can be as suspect here as ever).[78] But it's also possible Paul invented this tradition (whether deliberately or by the unconscious operation of his revelatory imagination, as we can infer from 2 Cor. 12:6–10 might often have happened) because he needed a replacement for the Passover as a symbol and a bond-creating ritual meal with which to integrate Jews and Gentiles. The original apostles then would not have objected (as they didn't to the rest of Paul's unique conclusions, as we see in Galatians 2), because it didn't contain anything contrary to their dogmas. For example, contrary to many a scholar's declaration today, they would entirely understand (as would any intelligent educated person then) that the ritual described was not *literal* cannibalism and thus would be in no way 'un-kosher' or 'immoral' or 'abhorrent' (the Catholic idea of *literal* transubstantiation would not be introduced for centuries yet).

This is a point made even more thoroughly by Alabi: "even if a preexisting tradition is present in Paul's Last Supper narrative, it is not impossible that Paul believed that he received a subsequent, independent revelation of this tradition," or that he claimed to; and even that tradition could itself have been revelatory (e.g., originally a revelation to Peter).[79] So even if we could make such distinctions (and we lack any evidence on which to), that still cannot recover a historical event from the scant data Paul provides. In the same fashion, that the ritual communicated to Paul related to a past event does not rule out a vision, either. After all, Jesus's resurrection was also a past event communicated after-the-fact (per 1 Cor. 15:3–8). On the theory that both events were cosmic, the ritual preceding the death and resurrection was performed only in secret to establish it (like casting a spell), and *then* communicated (1 Cor. 2:6–10; Romans 16:25–26).[80]

---

[78] On Paul's possible mendacity in such matters see: Carrier, *Historicity*, 536, 559 (cf. 131–34).

[79] Alabi, "Received from the Lord," 22–25 (24). Or the original is in *Didache* 9.

[80] All this, of course, assumes that Paul actually meant that Jesus performed this ritual "in the night" he was handed over, and did not mean "in the night in which [this informa-

Indeed, Alabi surveys and dispatches what appears to me to be every argument ever published against the conclusion that Paul is indeed saying that he received the Eucharist by revelation. For example, Alabi dispatches the oft-claimed assertion—that the Greek word Paul uses here for 'received', *paralambanô*, is a technical term from Rabbinical texts that designates only an *ultimate* source of a transmitted tradition—by demonstrating that everything claimed about that is false. Alabi shows that nearly all the examples scholars have cited as somehow establishing this also employ the term to refer to direct divine revelation, and in precisely the format Paul presents.[81] The remaining examples are then matched by others where that is meant *as well*. Which means the supposedly corresponding Rabbinical Hebrew word was demonstrably *also* used to refer to receiving information directly by revelation, and therefore *does not* distinctively indicate an ultimate source of a human tradition. That argument is therefore defunct.

It is specious to assume a connection between the Hebrew and Greek anyway, at least in the way this apologetical argument requires.[82] There is no example anywhere in the New Testament of *paralambanô* being used in the first-person singular to refer to oral tradition from a distant past teacher (Rabbinical or otherwise). In fact, I have yet to see an example of such a use in the whole of Greek literature. Whereas this is exactly the same word Paul uses, yet again in the first person singular, in Galatians 1:12 to refer to a revelation.[83] This evidence trumps any other. We should follow Paul's usage, when attempting to determine Paul's usage; not the Rabbinical (which, as just noted, doesn't exist anyway: it is identical to Paul's).[84] The same conclusion follows for attempts to argue that Paul's use of the Greek preposition *apo* for 'from' (in 1 Corinthians 11:23), instead of *para* (as in Galatians 1:12), is what indicates an ultimate and not immediate source. But the evidence shows no such distinction exists in Paul's usage. He uses them interchangeably, and appears even to prefer *apo* to *para* when his source is supernatural (and indeed in Galatians 1:12

tion] was handed down [to me or the first apostle]" (Carrier, *Historicity*, 560n63).

[81] Alabi, "Received from the Lord," 4–7.

[82] Alabi, "Received from the Lord," 5n12.

[83] Alabi, "Received from the Lord," 6–7.

[84] Again, see Carrier, *Historicity*, 516–17, 536 (cf. 553–54, 557–58).

para is only used to refer to *human* sources).[85]

Indeed, this apologetic (again depending on a premise that is provably false) overlooks the fact that if Paul actually meant what this argument avers, he would sooner have written that 'we' received it from the Lord, not 'I' received it from the Lord; or he would say it in the third person and with a more appropriate verb, for example 'as was handed down' or 'as the Lord handed down' (see Luke 1:2 or Acts 6:14). Instead, Paul chose wording that establishes himself *as* the tradent: from the Lord, to him, to them. Just as in Galatians. Which implies a vision, not a tradition.

Alabi ably dispatches several other attempts to argue against the revelatory interpretation of this passage. That Paul discusses revelations elsewhere differently is better explained by differences of context and purpose.[86] Lukan redaction is not usable as evidence to the point;[87] nor is Markan;[88] nor are Paul's other references to the Lord as his source;[89] nor is the mere fact that Paul later conferred with Peter.[90] Likewise, attempts to claim evidence of a pre-Pauline tradition in Paul's language in this passage are too circular to carry a point, and often rest on provably false claims about Pauline style, and are moot because a revelation could indeed have come to Paul in a voice other than his own, rendering such evidence incapable of proving otherwise.[91]

All this establishes two things. First, my position regarding this passage has gained, not lost, support since I published *Historicity* in 2014; and considerably so. Second, Alabi's analysis in particular shows not merely that it is as likely or even more likely that Paul is saying this information came by revelation (and not a historical event), but also that attempts to make this conclusion go away have never been sound but have always been specious and desperate. The apologetics Alabi doc-

---

[85] Alabi, "Received from the Lord," 7–9.

[86] Alabi, "Received from the Lord," 9–11.

[87] Alabi, "Received from the Lord," 11–12.

[88] Alabi, "Received from the Lord," 12–13. And see the previously referenced studies establishing Mark is adapting Paul's words into a narrative, and not the other way around.

[89] Alabi, "Received from the Lord," 14–15.

[90] Alabi, "Received from the Lord," 16.

[91] Alabi, "Received from the Lord," 16–22.

uments as deployed to rescue the passage for historicity span a whole scattershot of obscure and convoluted arguments, every one of which either self-evidently illogical or dependent on false claims about the facts. True conclusions do not require this kind of response. The sheer number of solely implausible arguments is itself evidence that the apologetical stance is the one that is false. We should acknowledge this. We should be reading Paul at exactly what he said, and not try to invent mountains of implausible or false claims to get him to have said something else. Which is a point I will expand upon in chapter four.

Did Thallus Prove Jesus Existed?

Not only has my position on the Gospels and Epistles gained support, but so have my positions on evidence outside the Bible. The easiest example is the chronologer Thallus. I ruled him out as a source because there was no evidence that he wrote before the Gospels or that he even mentioned Jesus.[92] I presented the evidence for this in a prior study.[93] That study has received a response from Jobjorn Boman worth noting, though not one affecting any conclusion regarding historicity.[94] Boman adds a lot of useful information of value to anyone studying the case; and he argues for an alternative thesis to mine: that Thallus never wrote anything about Jesus because his chronology ended a century before the time of Jesus; and that what I conclude is a quotation of Thallus in Eusebius is just a duplicative 'brief' of Phlegon. I am not convinced by Boman's argument, but I agree it's plausible. And either way, his study also eliminates Thallus as a source for Jesus.

Does Josephus Prove Jesus Existed?

Two important works surveying the sources for Jesus came out since *Historicity* was published that I would certainly have cited there. The

[92] Carrier, *Historicity*, 346–47.

[93] Richard Carrier, "Thallus and the Darkness at Christ's Death," *Journal of Greco-Roman Christianity and Judaism* 8 (2011/2012), 185–91.

[94] Jobjorn Boman, "Comments on Carrier: Is Thallus Actually Quoted by Eusebius?" *Liber Annuus* 62 (2012), 319–25.

first (which I have cited sections of already) was the three-volume collection *The Reception of Jesus in the First Three Centuries*; and the second, the ensuing work of Margaret Williams.[95] Both add a considerable amount of useful background, contextual, and interpretive information on the sources for Jesus outside the Bible. And yet neither work reaches many conclusions not already adopted or adequately questioned in my or Lataster's work. For example, the entry on Josephus by Jan Willem van Henten in *Reception* is woefully out-of-date, cites almost no recent work, and fails to consider hardly any of the relevant evidence.[96]

The few arguments in those volumes still requiring a response I'll deal with in coming sections or chapters. But of first interest is the position of Williams regarding the utility of Josephus as a source for Jesus, which agrees with mine.[97] She concludes that the material in Josephus "has suffered so badly through subsequent Christian 'editing' that Josephus's original words (assuming that there is a genuine Josephan core to this evidence) can no longer be identified with confidence," and therefore it is of no use for establishing the historicity of Jesus.[98] She doesn't even include Josephus in her study. Which would suggest she doesn't even think the 'James' passage in Josephus (the 'minor' testimonium) is worth comment either.

Other recent work on this material confirms our suspicions. Chris Hansen has criticized the use of extrabiblical evidence for Jesus across the board, Josephus among them.[99] Hansen is no fan of mythicism, yet

---

[95] Chris Keith, Helen Bond, Christine Jacobi, and Jens Schröter (eds.), *The Reception of Jesus in the First Three Centuries*, 3 vols. (T&T Clark, 2019); Margaret Williams, *Early Classical Authors on Jesus* (T&T Clark, 2022). By contrast, *The Jesus Handbook* (ed. Jens Schröter and Christine Jacobi; Eerdmans, 2022; German: Mohr Siebeck, 2017) I found to be useless, inadequate on every topic it approaches, with bibliographies and discussions already decades out of date. For example, its section on Tacitus discusses no scholarship at all from the 21st century, and its discussion of Josephus completely omits the work of Goldberg and Hopper, and does not accurately describe the results of Olson (all of whom will be discussed here shortly). And it does not cover the debate on the historicity of Jesus at all.

[96] Jan Willem van Henten, "Testimonium Flavianum," in *The Reception of Jesus in the First Three Centuries, Volume 1: From Paul to Josephus* (ed. Helen Bond; T&T Clark, 2019), 365–70.

[97] Carrier, *Historicity*, 332–42; see Lataster, *Questioning*, 36–38, 192–202.

[98] Williams, *Early Classical Authors*, 54.

[99] Chris Hansen, "Jesus' Historicity and Sources: The Misuse of Extrabiblical Sources

concludes as I do that none of these sources can be used as evidence for Jesus, because they are all fatally compromised by being either suspect or derivative, or both. This has been confirmed for the James passage (the 'minor' testimonium) by Nicholas List and Nicholas Allen.[100] While in *Historicity* I already cited the studies of Olson and others on this point for the 'major' testimonium.[101] But studies reinforcing the same conclusion have only proliferated since.

Besides Hansen, List, and Allen, one of the most important demonstrations of the wholesale interpolation of the major testimonium is now the work of Paul Hopper.[102] Hopper perfects and improves on an argument I independently made that renders incredible even supposed 'reconstructed' versions of the Testimonium Flavianum: that the text completely violates Josephus's discourse style—and even more so in every shortened, trimmed, or hypothetically 'revised' version scholars have proposed. Hopper's point is not just to compare the grammar and vocabulary (which Olsen has already extensively proved is not Josephan but in fact Eusebian; which I then argued could mean either Eusebius *or* his tutor Pamphilus produced it), but the style of narration itself. In other words, when we compare the Testimonium Flavianum with every other example in the works of Josephus of how he tells stories, we find

---

for Jesus and a Suggestion," *American Journal of Biblical Theology* 22.6 (2021), 1–21; and especially "Reception of the Testimonium Flavianum: An Evaluation of the Independent Witnesses to Josephus' Testimonium Flavianum," *New England Classical Journal* 51.2 (2024), 50–75.

[100] Nicholas List, "The Death of James the Just Revisited," *Journal of Early Christian Studies* 32 (2024), 17–44; Nicholas Allen, "Josephus on James the Just? A Re-Evaluation of *Antiquitates Judaicae* 20.9.1," *Journal of Early Christian History* 7.1 (2017), 1–27; and Hansen, "Jesus' Historicity," 6. My study of the minor testimonium remains the most comprehensive demonstration of its interpolation: Richard Carrier "Origen, Eusebius, and the Accidental Interpolation in Josephus, *Jewish Antiquities* 20.200," *Journal of Early Christian Studies* 20.4 (2012), 489-54. And I add yet more to it here in chapter ten. But List's study valuably adds far more discussion of its context.

[101] Ken Olson, "A Eusebian Reading of the Testimonium Flavianum," in *Eusebius of Caesarea: Tradition and Innovations* (ed. Aaron Johnson and Jeremy Schott: Harvard University Press, 2013), 97-114; "The Testimonium Flavianum, Eusebius, and Consensus," *Historical Jesus Research* (13 August 2013) at tinyurl.com/mr2uehpc; and "Eusebius and the Testimonium Flavianum," *Catholic Biblical Quarterly* 61.2 (1999), 305-22.

[102] Paul Hopper, "A Narrative Anomaly in Josephus: *Jewish Antiquities* xviii:63," in *Linguistics and Literary Studies: Interfaces, Encounters, Transfers* (ed. Monika Fludernik and Daniel Jacob; de Gruyter, 2014), 147–69.

the Testimonium wholly alien. For example, it tracks none of his ubiquitous techniques of explanatory and causal narrative; and 'revised' versions of the text do so even less, and thus are even less likely to be what Josephus wrote. Hopper also finds numerous and substantial violations of Josephan verbal syntax (his typical use of aspects, tenses, participles, nominalizations, and conjugations).

One could add to all this, following Hopper's own method of discourse analysis, that we actually have several examples of how Josephus writes about messianic pretenders, and all of them conform to a common structure—none of which can be found in the Testimonium.[103] In every case (The Samaritan; The Egyptian; John the Baptist; Theudas; and a general accounting of 'imposters') Josephus conspicuously avoids ever using the word Christ or Jesus (i.e. Joshua), yet depicts them as promising or alluding to an apocalyptic redemption of Israel through an act deliberately reminiscent of the *original* Joshua. Which means Josephus expected his Jewish readers to get the hint (a messiah emulating the patriarchal 'Jesus' as national redeemer), but at the same time wanted to conceal that from his Gentile readers, who wouldn't get the hint. Since every other time he relates such figures Josephus does not mention but conceals their status as 'messiahs' (Christs) and 'Jesuses' (Joshua-emulators), we can be certain nothing in the Testimonium derives from Josephus, who would have mapped the same model to the Christian Jesus: he would have avoided using the words Jesus and Christ, and would have described him doing something emulative of the original Joshua (and *then*, like the others, coming to an ignominious end). Likewise, we have several examples of how Josephus describes sects (such as the Pharisees, the Sadducees, and the Essenes), and those passages all follow the same blueprint in how he describes their beliefs and what distinguishes them. Yet the Testimonium follows none of that blueprint, despite clearly purporting to describe another Jewish sect. It therefore cannot be by Josephus.

If all of that were not enough, we have a clincher on the other side of the analysis: what the Testimonium *does* look like. Hopper noted it looks suspiciously a lot like Christian creeds in its structure and genre, and thus can only have been written by a dogmatic Christian. And indeed

[103] Carrier, *Historicity*, 68–71, 245–46.

it turns out that there is an even more specific source than that. I had already cited the work of Gary Goldberg establishing that the Testimonium Flavianum is entirely constructed from the Emmaus narrative in Luke.[104] As I noted in *Historicity*, Goldberg proves "nineteen unique correspondences between Luke's Emmaus account and the Testimonium Flavianum, all nineteen in exactly the same order," and a twentieth out of order. The significance of this is twofold: (1) whoever wrote it (and not some later redactor of it) used Luke reverently as their base text; and (2) once we remove every element of it thus explained, no elements remain to survive as a previous ('more original') version of the text. Goldberg's study alone thus refutes all attempts at proposing a hypothetical 'reconstructed' version of the Testimonium Flavianum to rescue any of it as authentic. Every component of it is original. We do *not* have a redaction that can be hypothetically trimmed down into something else. This is also proved by Hopper from a structural perspective; and by Olsen from a stylistic perspective. With three complete carpet bombings of scholarly hopes to save *something* here, those hopes really need to be binned. Josephus wrote nothing about Jesus.

Goldberg, aware of what he had wrought, attempted the only recourse left to the apologist: to argue Josephus reverently employed the Gospel of Luke, and wrote the entirety of the Testimonium as we have it.[105] But his effort there is based on dubious argumentation already thoroughly refuted by the findings of Olson, Hopper, and myself.[106] Of course, abundant evidence indicates Luke used the *Antiquities* of Josephus as a source, and *not* the other way around.[107] So Goldberg's thesis is already unlikely. But his approach is not even logical, consisting entirely of showing the testimonium conforms to ancient standards of paraphrasing—and then claiming this proves Josephus must have done it, without ever examining whether these standards were *commonly* em-

[104] Gary Goldberg, "The Coincidences of the Testimonium of Josephus and the Emmaus Narrative of Luke," *Journal for the Study of the Pseudepigrapha* 13 (1995), 59-77. See Carrier, *Historicity*, 333n81.

[105] Gary Goldberg, "Josephus's Paraphrase Style and the Testimonium Flavianum," *Journal for the Study of the Historical Jesus* 20 (2022), 1–32.

[106] See my analysis in Richard Carrier, "Goldberg's Attempt to Rehabilitate the Testimonium Flavianum" (11 September 2023) at richardcarrier.info/archives/24794.

[107] Carrier, *Historicity*, 267 (and see note here in chapter ten).

ployed by ancient paraphrasers and thus not particular to Josephus. He also ignores all the evidence against him (linguistically from Olson, discursively from Hopper, and contextually from myself and others). The end result is that the case for Josephus even having mentioned Jesus is now substantially worse than it was even when I published, and ironically even *because* of Goldberg's demonstration that the major testimonium was composed entirely as it is by someone paraphrasing Luke 24. And just as with Goldberg's subsequent attempt to use this fact to restore its authenticity, all attempts to rescue any form of either of the two passages in Josephus rely on ignoring all the evidence and arguments already refuting them, *even in Goldberg*. Which is yet another sign of the defense of a dogma rather than objective scholarship.

The irony is that this conclusion isn't even necessary in order to argue against this evidence being of any use for establishing the historicity of Jesus. As I explain in respect to the reference to Jesus we now find in the *Annals* of Tacitus (in the next chapter), it is enough to note that even if Josephus wrote the Testimonium Flavianum, exactly as we have it (or in any redactable form), it still cannot be established to be independent of the Gospels—and indeed, Goldberg has *proved it wasn't*. Therefore it has no value as evidence.[108] To have that we would need evidence (not mere conjecture) that Josephus 'fact-checked' his sources on this point rather than simply slavishly repeated them; but Goldberg's study demonstrates the author of the entire Testimonium (whether that was Josephus or not) chose to slavishly repeat them. The Testimonium therefore has no value as evidence even if it is authentic. This includes all attempts to reconstruct it, modern and medieval. Even the Agapius paraphrase has long been proved a redaction of the Eusebian text.[109]

All the same goes for the minor testimonium, where our text says a certain executed James was the brother of a Jesus 'called Christ'. That

[108] See Carrier, *Historicity*, 256, 342–46. Which also renders moot T.C. Schmidt's apologetical case for authenticity in *Josephus and Jesus: New Evidence for the One Called Christ* (Oxford University Press, 2025) which came out as this book was already going to press. I will address it in a future article.

[109] Carrier, *Historicity*, 336–37, summarizing, among other experts concurring, the crucial study of Alice Whealey, "The Testimonium Flavianum in Syriac and Arabic," *New Testament Studies* 54 (2008), 573-90.

phrase is almost certainly interpolated there, the whole affair originally being a story about a different Jesus than ours, as now several scholars concur (as I'll discuss in chapter ten). But even if it wasn't, it still can't help us establish a historical Jesus, because we can't establish that Josephus knew (or even would or could have known, or even cared) what sort of 'brother' James was to Jesus (a problem I will also explain in chapter ten).[110]

Meanwhile, continuing attempts to resist these conclusions do not pass any test of logic. For example, David Allen and Steve Mason have both inexplicably argued that the major testimonium can only have been edited and not wholly forged by a Christian because forgers do not emulate the vocabulary of their target text in any respect.[111] But in fact 'mixed texts' (a verbal and stylistic hybrid of the forger's and the target's text) are *the norm* for forgeries, not the exception.[112] As Ehrman succinctly put it, "it is easy to take over the words of another writer," and we see this even in the forgery of 3 Corinthians, which no one doubts is fake yet "a large number" of "Pauline words and phrases are scattered throughout" it.[113] The same we can expect to be the case for the major testimonium: its forger will have attempted to emulate Josephan vocabulary and not to sound like themselves, and will only fail in some respects, not in all. Which is exactly what we observe. So there is no logical way to derive from this fact that the forger only edited an existing text. Maybe they did; but that will not be shown by this state of the text. All of Allen's

---

[110] Likewise mooting Schmidt's argument in *Josephus and Jesus*.

[111] David Allen, "A Model Reconstruction of What Josephus Would Have Realistically Written about Jesus," *Journal of Greco-Roman Christianity and Judaism* 18 (2022), 113–43; Steve Mason, "Jewish Sources: Flavius Josephus," in *The Jesus Handbook* (ed. Schröter and Jacobi; Eerdmans 2022), kindle loc. 3922–4054. See also: David Allen, "A Proposal: Three Redactional Layer Model for the Testimonium Flavianum," *Revista bíblica* 85 (2023), 211–32, and "How Josephus Really Viewed Jesus," *Revista bíblica* 85 (2023), 333–57; and Chris Hansen, "A Response to David Allen's 'A Model Reconstruction of What Josephus Would Have Realistically Written about Jesus'," *Journal of Greco-Roman Christianity and Judaism* 19 (2023), 94–103.

[112] Evident throughout Ehrman, *Forgery and Counterforgery*. But see also: Don Foster, *Author Unknown: On the Trail of Anonymous* (Henry Holt, 2000); Joe Nickell, *Detecting Forgery: Forensic Investigation of Documents* (Rowman & Littlefield, 1996), 104–07; and Kenneth Rendell, *Forging History: The Detection of Fake Letters and Documents* (University of Oklahoma Press, 1994).

[113] Ehrman, *Forgery and Counterforgery*, 158, 428–29.

and Mason's arguments suffer the same fatal illogicality as this, while essentially ignoring all the evidence against their conclusion that I just surveyed.[114] Such is the state of the debate.

Ultimately, the case for relying on Josephus to argue for the historicity of Jesus is worse off now than when I published, having received multiple new blows (most especially from Hopper). Any resistance to this conclusion can now only be dogmatic or illogical.

Does Suetonius Prove Jesus Existed?

Christian apologists have continued attempts at arguing Suetonius's reference to the rioter Chrestus really, somehow, refers to Jesus.[115] This is a doomed project for historicity anyway, since even if that was a completely garbled account of some obscure event involving Christians, it was clearly so poorly understood or described that it can contain no usable data regarding the historicity of Jesus.[116] But I am delighted to notice that, since I published, these attempts have been quite thoroughly dashed by Margaret Williams, whose destruction of this passage as a usable source is in my view conclusive.[117]

Does Mara bar Serapion Prove Jesus Existed?

The same fate has befallen all attempts to recover the letter of 'Mara bar Serapion' as evidence for historicity. I had already dismissed that as useless on the conclusions of prior scholars.[118] But now Margaret Williams, Kathleen McVey, and Catherine Chin have decisively removed it from play, demonstrating that it is more probable than not that the Mara bar

---

[114] Reviewing all their errors and omissions here would be more tedious than economical (likewise for Schmidt's case in *Josephus and Jesus*). But for readers who wish to, see Richard Carrier, "Mason on Josephus on James" (17 May 2020) at richardcarrier.info/archives/16715, and "Allen's New and Illogical Theory of the Testimonium Flavianum" (6 May 2024) at richardcarrier.info/archives/27782.

[115] See my following section on Tacitus and discussion in the next chapter.

[116] Carrier, *Historicity*, 347–49 (cf. 275, 295, 344).

[117] Williams, *Early Classical Authors*, 105–19 (on Suetonius generally: 98–122; and with further context pertaining to Chrestus: 196–205).

[118] Carrier, *Historicity*, 275.

Serapion letter was a fourth century Christian school exercise and thus neither independent nor early.[119]

Does Tacitus Prove Jesus Existed?

In *Historicity* I concluded that even if the reference to Jesus (as 'Christ') in the *Annals* of Tacitus was entirely authentic it has no use for establishing historicity because it cannot be shown to be independent of Christian informants relying on the Gospels. There is no evidence Tacitus 'fact checked' what he was told; and what he was told was too amusing to his perspective to question.[120] Margaret Williams, Chris Hansen, and Ivan Prchlík now concur.[121] There has been no rehabilitation from this point since. However, the unrelated question of whether Tacitus even mentioned Christ in the first place (which my argument in *Historicity* did not depend on) has also received a lot of attention since I published, both for and against. But as that is tangential and involves an engagement with critics, I will address that debate in the next chapter.

Were There Christians Who Placed Jesus in a Different Century?

There has also been some (albeit more ambiguous) development relating to my treatment of Epiphanius as corroborating the Talmud's attestation of a Christian sect east of the Roman Empire placing the life and death of Jesus a hundred years before Pontius Pilate, indeed removing Roman involvement with Jesus entirely. Which is a reason Christian Brady now

---

[119] Margaret Williams, *Early Classical Authors*, 4; Catherine Chin, "Rhetorical Practice in the Chreia Elaboration of Mara bar Serapion," *Hugoye: Journal of Syriac Studies* 9.2 (2006), 145–71; Kathleen McVey, "A Fresh Look at the Letter of Mara bar Serapion to His Son," *Orientalia Christiana Analecta* 236 (1990), 257–72, and "Mara bar Serapion," in *The Reception of Jesus in the First Three Centuries, Volume 3: From Celsus to the Catacombs* (ed. Chris Keith: T&T Clark, 2019), 71–88.

[120] Carrier, *Historicity*, 342–46 (cf. 349); Lataster, *Questioning*, 203–04, 397–98.

[121] Williams, *Early Classical Authors*, 16 (esp. n. 76); Hansen, "Jesus' Historicity," 9–10 and "The Problem of *Annals* 15.44: On the Plinian Origin of Tacitus's Information on Christians," *Journal of Early Christian History* 13.1 (2023), 62–80; Ivan Prchlík, "Tacitus's Knowledge of the Origins of Christianity," *Acta Universitatis Carolinae: Philologica* (2017), 95–110 (Prchlík does consider the *possibility* the information is historical and not dependent on the Gospels, but presents no evidence that that is any more likely).

concludes that the Talmuds "are unlikely to preserve first-century traditions about Jesus" and are therefore unusable as evidence for historicity.[122] Though of course I aver this flexibility of where in history to put Jesus remains evidence *against* historicity.[123] But the question has been raised whether Epiphanius corroborates this fact (in *Panarion* 29). Andrew Jordan discusses alternative readings of that text but agrees mine is plausible, and that the evidence overall does suggest a Christian sect preaching this.[124]

By contrast, Gavin McDowell (unaware of my arguments or Jordan's) attempts to defend a contrary interpretation.[125] But his case rests entirely on the implausible assertion that the relevant section of Epiphanius was 'not' dating Jesus to the time of Jannaeus—yet it plainly does—and McDowell gives no good reason why we should follow his assumption and not the actual wording of Epiphanius, which McDowell correctly quotes as "the rulers in succession from Judah came to an end with Christ's arrival" and "after his birth in Bethlehem of Judaea the order [of priest-kings] ended and was altered in the time of Alexander [Jannaeus]" (Epiphanius, *Panarion* 29.3.3).

McDowell appears to be confusing this passage as a statement of Epiphanius's own beliefs, rather than a description of the beliefs of the Nazorian sect, and thus McDowell argues it is absurd that Epiphanius would believe that. But this passage only appears in Epiphanius's description of that sect's beliefs. Though it is garbled up (possibly by scribal errors omitting connective text) with his own digression on a separate question (of why the first Christians were, supposedly, called 'Jessaeans'), as Jordan suggests (and I concur), it appears Epiphanius meant (and probably originally wrote) this digression to be attacking the Nazorians' overly "literal interpretations of the messianic kingdom and dynastic

---

[122] Christian Brady, "Talmudim," in *Reception of Jesus, Volume 3: From Celsus to the Catacombs* (ed. Chris Keith; T&T Clark, 2019), 89–101 (89).

[123] Carrier, *Historicity*, 281–88.

[124] Andrew Jordan, *Jesus the Nazarene: The Talmud and the Founder of Christianity* (Resource Publications, 2023), 25–26 (n4), 176–77 (n127). Regarding the Talmudic story see also: Daniel Barbu and Yaacov Deutsch (eds.), *Toledot Yeshu in Context: The Jewish "Life of Jesus" in Ancient, Medieval, and Modern History* (Mohr Siebeck, 2020).

[125] Gavin McDowell, "The Alternative Chronology: Dating the Events of the Wagenseil Version of Toledot Yeshu," in Barbu and Deutsch, *Toledot Yeshu in Context*, 59–80 (79–80).

succession."[126] Otherwise Epiphanius's exact wording is literally inexplicable. Epiphanius states his own position clearly, as that "after Alexander this heritage from the time of Salina...died out under King Herod and the Roman Emperor Augustus" (*Panarion* 29.3.4–6), thus he believes (as McDowell rightly says) that Jesus was *actually* born then. His preceding declaration that Jesus was born under Jannaeus therefore must be his description of the view he is here *opposing*, which can only be the view of the people he is talking about in that chapter. The notion that Alexander Jannaeus came *after* the birth of Jesus is therefore the position Epiphanius is *disagreeing* with; and hence the position he is attributing to the Nazorians.

The received text is admittedly confusing; but the dropping of a single word could explain everything—a single particle or conjunction (any version of 'but' or 'however') separating line 3 from 4 would restore the obviously intended sense. Such a loss of a couple letters would not be unlikely: the manuscripts are rife with such errors (several even in this same section).[127] We might also have lost a sentence before or in paragraph 3 (more explicitly identifying it as the Nazorian solution to the scriptural problem Epiphanius had just mentioned at the close of the preceding paragraph at *Panarion* 29.2.6). Manuscripts even indicate missing material here.[128] But at the very least a dropped particle (a simple *de*, for example), toward the beginning of line 4 is likely. Otherwise, there is no other way to make sense of the sentence in question. It too flatly contradicts what Epiphanius himself says, both here and in many other places (as McDowell rightly demonstrates). And my reading (which Jordan agrees is plausible) is the only intelligible reason why this digressive argument exists precisely here, in Epiphanius's description of the Nazorians; while McDowell's reading makes no sense of this.

By contrast, the suggestion (also mentioned by Jordan) that the Talmud's misdating of the Christian account could have resulted from an error in the transmitting of legends implausibly assumes Christians no longer existed for the Talmudists to describe the beliefs of—otherwise,

---

[126] Jordan, *Jesus the Nazarene*, 26.

[127] Karl Holl, *Epiphanius (Ancoratus und Panarion)*, vol. 1 (Hinrichs, 1915), 323.

[128] Ibid. Holl indicates a gap (he suggests of a few words) with an asterisk (per the key after his forward) in the middle of § 29.3.3 (line 13).

this error would be impossible. Their polemic would be immediately shredded by any passing Christian as getting the entire century wrong, and not even knowing Pontius Pilate was indeed *creedally* Christ's crucifier, not a stoning by the Sanhedrin; and so on. Transmission errors require the information to be so ancient as to be uncheckable; and that cannot describe the situation of the Talmudists, who were surrounded by Christians, indeed Christianity was flourishing where and when the Babylonian Talmud was composed.[129] The Talmud therefore can only be describing the beliefs of actual Christians that they were polemically interacting with at the time. Certainly they also would also have known Christians preaching our more familiar Roman chronology; but they would already be rebutting that by presenting the pre-Roman chronology as if actual (thereby killing two sects with one stone).

This novel chronology appears outside the Roman Empire (which might be why no such information survives from the Jerusalem Talmud), and though (as just noted) standard Christian chronologists surely also existed there (representing the 'Gentile' Church), the evidence in Epiphanius suggests the Talmud is targeting the only sect still claiming to be Jewish, and therefore their most direct competitor—or even (in their eyes) the most authentic version of the Christian religion: the Torah-observant Nazorians. This would entail the non-standard chronology is *theirs*, and thus why the Torah (and for different reasons, as Jordan and I observe, Epiphanius) attacks *that* version of Christianity, rather than the standard one. This is the only plausible reconstruction of all the surviving evidence. It is the only probable one, too, given that, otherwise, we'd have to assume a remarkably improbable coincidence between the Talmudic attack on Christianity and Epiphanius's mention of the exact same chronology in his attack on Jewish Christians (the Nazorians) known to reside near the region of Babylonia (per *Panarion* 29.7.7).

[129] Adam Becker, *Fear of God and the Beginning of Wisdom: The School of Nisibis and the Development of Scholastic Culture in Late Antique Mesopotamia* (University of Pennsylvania Press, 2013); Michal Bar-Asher Siegel, *Early Christian Monastic Literature and the Babylonian Talmud* (Cambridge University Press, 2013).

Barabbas and the Nazorians

I also argued that Mark invented the Barabbas myth to depict Jesus mistakenly treated as the scapegoat, while intimating that the secret to salvation lies in recognizing that he is *actually* the goat of atonement, and Barabbas (explicitly a representative of murder and rebellion, and hence militant messianism) is the doomed sin-bearer meant to be the scapegoat (and thus 'the people' choose the wrong goat).[130] I already cited abundant scholarship concurring; but to that we can now add two studies by Hans Moscicke.[131] I also argued that the epithet 'Nazarene' (more properly 'Nazorian') probably did not originally refer to an origin at Nazareth.[132] This, too, has support now in the work of Christophe Lemardelé, who concludes its original cultic meaning most likely was in some sense of 'the guardian' or 'the keeper', perhaps of sacred truths or secrets or souls, as I argued before.[133]

Did I Miss Any Evidence from the Early Epistles?

So all the evidence I had surveyed warranting doubt is now in a stronger position than ten years ago. Which means only one last question remains: did I miss any evidence? There isn't anything after the Jewish War. But maybe I missed something in the pre-War evidence. So after I published *Historicity* I broadcast a call for any possible passages in pre-War Epistles that my study might have missed. Only two came to anyone's mind (one from Paul and one from Hebrews).[134] Both illustrate

---

[130] Carrier, *Historicity*, 402–08, 425 (cf. 143–45, 210n146, 433, 443, 447n122).

[131] Hans Moscicke, *Goat for Yahweh, Goat for Azazel: The Impact of Yom Kippur on the Gospels* (Fortress, 2023) and *The New Day of Atonement: A Matthean Typology* (Mohr Siebeck, 2020).

[132] Carrier, *Historicity*, 282, 400–01 (see also the index; and *Proving History*, 142–45).

[133] Christophe Lemardelé, "The Hebrew word [NAZIR] in Greek: From the Septuagint to the Christian Authors," *Semitica et Classica* 8 (2015), 1–6. Even ancient Christians thought the word related in some sense to the protection of sacred truths: Carrier, *Proving History*, 142–43.

[134] See Richard Carrier, "Desperately Searching the Epistles for Anything That Attests a Historical Jesus" (20 March 2017) at richardcarrier.info/archives/12220. On the opposite end of this question, my doubts about the authenticity of Philemon (Carrier, *Historicity*, 252, n. 13) are much strengthened now by Chris Hansen's study *The Empty Prison*

a general point: in Ch. 11 of *Historicity* I often explain evidence in Paul with passages exemplifying a point, without listing every example of the same concept being voiced in Paul. Yet any further examples of his saying the same thing would meet with the same analysis.

For instance, I showed that Paul says he regularly received information from an (obviously imaginary) Jesus by direct revelation, and therefore unless he says otherwise, anytime he says he received any information from Jesus, we cannot conclude that he means anything other than revelation (whether his own or some prior apostle's).[135] Which remains true even if he did—for if he does not say so, then we cannot claim to know, and therefore any reference to such information is not evidence for historicity. To get *that* we would need an instance of Paul making clear that he did not mean 'by revelation'. And there isn't one. The same reasoning holds for the two instances proposed: Hebrews 4:15 and Galatians 4:29. I would now add those to my treatment of related passages (and to *Historicity*'s scripture index), as instances of ideas Paul discusses several other times that I already did address. So these require only a brief address here.

Galatians 4:29 isn't about Jesus. It simply says '*At that time* the son born according to the flesh persecuted the son born by the power of the Spirit. It is the same *now*', meaning Paul's Jewish opponents (who embrace the domain of the flesh) are now persecuting the Christians (who embrace the domain of the Spirit), just as (in myth) Hagar's son persecuted Sarah's. Neither statement pertains to Jesus ('at that time' means before Jesus; and 'now' means after). Jesus did enter the domain of flesh (assuming a body of flesh) to die; but Paul is not here saying Jesus therefore persecuted anyone, or even that Jesus clung to the domain of flesh—Paul's whole point is that Jesus wore flesh briefly only to kill it off, and thus now has entered the domain of the Spirit as all Christians must.[136] Jesus is thus *not* doing what Ishmael did or orthodox Jews 'now' do, *even though* he wore a body of flesh (as Christians 'in the Spirit' still

Cell: The Authenticity of Philemon Reconsidered (Wipf & Stock, 2024). But that is moot here as it contains no material relevant to the historicity of Jesus.

[135] See: Carrier, *Historicity*, 137–41 and 146 ('elements' 16 and 19 of our background knowledge); which informs my analysis of this point in *Historicity*, 553–57 ('Things Jesus Said').

[136] Galatians 4:24–26 (cf. 5:1); Carrier, *Historicity*, 577–82.

do). Jesus is thus being placed in parallel to Isaac and the Christians, and in opposition to Ishmael and hardline Jews.

Then, according to the NIV, Hebrews 4:15 says "we do not have a high priest who is unable to empathize with our weaknesses, but we have one who has been tempted in every way, just as we are—yet he did not sin." One might assert that this implies a historical Jesus, imagining the temptation scene in the Gospels, which set this temptation on Earth, even though that's an obviously mythical tale, allegorizing the very concepts captured by this and other verses like it.[137] But Hebrews does not reference any such particular story; it is ambiguous as to where the temptation took place or what it consisted of. Translations conceal this by presuming a reference to the Gospels. But the actual Greek more literally says "we do not have a high priest who is unable to sympathize [*sympathêsai*] with our weaknesses, but one who has been tested [*pepeirasmenon*] according to everything [*kata panta*], in the same way, without sin [*chôris hamartias*]." Read in the original language, that is simply a restatement of another passage I did discuss:

> The notion that Jesus had to 'become like his brothers in all respects' (Heb. 2.17) is sometimes adduced as evidence a historical Jesus is meant, but this does not follow, nor is it all that plausible. This phrase is very strangely worded if a regular man is meant ... You do not normally describe this as a supernatural preexistent being 'becoming like' [*homoioô*] a human. And 'in all respects' translates the phrase *kata panta*, 'according to everything', in other words, everything that matters to being someone's 'brother', a fact known only from scripture. Thus, to make the scripture true, Jesus had to be sufficiently 'like us' in all the respects that would establish us as his brothers. Therefore (at least [the Hebrews] theologian is inferring) [Jesus] 'must' [*opheilô*] have put on a body of flesh so he could be tempted and suffer and die like us. Here Jesus is not being 'born' as one of us but simply 'becoming sufficiently like' us. And it appears we know this happened only because it's theologically required by scripture and logic. A cosmic supernatural event of donning a human body fits this way of speaking well enough, and arguably better.
>
> This likewise explains why they imagined that their calling to join this new religion (their *homologia*, 'agreed-upon creed') came 'from

[137] Carrier, *Historicity*, 468-69.

> heaven' and not from an earthly ministry (Heb. 3:1). After that we again get quotations of scripture and still not a single quotation from a historical Jesus.[138]

Hence his temptation 'according to everything' is simply a restatement of this same point, which most likely refers to what is simply stated in Phillipians 2:6-8: that Jesus was tempted to acquire all the power of God and to declare himself his equal (much as Satan had done), but voluntarily refused, allowing himself to become (instead) weak and powerless, submitting fully as a 'slave' to the natural order.[139] Which is just like us, because we too face the temptation to put other goals and rewards before God, to prioritize our own gain, to put *ourselves* before God and His word—the fundamental sin that all particular sins are just iterations of. That's the way in which the earliest Christians, who crafted the Philippians hymn, imagined that Jesus experienced 'all temptation'. He resisted all possible offers of power, and he voluntarily suffered for that refusal all the way to the point of dying. That's already explicitly in the cosmic version of the incarnation stated in Philippians 2, where no visit to Earth is mentioned, nor required. Just as Satan was tested and failed, so Jesus was tested and passed. But he passed by taking on a mortal body and thus all the burdens of temptation and suffering that entailed, allowing him to sympathize with mortal beings. And since Satan's test occurred in the heavens, so could Jesus's.

Has Any Background Knowledge Changed?

So, the evidence (as surveyed in the later chapters of *Historicity*) has been nothing but bolstered. What about the background evidence (as surveyed in the earlier chapters of *Historicity*)?

Just as I noted earlier that Hezser and Walsh have since confirmed that my use of 'outer space' (that ancient references to heaven refer to what we mean now by outer space) belongs in our established background knowledge, the same has happened to other items I put there

---

[138] Carrier, *Historicity*, 547–48.

[139] Carrier, *Historicity*, 535.

that others have tried to contest. To date none of my proposed background knowledge has been overturned; while much of it has been reinforced. Only one thing has changed (see chapter six). And I now believe the interpolation in 1 Thessalonians 2 did not include verse 13 (which is thus original), and in a forthcoming book I extensively shore-up the case for the interpolation of verses 14–16 against more recent attempts to restore them.[140] But otherwise, scholarship has left my survey of background knowledge either unchanged or even more secure.

This is important because you have to put evidence into its context before interpreting it correctly, or correctly assessing the probability of it coming to be (and remaining) extant on competing theories (such as of Christian origins). But everything I document as 'background facts' in chapters 4 and 5 of *Historicity* is itself equally likely to have been a fact whether Jesus existed or not; therefore none of it is evidence for *or* against the historicity of Jesus. Critics have commonly overlooked this point, and then in a kind of intellectual panic have treated what they consider the most dangerous elements of my stated background knowledge as if I had presented it against the historicity of Jesus. They then feverishly try to rebut it, even though nothing I said there is even arguable—even when I stated something there *is* arguable, that statement is itself not arguable; likewise everywhere that I state a thing as only plausible and not an established fact. Such distinctions are often elided by critics, who pretend that when I said something was plausible, I instead said it was an established fact; or that when I said something was *either* plausible *or* an established fact, that I only said the latter; and so on. I cannot do anything about this. If my actual arguments are going to be disingenuously straw-manned by my critics, that is their sin, not mine. But what I can do is disabuse my readers of these critics' disinformation.

For example, if our model of Christian origins without a historical Jesus requires the phrase 'brother of the lord' to refer to fictive kinship rather than biological, then that would be improbable as merely an assumption, and thus *would* reduce the probability of finding such phrases in the first generation of Christian texts, and thus turn such references into evidence against our model. That is, unless there is background ev-

[140] Richard Carrier, *The Probabilistic Argument for Interpolation in 1 Thessalonians 2:14–16*, which updates and supersedes what I argued in Carrier, *Historicity*, 566–69.

idence that that fictive notion was a fact at the time, and not something we are merely assuming or proposing (a methodological point I will explain more in chapter five).[141] And lo, the evidence of this being a fact at the time is conclusive (as I'll explain again here in chapter ten). So, in actual fact, this phrase is expected and no longer improbable.

That, by itself, does not mean the proposed model is correct, only that it is not rendered improbable by that specific evidence. If we cannot tell whether Paul meant 'brothers of the Lord' fictively or biologically, then the mere fact that he used that phrase is of no use in determining whether Jesus did or did not exist. Moreover, even if we could prove Paul never meant it biologically (which we do not have to do; we only need prove that we can't tell whether he did), by itself that would not argue Jesus did not exist, because that would merely mean Jesus (in historical reality) had no brothers (at all, or in the Christian movement at the time) or that early Christian authors just never had occasion to talk about them. It becomes evidence against the historicity of Jesus only when placed in conjunction with other known facts (as I discuss in chapter ten).

Hence background knowledge is not evidence for or against the historicity of Jesus. It's just as expected on either. But it can affect how we estimate the probability of any evidence proposed for or against the historicity of Jesus. In that example, that Christians regarded themselves all to be the brothers of the Lord is a background fact; that Paul mentions 'brothers of the Lord' is then the evidence we must estimate the probability of. Without that background fact, that evidence's probability is low on any theory other than that Jesus was a real historical person, because we do not expect imaginary people to have brothers Paul could meet. But its probability is *not* low on the theory that Jesus was a real historical person, because real people do often have brothers. However, once we acquire the background knowledge that Christians adopted the idea of their all being Jesus's brother (at least after baptism, which was literally for them an adoption ceremony), then the probability of this evidence (that Paul mentions 'brothers of the Lord') is no longer low. It is then exactly the same whether Jesus existed or not—because now we know that *both* an imaginary Jesus *and* a real

[141] Carrier, *Historicity*, 108 ('element' 12 of our background knowledge).

Jesus would have brothers for Paul to refer to.

Which means there is still a rhetorical logic behind a critic's need to get inconvenient background knowledge to 'go away'. But alas, none of my forty-eight elements of background knowledge have been successfully challenged as actually presented and used in my study (as, for example, I show in chapter six); whereas the most (needlessly) controversial of them have only been reinforced by yet more studies since I published (and others before). So here I will survey the studies I would have cited or discussed had they existed then (or had I been aware of them). Indeed, in many cases I did not believe anyone would be so uninformed or disingenuous as to challenge them, so I did not endeavor to list every study confirming every single one. But since critics have attempted to claim no such studies exist (or even that there are imaginary studies refuting them), I now know I must refute such disinformation by citing them all—however tedious that is to readers who already know this should never have been necessary.

Not every instance relates to debunking the rhetoric of critics, however. For example, (wisely) no one challenged my stated background knowledge that "voluntary human sacrifice was widely regarded (by both pagans and Jews) as the most powerful salvation and atonement magic available," such that "any sacred story involving a voluntary human sacrifice would be readily understood and fit perfectly within both Jewish and pagan worldviews of the time," rather than be embarrassing or a marketing setback.[142] There I surveyed the Roman concept of *devotio*, the 'Maccabean martyrs' tradition in Judaism, similar traditions in Hellenism, and even the actual philosophy of it as articulated by Plato. Now I'm delighted to see that a mainstream study by Joel Watts confirms my every point, even using some of the same examples.[143] I would now cite it.

Similarly, I would now include citations of more recent work on an array of my cited background data:

- The 'mystery religion' characteristics of Christianity. I argued these were entirely, though still significantly, generic (with specific char-

[142] Carrier, *Historicity*, 209–14 ('element' 43).

[143] Joel Watts, *Jesus as Divine Suicide: The Death of the Messiah in Galatians* (Pickwick, 2019).

acteristics being the Jewish framework the Christians brought in to their adaptation).[144] Which is now another conclusion also gaining support from numerous studies.[145]

- The reality (and nature) of early high Christology. I already cited abundant scholarship (and primary evidence) supporting this element.[146] But since I published, a slew of studies has confirmed it.[147]

---

[144] Carrier, *Historicity*, 96–124 ('elements' 11, 12, 13, and 14 of our background knowledge).

[145] See Andrew Ballard, *To Know All Mysteries: The Mystagogue Figure in Classical Antiquity and in Saint Paul's Letters to the Corinthians* (Fortress, 2022); Andy Hilton, "Christian Mysteries," in Andy Hilton, *Anthropology and Mysticism in the Making of Initiation: A History of Discourse and Ideas for Today* (Brill, 2019), 111–25; Birger Pearson, "Mystery and Secrecy in Paul," in *Mystery and Secrecy in the Nag Hammadi Collection and Other Ancient Literature: Ideas and Practices (Studies for Einar Thomassen at Sixty)* (ed. Christian Bull, Liv Lied, and John Turner; Brill, 2011), 287–302; and Paul Linjamaa's section 'On the Mysteries and Levels of Initiation in Paul's Generation of Christians' in Paul Linjamaa, *The Ethics of The Tripartite Tractate (NHC I, 5): A Study of Determinism and Early Christian Philosophy of Ethics* (Brill, 2019), 159–84.

[146] Carrier, *Historicity*, 92–96 (part of 'element 10' of our background knowledge). I had already cited as concurring: Adela Yarbro Collins and John Collins (eds.), *King and Messiah as Son of God: Divine, Human, and Angelic Messianic Figures in Biblical and Related Literature* (Eerdmans, 2008); Charles Gieschen, *Angelomorphic Christology: Antecedents and Early Evidence* (Brill, 1998); Margaret Barker, *The Great Angel: A Study of Israel's Second God* (Westminster/John Knox Press, 1992) and *The Great High Priest: The Temple Roots of Christian Liturgy* (T. & T. Clark, 2003), 60–62, 210–12; Craig Evans, "The Recently Published Dead Sea Scrolls and the Historical Jesus," in *Studying the Historical Jesus: Evaluations of the State of Current Research* (ed. Bruce Chilton and Craig Evans; Brill, 1994), 563–65; and (indirectly) Alan Segal, *Two Powers in Heaven: Early Rabbinic Reports about Christianity and Gnosticism* (Brill, 1977).

[147] We can now also cite as concurring: Bart Ehrman, *How Jesus Became God: The Exaltation of a Jewish Preacher from Galilee* (HarperOne, 2014); Andrei Orlov, *The Glory of the Invisible God: Two Powers in Heaven Traditions and Early Christology* (T&T Clark, 2019); Angela Costley, *Creation and Christ: An Exploration of the Topic of Creation in the Epistle to the Hebrews* (Mohr Siebeck, 2020); Chris Kugler, *Paul and the Image of God* (Fortress, 2020); Peter Schäfer, *Two Gods in Heaven: Jewish Concepts of God in Antiquity* (Princeton University Press, 2020); Ruben Bühner, *Messianic High Christology: New Testament Variants of Second Temple Judaism* (Baylor University Press, 2021). Also supporting has always been Susan Garrett, *No Ordinary Angel: Celestial Spirits and Christian Claims about Jesus* (Yale University Press, 2008); and even Larry Hurtado, *One God, One Lord: Early Christian Devotion and Ancient Jewish Monotheism* (Fortress, 1988), who only objects (for reasons hard to follow and of no actual relevance to the issue) to the use of the word 'angel' or even 'archangel' to describe the pre-existent Jesus, but otherwise affirms and documents every pertinent point.

- That Judaism (even in Palestine) was influenced by Hellenism (culturally, ideologically, religiously, and philosophically). Besides the studies I already cited,[148] I would now add many new studies confirming the point.[149] There are also challenging new studies regarding the origins of the Hebrew Bible that document pertinent background on this point even if you disagree with their thesis (on which I take no position myself).[150]

- The 'translation fable' mythotype Jesus belongs to.[151] For that I cited (among other things) a 2010 study by Richard Miller.[152] He has since

---

148 Carrier, *Historicity*, 164–75 ('elements' 30, 31, and 32 of our background knowledge).

149 James Aitken and James Paget (eds.), *The Jewish-Greek Tradition in Antiquity and the Byzantine Empire* (Cambridge University Press, 2014); Thomas Thompson and Philippe Wajdenbaum (eds.), *The Bible and Hellenism: Greek Influence on Jewish and Early Christian Literature* (Acumen Publishing, 2014); Pieter Hartog and Jetta Jokiranta, "The Dead Sea Scrolls in Their Hellenistic Context," *Dead Sea Discoveries* 24.3 (2017), 339–55, and Benjamin Wright, "Were the Jews of Qumran Hellenistic Jews?" *Dead Sea Discoveries* 24.3 (2017): 356–77; Katell Berthelot, *Jews and Their Roman Rivals: Pagan Rome's Challenge to Israel* (Princeton University Press, 2021); Sylvie Honigman, "In Search of a New Paradigm: Judean Literature as a Crucible of Appropriations from Multiple Imperial and Native Temple Cultures in Hellenistic Times," *Journal for the Study of Judaism* 53.4–5 (2022), 489–523. See also the updated survey of Erich Gruen, "Judaism in the Diaspora," in *Early Judaism and Its Modern Interpreters*, 2nd ed. (ed. Matthias Henze and Rodney Werline; SBL Press, 2020), 69–91 (cf. Carrier, *Historicity*, 66n14).

150 Besides the surprising case made from physical evidence by Yonatan Adler, *The Origins of Judaism: An Archaeological-Historical Reappraisal* (Yale University Press, 2022), there have been numerous literary studies arguing Hellenistic influence even on the Hebrew Bible (and on the intertestamental literature of Palestine): Philippe Wajdenbaum, *Argonauts of the Desert: Structural Analysis of the Hebrew Bible* (Routledge, 2011); Russell Gmirkin, *Berossus and Genesis, Manetho and Exodus: Hellenistic History and the Date of the Pentateuch* (T&T Clark, 2006), *Plato and the Creation of the Hebrew Bible* (Routledge, 2019), and *Plato's Timaeus and the Biblical Creation Accounts* (Routledge, 2022); Niels Peter Lemche, "How Does One Date an Expression of Mental History? The Old Testament and Hellenism," in *Did Moses Speak Attic? Jewish Historiography and Scripture in the Hellenistic Period* (ed. Lester Grabbe; Sheffield Academic, 2001), 220–24, and "On the Problems of Reconstructing Pre-Hellenistic Israelite (Palestinian) History," *The Journal of Hebrew Scriptures* 3.3 (2001), 1–14.

151 Carrier, *Historicity*, 225–29 ('element' 47 of our background knowledge).

152 Richard Miller, "Mark's Empty Tomb and Other Translation Fables in Classical Antiquity," *Journal of Biblical Literature* 129 (2010), 759–76.

produced a far more extensive study documenting dozens of examples of that mythotype, which I would surely now cite in support of it.[153]

- That the ancient world was awash with the trope of 'dying-and-rising' gods and heroes, to the point that a Jewish variant was actually expected. I cited abundant scholarship and evidence on this point already, refuting every challenge one might find.[154] But many more studies have appeared or come to my attention corroborating my results.[155] No countermanding studies have been published in the last twenty-five years.[156] It would appear the entire literature of the field has now moved to my position on this.

- That some segments of pre-Christian Judaism had already developed—or plausibly could have developed—an expectation of a dy-

---

153 Richard Miller, *Resurrection and Reception in Early Christianity* (Routledge, 2014).

154 Carrier, *Historicity*, 56–58, 168–73. I cited as concurring: Tryggve Mettinger, *The Riddle of Resurrection: "Dying and Rising Gods" in the Ancient Near East* (Eisenbrauns, 2013); Pirjo Lapinkivi, *The Neo-Assyrian Myth of Ištar's Descent and Resurrection* (Eisenbrauns, 2010); Mark Smith, *The Ugaritic Baal Cycle* (Brill, 1994); and Bojana Mojsov, *Osiris: Death and Afterlife of a God* (Blackwell, 2005), 38–53.

155 Besides Miller, *Resurrection*, Lataster, *Questioning*, 230–33, and Carrier, *Historicity*, 56–58 and 168–73, studies affirming my position now include: Richard Clifford, "Phoenician Religion," *Bulletin of the American Schools of Oriental Research* 279 (August 1990), 55-64; Dag Øistein Endsjø, *Greek Resurrection Beliefs and the Success of Christianity* (Palgrave, 2009); Noga Ayali-Darshan, "The Death of Mot and His Resurrection (KYU³ 1.5 II, V) in the Light of Egyptian Sources," *Ugarit Forschungen: Internationales Jahrbuch für die Altertumskunde Syrien-Palästinas* 48 (2017/2019), 1–20; John Granger Cook, *Empty Tomb, Resurrection, Apotheosis* (Mohr Siebeck, 2018); Paola Corrente, "Rethinking Frazer's Dying Gods: New Perspectives on the Death and Resurrection Pattern in Ancient Mediterranean Myths," *Annali di Scienze Religiose* 15 (2022), 345-363 and "The Gods who Die and Come Back to Life: The Orphic Dionysus and His Parallels in the Near-East," *Tracing Orpheus: Studies of Orphic Fragments* (ed. Miguel Herrero de Jáuregui et al.; De Gruyter, 2012), 69–76; and Paul Rovang, *The Archetype of the Dying and Rising God in World Mythology* (Lexington, 2023). Also pertaining is Nathan Nadeau, "Greek Resurrection Beliefs and the Resurrection of Jesus in the Gospel of Luke: Contexts for Consideration," *McMaster Journal of Theology and Ministry* 22 (2020–2021), 120–67 (135–38).

156 The last attempt at one (and the only one usually cited) is Jonathan Z. Smith, *Drudgery Divine* (University of Chicago Press, 1994), which fails to mention most of the evidence we've all collected and is the specific target of refutation by Rovang and Corrente.

ing messiah, and that this was not foreign or inconceivable even to mainstream pre-Christian or post-Christian Jews.[157] Opposition to this conclusion still lingers, often with little in the way of argument.[158] But it is so extensively supported by experts across the field now, both before and after I published, that there is no reasonable opposition left to maintain.[159] That includes dozens of scholars from the last decade,[160]

[157] Demonstrated with evidence in Carrier, *Historicity*, 73–87 ('elements' 5, 6, and 7 of our background knowledge), and corroborated by Lataster, *Questioning*, 94–99, and the experts I already cited: Martin Hengel (with Daniel Bailey), "The Effective History of Isaiah 53 in the Pre-Christian Period," in *The Suffering Servant: Isaiah 53 in Jewish and Christian Sources* (ed. Bernd Janowski and Peter Stuhlmacher; William B. Eerdmans, 2004), 75–146 (103–05); and Daniel Boyarin, *The Jewish Gospels: The Story of the Jewish Christ* (The New Press, 2012), 132–33.

[158] For example: Bart Ehrman, *Did Jesus Exist? The Historical Argument for Jesus of Nazareth* (HarperOne, 2012), 292 (cf. 163–70 and 240); John Collins, *The Scepter and the Star: Messianism in Light of the Dead Sea Scrolls*, 2nd ed. (Eerdmans, 2010), 19 and 147–48 (cf. 128–48); John Collins and Adela Yarbro Collins, *King and Messiah as Son of God: Divine, Human, and Angelic Messianic Figures in Biblical and Related Literature* (Eerdmans, 2008), 80–82, 130–33; Géza Xeravits, *King, Priest, Prophet: Positive Eschatological Protagonists of the Qumran Library* (Brill, 2003), 66, 114–15, 143; Albert Hogeterp, *Expectations of the End: A Comparative Traditio-Historical Study of Eschatological, Apocalyptic and Messianic Ideas in the Dead Sea Scrolls and the New Testament* (Brill, 2009), 427.

[159] To be cited in following notes, all of whose conclusions or arguments I summarize in Richard Carrier, "Did Any Pre-Christian Jews Expect a Dying-and-Rising Messiah?," *Canadian-American Theological Review* (forthcoming).

[160] Jason Staples, *The Idea of Israel in Second Temple Judaism: A New Theory of People, Exile, and Israelite Identity* (Cambridge University Press, 2021), 163n79; David Mitchell (with a foreword by Robert Gordon), *Messiah ben Joseph* (Campbell Publishers, 2016), following up his earlier study "Rabbi Dosa and the Rabbis Differ: Messiah ben Joseph in the Babylonian Talmud," *The Review of Rabbinic Judaism* 8.4 (January 2005), 77–90; Gabriele Boccaccini, *Paul's Three Paths to Salvation* (Eerdmans, 2020), 101; John Goldingay, *Daniel* (World Biblical Commentary; Zondervan, 2019), 261–62; Joseph Angel, "Enoch, Jesus, and the Priestly Tradition," in *Enoch and the Synoptic Gospels: Reminiscences, Allusions, Intertextuality* (ed. L.T. Stuckenbruck and G. Boccaccini; SBL, 2016), 285–316 (299); Anathea Portier-Young, *Apocalypse against Empire: Theologies of Resistance in Early Judaism* (Eerdmans, 2014), 272–76; Dean Ulrich, "How Early Judaism Read Daniel 9:24-27," *Old Testament Essays* 27.3 (January 2014), 1062–83.

the previous decade,[161] and nearly every decade prior.[162] This element is now firmly established, such that objections to it now can only be dogmatic rather than empirical.

---

161 Sook-Young Kim, *The Warrior Messiah in Scripture and Intertestamental Writings* (Cambridge Scholars Publishing 2010), 80–82, 146, 226, 263; Jintae Kim, "Targum Isaiah 53 and the New Testament Concept of Atonement," *Journal of Greco-Roman Christianity and Judaism* 5 (2008), 81–98, supported by Jintae Kim, "The Concept of Atonement in the Fourth Servant Song in the LXX," *Journal of Greco-Roman Christianity and Judaism* 8 (2011-2012), 21–33; John Bergsma, *The Jubilee from Leviticus to Qumran: A History of Interpretation* (Brill, 2007), 277–91, 282–83, 288–90; Rick Van de Water, "Michael or Yhwh? Toward Identifying Melchizedek in 11Q13," *Journal for the Study of the Pseudepigrapha* 16.1 (2006), 75–86; George Brooke, *The Dead Sea Scrolls and the New Testament* (Fortress, 2005), 150–51, 160–61; Hengel and Bailey, "Effective History"; Jostein Ådna, "The Servant of Isaiah 53 as Triumphant and Interceding Messiah: The Reception of Isaiah 52:13–53:12 in the Targum of Isaiah with Special Attention to the Concept of the Messiah," in Janowski and Stuhlmacher, *Suffering Servant*, 189–224 (191 and 219–220); Craig Blomberg, *The Historical Reliability of John's Gospel: Issues and Commentary* (IVP Academic, 2001), 79; Etienne Nodet, *Le fils de dieu: procès de Jésus et évangiles* (Cerf, 2002), 199–202.

162 Marshall Johnson, *The Purpose of the Biblical Genealogies: With Special Reference to the Setting of the Genealogies of Jesus* (Wipf and Stock, 2002), 120–38; Israel Knohl, *The Messiah Before Jesus: The Suffering Servant of the Dead Sea Scrolls* (University of California Press, 2000), 26, 48, 74, 120n61; Michael Wise, *The First Messiah: Investigating the Savior Before Jesus* (HarperOne, 1999), 223–32; Craig Evans, "From Gospel to Gospel: The Function of Isaiah in the New Testament," in *Writing and Reading the Scroll of Isaiah*, vol. 2 (ed. Craig C. Broyles and Craig A. Evans; Brill, 1997), 651–91 (659–60); Florentino García Martínez, "Messianic Hopes in the Qumran Writings," in *The People of the Dead Sea Scrolls* (ed. Florentino García Martínez and Julio Barrera; Brill, 1995), 159–90 (170–72); Otto Betz, "The Servant Tradition of Isaiah in the Dead Sea Scrolls," *Journal for Semitics* 7.1 (1995), 40–56; Geza Vermes (with Timothy Lim), "The Oxford Forum for Qumran Research Seminar on the Rule of War from Cave 4 (4Q285)," *Journal of Jewish Studies* 43 (1992), 90–92 ('11QMelch, Luke 4 and the Dying Messiah'); Émile Puech, "Fragments d'un apocryphe de Levi et le personnage christologique. 4QTestLevi$^{c-d(?)}$ et 4QAJa," in *The Madrid Qumran Congress* (ed. Julio Trebolle Barrera and Luis Vegas Montaner; Brill, 1992), 449–501; Roy Rosenberg, "The Slain Messiah in the Old Testament," *Zeitschrift für die alttestamentliche Wissenschaft* 99 (1987), 259–61; Sydney Page, "The Suffering Servant between the Testaments," *New Testament Studies* 31.4 (1985), 481–497 (493); Bruce Chilton, *The Glory of Israel: The Theology and Provenience of the Isaiah Targum* (JSOT Press, 1982), 94; Roger Beckwith, "Daniel 9 and the Date of the Messiah's Coming in Essene, Hellenistic, Pharisaic, Zealot, and Early Christian Computation," *Revue de Qumrân* 10.4 (1981), 521–42; Jean Starcky, "Les quatres étapes du messianisme à Qumrân," *Revue Biblique* 70 (1963): 492; William Brownlee, "The Servant of the Lord in the Qumran Scrolls," *Bulletin of the American Schools of Oriental Research* 132 (December 1953), 8–15; Harold Luis Ginsberg, "The Oldest Interpretation of the Suffering Servant," *Vetus Testamentum* 63 (1953), 25–28.

- That schizotypality has a role to play in new religious movements across the ethnographic record. I already cited studies establishing this point.[163] More have been published since.[164]

- The legendary location of Eden (God's original 'garden') in the third heaven.[165] This demonstrates that places to be buried (even crucified) in the skies and heavens above were well present in ancient conception. I already adduced clear and considerable evidence for this; but abundant scholarship confirms it that I would now cite lest anyone doubt that.[166] Indeed even the text of *Joseph and Aseneth* confirms that

---

[163] Carrier, *Historicity*, 124–37 ('element' 15 of our background knowledge).

[164] Evan Murray et al., "The Role of Psychotic Disorders in Religious History Considered," *Neuropsychiatry* 24.4 (2012), 410–26; Rafael Wlodarski and Eiluned Pearce, "The God Allusion: Individual Variation in Agency Detection, Mentalizing and Schizotypy and Their Association with Religious Beliefs and Behaviors," *Human Nature* 27 (2016), 160–72; Aiyana Willard and Ara Norenzayan, "'Spiritual but not religious': Cognition, Schizotypy, and Conversion in Alternative Beliefs," *Cognition* 165 (2017), 137–46; Kylie Harris, Adam Rock, Gavin Clark, "Spiritual Emergence(y), Psychosis, and Personality: Investigating the Role of Schizotypy," *International Journal of Transpersonal Studies* 38.2 (2019), 1–30; Paul Hanel, Sarah Demmrich, and Uwe Wolfradt, "Centrality of Religiosity, Schizotypy, and Human Values: The Impact of Religious Affiliation," *Religions* 10.5 (2019), 1–17; T.M. Luhrmann, *How God Becomes Real: Kindling the Presence of Invisible Others* (Princeton University Press, 2020); Christopher Rowland, *'By an Immediate Revelation': Studies in Apocalypticism, Its Origins and Effects* (Mohr Siebeck, 2022).

[165] Carrier, *Historicity*, 180, 195 ('elements' 34 and 38 of our background knowledge).

[166] Robert M. Grant, "Early Christian Geography," *Vigiliae Christianae* 46.2 (1992): 105–11; Jacobus van Ruiten, "Garden of Eden—Paradise," in *The Eerdmans Dictionary of Early Judaism* (ed. John Collins and Daniel Harlow; Eerdmans, 2010), 658–61; Ulrike Mittmann, "11QMelch im Spiegel der Weisheit," in *The Dead Sea Scrolls In Context* (ed. Armin Lange, Emmanuel Tov, and Matthias Weigold; Brill, 2011), 413–35, and Ursula Schattner-Rieser, "Levi in the Third Sky: On the 'Ascent to Heaven' Legends within Their Near Eastern Context and J.T. Milik's Unpublished Version of the Aramaic Levi Document," in *Scrolls In Context*, 801–19 (807), adding a new source, 1Q21 37 1, to my own list (2 Cor. 12:2–4; 2 Enoch 8:1–8; and *Revelation of Moses* 37, also known as *Life of Adam and Eve*); Jean Delumeau, *History of Paradise: The Garden of Eden in Myth and Tradition* (University of Illinois Press, 2000), 24–28, who notes as well that ancient opposition to the idea proves its existence (16–17); Paula Gooder, "Eden and Beyond: Images of Paradise in Biblical and extra-Biblical Literature," *New Blackfriars* 83.971 (January 2002), 3-15; Rachel Elior, "The Garden of Eden Is the Holy of Holies and the Dwelling of the Lord," *Studies in Spirituality* 24 (2014), 63–118; Ken Penner, "The Tree of Life in Enochic Literature," in *The Tree of Life* (ed. Douglas Estes; Brill, 2020), 166–82. Attempting to argue against is John Levison, "Terrestrial Paradise in the Greek Life

Paradise (indicated there to be a lush and inhabited garden) exists in "heaven" (hence, outer space).[167] Studies by Matthew Walsh and Joel Rothman also support the general idea of objects and places existing at every level of heaven, including 'the firmament' (in such contexts referring to the 'expanse' between Earth and the first heaven, i.e. 'the atmosphere').[168] And even my readers have pointed out that we actually have a direct precedent for a crucifixion there, too: in the original version of the myth of Ixion, Zeus condemns him to an eternal crucifixion upon a wheel in the sky.[169]

- That the Christians were working from a wider base of texts they deemed 'scripture' than we have; and of the texts we do have, that their versions often said different things then than ours do now.[170] This was already established when I wrote, but a recent survey by Richard Horsley has reinforced it.[171]

---

of Adam and Eve," *Journal for the Study of the Pseudepigrapha* 28.1 (2018), 25–44, but he conflates later with earlier redactions of the texts: see Richard Carrier, "Adam's Burial in Outer Space" (6 July 2020) at richardcarrier.info/archives/16930, as well as the scholars just cited.

[167] *Joseph and Aseneth* 6.8, 16.21.

[168] Matthew Walsh, *Angels Associated with Israel in the Dead Sea Scrolls: Angelology and Sectarian Identity at Qumran* (Mohr Siebeck, 2019); Joel Rothman, *The Cosmic Journey in the Book of Revelation: Apocalyptic Cosmology and the Experience of Story-Space* (T&T Clark, 2023). See also Hezser, "Outer Space," and the sources and examples I already cited in *Historicity*.

[169] For the evidence, unrivaled still is the dissertation of James Leonard Boyce, *Ixion: Origins and Meanings of a Myth* (University of North Carolina at Chapel Hill, 1976). In addition to ancient texts confirming it like Pindar's second Pythian Ode and a remark in Euripides' play *Heracles* 1295–1298, Ixion's celestial crucifixion was also a popular subject in pre-Christian art. See: A.D. Trendall, *The Red-Figured Vases of Lucania, Campania and Sicily* (Clarendon Press, 1967), 338 §787; and Boyce, *Ixion*, 33–40, 92–99. In later myth its location was transferred to Hades; but even in first century Pompeii, art still depicted him crucified in the celestial hall of the gods, before the throne of Juno: see the dissertation of William Archer, *The Paintings of the Casa Dei Vettii in Pompei* (University of Virginia, 1981), 400–01. So even in that account, if his eternal wheel ended up in Hades, it was *after* his being attached to it in outer space.

[170] Carrier, *Historicity*, 88–92 ('element' 9).

[171] Richard Horsley, "Can Study of the Historical Jesus Escape its Typographical Captivity?," *Journal for the Study of the Historical Jesus* 19 (2021), 265–329.

- The 'ugly Jesus' tradition.[172] Which is not a very important point but is now the subject of a detailed study by Callie Callon.[173]

There are other examples I address elsewhere here—including my interpretation of angelology in Philo ('elements' 6 and 40, discussed in the next chapter) and the Rank-Raglan mytheme ('element' 48, discussed in chapter six). Contrary to the claims of critics, these too have only become more reinforced by subsequent studies in the field, on top of confirmations in more earlier studies than even those I cited.

More examples will be taken up in chapters three and four. Then the matter of what it actually takes to prove someone existed (from methodology to examples) will be addressed in chapters five and six; rethinking the question of Docetism and its relevance to this debate, in chapter seven; how ancient believers in a 'cosmic Christ' must have interpreted prophecies of messianic ancestry, in chapter eight; what Paul meant by saying Jesus was 'born of a woman', in chapter nine; and what Paul meant by 'Brothers of the Lord', in chapter ten. But first we must evaluate what few direct criticisms there have been to our original studies.

---

172 Carrier, *Historicity*, 223n176.

173 Callie Callon, *Reading Bodies: Physiognomy as a Strategy of Persuasion in Early Christian Discourse* (T&T Clark, 2019).

3

The Inadequacy of Critical Responses So Far

In this chapter I will summarize and evaluate the critical responses to *Historicity* and *Questioning*. The overall picture is of a field that is avoiding the question, and rather than engaging with our arguments or results, is merely pretending to. Which bodes ill for the presumption of historicity. Because a genuinely defensible theory would not require this behavior, much less produce nothing but.

A Digression on Tacitus

This is the case even for the least representative of that behavior: Margaret Williams' effort to rehabilitate the authenticity of a reference to 'Christ' in Tacitus. Even in that, she ignores evidence she is supposed to be responding to, or attempts to dispatch it with fallacies or even false statements of fact. And yet, as I already noted, in respect to what is actually pertinent—the question of whether Tacitus's reference to Christ, even if authentic, can be used as evidence for the historicity of Jesus (as opposed to merely that the Gospels had invented him by then)—Williams actually concurs with our conclusion that it cannot (as do others I discussed in the last chapter).[1] So in terms of historicity, Lataster, Hansen, Prchlík, and Williams represent another instance of my position becoming more rather than less corroborated since I published.

Nevertheless, a digression is warranted on the unrelated side-debate over the authenticity of Tacitus's alleged reference to 'Christ'. I did devote one paragraph in *Historicity* to the possibility that the one line in *Annals* 15.44 about 'Christ' being executed by Pilate under Tiberius was an accidental or deliberate Christian interpolation. And usually my critics pounce on that and ignore my actual argument, which was the other point (that it is of no use even if authentic),[2] which has never been soundly answered. But since publications debating the interpolation hypothesis have continued since, they are worth discussing here. These have been in response not to *Historicity* (which did not rely on this conclusion) but to my separate journal publication presenting the case for interpolation (which also cited several scholars coming to the same conclusion; once again, I am not alone on this).[3]

Robert Drews tries to thread the needle with a convoluted theory of how the 'Christians' in Tacitus's account represented a more diverse segment of Jewish enthusiasts for Jesus as the messiah than our extant Christianity, and thus merely designated a certain movement of messianic Jews generally.[4] He thus explains the Chrestus reference in Suetonius, for example, as a garbled reference to this same enthusiasm. It's an inter-

---

[1] Carrier, *Historicity*, 342–46 (cf. 349); Lataster, *Questioning*, 203–04, 397–98; Williams, *Early Classical Authors*, 16 (esp. n. 76) and *passim*; Chris Hansen, "Jesus' Historicity and Sources: The Misuse of Extrabiblical Sources for Jesus and a Suggestion," *American Journal of Biblical Theology* 22.6 (2021), 1–21 (9–10) and "The Problem of *Annals* 15.44: On the Plinian Origin of Tacitus's Information on Christians," *Journal of Early Christian History* 13.1 (2023), 62–80, arguing (as I do) that Tacitus would most likely have received his information from his friend Pliny, who received it from Gospel-reporting Christians; and Ivan Prchlík, "Tacitus's Knowledge of the Origins of Christianity," *Acta Universitatis Carolinae: Philologica* (2017), 95–110, arguing Tacitus received his information directly from Christians. Otherwise Hansen and Prchlík take positions on authenticity either similar to or already challenged by Williams so I won't explore them further here.

[2] I "assume the passage has *not* been tampered with," Carrier, *Historicity*, 344 (cf. 150n202, 340n95).

[3] Richard Carrier, "The Prospect of a Christian Interpolation in Tacitus, *Annals* 15.44," *Vigiliae Christianae* 68 (2014), 1-20 (reproduced in Carrier, *Hitler Homer Bible Christ*).

[4] Robert Drews, "Judaean *Christiani* in the Middle Decades of the First Century," *Journal of Early Christian History* 13.2 (2023), 1–20.

esting speculation, but there is no evidence for anything Drews argues, other than the generic plausibility of 'Christus/Chrestus' and 'Christian/Chrestian' simply meaning 'Messiah' and 'Messianists' generally, which would actually entail no connection to our Christians at all. You could pull every speculation regarding Jesus that Drews advances from his article, and it would remain a coherent defense of these references in Tacitus and Suetonius not even being to our Christians in the first place (which is essentially my own view).

Which doesn't help a defense of the historicity of Jesus, particularly given the case made by several scholars now that Tacitus *invented* the persecution narrative he relates, whether entirely, or by conflating stories about riotous messianic Jews being killed by Nero (i.e. Christians *generically*, as per Drews) with 'Christians' in the specific sense of followers of Jesus.[5] On this theory, Tacitus is the first to ever (and indeed erroneously) construct this story at all or to link the Neronian persecution it relates with *our* Christians (rather than an unrelated group of messianic Jews). This gets us nowhere toward reconstructing any usable evidence for Jesus, because Tacitus's account is then not only by definition unreliable, but all his information about Jesus is then even more likely to come from a late Gospel-influenced source and thus, again, has no independent value.

[5] Willem Blom, "Why the Testimonium Taciteum Is Authentic: A Response to Carrier," *Vigiliae Christianae* 17.5 (2019), 564–81; Chris Hansen, "The Problem of *Annals* 15.44," and "The Number of the Myth: A Defence of the Ahistoricity of the Neronian Persecution," *Journal of Early Christian History* 13.2 (2023), 1–21; Anthony Barrett, "The Great Fire," *The Emperor Nero: A Guide to the Ancient Sources* (ed. Anthony Barrett, Elaine Fantham, and John Yardley; Princeton University Press, 2016), 149–70 (164–65); Brent Shaw, "The Myth of the Neronian Persecution," *Journal of Roman Studies* 105 (2015), 73–100. Some of which also question whether Nero scapegoated Jews or Christians for the burning of Rome in any sense at all, which I take no position on, although that specific claim has met with responses: C.P. Jones, "The Historicity of the Neronian Persecution: A Response to Brent Shaw," *New Testament Studies* 63 (2016), 146–52, with an answer from Shaw, "Response to Christopher Jones: The Historicity of the Neronian Persecution," *New Testament Studies* 64 (2018), 231–42. See also Birgit Van der Lans and Jan Bremmer, "Tacitus and the Persecution of the Christians: An Invention of Tradition?" *Eirene: Studia graeca et latina* 53.1–2 (2017), 299–321; David Álvarez Cineira, "La Persecución Neroniana de los Cristianos Tras el Incendio de Roma (Tácito, *Anales* XV)," *Salmanticensis* 66.1 (2019), 7–50; and John Granger Cook, "*Chrestiani, Christiani, Χριστιανοί*: A Second Century Anachronism?" *Vigiliae Christianae* 74 (2020), 237–64. See Hansen, "Number of the Myth."

Of course I consider all of this moot in light of the evidence that Tacitus never wrote the key line motivating this debate; and even if he did, we can't establish his information is independent of the Gospels. But once we remove that line, pretty much all the arguments on either side of these debates collapse—or indeed even reinforce mine, insofar as they *also* argue the 'Christians' involved were generic messianists and not followers of Jesus. But maintaining that that line is authentic remains an essential lynchpin to several disputes. As typically has happened, attempts to answer the evidence against its authenticity generally ignore almost all of it—an inexplicable behavior from anyone genuinely interested in answering it. This happened twice since I published: in an article by Willem Blom, and in the chapter by Margaret Williams. Blom is the most censurable, sometimes even making false statements about what I did or did not discuss in my article on the matter, while otherwise repeatedly answering every item of evidence only with speculations meant to get rid of it rather than providing his own evidence that would elevate any of those speculations into pertinent facts.[6] Which is just apologetics, not history.

The fact remains unchallenged (even by Blom) that no Christian author—even those educated in Latin, even those familiar with Tacitus, even those writing entire accounts of Nero's persecution of Christians—had ever heard of Tacitus's association of Christians with the burning of Rome, until the forgery of correspondence between Paul and Seneca in the fourth century, which assumes that Nero persecuted *Jews* for the crime and Christians were merely caught up in the net. Which actually supports my conclusion regarding what Tacitus actually (originally) said.[7] Critics of Christianity had never heard of it either (it never comes up in, for example, Origen's treatise *Against Celsus*).

Suetonius also seems to be ignorant of any such connection. He mentions a Neronian persecution of Christians, but in no relation to the fire, but rather in a mundane list of moral legislation, not for the horrific crime of burning down Rome—a strange omission even if he thought (?) the accusation was false. Even Pliny the Elder, a contemporary (and

---

[6] Blom, "Testimonium." For my full analysis see Richard Carrier, "Blom on the Testimonium Taciteum" (29 September 2020) at richardcarrier.info/archives/17187.

[7] All the evidence I only brief here is explained in Carrier, "Prospect."

probably eyewitness) recorder of Nero's response to the burning of Rome, does not appear to have mentioned Christians or their beliefs in any such context (or at all). Otherwise, his greatest admirer—his nephew, adopted son, heir, and even *publisher*—Pliny the Younger, would not have been as ignorant of the matter as he avers (in *Letters* 10.96–97). Surely, for example, when he asked Trajan regarding what crimes Christians committed, their confession and conviction for having burned Rome to the ground would be pertinent data. And yet even Revelation evinces no such thing having happened. Despite its authors' evident familiarity with the burning of Rome (Rev. 18), they have no idea of any Christian persecution associated with it. To the contrary, they seem to credit it as God's punishment upon Nero for a *previous* persecution (note the framing of Rev. 18 by Rev. 17:12-14 and 19:1-4). Adding to all that, Tacitus himself says Nero's victims were 'called' (past tense) Christians (lit. Chrestians), and seems generally to assume their movement no longer exists. Which suggests he didn't imagine himself to be writing about our Christians. So, probably, he wasn't—particularly given all the other evidence. None of which Blom dispatches.

Williams has even less to say in response to this evidence, but at least her arguments are worth the bother of answering. Unlike Blom's, her arguments aren't already refuted by the study they are supposed to be rebutting. But they are still hobbled by the fact that Williams doesn't really pay attention to what she is supposed to be answering. For example, when commenting on *Historicity*, Williams credits to me the argument that Jesus should "have been attested in pagan sources" earlier than we have, when in fact I argue the contrary. Indeed, I say exactly the same thing regarding this that she does.[8] The same thing happens on this topic: Williams doesn't know that I don't count Tacitus as interpolated in my argument against historicity.[9] In *Historicity* I argued that it is useless

[8] Williams, *Early Classical Authors*, 5–11. I say the opposite of what she avers in Chapter 8 of Carrier, *Historicity* (e.g., "I will regard minimal historicity to be as capable of predicting this state of affairs as minimal mythicism, and therefore this silence" regarding Jesus in the historical record "does not affect the probability of either," 308; cf. item 'Documentary Silence' on 357; likewise Lataster, *Questioning*, 438). Though her monograph is generally quite good, even invaluable, it does make more than a few mistakes like this, even if most are trivial: see Richard Carrier, "Margaret Williams on Early Classical Authors on Jesus," *Richard Carrier Blogs* (30 November 2023) at richardcarrier.info/archives/26243.

[9] Williams, *Early Classical Authors*, 17; compare: Carrier, *Historicity*, 344 (cf. 150n202,

data even if authentic. Which is the same conclusion Williams reaches: that Tacitus "produces no new information about Jesus" and "his source" is "unknown" and could easily "have been both oral and Christian."[10] Indeed, her entire section on Tacitus generally agrees with and corroborates my every substantive point in *Historicity* regarding Tacitus as a source.[11] She thus corroborates my actual case.

Williams only challenges my unrelated argument for interpolation—yet does little to actually rebut it. She cites but never quotes my study of this, nor ever describes its argument, and never mentions or responds to the evidence it presents—except only in oblique ways. For example, consider Pliny the Elder. Williams knows Pliny didn't mention the Neronian persecution in his brief of the burning of Rome in his *Natural History*, and she rightly explains that as a casualty of his brevity there (indeed Pliny doesn't mention *any* culprits there).[12] But Williams never even mentions (much less answers) the fact that if there were an account of such Christian prosecution and criminality in Pliny the Elder's separate *History* of this event (as there absolutely would have been), then for Pliny the Younger not to know of it in his correspondence with Trajan is simply too improbable to credit. That it is merely 'possible' this somehow got overlooked or forgotten (or even suppressed—by both Pliny and, more inexplicably, Trajan as well) does not answer the point regarding its *improbability*. This is evidence. And it stacks with the other evidence. Which all points in the same direction.

What about Suetonius's ignorance? Williams concludes Suetonius even used the *Annals* of Tacitus as a source, making his omission of this event even more inexplicable.[13] Williams explains this away by (again) merely conjecturing that Suetonius must have been merely duplicating material—so that, inexplicably, his reference to Christians under a raft of mundane moral legislation actually referred to the fact of their being executed for burning Rome to the ground.[14] But that is precisely what

---

340n95).

[10] Williams, *Early Classical Authors*, 16 (esp. n. 76).

[11] Williams, *Early Classical Authors*, 50–97; cf. Carrier, *Historicity*, 342–46.

[12] Williams, *Early Classical Authors*, 69, 70.

[13] Williams, *Early Classical Authors*, 99, 115, 120.

[14] Williams, *Early Classical Authors*, 69, 71.

he does not do. He does not repeat *anything* about the Christians in his account of the fire—nor vice versa. He is *not* duplicating anything. He does not seem at all aware of any connection. It's hard to fathom why Suetonius would consider mass murderers to be a mere victim of public morals legislation. That is simply improbable—unless Suetonius had no knowledge of Christians being connected with the fire. Williams offers no rebuttal to this point. Her suggestion of a 'possible' way this oversight could have occurred does not at all address its improbability, which is the actual point she is supposed to be answering. Confusing 'possible' with 'probable' is an oft-repeated error of apologists, as I'll illustrate here and in coming chapters. But for example, on this point Prchlík attempts to argue that it's 'possible' Pliny didn't read his beloved adoptive father's *History*.[15] But that is not even believable, much less probable. Pliny himself *published* that book, as reported in its dedication, which says "it has been long completed and its accuracy confirmed, but I have determined to commit the charge of [publishing] it to my heirs," which means the Younger Pliny (his heir), who even wrote of his love for his father's books.[16] It's inconceivable that he never read them.

What about the ignorance of all other Christian authors, for centuries, including the authors of entire accounts of persecution under Nero? Williams does not even list the devastatingly improbable raft of examples.[17] All she has to say on this is that maybe we have one isolated reference to the event in 1 Clement—which all other Christian authors also somehow missed for centuries.[18] This isn't really an answer. It still fails to explain why all other Christian authors, even relaters of the Neronian persecution, had never heard of it; or why the first time it ever really comes up, it is in a fake source (the *Letters of Paul and Seneca*), centuries later, that even assumes the targets were Jews and Christians merely included. But it's also false. 1 Clement never refers to Nero, the burning of Rome, or arson charges—nor to Christians being burned, crucified, or eaten by dogs. Williams falsely claims that Clement alludes to these things with his mythical parallel to the 'Danaids and Dircae', none of

---

[15] Prchlík, "*Auctor Nominis,*" 101n42.

[16] Pliny the Elder, *Natural History*, 1.ded.; Pliny the Younger, *Letters* 3.5.

[17] See Carrier, "Prospect."

[18] Williams, *Early Classical Authors*, 71–73.

whom were burned, crucified, or eaten by dogs.[19] Clement never even says the persecutions he is referring to occurred in Rome. So it is impossible for this text to corroborate the story in Tacitus. I am also certain 1 Clement isn't even referring there to methods of persecution in the first place.[20]

So the evidence—the one piece of evidence—that Williams claims to have against our mountain of evidence to the contrary literally does not exist. This bodes ill for her cause. It's all the worse that 1 Clement 5–6 does not put even the deaths of Peter or Paul in Rome (the latter's death Clement appears to place in Spain, the actual "limit of the West"), yet later Christians could easily have *mistaken* Clement for having *implied* that, which would then explain how legends of a Neronian persecution arose (involving the murder of 'Peter and Paul'), which make no mention of the arson tale.[21] 1 Clement in that case would evince exactly the opposite of what Williams wants: here is the origin of the Neronian legends; not Tacitus's account, which no one had heard of.

The same thing happens when Williams tries to cite Sulpicius Severus (*Chron.* 2.29.1) as attesting to the suspect line in Tacitus—but he does not.[22] He also wrote after the publication of the forged correspondence of Paul and Seneca. Williams has confused here the single-line interpolation theory, with the entire-narrative interpolation theory (which I oppose, not endorse). That the entire scapegoat narrative in the *Annals* is fake is very improbable for all the reasons Williams herself explains.[23] Only the one line about Christ is open to reasonable doubt. And the passage in Severus does not challenge the conclusion that that one line was interpolated. For the line we'd need him to quote or paraphrase isn't present in his account. His account only challenges the claim that the entire narrative was interpolated. Which means Severus may simply have imported assumptions from the forged correspondence of Paul and Seneca (or even legends spreading therefrom) into his summary of Tac-

[19] Williams, *Early Classical Authors*, 72.

[20] Richard Carrier, "Interpreting 1 Clement's Supposed Descriptions of Fabulous Murders" (30 November 2023) at richardcarrier.info/archives/26310.

[21] Carrier, *Historicity*, 309–10.

[22] Williams, *Early Classical Authors*, 70n105.

[23] Williams, *Early Classical Authors*, 68–74.

itus. Or he could even have simply assumed on his own that 'Chrestians' was an error for 'Christians', just as Orosius did with 'Chrestus' in his paraphrase of Suetonius.[24] After all, Williams herself recognizes *that* was an error by Orosius; yet her same reasoning would entail it is as likely that Sulpicius made the same mistake.[25]

What about the ignorance of this event in the Christian book of Revelation, despite that being reasonably dated barely thirty years after the event?[26] Williams has no reply. What about Tacitus referring to people as 'in the past' having called Nero's victims Chrestians? Williams has no reply. What about the fact that the first *actual* mention of this event is in the forged letters between Paul and Seneca that assume the victims were principally Jews and only incidentally included Christians? Williams has no reply. Yet she knows that evidence exists, and agrees it did not derive from Tacitus.[27]

So Williams has no credible arguments to counter any of the evidence against the authenticity of that one suspect line. Meanwhile, in favor of its authenticity, Williams only advances circular arguments, and sometimes even gets basic facts wrong. For example, she praises the supposed literary elegance of Tacitus's referencing the fate of Christ in comparison to the fate he then describes of (what would then be) his followers.[28] But this presumes there were fates to compare; which circularly presumes Tacitus wrote this passage about Christians, and not about continuing devotees of Chrestus (or just messianic Jews generally). But if that's all he did, he'd have had no fate to compare, and thus won't have written this line. Whereas a Christian scribe would obviously gloss Jesus as the one executed by Pilate under Tiberius. So we cannot claim any great coincidence between this insertion and the executions to follow; that is an inevitable outcome on the interpolation hypothesis. It therefore evinces no literary art from Tacitus.

Even worse than Williams' circular argumentation is that her premise is also factually false: if that line were authentic, then Tacitus con-

---

[24] Orosius, *Histories Against the Pagans* 7.6.15–16.

[25] Williams, *Early Classical Authors*, 202–03.

[26] Carrier, *Historicity*, 264; "Prospect," 281–82.

[27] Williams, *Early Classical Authors*, 70.

[28] Williams, *Early Classical Authors*, 67.

spicuously *avoided* comparing the two fates, exactly the contrary of what Williams' hypothesis predicts. For Tacitus mentions the Neronian victims were 'crucified' (*crucibus adfixi*), yet gives no such notice for Jesus, who is simply 'put to death' (*supplicio affectus*), which could imply a beheading for all his readers knew, or even a military action; the text says nothing of Jesus's social rank or crime or the circumstances of his killing. Even more bizarre is the fact that Williams claims Tacitus did not say Jesus 'was crucified' because he would never mention 'crucifixion' because that was 'beneath' him.[29] Yet he does mention crucifixion, just a few lines later, precisely where Williams wants to inexplicably claim Tacitus was being literarily artful (and even more explicitly elsewhere: see *Annals* 14.33). So the one 'ingenious' parallel Tacitus could have drawn here, he didn't; and this cannot be for the reason Williams invents. So Williams is simply wrong, on both her facts and her logic.

Much the same happens with Williams' attempt to explain away the contradiction between the movement being called the *Chrestiani* (which she agrees Tacitus spelled thus) and being named after *Christus*. She wants this to be a 'joke', that Tacitus is inexplicably here just making fun of the Roman people for no narratively relevant reason (and without explaining the point so as to make clear that that is even what he is doing).[30] That presumes intentions behind the text that we have no access to, and against the grain of its context. You need evidence *for* your auxiliary hypothesis; you can't just make things up.

For example, a simpler explanation of why Tacitus appears inexplicably to 'explain' the *Chr[e]stiani* name by appealing to *Chr[i]stus* is that the *Christus* line wasn't there—because everyone knew who Chrestians were. Which is exactly what Williams herself suggests as an explanation for why Suetonius devotes no space to explaining who Chrestus was in his own reference to the same movement.[31] We can even expect that Tacitus had already covered the Chrestians himself in his earlier volume on Claudius (now lost), even more necessitating no further explanation here, beyond the reference he does indeed give (that they are the folks that people 'called' Chrestians—such as, perhaps, in a prior volume of the

[29] Williams, *Early Classical Authors*, 134, 137.

[30] Williams, *Early Classical Authors*, 68, 79.

[31] Williams, *Early Classical Authors*, pp. 201–02.

Annals). The theory that Tacitus is making an off-point verbal joke at an illiterate public's expense (while thus *literally* failing to explain the actual etymology of the name) requires an added assumption not otherwise in evidence.

By contrast, while Williams complains that we have no other evidence for devotees of Chrestus continuing into the reign of Nero,[32] unlike her claim about Tacitus telling an impertinent joke, we do have evidence the Chrestians, as in 'people who follow Chrestus', existed: Suetonius says they did; and he says nothing of their ceasing to exist. They just get expelled from Rome; not wiped out by a military action, for example. And based on other cases, we know imperial expulsions rarely lasted more than a year, much less survived entire administrations.[33] So by Nero's time they could easily have been back, or gained new followers, or both—or even returned illegally to do the deed, or just to make a living (it's not as if 'illegal immigrants' are not a thing). So should we believe the people instigated to riot in Rome some ten years earlier ceased to exist in so short a time? That is what would require an assumption not in evidence, not the other way around. Williams herself admits these people remained so well known even a century later that Suetonius didn't even have to explain what he meant. So neither would Tacitus. Which means they stuck around long enough to become legendary.

Hence this becomes another circular argument. We have to *presume* Tacitus himself is not giving us evidence for the Chrestians' continuing presence in order to argue that there is no evidence for the Chrestians' continuing presence. Because otherwise, Tacitus is literally telling us there were folks still around in Nero's time whom people were calling Chrestians. So those Chrestians definitely existed. The only question is who they were. And when it comes to the possibility that they were not devotees of *Christus* but of *Chrestus*, we are not just 'making up' a Chrestus to explain this. We know there was a very well known Chrestus who could command enough devotion to instigate riots in Rome. And

---

[32] Williams, *Early Classical Authors*, 68.

[33] Leonard Victor Rutgers, "Roman Policy towards the Jews: Expulsions from the City of Rome during the First Century C.E.," *Classical Antiquity* 13.1 (1994), 56–74; Birgit van der Lans, "The Politics of Exclusion: Expulsions of Jews and Others from Rome," in *People under Power: Early Jewish and Christian Responses to the Roman Empire* (ed. M. Labahn and O. Lehtipuu; Amsterdam University Press, 2015), 33–77.

it is not likely that his fame would have lasted into the second century if there were not inspired followers of him at least for a time (especially to scapegoat for civic arson). And in Latin those people would be called Chrestians.

Unlike Williams' assumption of an unstated joke, this is not an assumption: it is an evidence-based inference. You can say it is still somewhat presumptive, but it is nowhere near as presumptive as the notion of an unmotivated 'joke' appearing just here, and just in time to conveniently make facts you don't like go away. For unlike that presumption, which is *pure* speculation (and one contrary to sense), that Tacitus was originally talking about lingering devotees of Chrestus with a proven record of urban violence stands on a large body of evidence (which I just surveyed). So that there were still devotees of Chrestus for Nero to round up a mere ten years after they rioted there is implied by all the evidence we have. Whereas Williams' convenient notion of a pointless joke isn't implied by any evidence at all.

Another fallacious argument is Williams' noting that the questioned line uses alliteration, something Tacitus was fond of.[34] But since all Latinists were fond of it, that cannot argue for Tacitus as its author over any other student of Latin. Williams admits the line is a mere 'epexigetical clause'.[35] Which is precisely the kind of thing that ended up as a marginal gloss, which we know is the kind of thing often pulled into a text over time.[36] So the fact that this one exhibits alliteration does not tell us who wrote it.

And that completes the entire gamut of arguments Williams attempts in order to restore the authenticity of this one suspect sentence about Christ in Tacitus. Her arguments are all illogical—some even depending on provably false premises, others on unproven ones. And yet against her stands a considerable amount of evidence that validly renders the authenticity of that line improbable. I do not believe it can be rescued. But even so, it's moot to the question of the historical Jesus. Even granting it's authentic, Williams herself agrees it offers us no corroborating evidence for a historical Jesus—just as I concluded. Which means,

---

[34] Williams, *Early Classical Authors*, 79.

[35] Williams, *Early Classical Authors*, 53n18.

[36] Carrier, "Origen," 490–91.

once again, my position has gained, not lost, support. But as you'll see shortly, how Williams handled the remaining dispute (with poor, illogical, incomplete, and incorrect argumentation) fits the trend of critics of our case generally.

Critics of *Historicity* and *Questioning*

As noted earlier, there are two academic studies now doubting historicity, by myself and Lataster. There are no comparable studies defending it. And the only formal academic responses to our studies have been apologetical or even dishonest. As Lataster concluded, "every single one of them completely ignored our most salient points," relied on "mischaracterising our work" or even "attacking the person instead of the argument," and none "add anything substantial to the debate."[37] This would suggest that historicity cannot legitimately be defended.[38]

Most responses are not even arguments but what we call in debate parlance 'punts'. This or that scholar will simply 'declare' our studies refuted by citing one or another critical review, with no evidence of their even having read that review, much less evaluated its arguments relative to the original studies they are supposed to be critiquing.[39] It is just as

[37] Lataster, *Questioning*, 463n20.

[38] The rest of this chapter adapts material from Richard Carrier, "What Is Now Needed to Defend the Historicity of Jesus" (forthcoming).

[39] See, for example: Brandon Massey, "The Quest for the Historical Jesus, 2000–2023," *Journal for the Study of the Historical Jesus* 21 (2023), 75–161 (160–61); Simon Joseph, *A Social History of Christian Origins: The Rejected Jesus* (Routledge, 2022), 2, 14–15; Dale Allison, *The Resurrection of Jesus: Apologetics, Polemics, History* (T&T Clark, 2021), 20n66; Craig Blomberg and Darlene Seal, "The Historical Jesus in Recent Evangelical Scholarship," in *Jesus, Skepticism, and the Problem of History: Criteria and Context in the Study of Christian Origins* (ed. Darrell Bock and J. Ed Komoszewski; Zondervan Academic, 2019), 43–66 (44–45); Jonathan Bernier, *The Quest for the Historical Jesus after the Demise of Authenticity: Toward a Critical Realist Philosophy of History in Jesus Studies* (T&T Clark, 2016), 57n6; and David Neal Greenwood, "The *Alethes Logos* of Celsus and the Historicity of Christ," *Anglican Theological Review* 96.4 (2014), 705–713, who demonstrates he didn't even read the study he references because he does not know his argument is already answered there (Carrier, *Historicity*, 354–56; cf. 275, 301–02, 350–01). Greenwood, Bernier, and Blomberg and Seal also published before Lataster, thus failing to anticipate that *Historicity* would be formally corroborated. Others simply ignore our studies altogether, e.g. *The Jesus Handbook* (ed. Jens Schröter and Christine

evident that few scholars who disagree with either monograph have even read them; and even those few who have, do not honestly or correctly describe their contents, much less respond to their actual arguments.

The most typical maneuvers are to (1) misstate an argument and rebut that, rather than any actual argument in either study; or to (2) restate the evidence or argument already rebutted in either study, as if merely repeating a refuted argument can restore it (rather than *actually* restoring it by responding to its rebuttal); or to (3) simply ignore essential arguments altogether, pretending they don't exist and thus require no response. Occasionally these tactics are combined with (4) professional dishonesty—making or implying false statements of fact—or (5) traditional apologetics: specious or fallacious rhetoric designed to make a position sound as though it has been defended when in fact it has not. I will here survey a representative sample demonstrating the point.

The end result is that to this day there is still no response to either Lataster's 2019 study or my 2014 study—as in, a critique that acknowledges either study's actual argument (and its corresponding evidence), and addresses it in any meaningful way. This is inexplicable for a position that is supposed to be easily defended. The truth would not require such tactics; yet after being given ten years to produce a real defense, and failing, the guild seems to have implicitly conceded that historicity is a dogma whose doubtfulness is only to be made to go away, rather than actually disproved. As a rule, refutable propositions get refuted; but ten years of evasion across an entire field of study can only mean one thing: there is no refutation. This is now the strongest evidence that the historicity of Jesus is no longer genuinely credible.

Readers might disbelieve my account of this, but if you sincerely wish to know whether what I describe is true, then you know what you have to do to verify or falsify it: read the critiques (as here cited), and compare what they say with the actual studies they are supposed to be responding to. You will then discover everything I am recounting. You can then see for yourself who is telling the truth. Or you can go on scoffing at and denying everything I am saying, without having checked—and thereby admit your position is dogmatic and not empirical. There will be no more

---

Jacobi; Eerdmans, 2022; German: Mohr Siebeck, 2017) provides an entire chapter on historicity that doesn't even mention them.

solid proof of my point.

Of course one scholar, Lataster, has formally published in support of my results, with three peer-reviewed articles (listed in chapter one) that led to his peer-reviewed monograph with Brill, *Questioning the Historicity of Jesus*. And several have published formal articles calling for more attention to be paid to the issue than has been (also listed in chapter one). But on the critical side, there have been only four formal responses to my study; and only two to Lataster's. Peer-reviewed critiques of *Historicity* have been published by Christina Petterson, Daniel Gullotta, Simon Gathercole, and M. David Litwa.[40] Apart from that, five critiques of isolated arguments within *Historicity* (and one critical review of *Jesus from Outer Space*) have also been published by Chris Hansen.[41] Though none address its overall thesis, they should be included in any assessment of its critical response.[42] There are also two co-authored studies forth-

---

[40] Christina Petterson, "*On the Historicity of Jesus*," *Relegere* 5.2 (2015), 253–58; Daniel Gullotta, "On Richard Carrier's Doubts: A Response to Richard Carrier's *On the Historicity of Jesus: Why We Might Have Reason for Doubt*," *Journal for the Study of the Historical Jesus* 15.2–3 (2017), 310–46; Simon Gathercole, "The Historical and Human Existence of Jesus in Paul's Letters," *Journal for the Study of the Historical Jesus* 16.2–3 (2018), 183–212; and M. David Litwa, *How the Gospels Became History: Jesus and Mediterranean Myths* (Yale University Press, 2019), 22–45. I am not counting Marko Marina, "Povijesni Isus i miticizam: kritička analiza teorije Richarda Carriera," *Diacovensia* 30 (2022), 215–35, because it appears to be a poorly informed plagiarism of the others (particularly Gullotta and Gathercole), adding nothing to them and evincing ignorance of the actual arguments in *Historicity* and even the existence of *Questioning*.

[41] Chris Hansen, "Book Review. Raphael Lataster. *Questioning the Historicity of Jesus*," *McMaster Journal of Theology and Ministry* 21 (2019–2020), R75–79; "You Invent for Yourselves a Trypho: Addressing Radical Reinterpretations of *Trypho* and Canonical and Non-Canonical Scriptures," *The American Journal of Biblical Theology* 23.4 (January 2020), 1–28; "Lord Raglan's Hero and Jesus: A Rebuttal to Methodologically Dubious Uses of the Raglan Archetype," *Journal of Greco-Roman Christianity and Judaism* 16 (2020), 129–49; "Romans 1:3 and the Celestial Jesus: A Rebuttal to Revisionist Interpretations of Jesus's Descendance from David in Paul," *McMaster Journal of Theology and Ministry* 22 (2020–2021), 31–60; "Book Review. Richard C. Carrier. *Jesus from Outer Space*," *McMaster Journal of Theology and Ministry* 22 (2020–2021), R1–6; "Re-Examining the Pre-Christian Jesus," *Journal of Early Christian History* 12.2 (2022), 17–40.

[42] There was a review of *Outer Space* by William Chavez for the online *Review of Biblical Literature* (March 2024) at www.sblcentral.org/home/bookDetails/1000407 but I will not address it here, as it contained no relevant critique of the study it summarized, consisting entirely of complaining about the aesthetics of the popular market style of *Outer Space*, and its omission of footnotes and demonstrations that are in fact in the corresponding study.

coming that warrant attention (which I will address in chapter six).[43]

By contrast, there have been only two peer-reviewed responses to Lataster's *Questioning*: one generally positive review by Milad Milani; and one negative review by Chris Hansen that I will assess with Hansen's other critiques below, which together represent something of a disingenuous campaign to make doubting historicity go away.[44] Although there is one notable exception. Hansen has published in support of two positions maintained in *Historicity* and *Questioning*: our conclusion that all the evidence outside the Bible (such as in Tacitus) is incapable of supporting historicity, being either dubious or derivative; and our conclusion that Jesus's baptism by John is also doubtable as history (see next chapter).[45]

Daniel Gullotta

Gullotta makes many arguments that are irrelevant to the issue in dispute. For a paradigmatic example of what I mean: Gullotta devotes four pages (over a tenth of his article) to complaining about my reliance on Dennis MacDonald's Homeric-emulation theory of the Gospels, a complaint that is not only disingenuous (as I noted in chapter two, MacDonald's thesis has growing support and is no longer 'fringe' as Gullotta falsely implies; and Gullotta's critique of it is just as disingenuous as of

---

[43] Kamil Gregor and Christopher Hansen, "Mytho-Historical Heroes: The Raglan Archetype in Application to Ancient Mediterranean Persons," *Literature & Aesthetics* (forthcoming), to which I reply in Richard Carrier; "John Wick vs. Jesus and the Logical Significance of the Tragic Hero-King Genre: A Response to Gregor and Hansen" (forthcoming); and Kamil Gregor, Christopher Hansen, and Brian Blais, "The Prior Probability of Jesus Mythicism Re-evaluated in Light of the Gospels' Dramatic Date," *Journal of Early Christian History* (forthcoming), to which I reply in Richard Carrier, "On the Causal Irrelevance of Dramatic Date to the Likelihood of a Story's Historicity: A Reply to Gregor, Hansen, and Blais" (forthcoming).

[44] Milad Milani, "Raphael Lataster: *Questioning the Historicity of Jesus*," *Journal of Religious History* 45.2 (2021), 354–55; Chris Hansen, "Book Review. Raphael Lataster. *Questioning the Historicity of Jesus*," *McMaster Journal of Theology and Ministry* 21 (2019–2020), R75–79.

[45] Chris Hansen, "Jesus' Historicity and Sources: The Misuse of Extrabiblical Sources for Jesus and a Suggestion," *American Journal of Biblical Theology* 22.6 (February 2021), 1–21, and "The Indisputable Fact of the Baptism: The Problematic Consensus on John's Baptism of Jesus," *Literature & Aesthetics* 33.1 (2023), 1–18 (cf. Carrier, *Proving History*, 145–48, and *Historicity*, 688, index, 'John the Baptist').

my work), but also false: I did not rely on MacDonald's thesis at all.[46] I merely mention it in asides, totaling less than four pages of material; my chapter making the case for the Gospels as myth is 122 pages long.[47] I instead relied on the entirely mainstream theory that the Gospels emulate the Septuagint (and Jewish legends and apocrypha). A point to which Gullotta devotes not even a single sentence.

This captures the entire apologetical nature of Gullotta's approach to this debate: he ignores my actual argument (pretending it doesn't exist and therefore warrants no reply), invents an argument I did not make (that the Gospels are fiction 'because' they emulate Homer), and makes factually false statements, not only about MacDonald's work (that MacDonald's conclusions are 'farfetched', after interacting with none of MacDonald's actual arguments and evidence for any of the conclusions Gullotta wishes to dispute), but also about my work (that I based my case for the Gospels being myths on—indeed, Gullotta implies, *solely* on—MacDonald).

Gullotta thus commits all five sins here: (1) he misstates my argument and rebuts the argument he thus invented, rather than the actual argument I made—which was to an entirely mainstream conclusion (that the Gospels are emulative mythographies), and by an entirely mainstream route (that the Gospels adapt Jewish and Biblical myths and legends into stories about Jesus); (2) he restates arguments already rebutted by myself and MacDonald, as if we had not already rebutted them—and thus evades our actual arguments in defense of our respective positions, rather than responding to them; and (3) he thus ignores all our actual arguments and evidence, never responding to them. He also (4) makes false statements (about what I argued, about what MacDonald argued, and about the academic status of MacDonald's thesis). And (5) he engages in specious rhetoric (arguing guilt by association, even though this material is irrelevant to the actual argument I made, yet this creates the appearance of substantively responding to my study).

The entirety of Gullotta's critique is like this. Anyone who cares to evaluate it can check all his other claims against mine and see which

---

[46] Gullotta, "Doubts," 336–40.

[47] Carrier, *Historicity*, 396n17, 399n25, 417n63, 422n68, 436, 438, 440, 442 vs. Carrier, *Historicity*, 387–509.

is sound and which specious. You'll get the same results, item by item. Gullotta identifies six overall objections to the case I made in *Historicity*, devoting one section of his article to each. We covered one already—that 'the Gospels can't be mythologies, because Dennis MacDonald is wrong about everything', which as just noted isn't even a cogent argument.

For the remaining five:

- Gullotta does the same thing with the 'Brothers of the Lord' argument. He ignores all the actual arguments and evidence I presented, pretends all that doesn't exist, and rests his case on a series of rhetorical questions I actually answered in detail, as if I didn't answer them at all or hadn't even thought of them (see chapter ten for the actual arguments and evidence here that Gullotta—*and the field as a whole*—is supposed to be responding to).[48]

- Gullotta does the same thing with my use of the 'Rank-Raglan hero-type' to derive a prior probability that someone 'like' Jesus would be historical. He again rests his argument on a series of rhetorical questions I already answered, as if I hadn't; and avoids every pertinent thing I actually argued (see chapter six for the actual arguments and evidence here that Gullotta—*and the field as a whole*—is supposed to be responding to).[49]

- Gullotta does the same thing with the question of who Paul said killed Jesus or where. He does not respond to any of my arguments regarding that.[50] He simply repeats the arguments that I rebutted, as if I had never even thought of them (much less responded to them).

- Gullotta does the same thing with the question of whether Paul actually mentions Jesus having an earthly family.[51] He ignores all the arguments I already make *in rebuttal to* the arguments Gullotta sim-

[48] Gullotta, "Doubts," 335.

[49] Gullotta, "Doubts," 340–44.

[50] Gullotta, "Doubts," 331–34. Compare: Carrier, *Historicity*, 563–70; and my discussion of the scholarship on this point here in chapter two.

[51] Gullotta, "Doubts," 328–32.

ply repeats, regarding Paul supposedly referencing a father (on which see chapter eight for the actual arguments and evidence here that Gullotta—*and the field as a whole*—is supposed to be answering) and a mother (on which, likewise, see chapter nine).

- Gullotta does all the same with the question of whether Philo knew Jesus to be the name of an archangel already in pre-Christian Jewish tradition.[52] Which I didn't even use as evidence for doubting the historicity of Jesus.[53] I'll say more about this later when I discuss Hansen's treatment of this question.

In each case, the effect is functionally libelous: Gullotta misleads his readers (and thus his peers; and thus the entire field of Jesus studies) into the false impression that I did not think of (and thus in my study had no answer to) any of his arguments, and that I therefore had no arguments or evidence for him to answer. And accordingly, he answers none of them. The result is that he has not defended historicity at all. He has *avoided* defending it; while (instead) crafting the false impression that he did. Why?

Another takeaway from this is: *this is all Gullotta has*. This evasive rhetorical mess is all the evidence that historicists have to present for their dogma. Had there been anything better, surely Gullotta would not have overlooked it. Which should worry any objective observer of this debate.

Simon Gathercole

Gathercole's focus is only on the Epistles of Paul. But his rhetorical tactics are identical to Gullotta's.

For example, on whether Paul actually said Jesus had a human mother in Galatians 4 (see chapter nine), Gathercole claims "the only real solution for the mythicist is to regard" Paul's statement "as an interpolation."[54] This looks like lying to me. It would be a lie not only with respect

52 Gullotta, "Doubts," 326–28.

53 Carrier, *Historicity*, 200–05.

54 Gathercole, "Historical and Human," 188.

to mythicism generally (because that is not the only explanation mythicists have offered), but also with respect to my study specifically, which explicitly *rejects* the interpolation hypothesis and explores two others instead: a prophetic-cosmological explanation, and an allegorical-metaphorical explanation.[55] It should be noted that Gathercole offers no rebuttal at all to the interpolation hypothesis *either*. He merely scoffs at it—which is conspicuously the *absence* of an argument. And yet there *is* an argument to consider (made by Lataster), and though it doesn't convince me, I admit it must be met before rejecting it.[56] But Gathercole never responds to either of my explanations, either. He instead misleads his readers into concluding my study never discussed them—effectively telling them that I, too, must have proposed it was an interpolation. Let that sink in. This dishonesty is not only censurable in itself, but it is also the device by which Garthercole avoids ever mentioning my study's actual arguments regarding this passage, and thence avoids ever responding to them. He has thus not defended historicity. He has again *avoided* defending it; while making it merely *seem* like he defended it. Why?

That exhibits all five sins again. Gathercole misrepresents my argument as something else (and thus gives no answer to what I did argue); he restates arguments I already rebutted as if I hadn't (and thus gives no answers to my rebuttals); he ignores the actual arguments he is supposed to be rebutting (addressing none of the evidence presented); he plies his readers with false statements of fact (about my study and mythicists generally); and his resulting output is entirely specious (all this bluster appears to falsely imply our incompetence, while avoiding answering any actual argument we made against his position; yet he gives the false impression of having done so).

Gathercole does the same thing everywhere else he addresses any pertinent argument in *Historicity*. For example, compare his treatment of how Jesus could be a mortal human Davidic heir with ours;[57] his

---

[55] Carrier, *Historicity*, 575–82. I reject interpolation hypotheses generally (pp. 349, 532n36, 535, 591n103) and require considerable evidence for them (pp. 332–42, 344, 569n73).

[56] Lataster, *Questioning*, 265–58.

[57] Gathercole, "Historical and Human," 195, 202; compare: Carrier, *Historicity*, 575–77, and Lataster, *Questioning*, 421–24. See my discussion here in chapter eight.

treatment of how Paul could refer to 'brothers of the Lord' with ours;[58] and his treatment of how the Eucharist tradition could have arisen with ours.[59] Sometimes he doesn't even give an argument at all. For example, he says my prophetic-cosmological explanation of Paul's 'seed' language in Romans 1:3 is not 'so easily read out of this scripture' but he gives no argument for that assessment, never even mentions nor addresses what my argument was, and doesn't even identify what 'this scripture' is that he and I are referring to—despite having just listed six other verses.[60] In every case, Gathercole simply ignores our arguments and evidence, presents arguments we already rebutted, does not answer those rebuttals (or even mention them), and pretends he has still somehow defended historicity from our reasons to doubt it. Why?

If this is the only way to defend the historicity of Jesus, then we should reject the historicity of Jesus. It is only a dogma now; an obsolete paradigm the guild refuses to abandon.

M. David Litwa

Litwa's critique is not only worse than those, but it qualifies as bizarre. He devotes ten pages to answering *Historicity*.[61] Yet he spends the first two of them with an emotionally charged complaint that I am an enemy of Christ assaulted by demons.[62] For the record, I'm not.[63] After that, Litwa deploys the usual unhelpful apologetics about the 'Rank-Raglan' hero-type (from which I derived a prior probability of someone *like* Jesus being historical in the ancient Mediterranean) and the 'dying-and-ris-

[58] Gathercole, "Historical and Human," 193–94, 209; compare: Carrier, *Historicity*, 582–92, and Lataster, *Questioning*, 100–01, 141, 301, 308–21, 367, 414, 424–27. See my discussion here in chapter ten.

[59] Gathercole, "Historical and Human," 191, 212; compare: Carrier, *Historicity*, 557–66, and Lataster, *Questioning*, 322–23, 418–19. See my discussion here in chapter two.

[60] Compare Gathercole's claim, in "Historical and Human," 192n32, that my explanation is not "so easily read out of this scripture," with Carrier, *Historicity*, 576–77. And see my discussion here in chapter eight.

[61] Litwa, *Gospels*, 22–45 (on historicity generally), 33–43 (on *Historicity* specifically).

[62] Litwa, *Gospels*, 34.

[63] Richard Carrier, "Litwa's Confused Critique of Mythicism" (29 April 2020) at richardcarrier.info/archives/16658.

ing' hero-type (which, you will not learn from Litwa, I never used as evidence against the historicity of Jesus). Like Gathercole and Gullotta, Litwa never explains what my argument in these cases even was, nor rebuts anything I actually argued about them, while simply repeating arguments I already refute in *Historicity*, yet without mentioning or answering those refutations—then pretends he has dispatched my results. For the truth (which you will not get from Litwa), see my discussion of the academic status now of the 'dying-and-rising' hero-type here in chapter two, and my discussion in chapter six of how I actually employ the 'Rank-Raglan' hero-type—and for the fact that it remains a standard mythotype accepted across folklore and mythology studies, and is not something I pulled out of some obsolete past.

Indeed Litwa is my most dishonest critic yet in print. He repeatedly makes false statements about the contents of *Historicity*, and rests thereon his entire critique of it. He claims I conclude that the *Ascension of Isaiah* predates Paul.[64] I do not.[65] He claims I count Jesus as having married a princess (the Church) to up-score him as a Rank-Raglan hero.[66] I do not.[67] He claims I argue that demons "affixed" Jesus as "a spiritual being to a spiritual cross" and that "this spiritual [Jesus] could die."[68] I do not.[69] He claims that I do not explain how demons could crucify Jesus or how Jesus could celestially die.[70] I do.[71] He claims that I never answer the complaint that, e.g., "Trees do not grow in the sky."[72] I do; with examples.[73] He claims that I "did not address any of [Enrico] Norelli's ar-

[64] Litwa, *Gospels*, 38.

[65] Carrier, *Historicity*, 36-37, 47-48. Indeed Litwa does not interact with my actual arguments regarding this text at all: Carrier, *Historicity*, 48, 322–23, 357.

[66] Litwa, *Gospels*, 37.

[67] Carrier, *Historicity*, 233.

[68] Litwa, *Gospels*, 38.

[69] Carrier, *Historicity*, 687, index, 'incarnation: of Jesus'.

[70] Litwa, *Gospels*, 38.

[71] Carrier, *Historicity*, 184–97.

[72] Litwa, *Gospels*, 38.

[73] Carrier, *Historicity*, 195–98.

guments" regarding the *Ascension of Isaiah*.[74] I do.[75] He claims that I rely on the outdated work of James George Frazer.[76] I do not.[77] He claims "Carrier leaves unexplained…how [the] extremely ancient story" of the Sumerian Inanna's crucifixion and resurrection "could have actually influenced the gospel writers."[78] I do not.[79] He claims that I never address the apparent historicity of the name 'Jesus'.[80] I do.[81]

And so on. Why does Litwa have to ignore all the actual arguments and evidence he is supposed to be addressing, *and* appear to tell an unprofessional string of lies instead, in order to defend the historicity of Jesus? Because, let's be honest: he wouldn't *if he didn't have to*. Yet there is only one reason he would have to: there is no *legitimate* way to defend the historicity of Jesus. That this is what critics have had to resort to is more informative than my and Lataster's entire studies—the studies whose content everyone is avoiding any real discussion of.

Chris Hansen

Which includes Chris Hansen, a prolifically published amateur. So far Hansen has never published any response to *Historicity*. She dances around it by responding to other targets of her rhetoric. The closest she has come is to critically review Lataster's study and my pop market summary, to which again she employs the same evasive and uninformative apologetical approach.[82]

For example, Hansen deploys an appeal to emotion rather than rea-

[74] Litwa, *Gospels*, 38.

[75] Carrier, *Historicity*, 36–48 addresses every effectual argument one could find in Norelli's work; and cites Norelli at 36n1 (as the corresponding volumes of the *Corpus christianorum* in the first edition of 2014; and under the name 'Norelli' in the revised edition of 2023).

[76] Litwa, *Gospels*, 39.

[77] Carrier, *Historicity*, 168–73.

[78] Litwa, *Gospels*, 39.

[79] Carrier, *Historicity*, 46–47, 169–170.

[80] Litwa, *Gospels*, 42.

[81] Carrier, *Historicity*, 688, index, 'Jesus (the name of)'.

[82] Hansen, "*Questioning*" and "*Outer Space.*"

son when she complains that Lataster "accuses the late Maurice Casey of being a liar" and "a bad researcher," without examining whether those accusations are supported by evidence, or even mentioning what Casey said that Lataster found to be dishonest.[83] The only claim I think Hansen could be referring to is Lataster's observation that when Casey says "mythicists try to date the Gospels as late as possible," any honest and competent operator would know this is false.[84] Yet Casey does say this.[85] And Casey should have known it is false, because the mythicists Casey principally attacks accept mainstream dates for the Gospels.[86] You will find Lataster's entire critique of Casey detailed and well argued.[87] Hansen evidently could find no real fault with it, so she issued a disingenuous complaint designed to have an emotional effect but which addresses no pertinent evidence, nor is even pertinent to its thesis. As you will be noticing by now, this has become a standard tactic in academic responses to doubting historicity.

Notice the vacuous approach there: rather than defend Casey against an allegation of dishonesty, Hansen merely complains that he got caught being dishonest. Which does not advance the discussion in any way; it avoids it. And it is designed to manipulate and deceive: to turn readers against Lataster with a fallacy of 'poisoning the well', while falsely alleging that Lataster's case depends on a false allegation (which it doesn't). Hansen likewise attempts a critique of Lataster's treatment of Marcion's possible editing of Galatians that ignores most of Lataster's arguments,

---

[83] Hansen, "*Questioning*," R75, referring to Maurice Casey, *Jesus: Evidence and Argument or Mythicist Myths?* (London: T&T Clark, 2014), discussed here in chapter one.

[84] Lataster, *Questioning*, 102, the only occasion I could find.

[85] Casey, *Jesus*, 43–45.

[86] Casey focuses a lot on Earl Doherty, yet Doherty not only stays within standard bounds in dating the Gospels, he even argues *against* attempting to date them later: Earl Doherty, *The Jesus Puzzle: Did Christianity Begin with a Mythical Christ* (Canadian Humanist Publications, 1999), 193–97, and *Jesus: Neither God Nor Man: The Case for a Mythical Jesus* (Age of Reason Publications, 2009), 403, 752–54. Casey also focuses a lot on Richard Carrier, *Not the Impossible Faith: Why Christianity Didn't Need a Miracle to Succeed* (Lulu, 2009), which does not argue against the historicity of Jesus but was the only publication Casey could critique at the time, yet it repeatedly asserts standard date ranges for the Gospels (pp. 51, 202–05, 297–98), as still: Carrier, *Historicity*, 264–70; likewise Lataster, *Questioning*, 102, 105–06.

[87] Lataster, *Questioning*, 99–126.

and describes the rest incorrectly.[88] So, once again, a critic evades the arguments, and then misrepresents to us that they have been dispatched. Again, I am not persuaded by Lataster's argument on that point. But I would rather have an actual critique of it. Lataster also frames this as a disjunctive argument ('either' the tampering he suspects occurred 'or' we are left with something else being the case), and Hansen neither tells us this, nor addresses the second lemma of the disjunct (which correlates to my own treatment of Galatians). Again, Hansen's concealing and evasive approach to what Lataster actually argued does not advance the discussion. It avoids it.

Even when there is an argument to assess, you will find it is too poorly reasoned to be effectual. For example, Hansen argues that if Marcion retained 1 Thessalonians 2:14–16, then those verses must be authentic; as if unaware that as much as seventy years could separate Paul's authorship of that Epistle and Marcion's acquiring any version of it.[89] Similarly, Hansen claims Lataster "fails to note that the current consensus" favors the authenticity of that passage, as if confusing 'some scholars supported it of late' with 'the entire field agrees with them', and ignoring the fact that Lataster's argument proceeds from that passage's authenticity being 'in question', not its being 'disproved'.[90] Which is also where Hansen's ignoring of the study Lataster is evaluating becomes a methodological problem: Hansen doesn't address any of my arguments regarding these verses, even though they address all of the arguments Hansen thinks have restored them.[91] So once again, Hanson's review misrepresents the state of this question rather than advancing it.

Employing all these same tactics, at no point does Hansen sincerely engage with any of the arguments in Lataster's study. The same happens in her treatment of *Jesus from Outer Space*, my pop-market summary (once again avoiding my actual study).[92] That is full of the same kind of disingenuous rhetoric and failure to engage. Once again Hansen goes for

---

[88] Hansen, "*Questioning*," R77. Compare: Lataster, *Questioning*, 265–70, 312–20.

[89] Hansen, "*Questioning*," R77.

[90] Lataster, *Questioning*, 77–78, 318, 419–20.

[91] Carrier, *Historicity*, 566–69. And for the most complete treatment yet, see my forthcoming study *The Probabilistic Argument for Interpolation in 1 Thessalonians 2:14–16*.

[92] Hansen, "*Outer Space*."

emotion rather than reason by pursuing a well-poisoning fallacy: telling their readers that I said "conservative Christian scholars are 'fanatics'."[93] I did not.[94] And Hansen misrepresents my work, for example saying I merely 'claimed' that "Philo of Alexandria had a celestial Jesus as his Logos."[95] I did not merely claim this; I argued for it.[96] Indeed, my position is based on a mainstream understanding of the text. Just like Gullotta, Hansen never even mentions, much less responds, to my arguments on this point. Hansen fails to do this even in an article she published that was supposed to be entirely on that question.[97] I presented several arguments for understanding certain passages in Philo (particularly but not only his remarks on Zechariah 6:12 in *Confusion of Tongues* 62–63) and their implications for pre-Christian angelology. Instead of addressing any of those arguments, Hansen purports to refute my argument that "a god named 'Jesus' was worshiped prior to the development of Christianity," an argument I never made.[98] I never mentioned 'worship', nor even 'a god' in the sense Hansen means. Hansen means 'god' as distinct from 'angel', whereas I operationally defined 'deity' or 'god' the way ancient pagans did, as *including* angels, archangels, and demons (*daimonia*, 'divinities').[99] But I still never use that word in respect to Philo's discussion of this angel.

So Hansen's entire thesis isn't even relevant to my argument. But even worse, none of my arguments for an 'archangel' already named 'Jesus' are even mentioned in Hansen's article—literally not even one of them—*much less* rebutted. Nor does Hansen make any substantive challenge to the rest of my argument: that the angel existed in lore and was mapped onto Jesus from the earliest known time *regardless* of its name—an entirely mainstream view (see my discussion of high Christology in the previous chapter). So Hansen avoided my entire argument, in an ar-

---

93 Hansen, "*Outer Space*," R1.

94 Carrier, *Outer Space*, 8.

95 Hansen, "*Outer Space*," R1.

96 Carrier, *Outer Space*, 32; the concordance to which references Carrier, *Historicity*, 200–05. See my forthcoming article "Evidence in Philo of a Pre-Christian Archangel Named 'Jesus'."

97 Hansen, "Re-Examining," p. 33.

98 Hansen, "Re-Examining," p. 33.

99 Carrier, *Historicity*, 60.

ticle entirely devoted to that argument. Evasion rather than engagement; all falsely represented as a rebuttal.

This is oddly identical to Gullotta, who did exactly the same thing.[100] He exhausted several pages arguing against my specific conclusion that the angelic figure Paul identified Jesus to be was probably already known by the name 'Jesus' (i.e. Joshua) in at least some esoteric Jewish understanding, yet never once mentions (and thus never once rebuts) any of my arguments to that conclusion—while also, like Hansen, ignoring all the other attributes this angel shares with the early Christian Jesus. It is also the case that neither Hansen nor Gullotta mention to their readers that I do not use any of this to argue against the historicity of Jesus; it is merely a component of our background knowledge, equally expected whether Jesus existed or not, and entirely compatible with both models of Christian origins. A historical Jesus could just as easily have been believed to be an incarnation of this angel. Indeed, his name could even have been changed (by himself or his devotees) to suit this interpretation (as one might infer from Philippians 2:9–11)—since 'Jesus' was already an overly convenient name for God's appointed savior, and thus might not have been the real man's original name.[101] It's just as possible that his coincidentally already having so convenient a name added to the conjunction of causes leading him or his devotees to believe he was God's appointed savior—and thus was even an incarnation of the corresponding angel.[102] So the prior existence of this angel in Jewish lore is no direct threat to the historicity of Jesus.

Moreover, apart from the name 'Jesus' (which evidently emotionally disturbs my critics beyond any degree I could have imagined), I have demonstrated beyond doubt that Philo knew of an archangel that had 'many names' and ten peculiar characteristics, all of which the earliest Christians associated with their Jesus.[103] Both the Christian Jesus and

---

[100] Gullotta, "Doubts," 326–28.

[101] Carrier, *Historicity*, 688 ('Jesus (the name of)').

[102] As I explicitly say in Carrier, *Historicity*, 209, 239–40 (cf. 3–4, 33–34, where I explain the historical Jesus need only be a "man at some point named Jesus").

[103] That Philo of Alexandria's archangel shared all ten is established across several texts: *On the Confusion of Tongues* 62–63, 97, 146–147; *On Dreams* 1.215, 1.239, 2.45; *On the Giants* 52; *On the Creation* 31; *On Agriculture* 50–52; *Questions and Answers on Genesis* 2.62, 2.126; *The Special Laws* 1.81; *On Flight and Finding* 101; *Who Is the Heir of Things*

the angel known to Philo were:

1. the firstborn son of God (Rom. 8:29; Heb. 1; Col. 1:15);
2. God's agent of creation (1 Cor. 8:6; Heb. 1; Col. 1:12–20);
3. the high priest of God's celestial temple (Heb. 8–9);
4. the image of God (2 Cor. 4:4; Col. 1:15);
5. God's chosen cosmic overlord (even literally the *Kyrios*, 'Lord': 1 Cor. 8:6; 2 Cor. 3:18; Phil. 2:6–11; Heb. 1);
6. a spiritual counterpart to Adam (1 Cor. 15:45-49);
7. the prime intermediary between God and men (Rom. 8:34; Heb. 8:6);
8. a celestial agent of atonement (Rom. 3:25; 1 Cor. 15:3; 2 Cor. 5:19; Heb. 8–9);
9. and the standard that mortals ought to imitate (Rom. 8:29; 1 Cor. 11:1, 15:49; 2 Cor. 3:18);
10. and they share the appellations of 'Logos' and 'Paraclete' (John 1:1, 14:6, 14:26, 15:26, and 16:7; 1 John 2:1), and though these two names are only attested for Jesus later, they as likely were assigned to him from the start, given all the other correlations (which are improbable otherwise).

That this angel already had the name Jesus would be an eleventh coincidence; but ten is already beyond any credibility—other than by a causal relationship: either from Philo to Christianity or from Jewish angelology to both Philo and Christianity independently (the remaining possibility, that Christianity influenced Philo, is not credible on the evidence extant). This is a significant fact that must be accounted for in any model of Christian origins, historicist or not. It is not something to be ignored with specious handwaving over what names this angel already had.

Meanwhile, that Philo did indeed believe one of this archangel's 'many names' to already be 'Jesus' (evidently without any knowledge of a sect claiming this angel had *also* become incarnate, died, and rose from the dead—these would be later Christian innovations) is evinced by sev-

Divine? 205–206; *On the Life of Moses* 2.99, 2.134–135; and *On Allegorical Interpretation* 3.96.

eral lines of evidence. I detail them elsewhere.[104] But in brief, there are two improbable coincidences. First, Philo says Zechariah 6:12 "fittingly" designates the "archangel of many names" the *Anatolê* (which means 'rising', 'arising', or 'east') because that angel, too, is God's firstborn son and agent of creation—and, we know from Philo's remarks elsewhere, God's celestial high priest. Which only makes sense if Philo understood the 'high priest' named Jesus 'son of Jehozadak' ('son of God the Righteous') in Zechariah 6:12 was the one being called *Anatolê* (otherwise there is no reason for him to think the appellation "fitting" there). And second, it is also improbable that Philo would peg a passage of the Bible whose only named figure is "Jesus the son of God" as referring to the son of God: the archangel "of many names" that also (just by coincidence) shares all the same peculiar attributes with the Christian's starlord, and also (just by coincidence) that savior would *also* be named Jesus.

To deny this requires embracing two quite improbable coincidences, whereas accepting that Philo says exactly what he appears to say requires leaning on none. But clinching my argument is the fact that to read the *Anatolê* in Zechariah 6:12 as indeed the man there named Jesus is agreed by a majority of Zechariah scholars as its most common reading in the time of Philo. Because regardless of Zechariah's original text or intent, by the time of Philo this passage was often being read exactly as I said. My position is not only mainstream, it's the mainstream *consensus*.[105]

[104] For the latest and most extensive case, taking into account every argument attempted by Hansen or Gullotta, see Carrier, "Evidence." For the briefer case that Gullotta and Hansen are reacting to (but essentially ignoring), see Carrier, *Historicity*, 200–05.

[105] See: Mark Boda, *The Book of Zechariah* (Eerdmans, 2016), 384–85, 396–97; Anthony Robert Petterson, *Behold Your King: The Hope For the House of David in the Book of Zechariah* (T&T Clark, 2009), p. 101; Daniel Sadananda, *The Johannine Exegesis of God* (de Gruyter 2004), p. 31; Frank Holbrook, "Christ's Inauguration as King-Priest," *Journal of the Adventist Theological Society* 5.2 (1994), 136–52; Meredeth Kline, "The Structure of the Book of Zechariah," *Evangelical Theological Society* 34.2 (1991), 179–93; Carroll Stuhlmueller, *Rebuilding with Hope: A Commentary on the Books of Haggai and Zechariah* (Eerdmans, 1988), 79; Beth Glazier-McDonald, "Malʾak habbərît: The Messenger of the Covenant in Mal 3:1," *Hebrew Annual Review* 11 (1987), 93–104; Bruce Malchow, "The Messenger of the Covenant in Mal 3:1," *Journal of Biblical Literature* 103.2 (1984): pp. 252–55; Margaret Barker, "The Two Figures in Zechariah," *Heythrop Journal* 18.1 (1977), 38–46 (41–42); Cameron Mackay, "Zechariah in Relation to Ezekiel 40–48," *Evangelical Quarterly* 40.4 (1968), 197–210 (208); Wayne Meeks, *The Prophet King: Moses Traditions and the Johannine Christology* (Brill, 1967), 71–72; Harry Orlinsky and Norman Snaith, *Studies on the Second Part of the Book of Isaiah* (Brill, 1967), 246–47. See also:

Hansen and Gullotta not only withhold this fact from their readers, but falsely claim it not to be the case. They instead attempt to argue that Philo would have read the text in its originally intended sense (prior to all intertestamental corruption and reinterpretation of the text), as calling the king Zerubbabel the *Anatolê*, someone whose name no longer appeared in the text when Philo read it. This is not a plausible argument, for many reasons—that is not how the text was usually being read at that time; it is not what the text said at that time; and Philo clearly is not reading the text in its original sense at all, as he thinks it refers to a cosmic archangel, not a historical person, least of all a long-dead king. But it is also not plausible for the reasons I actually gave in my study: those two coincidences are too improbable—unless Philo means what we understand him to mean.

Hansen and Gullotta never mention any of these things—not even my arguments, the very arguments they are supposed to be answering but chose to conceal and evade instead. But it is all the more appalling that they conceal the fact from their peers that the passage was *regularly* being read at the time as I said it was, as the vast majority of scholarship on Hellenistic readings of this passage confirms. Which means Hansen and Gullotta are disinforming their readers twice over: by concealing (and thus evading) my actual arguments to this conclusion; and by falsely reporting the state of scholarship on this passage of Zechariah (and thus the fact that, to their evident chagrin, it supports me).

Hansen's review of *Outer Space* is similarly full of disinformation. She claims, for example, that its fourth and fifth chapters "make the dubious argument from silence that is often found in mythicist works."[106] Which is false. Hansen has evidently confused a survey of the evidence we do indeed lack for Jesus in external sources, with an argument that he therefore did not exist—an argument I explicitly reject.[107] Hansen likewise employs the same disingenuous approach as Gathercole to my treatment of Romans 1:3, and as Gullotta to my treatment of Galatians 4:4: merely scoffing at one proposed explanation without mentioning the others (again overlooking the 'or' in a disjunctive argument), and ig-

---

Lataster, *Questioning*, 303–08.

[106] Hansen, "*Outer Space*," R2.

[107] Carrier, *Outer Space*, 80–81; likewise: Carrier, *Historicity*, 308, 356–57.

noring rather than responding to my arguments even for the explanation Hansen scoffs at.[108] Scoffing is not an argument anyway. It is representative of apologetic rhetoric rather than sincere engagement—another form of evasion.

Likewise, Hansen objects to my point that Jewish lore included an angel, named Laylah, specifically tasked with transporting sperm from men to God for review before returning it, establishing a proof of concept: that this is the sort of thing God and his agents were imagined capable of doing.[109] But Hansen's sole objection to this is to question 'where' God examines that sperm, an irrelevancy.[110] Hansen does the same with my arguments concerning the *Ascension of Isaiah*, claiming I have been rebutted, but not in what, and listing scholars who do not really address my arguments.[111] We see the same again when Hansen claims my "argument that Osiris is a dying-rising god has likewise been dismissed by Egyptologists."[112] But she cites only Stephen Thompson, who never mentions my argument or evidence.[113] Hansen thus conceals from her readers the fact that most Egyptologists agree with me, not Thompson.[114] Furthering the deception, Hansen claims Tryggve Mettinger is

---

[108] Hansen, "*Outer Space*," R2–R3. Even Hansen's entire article on that subject, "Romans 1:3," fails to mention my arguments, much less answer them (as noted below).

[109] Talmud, *b. Nid.* 16; now in the 2023 Revised Edition of Carrier, *Historicity*, 576n85.

[110] Compare: Carrier, *Historicity*, 171–90; and its revised edition (2023), 575–77. See discussion in chapter eight.

[111] Hansen, "*Outer Space*," R5. Critics often attack our reconstructions of this text, but I won't address it further here, since we don't count it significantly as evidence (Carrier, *Historicity*, 48, 322–23, 356–57), and they don't address our actual arguments regarding it anyway (Carrier, *Historicity*, 36-48, 540-45; Lataster, *Questioning*, 291–97, 331–32, 356–58, 414–15, 419), and even misrepresent the state of scholarship regarding it (our dating and description of the text matches the current majority consensus; our proposals regarding its redaction history are not unique in the literature; and we already address all objections otherwise raised there). The same position as ours was even recently argued by Arthur Droge in "Whodunnit? Paul's Peculiar Passion and Its Implications," in *Recovering an Undomesticated Apostle: Essays on the Legacy of Paul* (ed. C.B. Zeichmann and J.A. Egger; Montreal: McGill-Queen's University Press, 2023), 305–33.

[112] Hansen, "*Outer Space*," R3.

[113] Stephen Thompson, *Ancient Egypt: Facts and Fiction* (Santa Barbara: ABC-CLIO, 2020), 193–223.

[114] The resurrection of Osiris is still stated as a given in the entry on "Osiris" (written by Richard Gordon) in the *Oxford Classical Dictionary,* 4th ed. (Oxford University

my "only major source on the issue" of Osiris's resurrection, when in fact I present abundant primary evidence apart from Mettinger,[115] and in my formal study (referenced in *Outer Space* through its concordance) I cited Bojana Mojsov, S.G.F. Brandon, and Samuel Mercer.[116] There are now several more (see my discussion of the 'dying-and-rising' hero trope in chapter two).

And it's all like this. Hansen claims that "Kurt Noll has been inaccurately counted" in *Outer Space* as a doubter of historicity.[117] Which is false.[118] It's also irrelevant. Likewise, Hansen declares as if undisputed that no one in antiquity thought Romulus rose from the dead.[119] I adduced considerable evidence that some did.[120] Plutarch even equates the resurrection of Romulus to other resurrected heroes, leaving no doubt as to what he thought of it.[121] Which Hansen does not mention. And so on.

All of Hansen's critiques follow this same pattern. Hansen even misreports what her sources say. In her article questioning my use of the

---

Press, 2012), 1051–52. It is also still stated as uncontroversial in the latest online *UCLA Encyclopedia of Egyptology* (ed. Jacco Dieleman and Willeke Wendrich; Los Angeles: University of California, 2020), in an article by Mark Smith, "Osiris and the Deceased" (2008) at escholarship.org/uc/item/29r70244. See also Mark Smith, "Resurrection and the Body in Graeco-Roman Egypt," *Deuterocanonical and Cognate Literature Yearbook* (2009), 27–42; and Nadeau, "Greek Resurrection," 135–3.

115 Carrier, *Outer Space*, 117–19; cf. Tryggve Mettinger, *The Riddle of Resurrection: 'Dying and Rising Gods' in the Ancient Near East* (Eerdmans, 2013), 167–83; and "The Dying and Rising God: The Peregrinations of a Mytheme," in *Ethnicity in Ancient Mesopotamia* (ed. W.H. van Soldt; Nederlands Instituut voor het Nabije Oosten, 2005), 198-210, also now available in Tryggve Mettinger, *Reports from a Scholar's Life: Select Papers on the Hebrew Bible* (ed. Andrew Knapp; Penn State University Press, 2015), 114–32.

116 Carrier, *Historicity*, 171–72: Bojana Mojsov, *Osiris: Death and Afterlife of a God* (Oxford: Blackwell, 2005), 38–53; S.G.F. Brandon, "The Ritual Technique of Salvation in the Ancient Near East," *The Savior God: Comparative Studies in the Concept of Salvation Presented to Edwin Oliver James by Colleagues and Friends to Commemorate His 75 Birthday* (ed. S.G.F. Brandon; Manchester University Press, 1963), 17–36; and Samuel Mercer, *The Pyramid Texts* (Longmans & Green, 1952), which I confirmed holds true in the more recent work of James Allen, *The Ancient Egyptian Pyramid Texts*, 2nd Edition (SBL Press, 2015), 190, 224-25, 272.

117 Hansen, "*Outer Space*," R5.

118 Carrier, *Outer Space*, 26; likewise: Carrier, *Historicity*, 49, 352, 521.

119 Hansen, "*Outer Space*," R3.

120 Carrier, *Historicity*, 56–58.

121 Plutarch, *Life of Romulus* 28.4–7

Rank-Raglan mythotype, for example, Hansen asserts "Lord Raglan's work has since been widely dismissed by folklorists and mythologists," but cites only Rosemary Zumwalt and Alan Dundes.[122] You might think Hansen's citation of Dundes here strange given that I rely on the approving application of that mythotype to Jesus by none other than the same Alan Dundes.[123] So if you were thus inspired to check Hansen's citations, you'd find that they show Dundes *and* Zumwalt *endorsing* the mythotype I employ, not 'dismissing' it. They instead reject other theories Lord Raglan advanced that I never reference or rely upon (like cultic rituals underlying the mythotype). Having thus caught Hansen's false report, I tried to find *any* scholar 'dismissing' the mythotype. Instead, I repeatedly found it accepted without controversy.[124] Hansen thus misrepresents her sources and the field of folklore studies.[125]

Hansen also omits evidence that she must know contradicts what she is saying. Such as in Hansen's article attempting to challenge my interpretation of a passage in Justin's *Dialogue with Trypho*.[126] If you compare Hansen's response to what I argued, you will discover serious discrep-

[122] Chris Hansen, "Lord Raglan's Hero and Jesus: A Rebuttal to Methodologically Dubious Uses of the Raglan Archetype," *Journal of Greco-Roman Christianity and Judaism* 16 (2020), 129–49 (129), referencing: Rosemary Zumwalt, *American Folklore Scholarship: A Dialogue of Dissent* (Indiana University Press, 1988), 125–27, and Alan Dundes, *Interpreting Folklore* (Indiana University Press, 1980), 223-61 (231).

[123] Alan Dundes, *In Quest of the Hero* (Princeton University Press, 1990), 138–44; cf. Carrier, *Historicity*, 229–30.

[124] To cite a mere sample: Michael Fox, "From Folktale to Fantasy: A Recipe-Based Approach to Creative Writing," *Writing in Practice* 6 (2023), 131–43 (133); Kristian Frisk, "What Makes a Hero? Theorising the Social Structuring of Heroism," *Sociology* 53.1 (2018), 87–103; Anna June Pagé, "Deirdriu and Heroic Biography," *Studia Celtica Fennica* 15 (2018), 102–19 (103); Russell Frank, "Covering Captain Cool: The 'Miracle on the Hudson' as a Hero Tale," *Western Folklore* 72.1 (2013), 59–81 (61–62); Haya Bar-Itzhak, "The Legend of the Jewish Holy Virgin of Ludmir: A Folkloristic Perspective," *Journal of Folklore Research* 46.3 (2009), 269–92 (277); Tamar Alexander-Frizer, *The Heart Is a Mirror: The Sephardic Folktale* (Wayne State University Press, 2007), 171–72; William Hansen, *Classical Mythology: A Guide to the Mythical World of the Greeks and Romans* (Oxford University Press, 2005), 130, 351; Louis Feldman, "Josephus' Portrait of Moses," *The Jewish Quarterly Review* 82.3/4 (1992), 285–328 (311).

[125] This is repeated by Gregor and Hansen in "Mytho-Historical Heroes," though I suspect Gregor is a victim there, unwisely trusting Hansen.

[126] Hansen, "Trypho."

ancies.[127] For example, Hansen's principal argument proceeds from her claim that "Justin does not actually respond to an accusation that Jesus did not exist."[128] Yet Hansen never mentions the fact, central to my argument, that Justin actually 'responds' by disavowing the accusation that "we have not believed empty fables [*ou kenois episteusamen mythois*] or stories without any proof [*oude anapodeiktois logois*]," which indicates that doubting their savior's existence is indeed what the character of Trypho had just been made to propose.[129] This is even more obvious in its historical context (as I discover here in chapter seven). But to have omitted that line from her entire analysis is damning. Hansen does the same thing in her article on Romans 1:3, none of which addresses any of my actual arguments regarding that verse (see chapter eight).[130] And, as we saw before, Hansen did the same thing with my arguments regarding Philo. It's all evasion; no response—in some cases even relying on false statements: about the evidence, my arguments, and even Hansen's own sources.

Genuinely defensible positions do not require this behavior. So Hansen's entire project is an indictment of historicity as a dogma. Defensible positions would never require such a pervasive deployment of evasion and dishonesty.

Christina Petterson

Finally, Petterson's response is a mere book review that is brief and barely intelligible as a critique. More of her content is devoted to questioning my presumed motives than my arguments, and appeals to emotion rather than legitimate critique. For example, she offers such bizarre complaints as that I "[seem] to have a particular fondness for James Crossley," with-

[127] Carrier, *Historicity*, 350–51. My position also did not arise in a vacuum but builds on the previous suggestion of Robert Van Voorst, *Jesus Outside the New Testament: An Introduction to the Ancient Evidence* (Eerdmans, 2000), 15n35.

[128] Hansen, "Trypho," 13.

[129] Justin Martyr, *Dialogue with Trypho* 9.1, responding to the argument posed in *Trypho* 8.4. That Hansen's entire treatment of this subject is disingenuous is shown in my analysis in Richard Carrier, "On the Historicity of Jesus and the Rhetoric of Justin's Dialogue with Trypho" (25 March 2023) at richardcarrier.info/archives/23326.

[130] Hansen, "Romans 1:3." Compare: Carrier, *Historicity*, 575–82 (or indeed even Carrier, *Outer Space*, 171–90; or Lataster, *Questioning*, 267, 422–24).

out explaining why that is a problem, or in what sense it can even be true.[131] *Historicity* has an author index. You can confirm for yourself: Crossley is mentioned six times in nearly seven hundred pages; Dale Allison, by contrast, is mentioned forty.[132] Petterson likewise complains that I never cite "Richard Horsley's work…or Warren Carter's" in my background material regarding the political context of Christianity.[133] But she never explains what is wrong with that. How would Horsley or Carter correct anything there?

That all looks like *ad hominem*, albeit based on inside jokes I don't get. But even when she says anything that at least could pass as substantive, we get falsity. She complains that I argue early Christians were "schizophrenics suffering from hallucinations."[134] In fact I said the opposite, surveying the difference between schizophrenia and schizotypality, and citing several studies on the proven links between the latter and religious movements, and how this informs innovative revelation cults just like Christianity (and as I documented in the last chapter, even more research has confirmed my point since).[135] Of course, not only did I *document* that early Christians experienced hallucinations (or claimed to), but that is also a common position in mainstream scholarship.[136] As we have seen is typical of every critic, here Petterson never explains what my actual argument was, nor offers any real objection to it beyond moral panic. In the end, her review says literally nothing of any use to the debate. So we have yet another defender of historicity who actively avoids even mentioning much less answering our actual arguments, and resorts to specious apologetics instead.

Conclusion

Lataster found this same approach in earlier critics (particularly Bart Ehrman and Maurice Casey); and his deconstruction of their tactics is

---

[131] Petterson, "*Historicity*," 256.

[132] Carrier, *Historicity*, 673, 672.

[133] Petterson, "*Historicity*," 256; cf. Carrier *Historicity*, 153–64.

[134] Petterson, "*Historicity*," 255.

[135] Carrier, *Historicity*, 126.

[136] Carrier, *Historicity*, 134n181.

as applicable to these later critics.[137] They are all doing the same thing: dishonesty, evasion, rhetoric. Why, though? Why is no one actually mentioning, actually addressing, actually responding, to any of our actual arguments? Why are they publishing dozens of pages of the mere false appearance of having done that? Why do they *all* need to employ this tactic? Why was no one able to attempt any other, even in a fulsome ten years' time? Is the historicity of Jesus really that doomed as a hypothesis? Given the way it is still being defended—as we'll see in the next chapter—the answer appears to be 'yes'.

[137] For example, Lataster, *Questioning*, 262–350, 410–27. For my own take, see Richard Carrier, "Ehrman on Historicity Recap" (1 July 2021) at richardcarrier.info/archives/1794 and "Critical Review of Maurice Casey's Defense of the Historicity of Jesus" (3 March 2014) at richardcarrier.info/archives/4282.

4

An Inordinate Fondness for Suspiciously Bad Arguments

As was just demonstrated, the formal critical response to our studies and findings has not gone well. Without exception it has functionally ignored rather than responded to the challenges issued against the dogma of historicity. It is therefore entirely incapable of rescuing it. But there remain attempts to 'defend' that dogma without claiming to address our findings or arguments. And the fact that the arguments resorted to even in that context are remarkably poor is as telling as the behavior of the critics. When tasked to come up with a reason—any reason—to continue trusting in the assumption that there was a historical Jesus (and not an imagined revelatory being promoted by a growing shamanic class of apostles, only later promoted as a historical man), the arguments scholars have come up with are either illogical or factually dubious—sometimes both.

The Usual Stuff

We still have not been given any comprehensive study in defense of historicity. All that has happened instead—in spite of all the latest studies finding it dubious—is the evasive (and thus impotent) criticism surveyed in the last chapter, and the strange armchair speculating surveyed here. That was already the case before I published. I noted the embarrassing examples of E.P. Sanders inexplicably boasting that "the sources for Jesus are better . . . than those that deal with Alexander" the Great, and Bruce Chilton weirdly claiming miraculous knowledge of Jesus being a militant mystic in the entourage of John the Baptist.[1] Lataster's entire study catalogued scores of errors and absurdities from Bart Ehrman and Maurice Casey.[2] And in *Proving History* I surveyed numerous examples—and even widespread agreement—that the methods being used to 'prove' a historical Jesus are either illogical or illogically applied.[3]

None of the usual tropes can be trusted anymore to bolster historicity. Jesus's association with Nazareth was just as likely fabricated from scripture as his association with Bethlehem. The evidence attests the epithet derived from (a now lost) scripture (as Matthew 2:23 says), and did not originally refer to a person from Nazareth, but some other attribute.[4] Jesus's betrayal by Judas is just as likely (if not more likely) a fiction. Among other evidence, it is conspicuously unknown to both Paul and the author of 1 Clement, and unattested in either Hebrews or 1 Peter; it is also inherently incoherent as anything but myth, and appears only in mythologies.[5] So is John's baptism of Jesus (see below).

Similarly, Jesus not being portrayed as omniscient in the Gospels is not evidence he was real, either, because the idea that he was *the* omniscient Supreme Being (and not a created subordinate) was invented long after.[6] Nor is Jesus being portrayed as crucified evidence he was real, because ancient myths often attached humiliations, even ignominious

---

[1] Richard Carrier, *On the Historicity of Jesus: Why We Might Have Reason for Doubt* (Sheffield-Phoenix, 2014; rev. ed. 2023), 21–27.

[2] Raphael Lataster, *Questioning the Historicity of Jesus: Why a Philosophical Analysis Elucidates the Historical Discourse* (Leiden: Brill, 2019).

[3] Richard Carrier, *Proving History: Bayes's Theorem and the Quest for the Historical Jesus* (Prometheus Books, 2012), 121–205. See also chapters five and six here.

[4] Carrier, *Proving History*, 142–45, with *Historicity*, 400–01 (cf. 282), and supported by Christophe Lemardelé, "The Hebrew word [NAZIR] in Greek: From the Septuagint to the Christian Authors," *Semitica et Classica* 8 (2015), 1–6 (see chapter two).

[5] Carrier, *Proving History*, 151–55; with more evidence in *Historicity*, 311–14, 560–61 (and 438n105, 443, 453), and now in Richard Carrier, "Did Judas Exist?" (24 April 2025) at richardcarrier.info/archives/34055.

[6] Carrier, *Proving History*, 148–51, with *Historicity*, 92–96.

or embarrassing deaths, to their invented heroes; indeed, the idea of the unjustly abused or murdered hero was already a mythical trope within Judaism itself; and that specific form of submission and sacrifice for Jesus was already established from scripture and revelation from the beginning of the religion.[7] That no one gainsaid the invention of a historical Jesus also evinces nothing. It's not even true (see chapter seven). But we also don't expect any such observations to survive.[8] Who would preserve them? Christians preserved very little, and almost nothing that they did not want.[9] Whereas multiple attestation was just as routine for myth and fiction, so it cannot alone evince historical reality.[10] And plausibility is not probability.[11] Vivid narration was also a more common attribute of ancient myth and fiction than genuine historical writing.[12] Just compare literally *any* ancient work of fiction, fabricated history, or biography of a mythical person.[13] And claims of underlying Aramaic versions of Gospel pericopes or sayings have neither been credibly proved nor would help, as myth and fiction (and revelation) is just as capable of being written in Aramaic, which was also not spoken solely in early first century Palestine but all across the Middle East for centuries.[14]

These kinds of arguments have always been convoluted and desperate. In every case just listed, stacks of assumptions and leaps of logic are required, as well as a failure to compare alternative explanations of the same evidence. I've already documented that elsewhere (as cited here in footnotes), as have others (many of whom I cite in my own studies). What all these arguments lack is a straightforward connection between evidence and conclusion, leaving room for a lot of handwaving in between to get a predetermined result. This becomes the more starkly ob-

---

[7] Carrier, *Proving History*, 179–80; with *Historicity*, 46, 76, 209–14, 430–32, 610–11, 615–16.

[8] Carrier, *Historicity*, 248–52, 275–78, 349–56.

[9] See previous note, with Carrier, *Historicity*, 293–308.

[10] Carrier, *Proving History*, 172–75; *Historicity*, chs. 7, 9, and 10.

[11] Carrier, *Proving History*, 26–29, 101–02, 167–68, 175–82.

[12] Carrier, *Proving History*, 182–83; with, e.g., *Historicity*, 469–70, 500–04 (and the whole of chs. 9 and 10).

[13] For examples: Carrier, *Historicity*, 214-22.

[14] Carrier, *Proving History*, 185–86, with *Historicity*, 383–85, 402, 408–11, 465–58, 604 (cf. 266n24).

vious when you compare these, as arguments, with the way historians establish actually historical people (see chapter six): the approaches look nothing alike. Which means something strange is going on with Jesus.

Just as with the 'argument from consensus' (see chapter one), Jesus is not being treated by the same standard as other persons. For Jesus, the complete lack of the kinds of arguments we have for real people has spawned an entire industry for inventing convoluted ways to rescue him from the more obvious consequence of that fact. All Lataster and I have done is point this out.

"Baptism Mythology Proves Jesus Existed"

I won't revisit all those examples here; they are adequately treated where already cited. But as an illustration I will pause to examine a paradigmatic example, particularly because it is among those most often repeated, which is the Argument from the Embarrassment of Jesus Being Baptized by John. I am not the only one to have called this out as illogical in almost every respect.[15] The question is why it continues to be used, even knowing it is based on false premises and fallacious logic and is thus incapable of getting its desired conclusion.

The chief error here is in trying to evaluate Mark's invention of that myth by the standards of Christians from different eras (e.g., the 2nd or even 4th century) and different beliefs (e.g., that Jesus was literally 'God' and therefore could not have carried any stain of sin nor ever submitted to any authority; or the strict Torah-observant perspective that only Jesus, or the temple cult he replaced, could absolve anyone of sin). When reading Mark from within his own generation and ideology, there is nothing at all embarrassing about this myth—to the contrary, it is so extraordinarily convenient to his purposes as to render its fabrication *more* probable, not less. Mark has the famous John the Baptist literally declare Jesus his superior and successor! Fabricating celebrity endorse-

[15] Carrier, *Proving History*, 145–48, with Carrier, *Historicity*, 400, 422–23, 443 (cf. 32–33, 438n105, 453n132, 545–46). Others noticing the same things range from John Gager, "The Gospels and Jesus: Some Doubts about Method," *Journal of Religion* 54.3 (July 1974), 244–72 (262–63), to Chris Hansen, "The Indisputable Fact of the Baptism: The Problematic Consensus on John's Baptism of Jesus," *Literature & Aesthetics* 33.1 (2023), 1–18.

ments is the opposite of embarrassing. And as I've already demonstrated, Mark's version of the myth—the earliest version on record—is heavily constructed from mythological, literary, and scriptural tropes, which when removed leave no story left to remain as history. It is also entirely in accord with the Pauline doctrine of Christ's submission and humility (canonically declared in Philippians 2:6–11), as we expect from Mark. Remember my discussion in chapter two of abundant studies now demonstrating that Mark studiously reified Paul's teachings into narrative tales. This is a perfect example. Indeed, here Christ's submission reverses Satan's rebellion—which is why in Mark the temptation fable immediately follows the baptism fable.

As I've also pointed out before, anthropologists will recognize this tale as an etiological myth explaining the origin and meaning of baptism as a Christian ritual. Since that entailed Christians emulating Jesus (see Romans 6:2–10 and 8:14–17, 29; Galatians 3:26–29; and 1 Corinthians 12:13), there needed to be a story of Jesus undergoing the ritual for them to emulate (representing baptism as adoption by God and an analog to death and rebirth), and the most useful scenario for representing that would have been to invent an endorsement from none other than the Baptist himself. This does not argue for its historicity, but against it. Indeed, etiological myths are typically ahistorical fabrications. So we need a reason to believe this is an exception. And we don't have any.

When historians try to adduce some, nothing they produce is relevant—like the final redactor of the Gospel of John's evident displeasure with the story, causing them to delete it. That can prove the story was embarrassing to that specific editor, half a century later; but that cannot inform us about Mark, the originator of the story. There is no such evidence of embarrassment *in Mark*. Even Matthew's apologetical spin (in Matthew 3:14–15) is not in Mark, representing an evolution of polemics and apologetics *caused by* Mark's invention of the story; it is not anything *already present* in it. Self-evidently, Mark had no such concerns. Neither did Luke (Luke 3:21–22), which suggests Matthew's problem with the tale was a product of his peculiarly Torah-observant perspective, which neither Mark nor Luke shared. Here as in many other cases, we should be learning from the studies of Walsh, Trobisch, Litwa, and Vinzent (and others) discussed in chapter two, that when we stop treating the Gospels as gullible collections of lore and start treating them as the deliberate propaganda they actually are, many of our traditional conclusions collapse. Dogmas will not survive this revelation.

Needless to say, there is no argument of any like kind undergirding the historicity of any other ancient person. Such a convoluted attempt to get a historical person out of a patently mythical tale is peculiar to Jesus studies. That it depends on ignoring and fudging facts and logic to get that desired result is likewise peculiar to that field. But if we want real history, we need real arguments; not apologetics. Yet everything I just said about Mark's baptism fable should have long been obvious to every historian in this field. That it wasn't (and in too many cases still isn't) is what warrants concern—and a re-evaluation of our assumptions.

General Approaches

The usual arguments for historicity can be broken down into four general kinds: arguments from the Gospels; arguments from the Epistles; arguments from extrabiblical sources; and arguments from general implausibility. These are already treated in our studies—my monographs *Proving History* and *Historicity of Jesus,* and Lataster's *Questioning the Historicity of Jesus.*

Generally, the Gospels (and Acts) are demonstrably mythologies, and there is no way to establish that anything in them about Jesus is historically true (*Historicity*, chs. 9 and 10; *Proving History*, ch. 5). The mere possibility that something could be doesn't get you to historicity, because possibly is not probably.[16] Something in them needs to be proved, with evidence, to be more probable as a fact of the historical Jesus than as a fable or fiction about a theological Jesus. Note that we do not have to prove the reverse: merely *not being able to prove either* for any item removes it as evidence for either, and hence for historicity. Too often, historicity is defended by arguing that some passage 'could' derive from a historical fact about Jesus. That is logically incapable of supporting the conclusion. But also too often, historicity is defended by arguing for something indeed being more probable, exactly as needed, but on a faulty basis of facts or logic—like we just saw with the Argument from John the Baptist.

[16] On this fallacy (*possibiliter ergo probabiliter*) see Carrier, *Proving History*, 26–29.

Generally, the Epistles are demonstrably ambiguous at every single point where they could have evidenced historicity (*Historicity*, ch. 11). Scholars might claim Paul actively plays down a historical Jesus or that it was a point of embarrassment for him—*but there is literally no evidence of that* (a point I already covered in ch. 11 of *Historicity*). That is a modern myth. Which is suspicious in itself, but even in the best case doesn't get you to historicity, because, again, possibly is not probably. And again we do not have to prove the reverse: merely *not being able to prove either* for any item removes it as evidence for either, and hence for historicity. So we do not have to prove Paul *did* mean something allegorical when he refers to Jesus having a mother, for example (see chapter nine); we need merely prove that that is *as likely as* the contrary—in other words, that we can't tell. The burden of proving a reference more probable if Jesus existed falls on the historicist. Otherwise we are looking at the *absence* of evidence for historicity, not the presence of it, just as with the Gospels.

And generally, none of the extrabiblical evidence can be demonstrated to be independent of Gospel-inspired legends, and therefore cannot corroborate that any of those legends are true (*Historicity*, ch. 8). There is simply no evidence that they derived their material from any other source than the Gospels or Christians informed by the Gospels. The mere 'possibility' that any had some source independent of all that is logically incapable of supporting the conclusion. We need historicity to be *probable*, not merely possible. Because we already agree it's possible.

Which exhausts all the evidence one could claim for Jesus.

One of the most ineffectual versions of this approach is to defend the historicity of Jesus on the basis of *non-existent* sources, like 'Q' or 'M' or 'L' or the 'Signs Gospel', or a hypothetical lost edition of Josephus, and so on. Lataster's study focused a lot on the inability of that approach to reach a *probable* conclusion (as opposed to a merely 'possible' one), since a hypothesis that depends on a mere hypothesis remains a hypothesis (see next chapter).[17] While it is possible to establish a lost source as probably existing *and* that some key content probably was in it (rather than only might have been), this is still not the case for any source or claim posited for Jesus. Even John Kloppenborg, for example, one of the leading proponents of Q, set the probably of there being a 'Q' source at

[17] Lataster, *Questioning*, 39–72, 81, 102–05, 113–14, 130–40, 159, 175–91, 449–55, 461.

all at fifty-fifty.[18] Which means the historicity of Jesus, if it is based on that content, is *also* fifty-fifty (at best)—yet fifty-fifty is just another way of saying 'we do not know one way or the other'. It's only worse that establishing some content about Jesus *was* in some kind of 'Q' document *still* wouldn't get us to a historical Jesus, but to just another layer of mythology, which could as likely date decades after the fact and be based on no real sources either, just like the Gospels. Historicists need to *prove* otherwise, not *conjecture* otherwise.

That leaves claims that the non-existence of Jesus is simply 'implausible' for some reason or other. So far, no such argument survives scrutiny, whether logically or factually (*Historicity*, chs. 1 through 7). For example, claiming the non-existence of Jesus requires an improbable or implausible conspiracy theory is ineffectual because neither my theory nor Lataster's posits any conspiracy. Likewise, claiming it's implausible that any Jews (*any* Jews, mind you—meaning, no matter how unusual or fringe or counter-mainstream they were) would ever think of a 'dying messiah' theology unless forced to consider one by their chosen man's unexpected death fails as a matter of fact: as I discussed in chapter two, some did contemplate that, and others would, without any such impetus required. Paul already attests the early Christians claimed revelations had guided them to find this in scripture. And we do not need any other explanation for where it came from than the explanation Paul already gives us.[19] I've already shown that an imagined crucifixion would be just as politically attractive as a historical one.[20] The same happens to claims that Jesus had to have existed because the evidence we have for him is at least as good as we have for other people whose existence we don't doubt: there is literally no such person (see chapter six).

Sometimes these arguments exhibit simple failures of common sense. For example, you might hear that Jesus must have existed because all religions had founders. One obvious problem with that is: most religions' founders are mythical (for Islam, the angel Gabriel; for Mormonism, the angel Moroni; for the Jews, Moses; for the Cargo Cults, John Frum or

---

[18] Carrier, *Historicity*, 270n34. See: John Kloppenborg, "On Dispensing with Q? Goodacre on the Relation of Luke to Matthew," *New Testament Studies* 49 (2003), 210–36 (236; cf. 214–18).

[19] Carrier, *Historicity*, 137–43, 515–27, 543–46, 552–55.

[20] Carrier, *Historicity*, 153–63, and 209–14 ('elements' 22 through 29, and 43).

Tom Navy; for the Luddites, Ned Ludd; for the cult of Ganesh, well, Ganesh; for ancient Hercules cult, well, Hercules; and so on).[21] Christianity would thus still have an actual founder: Peter (analogous to Muhammad, Joseph Smith, Luddite activists, Melanesian shamans, whoever got Ganesh and Hercules cults started, and so on). It might then be claimed that only Jesus could radically innovate (in whatever way is supposed to be a radical innovation); but Peter, Paul, or any apostle is as likely to be a radical innovator as any Galilean or Judean, nor is it credible that only one person in a decade, or in a whole movement, will be clever or creative—the Christian movement could have developed early on in the hands of several clever and creative innovators. If a historical Jesus could do it, so could anyone of his generation—or any other. So maybe then it will be insisted that any person 'mentioned' many times within decades of their alleged life or earthly activity is going to be more likely historical than mythical, or some other claim like that. But for figures as rapidly and heavily mythologized as Jesus, that simply isn't true.[22] Remember Gabriel and Moroni, even Satan? Oft mentioned; never existed. Remember John Frum, Tom Navy, Ned Ludd? They were rapidly historicized. And we do not know that Ganesh and Hercules were not just as rapidly converted into historical persons, too; or that they couldn't have been. The idea that 'that can't happen' is refuted by it happening quite a lot. As I explained in chapter one, it unquestionably happened to *the risen* Jesus. So we cannot claim it can't have happened to the *pre*-risen Jesus.

There really are no other arguments for historicity than I have surveyed up to this point. They all fall into the same four categories, and they all fall to the same objections. Nevertheless, scholars keep trying, spitballing armchair notions whenever pressed.

---

[21] The attribution of the Quran as the sayings of the angel Gabriel, and the Mormon scriptures as provided by the angel Moroni, are widely known; that Ganesh and Hercules cults must have had human founders besides Ganesh and Hercules is logically undeniable. For the others: Carrier, *Historicity*, 9–11 (Ned Ludd) and 159–63 (John Frum and Tom Navy).

[22] Carrier, *Historicity*, 248–52. This error (of confusing timing with mythologization) occupies the entirety of the forthcoming critique by Kamil Gregor, Christopher Hansen, and Brian Blais, "The Prior Probability of Jesus Mythicism Re-evaluated in Light of the Gospels' Dramatic Date" in the *Journal of Early Christian History* (as I explain in chapter six).

Specific Approaches

Such are the general approaches to defending the historicity of Jesus and why they fail to be objectively convincing. Specific examples only illustrate the point.

"Names in the Gospels Prove Jesus Existed"

This is probably the most scandalous attempt to 'prove' Jesus really existed, because it borders on fraudulent, yet because no one checks so as to notice, I still see it repeated as if a fact: that the names of the people mentioned in the Gospels (and Acts) occur at the same frequency as real names did in Palestine of the time, therefore these stories must all be true because such an accurate spread of names cannot have been contrived as fiction. This originated with Richard Bauckham.[23] The claim is not merely false, it's *wildly* false.[24] This was already illustrated in studies by Kamil Gregor and Brian Blais, but I find it's even worse than they found it.[25] It's even refuted by Bauckham's own data.[26] In actual fact, the Gospels' peculiar *failure* to match real name frequencies among the people encountered is evidence their narratives *are* fabricated.

Here is the reality. Almost none of the names on Bauckham's list of real Jewish names appear in the Gospels. By contrast, while the name 'Jesus' (Joshua) was one of the most common names for Palestinian men,

---

[23] Richard Bauckham, *Jesus and the Eyewitnesses: The Gospels as Eyewitness Testimony* (Eerdmans, 2008; 2nd ed., 2017), 67-91.

[24] Bauckham is generally not a reliable operator: Carrier, *Historicity*, 397n20.

[25] Kamil Gregor and Brian Blais, "Is Name Popularity a Good Test of Historicity? A Statistical Evaluation of Richard Bauckham's Onomastic Argument," *Journal for the Study of the Historical Jesus* 21 (2023), 171–202, which is required reading on this question, and Kamil Gregor and Brian Blais, "Re-Examining Richard Bauckham's Argument from Name Popularity in Light of Apocryphal and Talmudic Evidence," *Journal for the Study of the New Testament* 47 (2024), 271–96, which expands on the point further. Their studies reinforce mine, and find many more errors besides those I mention. They are also expected to reply to a rebuttal just released at the time of this book's publication, though which their original studies and my present comments already answer: Luuk van de Weghe and Jason Wilson, "Why Name Popularity is a Good Test of Historicity: A Goodness-of-Fit Test Analysis on Names in the Gospels and Acts," *Journal for the Study of the Historical Jesus* 22 (2024), 184–214.

[26] Bauckham, *Jesus*, 67–84 (argument), 84 (conclusion), 85–91 (data).

somehow Jesus travels far and wide on a ministry of more than a year and never once meets anyone else named Jesus.[27] Even in the book of Acts, no one ever meets another Jesus in Palestine. The lone near-exception anyone meets is on Cyprus (Acts 13), and he is not even named Jesus (or indeed any common or even real name), but is portrayed as "the son of Jesus," and is not plausibly a real person.[28] The Gospels also ignore many other common names that mysteriously are missing (like Ananias, Jonathan, Manahem, and Annas), while including many bizarre names almost never heard of in Judea (like Nicodemus and Bartimaeus)—and yet still not even enough of those to match statistical reality (e.g. if rare names comprised a seventh of all names, we should expect a seventh or so of the names in the Gospels and Acts to be rare, yet there are substantially fewer than that).[29]

The Palestinian scenes in Acts alone get one or two of the common names missing from the Gospels back in—and yet still not credibly, as those names (like Ananias) were cribbed from histories or chosen for a fictional purpose—and still many expected names are missing in Acts (no Jonathans or Manahems or any others). Even a real name like Ananias appears *more* often there than it statistically should.[30] Only one in every thirty-two men should be so-named; yet Acts gives us three such men, and there are certainly not ninety-six named men in Acts (at all, much

[27] Even the probability that just one, Barabbas, *was* originally named Jesus in the Gospels, and thus had literally the exact same 'theological' name as Jesus ('Joshua, Son of the Father'), is evidence of fabrication to a purpose, not of historicity: Carrier, *Historicity*, 402–07.

[28] The name he does have, Elymas, is mythologically suited to the narrative and thus more probably than not fake: Daniel Glover, "'For That Is What His Name Means' (Acts 13:8): Luke's Etymology of Elymas the Magician," *The Catholic Biblical Quarterly* 84.4 (2022), 609–26.

[29] Gregor and Blais, "Name Popularity," 198–99 (they only count as rare names found only once elsewhere, like Bartimaeus; but their point carries even more for names appearing elsewhere only a few times, like Nicodemus, or names never elsewhere known, like Elymas).

[30] We get three men named Ananias in Acts, but one is a famous historical person inserted into the narrative (Acts 23:2, 24:1), most likely derived as color content from Josephus (Carrier, *Historicity*, 267–68, 385, 485–87); another is an obviously mythical person magically killed (presumably by God) to frighten readers into compliance with the author's communist program (Acts 5); and the third is a convenient reversal of the name of John the Baptist, in a scene emulating his (Acts 9:10–17, 22:12), and thus is likely also fake (Carrier, *Historicity*, 366).

less in Palestine). Similarly the frequency of the common names the Gospels include is not actually all that close to their frequency in ancient Judea, either. For example, there should be more men named Lazarus (Eliezer) and Matthew (Matthias), and fewer men named James (Jacob) or Simon.[31]

Some of this could be due to allowable statistical variation, because there are so few names in the Gospels and Acts to begin with.[32] But even if that did explain the data, it still allows no basis for Bauckham's conclusion. Because there is still no *apposite* match between the frequency of names we find in the Gospels and Acts and the documented name frequencies in first century Palestine. Deviations from what is expected are quite numerous, and run indiscriminately in both directions (many names appear too much; many, too little). And in too many instances these variations exceed what is even statistically credible—thereby, indeed, *disproving* Bauckham's thesis, not merely failing to establish it. Analysis shows "rare names are statistically significantly underrepresented" in this material, while "several of the most popular names are overrepresented"—both of which are "unlikely to occur in Bauckham's thesis" but entirely expected from a process of invention.[33]

Indeed, most of the common names used in the Gospels and Acts are actually mythically significant Biblical names (like Mary, i.e. Miriam, the sister of Moses; or Joseph, i.e. the Patriarch, and James, i.e. Jacob, better known as Israel) which are already expected for symbolic resonance in any Jewish mythology. Indeed they were popular among the population for the same reason they would be popular with Gospel mythographers. Which evinces a cardinal rule of historical method: you cannot argue your hypothesis is probable without comparing its predictive success to that of its strongest competitor. If the name distribution we actually find in the Gospels is predicted by their being myths, and *not* by their being histories, then this is evidence they are myths, and *not* histories.

Take James (lit. Jacob, hence Israel) as an example: Bauckham's own tables show this name is attested in extant records only 40 times, whereas

---

[31] Gregor and Blais, "Name Popularity," 199–200.

[32] As discussed throughout both studies by Gregor and Blais.

[33] Gregor and Blais, "Name Popularity," 202.

rare names (as a combined category) are attested over 500 times.[34] So across the Gospels and Acts there should be over ten times more men with rare names than men named James. But there isn't. Not even close. In fact rare names on Bauckham's table should appear ten times more often than the bizarre names the Gospels have instead, like Nicodemus or Bartimaeus—which names were obviously fictionally contrived to suit their role in the story.[35] The Gospels are thus *preferring* fake names to real ones. Personal names, both peculiar and commonplace, are already expected for mythical and fictional persons, whether they served an allegorical role or not, as many studies show.[36] And yet the distribution of names across the Gospels and Acts in no way matches reality (unless you posit a lot of statistical anomalies, which of course destroys Bauckham's argument). And their narrative distribution of names deviates from reality in precisely the ways expected if they were all contrived to a purpose. Does this mean none are historical? No. Rather, it means we cannot know—and therefore cannot claim—that any are. For example, we cannot prove 'Simon of Cyrene' was a contrived name; but neither can we prove it was not, leaving it unusable as data.[37] This is the same result I get for every other feature of the Gospels.[38]

So there is no argument for historicity here.

---

[34] Per prior note, I am counting more names as "rare" here (any zero, one, or single-digit frequency name in external sources) than Gregor and Blais do (names only attested once in external sources). And although Gregor and Blais, "Name Popularity," *also* find numerous errors in Bauckham's calculations of actual name frequencies (and their revised counts *worsen* his case), it is more significant that Bauckham should have noticed these incongruities *even with his own counts*.

[35] **Nicodemus:** Carrier, *Historicity*, 505n237; **Bartimaeus:** J.P. O'Connor, "'Spiritual Blindness' in the Bartimaeus Pericope (Mark 10:46–52): Toward Decentering Ableist Readings," *Biblical Interpretation* 20 (2023), 1–19. The Gospels' one **Lazarus**, though it was a common name in reality (Eleazar), is also a fake name there: Carrier, *Historicity*, 487–89, 503n234. And so on.

[36] See: Fred Burnett, "Characterization and Reader Construction of Characters in the Gospels," *Semeia* 63 (1993), 3–28; Bruce Metzger, "Names for the Nameless in the New Testament: A Study in the Growth of Christian Tradition," *New Testament Studies: Philological, Versional, and Patristic* (Brill, 1980), 23–45. See also the special issue of *Biblical Interpretation* 29.4–5 (2021), titled *Cognitive Linguistics and New Testament Narrative: Investigating Methodology through Characterization* (ed. Jan Rüggemeier and Elizabeth Shively).

[37] Carrier, *Historicity*, 444–52.

[38] Carrier, *Historicity*, 506–09.

"The Apostles' Illiteracy Proves Jesus Existed"

An example that isn't fraudulent, just poorly thought-out, is the Argument from Illiterate Fishermen, which goes something like this: 'the disciples can't have invented this religion out of scripture, because they were illiterate fishermen; therefore there must have been a real Jesus who did or inspired that'. This argument hinges on the assumption—which is actually a faith doctrine, derived from the mythology of the Gospels and Acts—that the apostles (particularly the top three men, the 'pillars' of Galatians 2:9: Peter, James and John) were illiterate (or indeed even fishermen). But why does any expert still believe that?

Even the Gospels don't ever really say this. Acts alone has one sentence claiming the apostles were illiterate (Acts 4:13). But Acts can't be trusted.[39] And there are sufficient reasons to doubt it on this point—just as we doubt legends that Mohammed was illiterate, and thus 'miraculously' wrote the Quran.[40] That was contrived to invent evidence his mission must have been divinely ordained; Acts' contrivance of illiterate apostles seems designed to the same purpose. And we know Christian theologians exploited that strategy.[41] And besides that immediate suspicion, there are two other problems with it.

First, all educated Rabbis were expected to ply a manual trade (and we know of ancient Rabbis who held such occupations as sandal-maker and stonemason); therefore 'being a fisherman' was not evidence of 'illiteracy'.[42] A later author or tradent could have mistakenly assumed it

---

[39] On this illiteracy claim specifically: Carrier, *Historicity*, 263–64, 440, 528–31; Richard Carrier, *Science Education in the Early Roman Empire* (Pitchstone, 2016), 137–38. That Acts is not reliable generally: Carrier, *Historicity*, ch. 9; and Richard Carrier, "How We Know Acts Is a Fake History" (21 April 2023) at richardcarrier.info/archives/23447.

[40] Andreas Görke, "Muhammad," in *The Wiley Blackwell Concise Companion to the Hadith* (ed. Daniel Brown; Wiley-Blackwell, 2020), 75–90 (85).

[41] See discussion and examples in Ryan Schellenberg, "τὸ ἐν λόγῳ ἰδιωτικὸν τοῦ Ἀποστόλου: Revisiting Patristic Testimony on Paul's Rhetorical Education," *Novum Testamentum* 54.4 (2012), 354–68.

[42] See Richard Carrier, *Not the Impossible Faith: Why Christianity Didn't Need a Miracle to Succeed* (Lulu, 2009), 51–70; Philip Alexander, "The Rabbis and Their Rivals in the Second Century CE," in *Christianity in the Second Century: Themes and Developments* (ed. James Carleton Paget and Judith Lieu; Cambridge University Press, 2017), 57–70; Gregg Gardner, *Wealth, Poverty, and Charity in Jewish Antiquity* (University of California Press, 2022), 21–37.

meant that (on the correct assumption that *most* fishermen were illiterate), and not realized the apostles were Rabbis, or whatever such persons were then called (and thus an exception to that inference); or, as with Muhammad, they could simply ignore that reality to spin a more miraculous story—trading on the idea that mere commoners could not do this unless it was a genuine miracle from God, ergo it was—or to control for class politics. Since a movement begun by educated elites might raise suspicion from the masses, the contrivance that the founders were 'really' illiterate commoners just like them becomes self-serving.

Of course, we also have no good reason to believe this report of their *occupation* is even true. Paul never mentions it; nor 1 Clement, Hebrews, or any early text (see chapter two). It comes only from Mark (all later authors simply borrowing the idea from him). It is thus telling that none are referred to or work as a fisherman in Acts.[43] It is too likely that the author of Mark invented this to construct a clever pun or literary allusion to be confident that he didn't. After all, Mark 1:17 introduces the notion of 'fishermen' as the 'fishers of men', which is sufficient to motivate inventing their being fishermen in the first place; and there are a lot of elements in Mark suggesting he needed them to be fishermen to get them repeatedly into boats and acting a lot like Odysseus's bumbling crew.[44] It remains contextually likely that the apostles, like Paul, practiced a manual trade as all educated Rabbis then did, regardless of what that trade was. Yet it is evident many a historicist has been unaware of this fact of the ancient Rabbinate, and thus are relying on the same faulty inference (or devotional desire) as the author of Acts. You simply can't get any assurance of their actual illiteracy here.

The second problem is greater. If Peter, James, and John were illiterate, Paul would have made hay of that fact all over his Epistles, continually and forcefully.[45] It is simply improbable that he never would. Because that would mean that he alone—and not they—could read the Scriptures, which he attests was essential to learning and demonstrat-

---

[43] On such unexpected omissions being evidence of historical facts: Carrier, *Historicity*, 385–86, 603–05 (cf. 368–80).

[44] Carrier, *Historicity*, 440 (Mk. 1:17: 'fishermen' = 'fishers of men') or 399 (fishermen = Odysseus's bumbling crew).

[45] Carrier, *Historicity*, 263–64, 440, 528–31.

ing the faith, and ascertaining its tenets.[46] And yet, instead, Paul always defers to them as his equals or veritable superiors.[47] The argument that they could not even *read* the Scriptures never comes up. That means Paul—and his congregations—knew the first apostles were just as educated as he was, and that they were deriving the creeds and doctrines of their new faith from the Writings as much as any other Rabbinical exegete. Which fact is also soundly proved if 1 Peter is authentic (see chapter two); conversely, this would also remove a key argument against the authenticity of 1 Peter (that Peter could not write it because he was illiterate); likewise James; and Jude, if we conclude its parallels with 2 Peter are the result of the latter using the former and not the other way around.

It's at least as likely, if not a certainty, that these apostles' illiteracy was a myth invented later. Because it has no contextual plausibility as history. Experts on ancient literacy have well documented that it is not possible that the kind of scriptural exegesis this sect's creeds and doctrines were based on could derive from a mere *ad hoc* recollection of scattered readings of scripture in public by the non-literate; and that thoroughly memorizing an extensive text was itself a years-long school exercise, not accomplishable by anyone bereft of an education altogether—and yet even if accomplished, actually *removes* their illiteracy as an argument for historicity, so it would be self-defeating for a historicist to insist on it.[48]

And yet 'the apostles were illiterate' is one of those things that just 'keeps being repeated' by historians in this field, while none ever stop to ask if it's even plausible, much less credibly evidenced—or even works

---

[46] For example: Romans 16:25–26; 1 Corinthians 15:1–8; Galatians 3:1. Likewise Gal. 3:8, 10, 13, 16, 22 and 4:22, 27, 30; 1 Cor. 1:19, 1:31, 2:9, 3:19, 4:6, 9:9–10, 10:7, 14:21, 15:45, 15:54; Rom. 1:2, 1:17, 2:24, 3:4, 3:10, 4:3, 4:23, 8:36, 9:13, 9:17, 9:33, 10:11, 10:15, 11:2, 11:8, 11:26, 12:19, 14:11, 15:3–4, 15:9, 15:21; and 2 Cor. 4:13, 8:15, 9:9.

[47] Galatians 1–2; 2 Corinthians 11:5–7; 1 Corinthians 1:11-13, 3:19-23, 4:1-9, 12:27-29.

[48] Raffaella Cribiore, *Gymnastics of the Mind: Greek Education in Hellenistic and Roman Egypt* (Princeton University Press, 2005); Thomas Brodie, *The Birthing of the New Testament: The Intertextual Development of the New Testament Writings* (Sheffield Phoenix Press, 2004), 2-79; Catherine Hezser, *Jewish Literacy in Roman Palestine* (Mohr Siebeck, 2001); William Harris, *Ancient Literacy* (Harvard University Press, 1991). See Carrier, *Historicity*, 397–98, 440–41, 465–67.

as an argument at all. The same would follow for a historical Jesus—he cannot have founded a sect based on scriptural exegesis if he was not the actual Rabbi the Gospels repeatedly label him as.[49] But that could at least be explained by his merely inspiring an educated entourage to build that religion on the foundation of his charismatic intensity and appeal to the masses; he himself needn't have been literate. But the apostles absolutely had to have been. Hence when Paul repeatedly says Christian beliefs were derived from revelation *and scripture* (as he clearly does in Romans 16:25–26 and 1 Corinthians 15:3–4), we have no evidence that that was not in fact the case. And that entails the first apostles (at the very least Peter) were literate.

Of course, even if we went against all plausibility and contrive the speculation that maybe all these guys were extraordinary savants and though illiterate nevertheless memorized the Scriptures, we then lose the argument we were trying to make in the first place. Because now we no longer need a real Jesus to inspire the religion: illiterate memorizers of the Scriptures can have built the religion out of the Scriptures as assuredly as the literate could. There is therefore no argument left here for the historicity of Jesus.

"People Knowing Jesus According to the Flesh Proves He Existed"

I have heard this from several scholars, but a paradigmatic example in print is James Tabor's argument that since Paul says "even if we have known Christ according to the flesh, yet now we know him no more" (2 Corinthians 5:16), then Paul knew people who met Jesus in life, and therefore Jesus was a historical person.[50] But Paul is referring to the Corinthians as a congregation (and indeed, all Christians everywhere)—not

---

[49] It need not matter if this term is anachronistic, i.e. even if 'Rabbi' as a term for 'teacher' (and thus an educated person) was invented later, one could still later apply it to Jesus (or any of his contemporaries also later described as a Rabbi) to thus describe them (just like the English word 'teacher', which also didn't exist when Jesus did). But on that possibility of anachronism see: Mark Verman, "Jesus as 'Rabbi/Rabbouni' and Mark's Use of Aramaic as Messianic Code Language," *Journal for the Study of the Historical Jesus* 21 (2023): pp. 1–34.

[50] James Tabor, *Paul and Jesus: How the Apostle Transformed Christianity* (Simon & Schuster, 2012), 3–4.

to the scant few people who once met Jesus, but to people who never had. Hence he means the *Corinthians* were the ones who once knew things "according to the flesh," not Jesus. This is not a reference to the incarnation at all, but to the transformation of Christians from a fleshly to a spiritual perspective (hence "we know *no* man according to the flesh," not just Jesus, because "if any man is in Christ, he is a new creature: the old things are passed away," 2 Corinthians 5.16–17).[51]

This is an example (one of many I addressed in *Historicity*) of scholars misreading verses out of context (and that means their textual *and* historical context; often even grammatical context), by allowing a faith-derived dogma to guide what they see in Paul's words—rather than operating as objective historians and thus ascertaining what Paul actually said. The historicity of Jesus is built on an edifice of misreadings like this. Which is another reason historicity is an obsolete paradigm: it is causing scholars like Tabor to misread their own source texts. There is no excuse for this anymore. Tabor is not a fundamentalist, and he is not contractually obligated to sell an apologetical line. And many translators already correctly render the sense here as "from now on we regard no one from a worldly point of view" and "though we once regarded Christ in this way, we do so no longer" (NIV; cf. RSV, ISV, NRSV, etc.). So it is not as if Tabor *shouldn't* have noticed he was misreading Paul. Yet he didn't. So pernicious are faith-dogmas in this field that even historians who have no faith-agenda at all fail to notice they are gullibly repeating mere dogmas of the faith as if they were facts. This is just one example. Other examples abound. Historians of Jesus really do need to stop and re-check all their assumptions.

"Paul's Referring to an Oral Tradition Proves Jesus Existed"

A similar thing happened to another open-minded scholar, Mark Goodacre. In our conversation on the *Unbelievable?* radio show (hosted by Justin Brierley), Goodacre said "what we have in places like 1 Corinthians 15" is that Paul "sets out what he has received from those who were in Christ—**as he describes it**—before him" (emphasis mine), which he

[51] Carrier, *Historicity*, 571.

then shared with the Corinthians.[52] I challenged this, noting that Goodacre had "mentioned that Paul said he received his tradition from those in Christ before him," but "that's not in the Epistles of Paul," in fact "Paul never says that he received the tradition from those in Christ before him; he only says he received it—he very adamantly says he received it—only from Jesus in a direct revelation," in Galatians 1, using "the exact same words" as in 1 Corinthians 15. But then Goodacre doubled down, insisting that (again, emphasis mine) "1 Corinthians 15 **clearly** sets out that" Paul "**says,** you know, he'd **received** these traditions **from** those that were in Christ before him" and passed that on to the Corinthians.[53]

This is similar to the Tabor phenomenon: Goodacre clearly believed that Paul actually said he received the gospel "from those who were in Christ before" him. I couldn't disabuse him of that myth. Of course that is nowhere in any letter of Paul. He never says he received anything (gospel or otherwise) from "those who were in Christ before" him, and the only times (and that's several times) he ever says *where* he learned such things, he references *only* scripture and revelation.[54] The phrase "those in Christ before me" appears to derive from Romans 16:7, in no relation to receiving anything, as in Galatians 1:17: both in chapters that explicitly *deny* receiving anything from them (in Romans 16:25–26 and Galatians 1:11–16).

I have found there are a lot of false beliefs scholars maintain as to what is in the letters of Paul. They are so trained in the faith-statements and assumptions of Christian apologetics (even if they themselves are secular) that they continue to maintain the historicity of Jesus on a basis of false beliefs like this. Often we will hear versions of the Goodacre claim, like 'Paul says he met the disciples' or at least 'other people who met Jesus in life', when in fact Paul never mentions disciples, only apostles like himself (e.g., 1 Corinthians 9:1–4, 15:3–8), and never mentions

[52] Justin Brierley, Richard Carrier, and Mark Goodacre, "Did Jesus Exist? Richard Carrier vs Mark Goodacre—Unbelievable?" *Unbelievable?* (December 2012) at tinyurl.com/y2p7yc95.

[53] Brierley, Carrier, and Goodacre, "Did Jesus Exist?" during minute 20. A similar argument is made by Robyn Faith Walsh in Derek Lambert and Robyn Faith Walsh, "Everything You Thought You Knew About The Gospels Is Wrong!" *Mythvision Podcast* (20 December 2021) at youtube.com/watch?v=PLKMcIz8Vd0, in minute 55.

[54] Carrier, *Historicity*, 135, 517, 535–38, 554 (cf. 594, 612; and, again, 137–46). See also the discussion of the Eucharist 'tradition' here in chapter two.

anyone ever even seeing Jesus until after his death—all of which evinces a contrary conclusion.[55] Yet that false claim is still repeated, even by experts. No one is stopping to check if those beliefs are even true. Paul instead keeps saying people met Jesus only in visions.[56]

One could still appeal to the more credible argument that Paul met the 'brothers' of Jesus or 'knew' he had biological parents, but for the present point that's just as ambiguous (see chapters eight, nine, and ten). After all, that the 'apostles' (those sent by epiphany) are even the same thing as 'disciples' (those who sat at Jesus's feet) is precisely what is doubtful, just as that 'brothers' (by spiritual adoption) ever meant the same thing as 'brothers' (by biological relation) is precisely what is doubtful. When you check, these conflations no longer appear to be so plausible. And there is nothing in Paul that supports them.

Indeed I used to believe all these same things. Until I checked and found they weren't true. I then realized I had to scrap *all* my assumptions and start over: I had to read the Epistles of Paul as if for the first time, to see what Paul actually says in them. And I found it isn't what scholars like Tabor and Goodacre keep assuming. It is often even the opposite of what they aver. Any defense of historicity must do the same, abandoning all assumptions and starting anew.[57] But since historians are not even aware which beliefs they hold *are* assumptions, they need to recheck their *every* belief against the evidence, to see whether they've been hoodwinked by Christian faith traditions, or whether their beliefs actually do accord with the evidence. I believe (as does Lataster) that when you do that, the credibility of historicity declines. Which needs to be acknowledged, not evaded.

It certainly must not be evaded by replacing evidence with dubious speculation. For example, Bart Ehrman has claimed that when Paul swears he learned the gospel by a vision alone (Galatians 1:11–16), the same as he implies for every other apostle (1 Cor. 9:1; 1 Cor. 15:1–8), he only meant his special adaptation to it (that Gentiles needn't go kosher), and that he learned *the rest* from human beings after all.[58] But that is

---

[55] Carrier, *Historicity*, 517–20, 532, 537, 544, 587–89.

[56] Carrier, *Historicity*, 524–27, 536, 553–54, 572.

[57] Carrier, *Historicity*, 512–14.

[58] Derek Lambert and Bart Ehrman, "Jesus vs Paul: The Origins of a Religious Schism in

impossible. Paul's entire argument there is that the gospel he received by revelation was *the same* gospel, not a different one (because Gal. 1:6–12 must be read in light of Gal. 2:2–7, 14); indeed Paul says the previous apostles added nothing to his gospel (Gal. 2:4–6); and as he uses exactly the same language here (Gal. 1:11–12) as in his delivery of the gospel altogether (1 Cor. 15:1–3)—in fact the formula is identical—he is therefore describing the same thing in both places.[59]

Moreover, Paul's entire argument in Galatians 1 entails that had he learned the rest of the gospel from men and not Jesus, he would be a fraud—not a real apostle, because he was not really 'sent by' Jesus (*apostelein*) but just cribbed the gospel from others, making him no special authority after all. This establishes that Paul has to mean here the *whole* gospel was learned by revelation, not just his modification to it, because otherwise the *rest* of the gospel he preached would be fraudulent, being 'received' from men and not Jesus. Just read Gal. 1:11–16, where Paul makes clear that he and the Galatians believe a gospel is only authentic if revealed, not learned; and that the gospel he received by revelation is the only one he preached everywhere.

Indeed the gospel Paul delivered to the Galatians *has* to be the same gospel he delivered to the Corinthians. So he has to be talking about the same gospel in both places. To the Romans Paul describes the entire gospel (and even *kerygma*) of Jesus as known only by revelation; and in none of his letters does he ever describe anyone learning it any other way.[60] Moreover, everywhere Paul defends his adaptation to the gospel (such as practically his entire letters to the Galatians and Romans) he only offers his own scriptural exegesis, and never a 'saying of the Lord'—indeed he never on such occasions quotes or even cites Jesus as his authority (apart from Scripture), even though he will do so in trivial cases when he has a pertinent revelation to quote (2 Cor. 12:1, 7–9; 1 Thess. 4:15–18; 1 Cor. 7:10–11). Which means Paul did not receive a special modified gospel from Jesus, but the same one as everyone else—*exactly as he says* (there is no "other gospel," Galatians 1:6–12)—and the rest was simply *his inter-*

Early Christianity," *MythVision Podcast* (9 June 2023) at youtube.com/watch?v=hJBb-zs-gX-s (from minute 6 to 8).

[59] As I already explained: Carrier, *Historicity*, 139, 516, 536.

[60] Rom. 16:25–26; likewise, in the original Greek, Rom. 10:14–18 (Carrier, *Historicity*, 554; and for all his letters, see 553–57 and 137-41).

pretation of it (see Gal. 3–4, which is defending the same gospel he insists he received only by revelation in Gal. 1–2). All of this should have been obvious. After all, what gospel could Paul have been preaching for three years in Arabia ("so that I might preach Him among the Gentiles...in Arabia," Gal. 1:13–18) but the *entire* gospel, and not just his one small mod to it? The latter would be nonsensical without the other. And how could Paul get away with claiming to the Galatians that his was *not* a different gospel than the original, if he was preaching that it *was* a different gospel than the original?

So when Paul says he preached the gospel he received only by revelation for years before even meeting with 'flesh and blood' to confirm it (Gal. 1:16, 20 and 2:2), he can only mean *the* gospel—the entire and same gospel of 1 Cor. 15:1–4. And Paul never describes any other gospel (even what Ehrman thinks was the 'original' gospel) being learned in any way other than by revelation, either, so we have no evidence on which to base Ehrman's speculation anyway. And speculations aren't facts. So the dogma that Paul ever claimed or even implied that he learned any 'gospel' from the apostles before him (or indeed that *any* apostle learned the gospel apart from revelation) is not only nowhere in evidence, it is repeatedly refuted by Paul's own words. So it is far time to put this dogma aside.

"Being Specifically 'Crucified' Proves Jesus Existed"

As I mentioned earlier (and already address in my original study) the mere fact of being crucified is no more likely for a real savior than a mythical one. But there is a more particular apologetic for historicity based on the specific use of the term 'crucifixion', as voiced by Bart Ehrman or Paula Fredriksen for example.[61] As this argument goes, Paul repeatedly refers to the 'crucifixion' of Jesus, and 'crucifixion' was an inherently Roman practice, and therefore it could never have described any other killers of Jesus than the Romans, which entails Paul believed Jesus was recently a real earthly man, a victim of imperial politics.

---

[61] Bart Ehrman, *Did Jesus Exist? The Historical Argument for Jesus of Nazareth* (San Francisco: HarperOne, 2013), 124; Paula Fredriksen, *Jesus of Nazareth, King of the Jews: A Jewish Life and the Emergence of Christianity* (Vintage, 2000), 217, 295.

The reasoning is sound. The problem is that the premise is not. No word existed in ancient Greek that was distinctive of any form of Roman execution. All the words Paul actually used were often used of Jewish executions, and the executions of other national cultures and eras.[62] Paul never links the execution of Jesus to anything distinctively Roman. In fact nothing Paul ever says requires it even to have been by humans, or on Earth (as I discussed in chapter two). The first we hear of it being specifically a *Roman* crucifixion is in the Gospels, none of whose accounts of that are historically plausible, and all of whose accounts of it are constructed from scriptural, mythical, and literary tropes.[63] But in stories outside the Roman Empire, Jesus is stoned by the Sanhedrin and hung on a plank in accordance with Jewish law—and a hundred years earlier, when Romans weren't even around.[64] Which also destroys all arguments of the form 'Jesus existed because the Talmud confirms it', another example of an argument scholars will repeat without having actually checked. But what this also shows is that this detail (of Jesus being 'crucified') was easily mapped to any context. It therefore does not imply historicity at all.

The same thing follows for the related argument that 'the rulers of this age' (in 1 Corinthians 2:8) must mean Romans. That simply isn't true. Any worldly authority performing legal executions could be so designated. And as many scholars have noted, this is an unusual phrase in a particular context that allows or even suggests that it means *demons*, not people (see my discussion in chapter two).

"Inability to Think of Another Explanation Proves Jesus Existed"

Another strange argument also comes from Mark Goodacre, in his crit-

[62] As I document, citing several scholars concurring, in Carrier, *Historicity*, 61–62. Plato describes crucifixion as commonplace (*Republic* 2.362a), and therefore not distinctively Roman (using a word more specific than Paul ever does: *anaskolopizô*, 'being set on-a-pole'), in a passage of direct interest to Christians (Carrier, *Historicity*, 211–12); while Paul chooses words from the Septuagint describing executions in non-Roman cultures and even Jewish executions (e.g. Esther 7.9; Deut. 21:22-23, cf. Gal. 3:13).

[63] Carrier, *Historicity*, 402–08, 422–26, 437–38, 441–43, 462–64, 493–94, 497–99, 501, 504 (cf. 515, 531, 563–65, 573).

[64] Carrier, *Historicity*, 281–89. See my discussion of this point in chapter two.

ical analysis of John Dominic Crossan's explanations of the contents of the Gospels as the reification of prophecy.[65] Goodacre's overall point is that Crossan seeks to explain the content of, say, the Gospel of Mark as entirely a construct from scripture, to turn a prophecy into a narrative; but Goodacre rightly observes that Crossan's procedure cannot explain every single pericope or detail in Mark, and so what remains unexplained could yet be there because it is historical.

Here Goodacre is attempting to articulate another 'criterion' by which to identify underlying history in the Gospels, something like a 'criterion' of 'lack of any other explanation', whereby if we can't explain something, odds then favor it being historical. One of Goodacre's examples is the 'names' of the women at the cross: Crossan can't derive them from prophecy; therefore they likely derived from history (or, at least, oral lore). But we already saw earlier what is wrong with that reasoning: myth and fiction routinely assigned names to people; therefore their having specific names cannot evince their historicity. Often we can even tell the names are fake; and I think we can in this case as well.[66] But even when we can't, we cannot therefore *assume* they are historical.[67] It remains as likely they are not (or even more so—as I will explain below, and further in chapter six).

Goodacre's treatment of Crossan is otherwise generally sound and valuable. But his argument to historicity still stumbles on two assumptions. It operates entirely from an assumption of historicity (rather than considering the alternative, and how it might explain the same evidence); and from an assumption that Paul said he got information about Jesus from the entourage of Jesus (and therefore, such information was in circulation), which, more than merely an unestablished assumption, is actually false. That both those assumptions are dubious I've already addressed. But what remains to address are Goodacre's faulty inferences

---

[65] Mark Goodacre, "Prophecy Historicized or Tradition Scripturalized? Reflections on the Origin of the Passion Narratives" in *New Testament and the Church: Essays in Honour of John Muddiman* (ed. John Barton and Peter Groves; T&T Clark, 2015), 37–51. For my full analysis see Richard Carrier, "Mark Goodacre on the Historicity of Jesus's Execution" (1 July 2021) at richardcarrier.info/archives/18498.

[66] See, for example, Carrier, *Not the Impossible Faith*, 312–21.

[67] See my discussion of Simon of Cyrene (Carrier, *Historicity*, 444–52), another of Goodacre's examples.

here: first, that if we cannot think of a reason a story or detail would be in Mark (or wherever), then it is more probably historical; and, second, that (for any example he might call up) indeed no one has yet thought of a reason that story or detail would be in Mark (or wherever). But in actual fact, often someone has—and the fault is simply that Goodacre didn't look for it or hadn't found it; while even when no one has, the conclusion still does not follow, owing to the precedents already established pointing in the other direction.

This is a failure produced by not studying the logic of probability (see chapter five), which is a fault common to almost all historians, but particularly Jesus historians. In this case, understanding how probability actually worked would produce the opposite conclusion: if most examples in a text are proven fabrications, then the prior probability favors any one example remaining in that text *also* being a fabrication. So absent evidence otherwise—evidence that you are looking at one of the exceptions to the trend—you should conclude *on* trend, not against. Hence in any case within a text where we cannot ascertain the origin or meaning of its details, we should assume it has a similar origin or meaning to *most* other things in that text.[68]

Hence, if we are looking at a modern detective novel set in New York, and cannot explain its description of a particular street there and its name (we can neither check what that street actually looked like or was called at the time), nor can we explain how the author came by that description or name, or what purpose those served in their story, then the last thing we should assume is that 'therefore' that street existed in New York and was named and looked as described. It's a detective novel. Most things in it are made up, not derived from real accounts of New York. Some are real. But *most* aren't. Therefore, any as-yet unidentified detail we find is more likely to *also* be made up and not real. That does not mean it cannot be real. Nor does it mean the probability it is real has to be particularly low. All it means is that it's *more likely* not to be.

Which 'does in' Goodacre's first mistaken inference. His second mistaken inference represents a failure of the more mundane scutwork of doing history generally. We cannot know or read everything. So we will often not know what has or has not been suggested to explain any partic-

[68] For a more detailed explanation of this point see Carrier, *Historicity*, 506–09.

ular detail in the Gospels—even when we try hard to find as many as we can, it simply is not possible to have found them all, as the literature in this field is vast and not as well databased as one would like. But working hard at this can result at least in a cross-trend that influences your judgment in respect to the first inference: not only, for example, is most of the Gospel of Mark constructed to a purpose and thus not likely historical (thus suggesting anything we are unsure about is more, not less, likely to be more of the same), but the more you check *the literature*, the more examples of well-argued explanations you will find—converging to the same conclusion: odds are, there is an explanation you haven't thought of.

This was my realization as I accumulated examples for my chapter on the Gospels in *Historicity*. More and more I found very good explanations for astonishingly large amounts of structure and details in all the Gospels. Yes, I found many poorly argued ones, too. But still many more well argued ones than I expected. I soon realized that my own lack of imagination was no guide in determining what to expect. Odds are, anything in a Gospel that still mystifies me will either fall to yet another such analysis somewhere, or was built on background assumptions obvious to a Gospel's author (and maybe even his intended audience) but that modern historians have long since lost access to. In other words, coming from both directions (the trend in the Gospels *and* the trend in modern scholarship), it is indeed the case that the last thing we should ever assume is that *anything* in a Gospel is historical. We need more than the lack of knowledge of why something is there. We need *positive evidence* that it is there because it is historical, and hence there for reasons *contrary* to both trends. Otherwise, odds are, it's *on* trend. Hence Goodacre's entire reasoning is unsound.

To illustrate what I mean, if you read his study you'll find that many of Goodacre's examples fail to take into account how Mark reifies the teachings of Paul (as noted in chapter two). His conclusion is thus based on overlooking good explanations for the content of Mark—it's not all 'reification of prophecy' as Crossan avers, and yet that does not mean 'history' is the only source left. Mark draws from not only prophecy, but prophecy as written in scriptures and variants (and interpretations and paraphrases of prophecy) that we do not have,[69] and from the Epistles

[69] Carrier, *Historicity*, 88–92 (e.g., that Mark used lost targumim: 408–10, 433, 562n66).

of Paul (and possibly other Christian Epistles we have *and* don't have, including lost Epistles of Paul and earlier versions of Paul's Epistles which we know contained more material),[70] and from Greek and Jewish literature,[71] and from philosophy and mythology and popular lore,[72] and from real history that otherwise never really connected to Jesus (or even Christianity at all),[73] and from a creative application of rhetorical storytelling the author of Mark will have learned in school.[74] You cannot just say 'it's either reified prophecy or history'. You have to get behind all the sources Mark employs. But we cannot always do that—many of his sources are lost now, and many will never have been written down at all, such as Jewish or pagan parables and proverbs, and the oral transmission of apostolic and post-apostolic revelations and doctrines and experiences, and Christian pesharim. So we cannot assume that even when we've checked everything we have access to, that *then* we can say it comes from history. We need more specific evidence than that. After all, would we really buy the argument that Hercules must have been historical because how otherwise can we explain someone inventing the story that he had to mop up horseflop?[75] No historian believes that story, even the ones who have no idea why it was contrived. The inference 'we cannot explain it, therefore it happened' therefore has no value.

Our assumption must favor the greater probability, and the greater probability will always be signaled by the trend. Do things *usually* end up confirmed as historical in Mark—or do they more usually end up confirmed as fiction? As with the labors of Hercules, the answer is 'usually fiction'. And what is the more usual is by definition the more probable—until you have specific evidence otherwise (see chapters five and six). For example, we can externally confirm Pontius Pilate and the High Priest Caiaphas were real and held office in Judea at the same time. But we trust that conclusion only because we *got* that external evidence.

---

[70] For examples: Carrier, *Historicity*, 280, 306–08, 311–13, 511.

[71] Countless examples are surveyed in ch. 10 of Carrier, *Historicity*.

[72] For examples: Carrier, *Historicity*, 56–58, 197–209, 214–34.

[73] For example: Carrier, *Historicity*, 428-30.

[74] For examples: Carrier, *Historicity*, 397–99.

[75] See the entry on the "Augean Stables" in *The Oxford Companion to World Mythology* (ed. David Leeming; Oxford University Press, 2005), 38.

Until we get the same kind of evidence for anything else in the Gospels, we *cannot* conclude anything in them goes against the trend.

This is the role of background knowledge in determining the probabilities of evidence and its explanations. We have two well-established background facts here: first, that the Gospels fabricate routinely (far more routinely than otherwise); and, second, that we cannot expect to know every intended meaning or idea behind every fabrication, sitting as we are thousands of years later, in a different culture, with almost none of the source materials and background knowledge Mark and his readers would take for granted. Those two facts together mean that our inability to think of an explanation is no longer evidence of there being none.

I originally discussed this point using the example of the '153' fishes in the Gospel of John, a story that obviously is not historical but had some symbolical meaning now lost to us or only tenuously guessable.[76] The same can be expected to be the case even when a story or detail's fictionality is not similarly obvious—like the tale that an unnamed minion of Jesus severed the ear of the high priest's servant,[77] to no evident outcome, which evolved into more elaborate legends later, including inexplicably assigning the crime to Peter (Mk. 14:47; Lk. 22:49–51; Mt. 26:50–52; Jn. 18:10–11), who somehow manages to never be sued or prosecuted or even denounced for it (Acts 2ff.); or the bizarre story of an unnamed (yet somehow simultaneously famous) woman who anoints Jesus's 'cadaver' before he is even dead, and with absurdly expensive perfume, whose monetary value is inexplicably even precisely stated (without any explanation of how anyone came by that knowledge).[78] The odds favor these being symbolical myths of some construction and not historical events. There is no other reason Mark would include them. But just because we cannot figure out the intended sense is no argument for their being real events (or even based on any)—because all the trendline evidence indicates that to be the least likely explanation.

Goodacre himself almost gets this point (but remains stuck in the

---

[76] Carrier, *Historicity*, 450–51, 505–06.

[77] This might connect with the LXX (Leviticus 21:18): see Mark McVann, "Conjectures about a Guilty Bystander: The Sword Slashing in Mark 14:47," *Listening* 21.2 (1986), 124–37; and Benedict Viviano, "The High Priest's Servant's Ear: Mark 14:47," *Revue Biblique* 96.1 (1989), 71–80.

[78] Carrier, *Historicity*, 452–53.

false dichotomy of 'either reified prophecy or history') when he addresses Crossan's argument that, while the women being at the burial and empty tomb is probably made up, their being at the crucifixion must be a historical fact "because the male disciples had fled." So, Crossan argued, "if the women had not been watching, we would not know even the brute fact of crucifixion (as distinct, for example, from Jesus being summarily speared or beheaded in prison)." Goodacre rightly identifies the flaw in Crossan's reasoning here, noting that Crossan's "basis for affirming" this is that "the male disciples had fled," but "there is no way Crossan can know this," since their flight derives from "a quotation of Zechariah 13:7, 'Strike the shepherd and the sheep will be scattered'," and therefore Crossan's argument "presupposes that an explicitly scriptural element in Mark's story is historical," rather than (as Crossan's own reasoning should determine) fictional.[79]

Of course we could just as well conclude that 'the brute fact of crucifixion' itself derived already from interpretations of Scripture (as elaborately illustrated in 1 Peter and explicitly stated by Paul) and thus *also* required no historical fact to vouch for it. But even as history it would have been a mater of public record (indeed broadcast and posted), requiring *no one* to have witnessed it. So Crossan's reasoning is swarming with logical fallacies. If Goodacre could take this insight and add to it the fact that reified prophecy is *not* the only place Mark gets stories and details for his mythography, he'd be where I am now: realizing we can't get to history this way. The Gospels are self-evidently far too fictional to vouchsafe *any* of their contents as history, without specific external corroboration. Which, for anything to do with Jesus, we do not have.

Not Understanding the Alternative

That covers the gamut of what's been attempted over the last ten years (apart from what we'll cover in coming chapters). You will notice it is all bizarre relative to any other historical person. That these convoluted and illogical efforts are needed at all suggests we should give up on the historicity of Jesus rather than continue defending it. It's an obsolete

[79] Goodacre, "Reflections," 45.

paradigm. So we need a new one. But there is one last argument I need to cover here: to keep insisting Jesus must have existed because there is no other plausible way of accounting for the origins of Christianity and its earliest (pre-Gospel) literature.

Variants of this argument always stem from not having read either of the peer-reviewed studies of this question to date, mine or Lataster's. For example, Robyn Faith Walsh declares as her reason to believe Jesus existed the fact that she cannot imagine Paul and the first apostles just making it all up, because that just never happens in human history.[80] I have to assume she means 'making up' the core story of the Gospels (of an actual earthly man touring Palestine, gaining crowds of followers, and being crucified by the Romans), because otherwise the history of religions affords *ample* examples of founders and their apostles making up *all sorts* of things. Islam and Mormonism are only the most famous examples of being rapidly founded on fabricated histories.[81] I myself gave the examples of the Luddite and Cargo Cult movements; even the Rastafarian movement—whose 'savior' did exist, but never did anything they claim and even continually disavowed their religion his whole life.[82] Yet it thrives to this day.[83] Even Walsh herself would have to agree the risen 'dinner party' Jesus was rapidly invented (see chapter one). And so on. So Walsh must mean, rather, an invention of a historical Jesus right out of the gate. But in that case I agree with her. I explicitly excluded that theory of origins from consideration, for exactly the same reason she does.[84] The only theory that has passed peer review is far more plausible, because it requires no fabrication at all during its first generation. It is also compatible with some fabrication, but only of a kind well documented to be commonplace (like authorities claiming to have visions

---

[80] Jacob Berman and Robyn Faith Walsh, "Paul Did NOT Make up JESUS," *History Valley* (22 August 2023) at youtube.com/shorts/U4mN9X7giq8.

[81] There remains no more complete survey of the Mormon case than David Fitzgerald, *The Complete Heretic's Guide to Western Religion Book One: The Mormons* (CreateSpace, 2013), whose bibliography is extensive; but see also the citations in chapter six (p. 225, n. 60). For Islam, see the relevant entries in Brown (ed.), *Companion to the Hadith*.

[82] Carrier, *Historicity*, 9–11 (Luddites), 18-20, 249–50 (Rastafarianism; likewise the Roswell myth), 159–63 (Cargo Cults), 352, 388n2 (Islam).

[83] Ian Boxill (ed.), *The Globalization of Rastafari* (Arawak, 2009).

[84] Carrier, *Historicity*, 53–55.

that in fact they did not, of mystical or celestial affairs which therefore by their very nature cannot be falsified).

Walsh's reason for maintaining an assumption of historicity sounds like 'I have not read the leading theories of historicity and don't know what they are'. Which is not a good reason. Try it out for any other religion. 'The angels Gabriel and Moroni must actually exist, because I cannot imagine Muhammad and Joseph Smith making them up'. 'Moses must have existed because I cannot imagine anyone getting away with inventing an entire biography of him'. 'John Frum and Ned Ludd must have existed because I cannot otherwise fathom where they came from'. 'The U.S. government must have a secret base containing an entire alien ship and the cadavers of its extraterrestrial pilots, because who would invent that and why would anyone believe them if they did?' 'Haile Selassie must be the one true messiah because his worshippers can't have made that up'. And so on.[85] Needless to say, this is not sound reasoning.

While it is surely the case that (as I think Walsh means to say) the kind of narrative contrived in the Gospels cannot have succeeded (since most of the proofs-of-concept that I just surveyed required considerable physical or temporal distance to succeed), the kind of account actually found in the Epistles of Paul *could*. Because that account fits the model of, for example, Mormonism and Islam: if Jesus began (and was preached in that generation) as the analog to Gabriel and Moroni—only seen by the elect, and only mystically, and thus not an earthly man whose reality could at such close distances and time be tested—then the religion could easily flourish just as Mormonism and Islam did. Indeed, those 'visions' (which may have been waking or dreaming or both) could even have been 'real', in the sense that those receiving them genuinely had those experiences and believed them real; but that needn't be the case.[86] I doubt either Muhammad or Joseph Smith and their apostles were relating genuine experiences; masses of people believed them all the same. But either way, ample precedents establish this could be what happened, leaving only the question of whether the evidence fits that model. And it does.

As for how that later transformed into legends of a historical Gali-

---

[85] See my survey of how rapidly these kinds of falsehoods get invented in Carrier, *Historicity*, 248–52 ('Rapid Legendary Development').

[86] See my discussion of the possibilities, based on scientific and historical studies of other religious movements, in Carrier, *Historicity*, 124–37.

lean a generation later, the model would then follow that of Ned Ludd, the Cargo Cults, or the Roswell saucer—or the 'resurrected dinner-party Jesus' as already covered in chapter one. Such transformations have happened in several other movements, and demonstrably in Christianity itself—e.g., with dinner-party Jesus, and a great deal else (because examples abound: Christians routinely fabricated their history).[87] So we cannot say it can't have happened in Christianity. To the contrary, the evidence suggests it not only could, but did: Jesus is only described as a mystically encountered being in Paul (and 1 Clement and Hebrews and even 1 Peter); and only historicized decades later, and anonymously at that—just like Ned Ludd and John Frum. Once you take into account what our theory *actually is*, it is no longer viable to argue that 'Jesus must have existed because there is no other plausible way of accounting for the origins of Christianity and its earliest (pre-Gospel) literature'. That is precisely the argument our studies refuted. So you can't just repeat that refuted proposition against them. You have to engage with their findings and arguments.

Concluding Remarks

We've seen the critics in the last chapter; and the typical defenders in this chapter. Together they keep prompting the same questions. Why are these awful contortions the arguments historians go to when they are tasked with defending the assumption that Jesus really existed? And why do we still trust in a historical Jesus when our best reasons to are so unconvincing?

Perhaps you will agree these have all been the weakest of tea, but that there really is still at least one argument that remains good: that Paul knew (or knew of) Jesus's earthly family. That's certainly a better argument than what we've seen so far. But in the end it still suffers all

---

[87] Apart from countless examples surveyed in Markus Vinzent, *Resetting the Origins of Christianity: A New Theory of Sources and Beginnings* (Cambridge: Cambridge University Press, 2023), see the examples in Richard Carrier, "The Rain Miracle of Marcus Aurelius: A Case Study in Christian Lies" (27 May 2017) at richardcarrier.info/archives/12480, and "How To Fabricate History: The Example of Eusebius on Alexandrian Christianity" (20 November 2020) at richardcarrier.info/archives/17358.

the same defects, as Lataster and I already explained in our respective studies, and as I'll explain again here in chapters eight through ten. But first I have to orient you in some principles of method and background knowledge. Because those, too, have been evaded, yet need to be grasped before we can ever develop a sound defense of a historical Jesus.

5

WHY HISTORIANS SIMPLY MUST LEARN MATH

> *If there is a field-related logic of historical thought, then working historians must help to find it. But they have contributed little of consequence in the past forty years. Their articles and books on the nature of history tend to degenerate into mere exhortations, or manuals on the mechanics of citation, or metahistorical mumbo-jumbo. Many academic historians regard methodological and logical problems with suspicion and even hostility. Incredibly, the word 'logic' is often a pejorative ... [the] appropriately ugly name for this prejudice: misology, or logic-hating. Its continuing existence among academic historians explains their failure to refine a logic of historical thought.*
>
> —David Hackett Fischer, *Historians' Fallacies*[1]

Fifty years later and Fischer's observation remains largely true.

[1] David Hackett Fischer, *Historians' Fallacies: Toward a Logic of Historical Thought* (Harper & Row, 1970), ix-xi.

The Problem of Method

I have to orient you in some principles of method essential to this debate, because those, too, have been evaded—usually with the excuse that math is too hard to learn. Just from the critics surveyed in chapter three: in their critical responses, Gullotta declares all the mathematics required "unnecessarily complicated and uninviting" and thus ignores it;[2] Petterson misspells Bayes' as "Bayle's" and complains for a whole page about how the math is too hard, and likewise ignores it;[3] Gathercole and Litwa simply ignore all math and logic entirely, even when it is essential to a point they want to make (such as why and how I use the Rank-Raglan hero class, or what could even be wrong with that),[4] while Hansen never engages with any mathematical point even when they mention one, which is almost never, until they teamed up with Kamil Gregor on the same Rank-Raglan question—and got it wrong (on which see chapter six).

But not understanding how math works is identical to not understanding how probability works. And not understanding how probability works is identical to not knowing how to do history at all. Because probability is inalienably mathematical. And all statements about historical fact are statements about probability—what is probable or improbable, what is more probable or less, what is most probable or least. And yet historians can rarely explain what logic justifies any of their assertions about probability. They just 'feel it in their gut' or something. And this is a scandal. We have an entire professional field of knowledge that can't explain why any of its conclusions are true.

If you already agree with me on this, you can skip the following bullets. But if you don't, I do have to pause on this: the excuse that learning the requisite math and logic to resolve this failure 'is too hard' is not sound for two reasons…

- First, historians accept that many skills they must acquire are hard—at the very least, mastering (usually several) ancient languages, but

---

[2] Gullotta, "Doubts," 325.

[3] Petterson, "*Historicity*," 254.

[4] Hansen, "Lord Raglan's Hero," 135–36.

even just reading (and writing) their own language at what is, in fact, a very high level of literacy; and the rest of what they do is a skill requiring years to develop to anything like an expert level. Moreover, 'it's too hard' is not a valid excuse to avoid learning something absolutely essential to your field of study. Since, as a historian, your field of study is almost entirely about determining probabilities, the logic and mathematics of probability is essential to your field of study. 'It's too hard to know what I'm doing or why any of it is correct' sounds silly for a reason.

- Second, the math and logic required is not even hard. In fact, you do not need to know any actual math (as in the mechanical tools of calculation) beyond the level of what constitutes sixth grade arithmetic in the American system (or 'Year 7' in the U.K. or the final year of *weiterführende Schule* in Germany), which is generally mastered by pre-teen children. You are (presumably) an adult. You can learn this. Some of the *concepts* might be more advanced, but even those do not go beyond undergraduate college level (or indeed A.P. level for high schoolers in America). In fact many private schools teach the requisite level of logic to the 7th and 8th grades, which correspond to ages 13 and 14. It really is not hard.

So let's talk about math.

Start with the Basics: Arithmetic

The easiest way to tackle calculations in probability is to use arithmetical fractions, based on what we call 'relative odds'. That is closer to how the human brain intuits probabilities, and it requires fewer steps. But this requires knowing how to convert odds into probabilities and back again.

For example, in *Historicity* I find the highest probability that someone *like* Jesus is historical is 1 in 3, or around 33% (100% divided by 3 and rounded to the nearest whole number).[5] That does not mean Jesus himself has that probability of existing. That still requires factoring in

[5] Carrier, *Historicity*, 235–53, 597–601.

any evidence we have for Jesus that might indicate differently. For example, even if people like Alexander the Great or Julius Caesar faced those same *general* odds of existing, the evidence we *specifically* have for those two men far overwhelms and reverses that conclusion (as we'll see in the next chapter).[6] Of course, even after accounting for all the myths and legends that grew over their legacy, Caesar was still not as heavily mythologized as Jesus, though we could say Alexander was.[7] But even when they do face those odds, that still would not mean they didn't exist. The evidence specific to them could decisively transform those odds—even if they started out in a class of people who usually didn't exist.

What I am talking about now is called a 'prior probability' or 'base rate'. It is the probability of a phenomenon happening or being true in general—in other words, what is 'usually' the case. Which in a sense measures how much evidence we'd need to conclude otherwise—how much more probable the evidence has to be to flip the odds in the other direction, to change what we expect into what is actually the case. This is the logic underlying all historical thought.

But I have still not actually stated the odds here.

The idioms '1 in 3' and '33%' state *probabilities*. To restate those in the form of *odds*, we would say '1 to 2' or '2 to 1 against' (or more succinctly 1:2 or 2:1, or 1/2 or 2/1, depending on the context). Because when we say 33% we mean one third of all possible probability. Hence '1 in 3' is counting off the total probability-space into three equal parts, and saying one of them corresponds to our queried result ('historical person') but two of them correspond to the converse result ('mythical person'), such as we find in the set of all heavily mythologized persons in the relevant period (which means, in this case, Greco-Roman antiquity). What I originally found the empirical data indicate for that set is simple. That someone in that set is a 'mythical person' is (*usually* and *at least*) twice as likely as someone in that set being a 'historical person'. Hence we can say 1 in 3 are historical. When we say this in the form of odds, the total is represented in the sum of the parts. So '1 in 3' becomes '1 to 2', where one and two sum to three, and one of those parts falls on one side ('historical person') and the other two parts fall on the other side ('mythical person').

---

[6] Carrier, *Historicity*, 252–53.

[7] Carrier, *Historicity*, 222–34; *Outer Space*, 111–51. I shall go into this more in chapter six.

So these two expressions ('1 in 3' and '1 to 2') are saying the same thing, just in different ways.

To convert one to the other requires a step of calculation: if it's 1 to 2 (or 1/2) odds, then it's a 1/3 probability (or, again, 100% divided by 3, which is 33%). To know that, you have to add the parts back together ('1 to 2' therefore means 1 + 2 = 3 parts), then put the part you are measuring the probability of on top of your new fraction, and put the sum (of all the parts) on the bottom, and so you get 1/3, from 1/(1 + 2). Plug 1/3 into your calculator and you'll see the result is 0.3333… (using an ellipses here to indicate the digits keep going). Which is 33.33% if we are rounding to the second decimal place, or just 33% if we are rounding to the nearest whole number. Notice that the percent symbol (%) is an almost literal abbreviation for '100'. Hence a percentage is just the decimal multiplied by a hundred. The percent symbol in fact means 'divide by 100 to get the true number'. Hence '/100' or '÷100' became abbreviated to %. So 33% divided by 100 gets 0.33, the actual number represented. Hence 0.3333 × 100 is 33.33 (you just move the decimal place by two, because of the two zeroes in '100' as signaled by the symbol '%'). Which we then write out as 33% (rounding to the nearest whole).

If the odds are the other way, for example 2 to 1 (or 2/1), the math is all the same. You just sum the total parts of the space again (2 + 1 = 3) and divide that into the side you are interested in knowing the probability of. So in this case, that would get you 2/3, from 2/(2 + 1), which is 67% (rounding to the nearest whole percent; or, in decimal notation, 0.6667, if we want to round, for example, to the fourth decimal place). You can also get that probability by subtracting the converse probability from the sum of all probabilities (which is always, axiomatically, 100%, because the probability is always 100% that any claim is either true or false, there being no other possibility).

This is because, when you have properly divided the options into two and they account for all possibilities, each probability is always the converse of the other. So when one side has a probability of 33%, the other must have a probability of 67%. So, 100 – 33 = 67; or 1 – 0.33 = 0.67, which means the same thing. Hence you should know that '100%' means a probability of 1 when you are measuring probability as a decimal (when, for example, you are displaying 1 in 3 as 0.33), which you have to do if you intend to do calculations. For example, 100% times 33%

is 33%—not 3300%. And the only way to figure that is decimally, hence 1 × 0.33 = 0.33. And don't worry if this is either surprising *or* obvious. I had to explain this to a room of Ivy League professors once, who didn't know how to multiply a probability. So you may be in good company. Or if I'm sounding *too* basic here, it's because, I know now, not everyone in the room has mastered these steps. That needs to change. But change begins here.

All the things I'm talking about—like fractions, percentages, rounding procedures—you can pick up in any sixth-grade math textbook. For that I genuinely recommend Danica McKellar's *Math Doesn't Suck*.[8] More advanced concepts that you might need (like the axioms of probability, or the law of total probability, or even Bayes' Theorem itself) you can acquire in even the most basic of undergraduate college textbooks, like Ronald Staszkow's *The Mathematical Palette*, which is a breadth study specifically designed for art majors scared of math.[9]

Okay. So far so good.

Here's the next step. If the *prior* odds that someone like Jesus existed are 1 to 2, then how do we determine the *final* odds that Jesus existed? In the simplest form of Bayes' Theorem (and I'll explain why we have to use that specific theorem later), the final odds equals the product of the prior odds and something called the likelihood ratio, which is another fraction.[10] Like so:

Prior Odds × Likelihood Ratio = Final Odds

[8] Danica McKellar, *Math Doesn't Suck: How to Survive Middle School Math Without Losing Your Mind or Breaking a Nail* (Penguin, 2008).

[9] Ronald Staszkow, *The Mathematical Palette*, 3rd ed. (Brooks/Cole, 2004), which includes probability theory (152–211) and statistics (212–79), though little of the latter is needed for ordinary historical reasoning. The most important concepts (like error margins and their relationship to confidence levels) I explain (with examples) in Richard Carrier, *Proving History: Bayes's Theorem and the Quest for the Historical Jesus* (Prometheus Books, 2012), index.

[10] Given my discovery of the scale of historians' fear of math, I would have devoted far more space to explaining the Odds Form in *Proving History*, but for those interested, it is referenced there (64, 69, 76, 284–85, and 328–29n25). I also provide a model for running Bayesian reasoning without even numbers or arithmetic at all (287), although that can't handle complex cases. The full expression of Bayes' Theorem I mostly employ in *Proving History* is simply what you get when you convert it to a calculation of probability rather than odds.

And, really, that's it. That's Bayes' Theorem.

So what's the second term in this equation? The likelihood ratio is not a simple expression of odds but a ratio between two probabilities: the probability of all the evidence we have existing if the hypothesis being queried is true; and the probability of all that same evidence existing if that hypothesis is false. Which in the latter case always means something *else* caused all that evidence—and that 'something else' would usually be the most pertinent competing hypothesis. Thus all empirical reasoning is necessarily contrafactual: you are always comparing two competing explanations of the same evidence, one that is true and one that is false, and simply trying to determine which is more likely which (and how much more likely). It is impossible to determine the probability of one of those theories, without determining the probability of the other. Because anytime you are saying your model (your theory) caused the evidence, necessarily you are also saying the competing model (whatever other ways that same evidence could have come about instead) did not. Therefore you always have to run the numbers even for hypotheses that are false. The outcome is the likelihood ratio, a ratio between them both. Which directly measures the strength of the evidence for your theory—against competing theories of the same evidence.

In *Historicity* I had to calculate the final likelihood ratio (of all the evidence together), but to make the procedure easier to test and critique, I broke it down into classifications of evidence (extrabiblical, Gospels, Acts, and Epistles) and into sub-classifications within each where necessary. For example, for the Epistles I listed eight kinds of evidence within the Epistles and calculated a likelihood ratio for each. Let's assume for this brief tutorial that that just happened to be the only evidence there was that could determine whether Jesus existed or not. In reality, of course, the other categories have to be considered, too. But that's just more of the same procedure; so to make learning that procedure easy, we'll assume only the one category of evidence exists for now.

Within the category 'Epistles' I broke the surviving information down into eight sub-categories of evidence. Then, on the *a fortiori* side ('the stronger' side, meaning the conclusion most against my theory, where I estimated every probability as far against it as I could reasonably believe), I determined two of those subcategories were equally likely on either theory—which two competing theories are 'Jesus existed' and 'Jesus was a myth'. One of those categories was the evidence regarding things Jesus said, where we cannot tell in Paul *where* Jesus said those things—in life or in postmortem dreams and visions (as in 2 Cor. 12:9–10); he just never *says* any were said during his life. The other was the evidence regarding the Eucharist, where (as noted in chapter two) it appears Paul claimed to have that from a vision—certainly it is undecidable with any confidence that he meant otherwise—but his having that one piece of information from a vision would not entail Jesus did not exist. In each case, the probability that Paul would say those things (as he actually says them in our extant record) is the same either way. If Jesus existed, Paul's ambiguity in both cases is expected. If Jesus didn't exist, Paul's ambiguity in both cases is also expected. Therefore, neither set of information is evidence for either conclusion.

I then found three subcategories of evidence *against* historicity—first, the weird silences across all of Paul's Epistles, and, second, the creedal statements in them that appear to predate those letters, and, third, all other early Epistles in the canon. I determined (again, *a fortiori*) that the best we could say is that these subcategories ranged in expectancy from 3/4 to 4/5, meaning each set of information was slightly less expected if Jesus existed, but not by much.

You can think of 3/4 as saying one of these oddities is three parts expected if Jesus existed but four parts expected if he didn't (so 'a little more expected'). Which means if we imagine them to be 100% expected if he didn't exist (because those silences are then exactly what we'd have), then they are only 75% expected if he did exist (if 4 parts makes 100, each part is 25, so 3 parts is 75). Which would mean there is still a 75% chance (it's therefore still likely) that those silences would be found there even if Jesus existed—it's just *more* likely if he didn't (by 25 percentiles). For another of these odd features of the Epistles I allow its likelihood to be at best 4/5, which is 4 parts likely if Jesus existed to 5 parts likely if he didn't (so, again, 'a little more expected'). Since 100 into 5 parts makes 20 each, 4 parts is then an 80% chance that that evidence would look like it does even if Jesus existed. In each case this is more generous than I actually believe to be the case. But it's as far as I believe the evidence allows us to go in support of historicity.

Let's assume only one of these subcategories of evidence existed, and at a 3/4 expectancy on historicity. For example, on a ratio of 3/4, if that evidence is 100% expected if Jesus didn't exist, then it is still 75% expected even if he did exist, which is still pretty likely. That evidence is therefore not strong evidence against his existence. But it does count a little against it. If we put 75 in ratio to 100 we get 75/100 which reduces to 3/4, because 75 is (3 × 25) and 100 is (4 × 25), so if you divide both sides of the fraction by 25, you get 3/4. Which is the same fraction, just reduced to its smallest expression (in whole numbers).

If there were only one such item of evidence that existed or carried any weight, then our final odds on Jesus existing would be 1/2 (the prior odds) × 3/4 (the likelihood ratio for that one item or set of evidence; or just 'the likelihood ratio' or even 'the evidence ratio', or as called in the Appendix the 'consequent odds'), which, arithmetically, is (1 × 3) / (2 × 4) or 3/8, and therefore 3 to 8 odds. Those would be our new odds—and if no other evidence changes it, that would be our *final* odds on Jesus existing. The prior odds have now been updated by the effect of one set of evidence. If we wanted to convert those odds into a probability that Jesus existed, then we'd follow the same procedure described earlier: add all the parts up (3 + 8 = 11) and divide that into the value for the side you are interested in: hence, 3/11, from 3/(3 + 8). If you run that through your calculator you'll see it comes out to '0.27…' or just 0.27 (rounding to the second decimal), which as a percentage is 0.27 × 100 and thus 27%.

But that wasn't the only evidence (neither in the Epistles, nor beyond). So many more arithmetical calculations were needed. But all of that—everything you are terrified of the moment you see it (such as reproduced in the Appendix here)—is just a repetition of the same simple steps I just walked you through.[11] Sticking with the Epistles as a category, the last three subcategories of evidence within that I actually scored *in favor* of historicity (at least on the *a fortiori* side; not on the other). Which are the three I devote chapters to at the end of this volume: whether Paul attests Jesus had a father; whether Paul attests Jesus had a mother; and whether Paul attests Jesus had brothers. I thoroughly addressed (then and now) the evidence and background information in

[11] Hence Petterson ("*Historicity*," 254) was terrified of the table in Carrier, *Historicity*, 600, even though that was all pre-teen arithmetic requiring no advanced calculator or skills. This is so even for the more daunting tables in Carrier, *Historicity*, 597–98, from which that derived.

each case, and demonstrated that, even at best, these are not strong evidence because of all the ambiguities surrounding them. Nevertheless, I concluded they *could* still be weak evidence for historicity.

Indeed I considered that these three facts might be stronger evidence than I just mentioned. I conclude each reference (in the form we actually have it) is twice as likely to come from Paul if Jesus existed than if he didn't. Hence each one scored 2/1 in favor of historicity. Which means, together, they score 8/1 in favor, because 2/1 × 2/1 × 2/1 = (2 × 2 × 2) / (1 × 1 × 1) = 8/1. That means these three references together are eight times more likely to survive in Paul's Epistles if Jesus really existed, than if he didn't. In effect, I am saying the non-existence of Jesus *might* not explain these very well. In truth, I think it's the other way around; so on the other side, the *a judicantiori* margin ('the more judicious' or 'more critical' side), I find that they don't support historicity at all. But erring as much as possible on the side of historicity, I conclude it *could* be otherwise—that in fact all this stuff could be eight times more likely on historicity.

If we now update our result with that, we get: 3/8 × 8/1 = 24/8; or if you want to spell it all out (as the prior odds times *both* likelihood ratios), then it's 1/2 × 3/4 × 8/1 = (1 × 3 × 8) / (2 × 4 × 1) = 24/8. Which reduces to 3/1 (because 8 goes into 24 three times). So the odds favoring historicity are now 3 to 1, for a probability that Jesus existed of 75%. Because 3 plus 1 makes 4, and 3 divided by 4 makes 0.75. Or in this case, you can just notice there are four parts, so each is one quarter, and 'three quarters of a dollar makes 75 cents'. Hence the only reason I reach a final conclusion almost the other way around (2 to 1 against historicity, for a probability that Jesus existed of only 33%) is that my conclusion factored in all the *other* sets of evidence that we have been ignoring here (both in the Epistles and beyond), which all either have no effect or reduce the odds of historicity to some degree; which in the end pull its probability down from 75% to 33% (a loss of over half).

The only reason those calculations look complicated, therefore, is because there is a lot of evidence to consider. This procedure has to be repeated for every one, and all of it tallied up. And the easiest way to organize that information all in one place is with the tables I present. Which look scary. But only if you don't understand the arithmetic. Now that you know how to read them, you can vet all my calculations yourself—even run your own, if your estimates of any pertinent probabilities differ from mine; even add new evidence-categories or subcategories, if you think I overlooked something. There is even an app for that now, called CHRESTUS, which includes a customizable Bayesian calculator.[12]

Although if your estimates for any categories of evidence do differ from mine, you still have to explain *why* they do. Why are you estimating a different probability or odds in each case than I ended up with? On what basis? And that is the fundamental point of all this: to get at why you believe what you do. In *Historicity* I gave my reasons, in each and every case. What are yours?

Why This Has to Be Bayesian

One of the most important books every historian should read is David Hackett Fischer's *Historians' Fallacies* (which I quoted at the top of this chapter). It is a valuable, entertaining, and wide-ranging survey of examples of expert errors in the field—which is crucial to experts who want to learn how to avoid errors in their field (and this is not coming from an outsider: Fischer himself is a professional historian). More importantly, Fischer's whole through-line is to pursue a single question: by what logic are *any* historians' conclusions justified? There must be one. Yet if we do not know what it is, then we cannot know whether any of their conclusions *are* justified, least of all when.[13] As Fischer points out, "assuming that this logic of historical thought does tacitly exist," as otherwise historical thought must be devoid of logic and thus *illogical* (and if that's the case, we may as well just pack it in), "the next question is to raise it to the level of consciousness," and thus start working out what that logic is, so that it is no longer tacit.[14]

Fischer aims to do this with a catalogue of fallacies, and examples illustrating them, all from top historians in their respective subjects (proving that this is a problem *in the guild* and not a matter of amateurs vs.

[12] See https://chrest.us.

[13] Fischer, *Historians' Fallacies*, xv–xxii.

[14] Fischer, *Historians' Fallacies*, xvi.

the guild: even the experts are failing here). But he wishes he could get at the underlying formula explaining them all—explaining, in fact, the fundamental logic of all historical reasoning. "The problem of locating a logic of historical thinking defies a direct approach," he thought, because "every attempt" up to his day had "failed of its objective."[15] But this is one thing that *has* changed since then: several of us have found what he was looking for. It's called Bayes' Theorem.

I have not been alone in demonstrating this. When I published my treatise establishing it, *Proving History*, I was not aware Aviezer Tucker had reached the same conclusion. His books now supplement mine in proving the point.[16] Since then, a number of scholars have joined us in recommending (some even insisting) that historians begin framing their arguments with Bayesian logic.[17] That human empirical reasoning gen-

---

[15] Fischer, *Historians' Fallacies*, xvi.

[16] Aviezer Tucker, *Historiographic Reasoning* (Cambridge University Press, 2025); summarizing Tucker, *Our Knowledge of the Past: A Philosophy of Historiography* (Cambridge University Press, 2004); preceding Richard Carrier, *Proving History: Bayes's Theorem and the Quest for the Historical Jesus* (Prometheus, 2012); which led to applications in Richard Carrier, *On the Historicity of Jesus: Why We Might Have Reason for Doubt* (Sheffield-Phoenix, 2014); which were evaluated in Raphael Lataster, *Questioning the Historicity of Jesus: Why a Philosophical Analysis Elucidates the Historical Discourse* (Brill, 2019). Tucker's review of *Proving History*—Aviezer Tucker, "The Reverend Bayes v. Jesus Christ," *History and Theory* 55 (2016), 129–40—concurs on this point, and only attempted a critique of my application of it to the historicity of Jesus, but since I made no such application of it there (and he never reviewed my application of it elsewhere), his critique of that element is largely impertinent (it is effectively answered in the actual subsequent study and in its assessments by Lataster): see Richard Carrier, "Tucker's Review of *Proving History* in the Journal *History & Theory*" (3 February 2016) at richardcarrier.info/archives/9619.

[17] Besides Tucker, Lataster, and myself, it is also directly advocated for employment in history now by: Theresa Heilig and Christoph Heilig, "Historical Methodology," in *God and the Faithfulness of Paul: A Critical Examination of the Pauline Theology of N.T. Wright* (ed. Christoph Heilig, J. Thomas Hewitt, and Michael F. Bird; Fortress, 2014), 115–50; Gard Jenset and Barbara McGillivray, *Quantitative Historical Linguistics: A Corpus Framework* (Oxford University Press, 2017); Barbara McGillivray, Jon Wilson, Tobias Blanke, "Towards a Quantitative Research Framework for Historical Disciplines," in *Proceedings of the Workshop on Computational Methods in the Humanities 2018* (ed. Michael Piotrowski; Université de Lausanne, 2018), 53–58; Myles Lavan, "Epistemic Uncertainty, Subjective Probability, and Ancient History," *The Journal of Interdisciplinary History* 50.1 (2019), 91–111; Nathan Nadeau, "The Philosophy of History and New Testament History: A Survey of the Former with Some Implications for the Latter," *Biblical Interpretation* 30 (2022), 374–97 (391–95); and the historians who have begun employing it in their work (in following notes).

erally should always be so framed has already long been argued.[18] And many historians in our field are starting to employ it.[19]

Historians unversed in (or even terrified of) math and logic often find this suspicious, because, not understanding it, they cannot distinguish fraudulent or mistaken uses of the process from sound ones. So they worry it is a technique that hoodwinks rather than advances understanding. But that is true of *every* method and *every* logic. The solution is to become acquainted with this method; indeed, to master the logic of it, so you cannot be duped or misled by improper uses of it—indeed, so you can evaluate and test *any* argument from *any* historian on *any* matter of fact, whether they framed their logic this way *or not*.

Bayes' Theorem itself has been formally proved.[20] Which means that

---

[18] For example: Michael Titelbaum, *Fundamentals of Bayesian Epistemology 1: Introducing Credences* (Oxford University Press, 2022); Mike Oaksford, Nick Chater, and Ulrike Hahn, "Human Reasoning and Argumentation: The Probabilistic Approach," in *Reasoning: Studies of Human Inference and Its Foundations* (ed. Jonathan Adler and Lance Rips; Cambridge University Press, 2008), 383–413; and David Hardman and Laura Macchi (eds.), *Thinking: Psychological Perspectives on Reasoning, Judgment and Decision Making* (Wiley, 2004).

[19] I provide a complete example teaching the method in Richard Carrier, *The Probabilistic Argument for Interpolation in 1 Thessalonians 2:14–16* (forthcoming). For other examples besides Lataster, *Questioning*, and Carrier, *Historicity*, and *Proving History*, 121–205, see: James Albertson, "An Application of Mathematical Probability to Manuscript Discoveries," *Journal of Biblical Literature* 78 (1959), 133-41; Winsome Munro, "Interpolation in the Epistles: Weighing Probability," *New Testament Studies* 36.3 (1990), 431–43; Raphael Lataster, "Bayesian Reasoning: Criticising the 'Criteria of Authenticity' and Calling for a Review of Biblical Criticism," *Journal of Alternative Perspectives in the Social Sciences* 5.2 (2012), 271–293, and "Questioning the Plausibility of Jesus Ahistoricity Theories—A Brief Pseudo-Bayesian Metacritique of the Sources," *Intermountain West Journal of Religious Studies* 6.1 (2015), 63–96; Efraim Wallach, "Bayesian Representation of a Prolonged Archaeological Debate," *Synthese* 195.1 (2018), 401–31; Christoph Heilig, *Hidden Criticism? The Methodology and Plausibility of the Search for a Counter-Imperial Subtext in Paul* (Fortress, 2017); Zachary Milstead, "Religion and Arguments from Silence," *European Journal for Philosophy of Religion* 10.3 (2018), 155–69; Nevin Climenhaga, "Papias's Prologue and the Probability of Parallels," *Journal of Biblical Literature* 139.3 (2020), 591–96; Nathan Nadeau, "The First Pauline Chronologist? Probably Not: A Review Essay of Ryan Schellenberg's 'The First Pauline Chronologist' from a Bayesian Perspective," *Journal of Greco-Roman Christianity and Judaism* 16 (2020), 150–82; and Mark Giacobbe, *Luke the Chronicler: The Narrative Arc of Samuel-Kings and Chronicles in Luke-Acts* (Brill, 2023).

[20] A.N. Kolmogorov, *Foundations of the Theory of Probability*, 2nd English ed. (tr. Nathan Morrison; Dover, 2018; orig. German 1933), 6–8; E.T. Jaynes, *Probability Theory: The Logic of Science* (Cambridge University Press, 2003), 112–15.

when its premises are true, its conclusion is necessarily also true. And its premises consist of three propositions, which happen to represent the entire content of every argument over fact, including historical facts. People rarely realize it, but all arguments over what happened in the past are really arguments over just these three numbers: the prior probability (how likely the thing claimed usually turns out to be true)—which measures what is sometimes colloquially referenced nonnumerically by such vague expressions as 'plausibility'—and the two consequent probabilities that comprise the likelihood ratio. Which measure how likely all the evidence is if the thing claimed is true, and how likely all that same evidence is if something else caused it instead.

People might avoid *saying* any of these numbers (or not even have to). But all their verbiage still conceals or implies these numbers. To describe any theory as 'implausible', for example, entails a numerical assessment of prior probability: that it is low, and not merely low, but very low, perhaps even fatally low—though by avoiding actually saying how low it is (much less how we know it is that low), this all too often becomes a fountainhead of equivocations, fallacies, and handwaving, as documented by Fischer. Likewise, to describe something as evidence 'for' one theory over another, or 'against' one theory over another, entails a numerical assessment of its relative likelihood: that the evidence is more likely (more expected) on one theory than the other. And the strength or weakness of any item of evidence is measured by the spread: the stronger the evidence, the larger the likelihood ratio it produces—so, the *more* likely it is on that theory than on its best competitor(s). But again, by avoiding actually saying how likely the evidence is on our theory, or any other (or how we know it is that likely, or that it is any less likely on an alternative explanation), this all too often becomes another fountainhead of equivocations, fallacies, and handwaving, also as documented by Fischer.

These statements can also simply be false. For example, a theory declared 'implausible' (i.e., 'possessed of a very low prior probability') might in point of fact not be. If there is ample evidence that relevantly similar things happened actually quite a lot (or often enough) in the context concerned, then that claim is indeed false. And we can know that it is false when we understand the logical connection between evidence and a claim's truth-value. What *makes* a claim to implausibility *true*? Well, the background information establishing its contextual frequency, and hence its prior probability. That's what. 'It's implausible that King Henry would conspire to secretly kill his predecessor King William II in order to gain his throne' is refuted by the abundant fact that people often do exactly that sort of thing in precisely those kinds of contexts. So it is not implausible at all. It might still have a low prior probability—such a scheme is, after all, not *so* common or routine that it is safe to *always* assume that it has happened in any succession in any monarchy in history—but it won't be so low that it can be dismissed out of hand. Checking the evidence is definitely still warranted.[21]

And even that prior probability rests on evidence: evidence of what is common, usual, or what at least happens even if rarely. The prior is a derivation from the data indicating the relative frequency of the phenomenon in question. For example, in at least comparable enough circumstances, how many monarchial successions caused by unexpected deaths have been the result of a conspiracy? That is not something we just magically intuit. It is reflected in real data. It is anchored to (and thus constrained by) *evidence*. We can never be precise. For example, we might never count them up, and even if we do, we know the frequency of successions resulting from a covert murder must exceed that of proven cases anyway (to account for all the *unproven* ones). But we can ballpark it reliably enough. And we can demonstrate empirically that it is a real phenomenon and not unique, nor so rare as to not even be looked into. Sometimes we can even narrow the 'reference class', or the most suitable set of comparable cases and how they proceeded, which guides our expectancies in any new case. For example, the frequency (hence, the prior probability) of covert murders arranging monarchial successions *generally* may be low; but the frequency of covert murders arranging monarchial successions *already involving a suspicious death* is going to be considerably higher, right?

By contrast, a claim such as 'when the book of Acts reports Jesus ascended into the clouds, this was the first recorded instance of the use of an air balloon as a conveyance' is *not* plausible—which means, the prior probability that an air balloon even existed then to be used, much less was used in that instance, is indeed so low we really don't need to

[21] This is a real example: Carrier, *Proving History*, 273–75.

investigate it. There are vastly more plausible explanations already aligning perfectly well with the evidence (chief among them being that the author of Acts is a liar). Perhaps if there were evidence (if, for example, the author of Acts did indeed meticulously describe an air balloon) we could then say the prior, no matter how low, is then nevertheless *overcome* by an even more favorable likelihood ratio: the probability of that author miraculously knowing in such detail what an air balloon even looked like is certainly substantially lower than the prior probability of otherwise-unattested ancient air balloons generally (since the *possibility* of air balloons is scientifically established, as is the innovative spirit of ancient inventors; so air balloons back then aren't *impossible*).

Notice I have never stated any actual numbers in all this. I have kept to general expressions—as historians usually do—such as 'low' and 'lower'. But even when that is perfectly reasonable to do (and most of the time it is), we must still *understand* that these expressions conceal real numbers, or ranges of numbers. For example, I cannot mean by 'low' a probability of 90%, or even 50%. And when we query what we would have to mean, by for example saying Jesus's use of an air balloon is too improbable to credit, we can discern our numerical intentions even more precisely. For example, we could not in that instance mean even a 1% probability, but some probability considerably lower—more like an odds of thousands if not millions to one against.

I won't belabor this point. I discuss ballparking and benchmarking and setting error margins (ranges of numbers in place of overconfidently precise ones) and other techniques of mathematical reasoning underlying colloquial English verbiage throughout *Proving History*. My point here is to illustrate that all empirical reasoning is already Bayesian—even when the reasoners don't know it. All of us are arguing over the prior probabilities of competing explanations of the evidence, or over one or the other (or both) of the likelihoods of that evidence. There is in fact nothing else being debated than those three things. I have already formally proved this.[22] But any attempt you might make to disprove it will accomplish the same realization: there really is nothing else historians are saying, than what they think the priors and likelihoods are; and the formal validity of Bayes' Theorem establishes that the only logically val-

[22] Carrier, *Proving History*, 106–14.

id relationship between those premises and any conclusion is the one mathematically described by that theorem. Therefore all historical reasoning is Bayesian.

It remains then only to ascertain in what ways, so we can pop the hood and get a look at the hidden underlying machinery—the hidden underlying logic—behind *any* argument to a conclusion of fact in history, whether your own or anyone else's. Because now you know the secret of why any conclusion in history logically *does* follow from its premises—if it does at all. And now you know what the premises actually are, so you can empirically test them, and ascertain how true or false they are.

Because the *real* premises are not statements like 'we have such-and-such evidence, and that proves such-and-such theory', since that does not even say why the conclusion follows from the premise. It simply 'declares' that it does, relying on some vague intuition that cannot be tested or queried. By contrast, the *real* premises behind any historical argument are these:

- Our proposed explanation is at least as plausible as, or is more plausible than, any other alternative explanation; or if it is less plausible, we aver it nevertheless has more evidence supporting it. **Translation:** So far as we know, our hypothesis has a prior probability equal to or greater than any other hypothesis; or if its prior is lower than any, that defect is reversed with evidence.

- Compared to any alternative (especially the most likely alternatives), our proposed explanation makes better sense of the evidence; or, at least, just as much sense of the evidence. **Translation:** The probability of the evidence resulting from our hypothesis is the same as or higher than the probability of that same evidence resulting from any other hypothesis being considered.

Both of these premises of course combine two sub-premises into one, as in each case two probabilities are being compared to produce a single outcome, a ratio between them (hence, 'prior odds times consequent odds equals final odds' states the entire theorem and thus models every argument about history). But the first ratio (the prior odds) is always predetermined by one or the other prior probability, since the sum of all priors must equal 1 (i.e. 100%) to account for all possible explanations. So once you know one prior probability, you already know the other is the converse of that. A converse probability is the total probability minus the contrary probability, so if the prior probability that a hypothesis *h* is true is 80%, then automatically the prior probability that it is false is 20% (since 100 – 80 = 20). But for the second ratio this is not the case. The *likelihoods* of the evidence can vary freely from theory to theory, and can even both *be* 1, i.e. the evidence can be 'just as' or even 100% expected on either competing theory at the same time.

I must note here that I have been speaking of binary cases where all alternatives are subsumed under one umbrella, so the probability-space is entirely split between your hypothesis and its negation, even though its negation may encompass a large range of alternative hypotheses (up to and including 'space aliens did it' or 'the evidence was all fabricated by The Matrix'). There are ways to break that space into three or more, to test multiple competing explanations against each other simultaneously.[23] But it's generally good enough to compare the best two hypotheses, when all the others are so implausible as to not even exceed our rounding error (so it's safe to act like they don't exist).

But back to binary cases. It is indeed possible for an explanation to be less plausible than another *but* have more evidence in its favor, and thus *end up* more probably true. This could be the case for the plot to kill King William II, for example, where most cases of even suspicious death aren't assassinations, but enough are that enough evidence can prove this one was. In which case the first premise that the proposed hypothesis is less plausible is a concession which is then answered with evidence, through the likelihood ratio produced by the next premise. But often the best theory wins on both premises: it has a higher or comparable prior (it's 'more usually what happens in contexts like this' or 'just as usually is'); and its evidential likelihood is greater ('the evidence, precisely as we have it, is more likely if this is what caused it, than if anything else did').

There are other possible outcomes. Like when a proposal has a higher likelihood ratio, but has such a low prior probability that its likelihood

---

[23] See Carrier, *Proving History*, 69, 247–50, 284–85, 329–30n27.

ratio is not large enough to reverse our expectations. There is evidence, just not *enough* evidence. For example, imagine if Acts described Jesus flying into the clouds holding onto a bag above his head. That would suggest knowledge of at least small balloons; but as evidence it is too weak (being too unspecific) to confidently signal a real conveyance. That evidence could thus increase the *probability* of the hypothesis that Jesus used an air balloon to ascend, but not enough to make that hypothesis *probable*. As a rule, the difference between the two likelihoods of the evidence (the likelihood on one theory and the likelihood on the alternatives) has to be greater than the difference between the priors in order to reverse 'what we usually expect' into something we didn't expect but that now has enough evidence to nevertheless believe.

In any case, both of these premises are often not even stated but merely hinted at or presumed, or buried under a collage of verbiage. But now you know to look for them. Because in questions of fact, every argument you will ever make or encounter is actually drawing its conclusion entirely from those two premises: the ratio of priors, and the ratio of likelihoods.

How Evidence Works

It should be apparent by now that when we talk about Bayes' Theorem in the context of history we are referring to a logical structure of argument (Bayesian *reasoning*) and not to some complex scientific analysis of data (Bayesian *statistics*). Although the latter can have applications in history, those do require advanced skills in mathematics, and are limited to questions that enjoy a large abundance of reliable data. We are thus not talking about that here. We are talking about *logic*. We mean merely that Bayes' Theorem proves how conclusions in history logically follow from their premises—and thus what kinds of premises sound conclusions require, and when conclusions are soundly reached at all.

Sometimes (indeed, most of the time) this never requires stating any numbers, as such precision is not mathematically necessary (as in the examples I just surveyed). But sometimes it does, and then it can implicate arithmetic, maybe even a lot of it, as the only way to trace out the actual logical structure of an argument, and thus evaluate it. This is especially the case in ambiguous cases, like the historicity of Jesus, where nothing (literally *nothing*) is clear cut, and historians have to rely overmuch on unstated assumptions and opaque structures of reasoning. Applying a simple Bayesian analysis to such arguments will then *expose* all those assumptions and structures to the light, allowing them to be evaluated. You can then see when—*and why*—an argument is unsound or invalid, and therefore should be rejected; *and* when an argument is instead valid and sound, and therefore should be acceded to. The rest of this chapter will take up important examples in the historicity debate to make this point clear, and to teach the skills needed to evaluate the arguments in the remaining chapters of this book (and, quite frankly, anywhere else in the field of history).

The first question to master is how evidence works. What makes something 'evidence' for or against something else? And what is it about evidence that increases or decreases the probability of a conclusion? In other words, why does 'evidence' have any such effect on a claim at all? What is the underlying logic? Once you realize the answer is Bayes' Theorem, you can then answer how evidence has that effect: by some body of evidence being more probable on one theory than on any other, that *theory* becomes more probable than it would have been without that evidence; and the more the probability of the evidence differs between that theory and any other, the *more* the probability of that theory increases. So when we say something is 'overwhelming evidence' for a theory, we are actually saying the likelihood ratio is overwhelmingly in its favor, and therefore is numerically large. And usually that's because the probability of all that evidence existing on any other explanation of it is extremely small (it's 'very unexpected'), but remains very high on our explanation.

Indeed, in most questions of history the disparity is so great that this doesn't even require math. For example, the probability that all the evidence we have for the reality of the Holocaust has been caused by something *other* than the Holocaust having actually happened is extraordinarily small, even vanishingly small. One would have to conjure numerous extremely improbable coincidences and feats, resulting in the mass fabrication of thousands of videotaped eyewitness testimonies (of victims, rescuers, and even perpetrators); countless vouchsafed German documents seized by Allied and Russian troops; countless photographs and court transcripts; as well as multiple entire death-camp archaeologies and forensic studies. The odds of all of this coming about, in such meticulously coordinated fashion, in any other way is easily hundreds of trillions to one against—and that's being *generous* to Holocaust deniers. There is thus no need to work out precisely what its probability is. We can already tell it will be as near to 100% as makes all odds.

Needless to say, if we had *that* kind of evidence for Jesus, you'd be reading a very different book from me now. If we had Pontius Pilate's court records, the memoirs of Gamaliel, first-generation inscriptions carved by the apostles proclaiming their gospel in no uncertain terms as coming from Jesus ben Joseph the Galilean executed by Pilate, humorous satires by contemporary traveling sophists curious about the whole Jesus movement, contemporary Rabbinical treatises and warrants, extensive interchurch correspondence and records (bills, contracts, minutes, account books—and not just copies, but the actual originals)—if we had all that, and it all pointed to the historicity of Jesus, then the historicity of Jesus would be a certainty. And that would still be *vastly* less than we have for the Holocaust, which enjoys, for example, a massive archive of video recordings of eyewitness testimonies and a far more extensive collection of documents and archaeology, with extensively triangulatable contents, than will even have existed in the first century, much less survived. And yet still the odds Jesus existed in that case would be trillions to one.

To be clear (and I have to keep repeating this because my critics keep pretending I'm not): I am not saying that we can doubt Jesus existed because we don't have that scale of evidence I just described. We don't have that scale of evidence for anyone in antiquity. My point is that that scale of evidence is less than we have for the Holocaust, and yet what we have for Jesus is *vastly less* than even that. So our certainty that Jesus existed must correspondingly be vastly less than that. It is therefore absurd to compare doubting the historicity of Jesus with doubting the Holocaust. That is not the evidentiary position we are in. Because the evidence for Jesus is so extraordinarily scant and problematic, it requires a great deal more careful attention to determine its logical effect. For the Holocaust, it's obvious. And even for the imagined Jesus scenario I just outlined, it would be obvious. But, for the situation we are *actually* in, it's not obvious. We therefore need to make sure we are correctly connecting whatever evidence we believe there to be, to whatever conclusion we think it entails. We have to be clear by what logic that conclusion follows from that evidence. We can't just handwave this.

And that begins with admitting that the probability Jesus existed is proportional to the difference between the probability that the evidence would exist if he did and the probability that that same evidence would exist anyway even if he didn't. And this requires attending to the evidence as it actually is, and not to embellishments upon it that more reflect what we had hoped it would be. We have to look at the actual facts; not assumptions or modern lore.

The logically correct way to reason from evidence to a conclusion is thus to assume that a hypothesis is true, and then ask how likely each particular piece of evidence you are looking at would be in that case. So you have to take that hypothesis seriously. You have to genuinely imagine it's true, for the sake of argument; and *then* think through how likely it is that it would generate the evidence we have. To do that correctly, wholly regardless of whether you think that hypothesis is probable or not, you must assume it is not only probable *but in fact true*. And you must do this for *both* competing hypotheses. In this way you generate two probabilities of the evidence, one for each hypothesis, measuring how expected the evidence is on each. The ratio between those two probabilities is then the strength of the evidence for one over the other. And that has its logical effect by being multiplied by the prior odds, giving us the final odds (or at least, the odds after adding in that evidence, if there is more evidence yet to add).

Which means if some item of purported evidence being considered is just as likely on either hypothesis, then it *isn't* evidence, whether for or against either hypothesis. And if it is evidence that is only slightly more likely on one hypothesis, then it only slightly increases the relative probability of it. And if that evidence is a lot more likely on one hypothesis, then it increases the probability of that hypothesis by a lot. And in both respects, accumulated evidence can have an accumulating effect.

Which further means that if we have evidence that is *extremely* unlikely on any hypothesis but the one we are considering, then that evidence may well stand as a sufficient proof of that hypothesis all on its own. For example, the ashes of Herculaneum, Italy, still preserve an entire intact library. All (or most) of its books are still there; charred, but now readable with advanced technologies. Pliny the Elder served as a naval commander in the same bay as Herculaneum (he even died heroically attempting to rescue victims of the same volcanic eruption as buried Herculaneum).[24] And in the close elite culture of the era he would very likely have been personal friends of that villa's family; and certainly politically close, enough to render it very improbable that some of his writings would *not* be found there. It could even include precursors to his own eyewitness *History of Rome*. That was not published until after his death and thus is not likely to be there.[25] But imagine if he had stashed a pre-publication copy there for safe keeping. There would then be a very good chance the whole thing, every volume, is still there, waiting for us to retrieve and read it; and that would be the nearest thing to an autograph original. But even if not that, then some of his earlier writings or correspondence on the matter, or some such history of Nero's reign, by *some* contemporary or other, is likely to be there. And that will surely contain a detailed accounting of the burning of Rome, and whom Nero punished for it—and whether its author thought they deserved it or not.

Pliny was there at the time. So will other historians have been.[26] For example, Cluvius Rufus, ex-consul and Nero's personal herald, wrote an extensive first person account of Nero's reign.[27] This stands good odds of being at Herculaneum, just waiting to be recovered (and to have been used as a source for Pliny's lost *History*). It is possible that, upon retrieving this, we will find in it something like this: an eyewitness's account of his own or a colleague's attendance at the trial or the first administrative hearing of Paul the apostle, in which account Rufus verifies that emissaries from Judea testified to the execution of Jesus ben Joseph for treason by Pontius Pilate, and that Paul and others claimed to be mystically re-

---

[24] See Carrier, *Historicity*, 295, 343–45, 475, 510–11.

[25] Pliny the Elder, *Natural History* 1.pr.20–21 (it was finished, but left to his 'heirs' to publish); cf. Pliny the Younger, *Letters* 3.5 ("A Continuation of the *History* of Aufidius Bassus, in thirty-one books").

[26] Far more books were published in antiquity than we have, at a pace ensuring several lost histories of Nero could be in this library: for calculations see Carrier, *Historicity*, 300n29. For example, we can be sure that at least a hundred scientists were publishing books every generation in this period, which entails hundreds of lost books per generation even in that rare field—and histories would outnumber this production several times, if not tenfold: Richard Carrier, *Science Education in the Early Roman Empire* (Pitchstone, 2016), 30–31.

[27] Carrier, *Historicity*, 295.

ceiving orders from that traitor's ghost.

Let's assume this volume's excavation will have been surrounded by sufficient security to ensure it wasn't a modern forgery snuck in, or at least to render that possibility very improbable. The probability of this record then existing in this artifact, if Jesus *didn't* exist, would be astronomically low. I'd wager it at no less than millions to one. Thousands to one if the site's security were poor and so our surety of the text's authenticity were lessened. But even if I updated my finding of a final 1/2 odds against historicity with a mere 1000/1 likelihood ratio from this new evidence, I would have to agree then that the final odds on Jesus existing would be 500 to 1 (1/2 × 1000/1 = 1000/2 = 500/1), for a probability of about 99.8% (500/(500+1) = 500/501 = 0.9980...). The existence of Jesus would then have been proved as certain as anyone need. All from just a single piece of evidence.

We don't have anything like this. Which is the problem. But the point here is to illustrate how evidence works: to say that something is evidence 'for' Jesus's historicity is to say that there is something *improbable* about that evidence *but for* Jesus having actually existed. However, if anything about the context makes that evidence *not* improbable anymore, then it is *no longer* evidence for his historicity. But it also wouldn't be evidence *against* his historicity, either. Which is crucial to understand, lest you be triggered by a confusion over this point: it is possible for some item of evidence to have no effect on the historicity of Jesus. Saying it does not make Jesus more probable *is not* saying it makes Jesus less probable. It simply is saying that that conclusion doesn't gain the probability you had hoped. Only when we have some item of evidence that is (to some degree) improbable *if* Jesus existed do we have evidence 'against' his historicity. For example, suppose Cluvius wrote that Paul and his Christians reported their belief to be, as confirmed by his accusers in court, that Jesus was a mystical being slain in the heavens and not yet come. That would pretty much end the historicity of Jesus as a hypothesis. Yet we don't have this sort of evidence, either.

So not having evidence for Jesus is not equivalent to having evidence against Jesus. Which means that knocking the probability of Jesus down on the conclusion that you had incorrectly raised it does not constitute presenting 'evidence against Jesus'. Hence here in chapter nine, my demonstrating that Paul is only speaking of mothers allegorically in

Galatians 4 does actually remove evidence *for* Jesus, but only because it never really was evidence for Jesus. So it does lower the probability of his existing, but only because you shouldn't have raised it on that evidence in the first place. The net effect of that result is that we simply don't know whether Paul thought Jesus had a real mother, because in the one place he speaks of Jesus having a mother, it turns out, he isn't talking about biology either way. That is therefore not evidence Jesus *didn't* exist. It's just not evidence anymore than he did.

Bayesian reasoning will help you understand such distinctions. As I wrote in *Historicity* in an effort to allay such confusions:

> [T]he most common, and wholly erroneous, way scholars look at arguments like [this] is to simply assume, *a priori*, that a particular interpretation is unlikely. But that is simply a measure of the strength of your bias. It is not a measure of any logically valid effect of that evidence on your conclusion. The question you should ask here is not 'Is that likely what Paul would have meant by that?' but rather, 'If Paul was in fact a mythicist, *is that likely what he would write*?' (and then 'If Paul was in fact a historicist, is that likely what he would write?', for the comparative probability).[28]

You must do both. That's how you control for your bias and get a logically valid result. That's the only way to argue *objectively* as a historian. Hence:

> [I]f a passage is already effectively 100% what we expect on mythicism, its likelihood on historicity cannot be any significantly higher (since 100% is as high as any probability can be), and thus the difference in those two probabilities will favor neither hypothesis, even at best (i.e. even if the passage is also 100% what we expect on historicity). … And if that passage or chapter or letter is not what we expect on historicity but looks a little weird in that case, then that probability has to be less than 100% (even if only a little), and that means the evidence argues against historicity (even if only a little).

So no matter how much you don't *like* the idea that Paul is only talking about allegorical mothers in Galatians 4, if it remains the case that Paul

[28] Carrier, *Historicity*, 512–14 (513).

would write exactly what he writes there if Jesus didn't exist, then you can't argue it is evidence that he did. If you genuinely assume Paul is not talking about biological mothers here, and *then* you see that everything he says is indeed exactly what he would say in that case, then you cannot argue he 'must' have been talking about biological mothers there. That follows even if you think this is *also* exactly what Paul would say if he knew Jesus did have a human mother. Because then it is 100% expected on *both* hypotheses. And that gets you a likelihood ratio of 1/1, which reduces to simply '1', which will have no effect on the probability Jesus existed. Because any value multiplied by one remains unchanged. It neither goes up *nor* down.

Impact of Background Knowledge

The probability of any piece of evidence, like the prior probability of a hypothesis, is impacted by background knowledge, which is contextual. For example, that someone flew into the clouds with a balloon has a far higher prior probability today than two thousand years ago. Conversely, that the first Christians would have had to make their beliefs conform to respected Jewish prophecies, even at the expense of resorting to bizarre solutions, is nigh 100% certain; whereas today, at least for mainstream Christians, that some new religious belief must match every Jewish prophecy pertaining is less necessary, and thus less commonplace in the development of Christian beliefs. Hence the Mormons did not strive very hard to get all their new ideas to conform to the entire panoply of Old Testament prophecy. But in antiquity, we can expect they would have.

One example that has come up in the debate over the historicity of Jesus is whether the original Christians—upon receiving a dream or vision of Christ informing them he'd been crucified and buried by dark celestial powers but raised back to life by God Almighty—would have balked, or even have conjured such an idea in their imaginations at all. Answering that question requires examining our pertinent *background knowledge*.

Today, heaven is a pristine supernatural place governed by God in another dimension of existence, not a material location we could travel to in a rocket or observe with a telescope. Jesus being killed by demons in outer space and buried there does not seem a likely contrivance in that context. But in antiquity, no such concept of the heavens existed, but one quite contrary. As I thoroughly documented, the ancient Jewish conception was of a layered heaven, physically accessible (even observable, although they lacked telescopes at the time), with ever-decreasing purity from the top (the realm of the stars, where God ruled directly) to lower and lower heavens (managed by decreasing ranks of angels), unto the lowest celestial sphere, which was the atmosphere of the Earth—the space below the moon then identified as 'the firmament', where Satan and his fellow fallen angels and their demon progeny resided, warred, and meddled in human affairs below (contrary to later belief that they resided under the ground—a notion not developed in Judaism or Christianity until after the first century).[29]

I documented that the popular imagination filled all those spaces with versions of everything on Earth, including thrones and halls and gardens, and wars (and hence deaths), and burials (see chapter two). In that context, a message that the messiah was killed and buried (and raised) *there* is not only intelligible, but resonant. It is thus no longer unexpected that a movement *then* would begin believing or even just preaching such a thing, particularly if that solved a number of pressing problems faced by Jewish messianism at the time (as evidence suggests it did).[30] So it cannot be argued that *that* would be contextually improbable at all.

The effect of background knowledge on what's likely or unlikely in that time and region is thus a crucial component of historical methodology, and must be attended to. It will affect all your estimates of probability in your premises.[31] Historians are already familiar with the notion of the folly of anachronistic reasoning or ignoring context or background

---

[29] Carrier, *Historicity*, 178–97. In original belief, Hell (if believed in at all) only existed after the end times and was tended by angels on behalf of God (Revelation 20:11–15; *Apocalypse of Pete*r 1–2, 20–21); the idea that Satan's brood would end up there, even rule there, likewise: Bart Ehrman, *Heaven and Hell: A History of the Afterlife* (Simon & Schuster, 2020).

[30] Carrier, *Historicity*, 153–63.

[31] For more on this point see Carrier, *Historicity*, 58–59, 236–36 (and index, 'background knowledge' and 'probabilities'); and *Proving History*, 79–81, 108–109, 239–42, 276–80 (and index, 'background knowledge' and 'probability').

data. All I am doing here is explaining the underlying logic of it—*why* it matters, and what effect it has on our reasoning about probability.

Cumulative Evidence and Dependent Probabilities

The effect of accumulating evidence has already been discussed: the likelihood ratios multiply. Hence having three and not merely one reference to the family of Jesus, each different and thus not a mere repetition of the others—some references supposedly to a father, one supposedly to a mother, and two supposedly to brothers, each with a different context and function (see chapters eight, nine, and ten)—are not accorded as all producing the same probability, but are multiplied. If each is twice as likely to be found in Paul's letters if Jesus existed than if he didn't, then that all three would is eight times as likely (2 × 2 × 2 = 8).

This logic does not always follow. Sometimes facts cited as evidence are not independent of each other, and we have to account for that. Sometimes, one fact is already entirely expected given another fact: everything Celsus said about the Christian Gospels is entirely expected once the Gospels existed, because he adds nothing to them, so nothing in Celsus is usable as evidence once we've already accounted for the Gospels.[32] In that case, the one fact (what Celsus wrote) can no longer have any effect on our concluding probability (that Jesus existed). Because what Celsus wrote is already entirely expected whether our hypothesis is true or false. Only the other fact matters: the production of the Gospels. Once we assess how likely *that* is, all other facts derived from it are accounted for, and so their contents cannot be counted twice. Other times the effect of dependence is not so complete: for example, that Paul tends often to use the vocabulary of family figuratively rather than literally (e.g., Gal. 3:29, 4:19, 4:24; 1 Cor. 4:15; 1 Thess. 2:7, 2:11) does increase the probability that he would do so again (such as in respect to Jesus), but not to a certainly (hence my conclusions in chapters eight, nine, and ten do not arrive at a certainty).

Likewise, since all the evidences we might cite are in some sense not independent of each other (references to a father, mother, and brothers

[32] Carrier, *Historicity*, 254–56.

could all share a common cause: Jesus having had a real family), our estimates of their probability must take that into account. For example, Paul mentions Jesus deriving from the seed of David in one place (Romans 1:3), and coming from the tribe of Jesse in another (Romans 15:12). But those constitute essentially the same statement. Neither is any less ambiguous than the other, and any explanation of the one would work equally well for the other. Therefore, those two items of evidence do not accumulate. If Paul believed Jesus was formed from the seed of David magically (like Adam) or metaphorically (like the Gentile 'seed' of Abraham in Galatians 3:16–18 and 26–29), then this would also make him the seed of Jesse (David's legendary father). So the second verse requires no additional explanation. If the first reference is 100% expected, then so is the second.

This needn't have been the case, of course. The authenticated text of Paul could have said Jesus 'was a descendant of Jesse according to his family's records', for example, and so even if the first passage (in Romans 1:3) remained ambiguous, this second passage would pick up a far stronger force, being sufficiently different that magical or metaphorical theories no longer explain it that well, which would still make Romans 1:3 entirely expected if Jesus did not exist, but would *not* make this version of Romans 15:12 as expected. Therefore, in that case, we would need a separate estimate of likelihoods for that passage. I would assign it a value of no less than dozens if not hundreds to one, accounting for the very unlikely probability of it being an interpolation (without evidence thereof).[33] And that would again bring the probability Jesus existed back to well near 100%.[34]

In *Historicity* all my estimated probabilities account for this dependency. For example, that Acts would repeat evidence in the Synoptic Gospels is 100% expected regardless of whether Jesus existed or not; therefore that evidence cannot add to the likelihood Jesus existed. For

[33] I demonstrate the base rate of interpolation in the New Testament cannot be much higher than 1 in 200 in Carrier, *The Probabilistic Argument for Interpolation in 1 Thessalonians 2:14–16* (indeed, 1 in 266; and if the verse in question can be established to have existed in the second century, then no higher than 1 in 800, that being the measurable base rate of interpolation per century).

[34] 1/2 ('our previous final odds Jesus existed') × 200/1 ('the effect of new evidence') = 200/2 = 100/1, for a probability of 100/101 = 99% (rounded), assuring the historicity of Jesus.

instance, its casual mention of Jesus still having a mother and brothers in Acts 1 affords us with no new evidence to weigh. It is simply a carry-over from the Gospels. If the Gospels made that up, then its repetition in Acts is just as made up. Had Acts specified an independent source for that information, then (like that hypothetical line about Jesse) we might be able to weigh it differently; but it doesn't. This is also why we can't use Tacitus or Josephus as evidence (see chapters two and three). They are just repeating other evidence we are already weighing the effect of; they therefore are adding no new evidence. By contrast, that Acts' public history (beginning in Acts 2) would never mention any family of Jesus (not even his supposed top-ranking brother James) remains independently *unlikely* if Jesus existed, *regardless* of the contrivances of the Gospels (indeed, all the more *because* of them).

So in my original study, all the probabilities estimated are already dependent probabilities accounting for these effects, and can be imagined as operating iteratively, from one category or subcategory to the next (each accounting for the last already having been considered), but are presented altogether for ease of reference and calculation.

Some Technicalities of Dependent Probabilities

Dependent probabilities do not always share the probability of their originating evidence. If Rom. 1:3 is 100% likely on an explanation that also applies to Rom. 15:12, then that dependency is total, and we have no resulting effect. But if Rom. 15:12 had read the way I proposed, then the two passages are mutually dependent on each other—we can then interpret Rom. 1:3 in light of that new version of Rom. 15:12; and so while the probability of Rom. 1:3 remains unchanged given mythicism, the probability of the new version of 15:12 would change substantially.

In mathematical terms, P(A and B) = P(B|A) × P(A) is the standard formula for a dependent probability. If Romans 1:3 is A and Romans 15:12 is B, then in our actual case, given the mythicist explanation of these passages, P(B|A) × P(A) = 100% × 100%. But in that hypothetical case I described earlier, even given the mythicist explanation of these passages, it could well be P(B|A) × P(A) = ½% × 100% = ½%. Thus, the dependency of Rom. 15:12 on Rom. 1:3 does not remove the impact that Rom. 15:12 independently has on our conclusion, even after its dependency is accounted for. The same goes for Rom. 1:3 but only in light of Rom. 15:12. So the probability of both verses is thus always just ½%, and not ½% × ½%. Once the effect of our new Rom. 15:12 is taken into account, Rom. 1:3 has no further effect. Because mathematically you must ensure you never count the same evidence twice.

It is important to understand this concept of dependent probability, because that might impact your own argument, or your critique of anyone else's. For example, if the order of evidence somehow changes my assigned probabilities, then I mis-ordered the evidence, and my calculations must be revised to account for the effect of one piece of evidence (like Paul's apparent references to Jesus's family) arising before (and thus influencing) another (like Mark's naming one of the brothers of Jesus 'James', the only place that ever occurs in the New Testament outside of that one vague reference in Paul, and the Gospels that merely copy and embellish this information from Mark). I believe I accounted for this dependency in all my estimates. But maybe you can catch some way that I didn't, and explain how that should alter my equations. I acknowledge all the evidence is mutually dependent in some way and only derive dependent probabilities for them accordingly, but for simplicity's sake I multiplied all the evidence with any measure of independence straight down the line on various tables. But if arranging the order of it all should alter any number there, then that needs to be addressed.

One way to check this is to use the iterative method I demonstrated earlier in this chapter: start with a prior odds, then multiply it by the likelihood ratio of one set of evidence, and use that final odds as the prior odds instead in the next equation, when you multiply that concluding odds against the likelihood ratio of the *next* set of evidence, doing the same thing; and so on—in each case taking the previous evidence into account as if it were now background knowledge. For example, once you have factored in the effect of the Gospels on the probability Jesus existed, and are now factoring in the effect of the book of Acts, that probability then takes the Gospels existing as we have them as a given, as much 'background knowledge' as any other contextual knowledge you employ (like, say, whether magical or metaphorical ancestry was a live option in the zeitgeist of that time).[35] This way you can confirm the impact of

[35] That all background knowledge was once 'evidence' in a previous run of the equa-

evidence in its chronological order, and see if its order changes anything (I did not find that it did, beyond what I already accounted for).

This also works if you are uncertain or even suspicious regarding how a prior probability has been determined. Because you can follow the above procedure by starting with 'even odds' (50/50, hence 1/1), which is called an 'uninformed prior' (the effect of assuming we don't know anything that makes one conclusion more likely than another). But if you do that, then you have to put all human knowledge back in as evidence at some point as you run the entire series of equations from scratch.[36] Of course, epistemologically, no one usually starts with *truly* uniformed priors, but with *relatively* uninformed priors, whereby all information (everything we know about the world) is still retained as background knowledge, but only what should have no effect on the specific conclusion in question. So we do include knowledge of logics, Cartesian knowledge of raw sensory data, general conclusions about the nature of the world or the period in question, and so on—our prior probability is always at least *that* informed. The goal is not to tediously exhaust your time building an entire worldview, but to remove all information that would make the prior probability of only the specific hypothesis being tested be higher or lower than its competitor, thus pretending you didn't know anything yet that would make either of those hypotheses any more likely than the other. But when you do that, you still have to put in all the information you just left out *eventually*.

This is because no 'final odds' calculation is valid that has omitted any relevant information. In Bayesian terms, the posterior probability is $P(h|e{\cdot}b)$, and the final odds are $P(h|e{\cdot}b)/P(\neg h|e{\cdot}b)$, where P means 'probability', h means 'the tested hypothesis is true', $\neg h$ means 'some other hypothesis is true instead', and the symbol '|' means 'given the truth of' what follows, the symbol '·' means 'and', and then e means 'evidence specific to our hypothesis' and b means 'all other human background knowledge'. So, $P(h|e{\cdot}b)$ is just a shorthand way of saying 'the probability that the tested hypothesis is true, given the truth of literally everything we know' and 'everything we know' is the sum of all background knowledge

tion (whether we explicitly ran that equation or not) see: Carrier, *Proving History*, 168, 182, 193, 239–42, 277–80, 327-–28nn19–22 (and index, 'iteration'); and *Historicity*, 59, 65n13, 240, 509.

[36] See ch. 6 of Carrier, *Historicity*.

and all other evidence. But this means it must be the case that *b* (the sum of all human 'background knowledge') and *e* (the sum of all 'evidence') must in turn sum to all available knowledge, such that no information can be excluded from the conjoined set of *b* and *e*.[37]

To put that in colloquial terms: you cannot conclude what's true, if you have left out *any* pertinent facts in arriving at that conclusion. Leaving things out to get your result is apologetics, not scholarship. So if you take anything out of *b*, you have to put it in *e*, and vice versa. Which is really the only difference between *e* and *b*: we put things in *e* to calculate what effect that information has on the probability, after which that information (which was previously designated *e*) is now simply in *b*.[38] Thus all of *b* is just what was in *e* in a previous (often only implicit) run of the equation. Hence if you iterate the inclusion of evidence one set of evidence at a time, updating the odds or probability each time, you are essentially folding each set of 'evidence' into the 'background knowledge' in the next run of the equation.

This also means that *e* and *b* cannot overlap. Because you can't count evidence or information twice. So if you include something in *e*, you must exclude it from *b*—and vice versa. For example, if you are using this method of iteration, then you must assess the effect of the Gospels on your running odds *before* you assess the book of Acts, because given the chronological order of their production, the Synoptic Gospels at least could have affected the content of Acts, but not vice versa. For this reason, you might even set the Gospel of John apart, and assess it separately after Acts, if you think any evidence in it matters. I did not think any evidence in John mattered, which is the only reason I did not assess it independently. But, for example, if you run the equation for the evidence in the 'Synoptic Gospels' *before* running it for the evidence in 'Acts', the formal representation of the first result would not simply be $P(h|e{\cdot}b)$ but $P(h|\text{Gospels}{\cdot}b)$, and of the formal representation of the second result would be $P(h|\text{Acts}{\cdot}b)$ where 'Gospels' is now in *b* (along with everything else that was), and its effect on the probability of *h* is already included from the previous calculation's result being carried over.

---

[37] In symbolic language you might write this as e·b or e∧b or e&b or e ∪ b.

[38] Just as when we calculate the effect on our final odds of some newly discovered evidence. See Carrier, *Historicity*, 59, 603–05.

But now its dependency effect also plays out: that the author of Acts is simply repeating information from the Gospels makes that information already expected regardless of whether it's true; hence that duplicated information from the Gospels cannot count twice now as if it were new evidence. With the 'Gospels predate and were used by the author of Acts' in our background knowledge, the probability of finding the same information in Acts becomes 100% regardless of whether Jesus existed or not. Its relative probability is now simply 1/1 (which reduces to just 1), *given* the existence of the Gospels as a source. That same information could already have increased (or even decreased) the probability Jesus existed. But if it did so, it will have done so in the first result, when the effect of the Gospels was assessed as *e*, but it will not do so *again* once thus folded into *b*. Hence evidence in Acts must be provably independent of the Gospels in order to have any new effect not already felt once that same information was accounted for in the Gospels.

In my tables in *Historicity* I accounted for but glossed over this underlying process, to make the math easier for the reader. But that means, for example, when I asses the effect of the evidence in Acts in *Historicity*, I did implicitly include the Gospels in *b* there, even though I only treat them as evidence in the next chapter. That I treated them in reverse order should not affect any results; but in the event that someone can show that it does, they need to be explicitly aware of what was only there implied, so they know how to test or correct any of my results.[39]

Theory Complexity and Prior Probability

One last general point regards the logical effect of making a theory more complex to get it to explain the evidence; and how to tell when this is just gerrymandering, or when it is a valid approach.[40]

[39] Notice I do not use symbolic terminology in the table (Carrier, *Historicity*, 386), but discuss this point colloquially (e.g., Carrier, *Historicity*, 360, 373), including when incongruities between Acts and the Gospels do constitute new evidence (e.g., Carrier, *Historicity*, 369–72, 385–86, 601–06). But for mathematicians I provide the full iterated equation for the historicity of Jesus symbolically indicating these dependency relations at richardcarrier.info/equation.pdf.

[40] See 'gerrymandering' in the index to Carrier, *Proving History*.

It is fairly common for historians, disappointed that the evidence does not fit their theory as well as they thought, to then invent 'epicycles' to add to their theory to *explain away* evidence, rather than actually explain it. This method is not inherently incorrect, as any theory must have some measure of complexity, especially when we lack a great deal of information, and some kind of causal conjectures must fill the gap. For example, we are not gerrymandering when we suppose that Julius Caesar did not use ships or have a winged horse when he crossed the Rubicon, and thus conclude that his reporting his infantry's movement from a town on one side of that river to a town on the other side constitutes 'crossing the Rubicon' even though he never uses those specific words.[41] But this process tends to be abused, too often becoming apologetics rather than sound reasoning. For example, if you conclude that the best explanation of Julius Caesar not saying the words 'I crossed the Rubicon' is because he was using an otherwise undocumented fleet of ships (that you just theoretically invented) and thus never did cross the river, you are gerrymandering. If you understand Bayes' Theorem, then you will be able to tell the difference—*and* be able to construct more plausible hypotheses.

A theory's complexity can affect its prior probability in either of two ways, or any combination of them: you can accept that all your additional ancillary hypotheses and suppositions are each not 100% certain to be true, and therefore *their* probability reduces the prior probability of your theory—and then hope to recover that loss with evidence particular to proving that your (now more complex) theory is nevertheless correct; or you can *demonstrate* (not conjecture, but prove with evidence) that each of your additional ancillary hypotheses and suppositions is already reasonably certain to be true, on background evidence alone, and therefore they have no noticeable effect on your theory's prior probability.[42]

For example, you can simply 'allow' the tremendous improbability of Caesar having but never referencing a fleet of ships or its use for transport (just to make your theory that he didn't cross the Rubicon nevertheless explain the evidence), and thus *reduce* the prior probability of your

[41] Julius Caesar, *The Civil War* 1.4.6, 1.8.1.

[42] For examples see my minimal theory construction in Carrier, *Historicity*, 31–35 (historicity) and 52–55 (ahistoricity).

theory accordingly—and then hope that some evidence turns up that is even more improbable unless he did indeed transport his army by ship. Or you can posit that Caesar and his infantry crossed the Rubicon even though he didn't specifically say so; and since that posit is inherently the most likely way he'd get from Ravenna to Ariminum, *your* supposition does not reduce the prior probability of your theory at all—because it is already made sufficiently probable on background knowledge alone (which knowledge includes the position of those towns in respect to that river, and how armies usually move, and the absence of any reference to Caesar having ships at the time, and all the other factors that would have made him unlikely to have them at the time).

Just as we saw, for example, with ancient Jewish assumptions about the celestial realm: as those are effectively 100% certain to have governed or influenced any thinking about a celestial messiah, our positing them as components of our theory does not lower its prior probability at all. Likewise our positing a hallucinatory or oneiromantic origin for Christian belief: both are well attested then as commonplace originators of religious beliefs, both among the first Christians and among ancient Jews and pagans generally. And so on. Conversely, supposing a passage that is unlikely on your theory has been interpolated, so as to make your theory likely again, must accept the improbability of interpolation, reducing the prior probability of your theory hundreds of times—which is only worth doing if there is so much evidence for that specific passage being interpolated as to overcome that low resulting prior.[43]

All of this is the function of the background chapters in *Historicity*. Most of that information establishes a variety of assumptions to be probable, not improbable. But as soon as your theory requires a component that *isn't* inherently probable, yet it *needs* to be probable (and not be merely possible or plausible), then the impact of its improbability must be mathematically felt. Sometimes, though, a supposition is only required as to what is *possible* or *plausible*.[44] In which case the only probability that has to be established is that it was at that time possible or plausible (see the discussion here in chapter eight). But even then it still

[43] As we can, for example, in the case of 1 Thessalonians 2:14–16: Carrier, *Historicity*, 566–69 (updated in Carrier, *The Probabilistic Argument for Interpolation in 1 Thessalonians 2:14–16*, forthcoming).

[44] See, for example, Carrier, *Historicity*, 65n13.

has to be probable *that it is* 'possible' or 'plausible'.

For example, if we really did need Galatians 1:19 (mentioning James as a 'brother of the Lord') to be an interpolation in order to explain its presence (if it's being there is otherwise so unlikely on our theory as to render our theory unlikely), and if we don't have any particular evidence of that verse actually being an interpolation (and its merely being unexpected 'on our hypothesis' doesn't count), then the prior probability of our hypothesis plummets in proportion to the improbability of that supposition. So, for example, if that supposition is two hundred times less likely, so must any conclusion be that depends on it. Which usually ensures that our theory won't be probable. Which is why you need evidence for it being an interpolation. You can't just posit that it is.

Some Technicalities of Theory Complexity

So these effects must also be accounted for mathematically. For example, if indeed the base rate for any verse being an interpolation is (let's say) 1 in 200, then if our theory only makes the evidence likely if we suppose a passage has been interpolated—and we have no specific evidence that it was—then we must multiply our prior odds by 1/200, making our theory two hundred times less likely than it would otherwise have been. And if we need *two* convenient interpolations, with no evidence for *either* being so, then this effect compounds: 1/200 × 1/200 = 1/40,000. We have then reduced the probability of our hypothesis forty thousand times. And so on.

Needless to say, we are not going to end up with a credible hypothesis this way. If we need a passage to be an interpolation, we need there to be very good evidence of it being so, such that our claim that it is one is not a mere assertion of the base rate ('maybe' it's an interpolation), but a statement that enjoys a near 100% certainty ('almost certainly' it's an interpolation). Either way, that probability must be a fact in our background knowledge—and our background knowledge can by then include the conclusion of a previous Bayesian analysis of that very question. If that probability is then as near to 100% as makes all odds, then concluding it was an interpolation has no measurable mathematical effect on the probability of our hypothesis. Whereas if the probability of our needed assumption is high but not that high—if, say, we can credibly argue it is at least 80% likely—then our hypothesis's prior probability must still be multiplied by 80%. In an odds format, that means our prior odds must be multiplied by 4/5 (80% = 80/100 = 8/10 = 4/5) to produce our theory's *actual* prior odds, now that we have added an uncertain complexity to it.[45] Whereas this doesn't happen for probabilities arbitrarily close to 100%, whose remaining improbability (which is the converse probability, as described earlier)—being then below even 1%—won't even show up in our math when we are rounding to a whole percentile. That's why we can disregard it. We can safely assume such facts without effect.

It thus matters how inherently likely a supposition is in the relevant context (and how likely it needs to be). Consider my debate with Fernando Bermejo-Rubio on whether the Gospels preserve fossils of originally militant actions and teachings of Jesus relating to his armed resistance—which the Gospel authors were actually keen to suppress in order to paint Jesus as an anti-militant pacifist instead.[46] I argued that ancient authors never, and therefore the authors of the Gospels would never, include any information that they did not see some value of—their every word serves a purpose, and if your theory cannot explain what that purpose was, then your theory does not explain the text.

Bermejo-Rubio and Tommasi did not understand my point. They instead just invented additional epicycles to 'explain away' the Gospels' inclusion of information against their own agenda, rather than explaining *why* those authors believed that information furthered their agenda. Hence they provide a correct list of ways information can indeed slip through that net.[47] Such as: inclusion by some overriding reverence for the source material; inclusion by some mistake (such as editorial fatigue, or failing to notice the problem); and inclusion by some overriding necessity (such as avoiding accusations of lying, maintaining a story's intelligibility, or apologetically addressing a spreading polemic). But they fail to recognize that you can't just make up a bunch of reasons; you need evidence that one of them actually happened in the case in question. Just as you can't just 'suppose' an interpolated passage in Paul; you need evi-

---

[45] Carrier, *Historicity*, 29, 53–55.

[46] Bermejo-Rubio, Richard Carrier, and Franco Tommasi, *Jesus: Militant or Nonexistent?* (Philosophy Press, 2025); cf. Carrier, "Thorough Fisk," and ch. 3 of Carrier, *Outer Space*.

[47] Bermejo-Rubio, Carrier, and Tommasi, *Jesus: Militant or Nonexistent?*, 115–16.

dence that it actually is an interpolation. Otherwise, you are *reducing* the probability of your hypothesis; not rescuing it, as you might mistakenly think. Hence, I fully agree with Bermejo-Rubio's list of ways that 'undermining information' can slip through an author's attention, including realized and unrealized embarrassment; and I even present examples of that in my own work—such as to explain why John cut Mark's Baptism narrative (as discussed in chapter four); or why Mark didn't realize the polemics that his invention of an empty tomb would cause (that Matthew then felt he had to address); or why the author of Acts didn't realize the problems his unexpected omissions would cause. However, I don't just 'suppose' this; I prove it with evidence.[48] I'll illustrate the difference in the next chapter, using an example from our debate. But here it's important to simply understand the underlying mathematics of why this is.

This again differs from when 'possibility' is the only matter in dispute: if someone claims something is impossible, then all you do need present are examples of it being possible in order to refute their claim (I survey an example of this in chapter eight). But when someone is claiming something is *improbable*, then you cannot merely present examples of it being possible; that will have no logical impact on their claim at all. You are then committing the fallacy of *possibiliter ergo probabiliter*, 'possibly, therefore probably'.[49] To respond validly instead, you must demonstrate your alternative to be *probable*, and that requires evidence specific to your claim—not just evidence of its possibility, but of its *probability*. Bermejo-Rubio and Tommasi never do this.

As you've seen, Bayesian reasoning operates on two premises: relative priors; and relative likelihoods. So whenever we face any crux in the Gospels, we need to first assess what is usually the case in them. The evidence that they *usually* are fabricating narratives and conversations to a purpose, often a deliberately cryptic one (as even admitted in Mark 4:11–13), establishes that for any passage we cannot explain, it is *probably* another instantiation of that, and not something else (as I discussed already in chapter four).[50] That is an assessment of the prior probability of that explanation, within that particular reference class (which is 'the

---

[48] Carrier, *Proving History*, 128 (Mark), and *Historicity*, 371–81 (Acts).

[49] See Carrier, *Proving History*, 26–29 (and index).

[50] And see chs. 9 and 10 of Carrier, *Historicity*.

Gospels' specifically; or even 'mythography' generally). Specific evidence could turn that around. But without that specific evidence, you can't turn it around. Just proposing a 'possible' way your hypothesis 'could' make sense of the passage does not make your hypothesis probable. You need evidence *supporting* your hypothesis. Although when *both* sides of an argument over the origination of a passage and its content have merely 'possible' explanations of it, and neither can show theirs to be more probable, then it is a wash: neither of you can affirm that it's one or the other. That removes that passage from the category of evidence—since then it's just as likely either way, and we simply don't know if it's evidence or not (like I found for Mark's introduction of Simon of Cyrene and his sons).[51]

So to get your explanation of a passage back in as evidence for something else (like, 'a militant Jesus' or 'a nonexistent Jesus'), then you need evidence that your explanation is more probable—and that requires evidence that is more probable on your explanation (than on any other). The possibility that your explanation is nevertheless incorrect is *already then accounted for* by the measure of relative likelihoods between the two explanations of that evidence. For example, if we could establish that it is 20% likely that the contents of 1 Thessalonians 2:14–16 would be as we find them if it were interpolated, *but* that those contents are only 10% likely if authentic, then the evidence still favors interpolation, by 2 to 1 (20%/10% = 20/10 = 2/1). But that won't increase the probability that Jesus didn't exist. That 1 Thessalonians 2:14–16 would be interpolated is as likely whether he existed or not. So it evinces neither. But that also means its being an interpolation won't *increase* the probability that he existed, either, because to have *that* effect we need the passage to be *more likely* authentic than interpolated (not just 'possibly'). Otherwise the evidence is as expected on either theory (whether Jesus existed or not), and thus its likelihood ratio for *the historicity of Jesus* is simply 1/1, which reduces to 1. And anything multiplied by 1 remains unchanged.

That is the difference between relying on an entirely unevidenced supposition (e.g., 'Galatians 1:19 was interpolated') and a supposition that is established to be at least as likely either way (e.g., 'it's 50/50 whether 1 Thessalonians 2:14–16 was interpolated'). If it went the other way around—if the balance of evidence left it more likely that 1 Thessa-

[51] Carrier, *Historicity*, 444–52.

lonians 2:14–16 was *authentic*, let's say by a margin of 3/2 (a 60% chance it's authentic)—*then* it would become evidence for historicity, adding a likelihood factor (also known as a 'Bayes factor') of 3/2, which accounts for the possibility it nevertheless is an interpolation *and* for the fact that it more likely *is not*. It accounts for both.

The reason this would increase the probability of historicity, whereas the alternative (let's say, a 40% probability of it being authentic) does not, is that the contents of 1 Thessalonians 2:14–16 are equally likely (equally expected) if that is an interpolation, but *not* equally expected (equally likely) if those verses are authentic. So to have any effect, the authenticity of a passage always has to be more likely; and even then its effect is still reduced by the remaining uncertainty of its authenticity.[52]

For example, if your proposed explanation makes all—and especially the strangest—contents of that passage entirely expected and therefore quite probable, and no other explanation performs as well at that, then you have evidence supporting your explanation (we'll see an example of this in chapter six). Your explanation is therefore probably true, or at least more probably true (assuming that that evidence is strong enough to overcome any prior probability there may be against it, of course).

[52] Mathematically (for those who want the more technical explanation), the impact of the evidence is contained within the probability of the evidence. So an asymmetry in impact (evidence that is 100% expected if inauthentic but not if authentic) has an asymmetrical effect. For example, if authenticity is 40% likely, and inauthenticity thus 60% likely, then nonhistoricity already predicts there is a 40% chance this evidence confirms historicity, but a greater 60% chance it doesn't confirm either. So we only have to account for the slight improbability of the contrary (the probability that the passage is authentic *and yet* Jesus still did not exist). If authenticity here favored Jesus's existence by a ratio of 99% to 0.9% (which is a hundred and ten times more likely), then the probability this evidence would be here because Jesus existed equals 0.99 / (0.99 + 0.009) = 99/99.9 = 0.99099, or 0.99 rounded. The passage is then 39.6% expected if Jesus existed (0.40 × 0.99 = 0.396) but still 60% expected whether he did or not (0.60 × 1 = 0.60), which is a negligible change of ratio (39.6/60 vs. 40/60: both simply round to 4/6). Since its inauthenticity is equally expected on historicity, the likelihood ratio simply devolves to 1/1 rather than 6/4 against historicity, because this being an interpolation is never evidence against historicity. But if authenticity were 60% likely (and all else the same), then it would indeed be 6/4 in favor of historicity. Again, it would be negligibly less than 6 to a solid 4, to account for the remote possibility that the passage is authentic *and nevertheless* Jesus didn't exist. But the effect of that remote possibility is again so small that we can ignore it—because we are rounding to whole percentiles, and even maintaining margins of error of several (even several tens of a) percent, and so variances of a fraction of a percent won't even show up in our math.

Otherwise, if your explanation of some item of evidence has *not* been proved more likely, then you are *explaining away* evidence rather than explaining it. And that necessarily makes your hypothesis less probable—the opposite of your intention, which was to try and get some evidence in that would make it *more* probable. But the only way to do that is to establish a greater probability of the evidence on your explanation than on another. And that cannot be accomplished by mere supposition. This is why it is not logically sound to make up a bunch of excuses to get your theory to fit the evidence; but it is logically sound to document facts (*not* suppositions) that actually do get your theory to fit the evidence.

Conclusion

All the conceptual difficulties here are not arithmetical (the math is relatively easy), but logical; and historians must learn logic. You need to be able to understand a chapter like this, because you need these concepts to understand why your own arguments regarding probability are sound (or not sound). It should be required of all history graduate students to master at least basic level logics, in particular how to derive conclusions from premises and fallacy-test their inference models, as well as the basic principles of probability logic as here described. 'But it just feels right in my gut' can no longer be an accepted mode of reasoning. You need to be able to explain why your conclusion follows from your premises. Indeed, you must be able to identify what your premises even are, and how they are distinguishable from your conclusions. Lataster already has much to say on this point in *Questioning the Historicity of Jesus*. As does Fischer in *Historians' Fallacies*, and Tucker in *Our Knowledge of the Past*, and myself in *Proving History*. As do the many others I cited in earlier notes who are applying Bayesian logic now to history specifically, and to human empirical reasoning generally.

The bottom line is that historians need to take math and logic seriously. Because it is the only way they can justify any of their conclusions about history. This means we need to take seriously how we determine and measure the initial plausibility of a claim—which in Bayesian reasoning is formally designated by its *prior probability*. This also means we need to take seriously how we determine and measure the impact of any purported evidence on the probability of a claim—which in Bayesian reasoning is formally designated by its *likelihood ratio*. Because a claim's prior odds times the likelihood ratio, of each item or batch of evidence, then gets you the final odds on your claim being true. And all these things in turn require us to understand how dependent probability works, how adding suppositions to a theory works, and how we account for all other possibilities, and the effect of background knowledge on every probability we estimate.

For example, what is gerrymandering and why is it not a valid mode of reasoning? And *when* is someone gerrymandering a hypothesis—because not all complex theories are gerrymandering; some are correctly using background knowledge to derive their likelihoods and priors, and correctly demarcating the space of probabilities, and correctly calculating the effects. There is a reason why Bermejo-Rubio's 'supposing' an author behaved a certain way is not a logically valid approach to determining what is likely, while getting the same conclusion by proving, with evidence, that they did is a logically valid approach. Which in turn requires understanding how, logically, evidence can even do that—what is it about a thing that logically increases the probability of a conclusion about it? Understanding this is essential to understanding all the mistakes we can make when doing it (as surveyed by Fischer, for example). And if we don't understand that, we cannot guarantee we ourselves are avoiding those mistakes. So you need to understand the logic of probability (and hence the mathematics—both conceptual and arithmetical). Which in matters of fact is always Bayesian.

You are already reasoning this way, even when you are not aware of it. Your every thought process, premise to conclusion, is Bayesian. But when you are not aware of this, mistakes in your reasoning become too easy to make. You need to know how to justify your assumptions about a claim's initial plausibility and how to justify when and whether any fact operates as evidence for or against it, and why and how that evidence can be called strong or weak. And you need that same knowledge to properly critique my or anyone else's arguments in academia. Bayesian logic provides the only reliable framework for all of this, even when you don't need to use any numbers or arithmetic.

Various aspects of how to do this properly—and avoid mistakes in the process—have been covered in this chapter. In the next chapter I will apply it all to some examples important to resolving the question of Jesus's historicity.

6

The Mathematics of Historical and Mythical People

In this chapter I will apply the logic of the last chapter to three important categories of analysis in the historicity debate: how to analyze the likely origin of Gospel stories and their content; how to prove someone existed in antiquity; and how to determine the average expected frequency of heavily mythologized persons being nevertheless historical—and why we have to actually do that (and not skip that step as if it didn't matter).

First Case in Point: The Two Swords Pericope

In the last chapter I discussed problems with the approach of Fernando Bermejo-Rubio. Let's consider a specific example from that debate: the strange tale of the mysterious 'two swords' in Luke 22:35–38. Which is found in no other Gospel, and seems hardly to make sense even where we find it. The rest of that chapter adapts tales originating from Mark and Matthew, depicting Jesus shutting down the high hopes of Judas, Peter, and the other apostles, in each case highlighting (to their incomprehension) some profound failure of theirs to come. Then, immediately before switching the scene to their climbing the Mount of Olives on the way to Jesus's eventual arrest and crucifixion (which sequence contains more admonishments of the apostles' failures and incomprehensions, and eventually brings to fruition all the other failures Jesus predicted), Luke has Jesus suddenly (and inexplicably) say this:

> Then Jesus asked them, "When I sent you without purse, bag or sandals, did you lack anything?"
>
> "Nothing," they answered.
>
> He said to them, "But now if you have a purse, take it, and also a bag; and if you don't have a sword, sell your cloak and buy one. [Because] it is written: 'And he was numbered with the transgressors'. And I tell you that this must be fulfilled in me. Yes, what is written about me is reaching its fulfillment."
>
> The disciples said, "See, Lord, here are two swords."
>
> "That's enough!" he replied.
>
> —Luke 22:35–38 (NIV)

What is happening in this scene? It makes no immediate sense as history or parable. In no way could 'two swords' be 'enough' for anything (not even to effect a robbery, least of all a rebellion); and yet why is it *two* swords? And why is Jesus, supposedly a pacifist, giving them a command to buy swords? And yet, why does he rescind that command as soon as they tell him they already have the two?

Bermejo-Rubio argues that this is evidence of a real armament program in Jesus's militant entourage, that Jesus did indeed order up an arsenal of swords, and this has just become garbled-up in transmission into this strange, unintelligible tale, one that no other author thought worth the bother of including.[1] Bermejo-Rubio provides no hypothesis explaining any of the details here. He just handwaves into existence the mere idea of a confused preservation of a militant past for this story. Which leaves it easy for Justin Meggitt to refute all his *ad hoc* suppositions and best him with a third possibility: that the pericope *is* garbled history, but *not* of a military armament program.[2] But Meggitt provides

---

[1] Fernando Bermejo-Rubio, "Changing Methods, Disturbing Material: Should the Criterion of Embarrassment be Dismissed in Jesus Research?" *Revue des Études Juives* 175.1 (2016), 1–25 (18–19).

[2] Justin Meggitt, "Putting the Apocalyptic Jesus to the Sword: Why Were Jesus's disciples Armed?," *Journal for the Study of the New Testament* 45.4 (2023), 371–404 (384–90).

no hypothesis explaining any of the details here, either. He, too, just handwaves into existence the mere idea of a confused preservation of a trivial fact, that many people often carried longknives for various reasons.

Mathematically, Meggitt's and Bermejo-Rubio's hypotheses split the probability-space shared by the overall theory that the passage is as it is because it preserves some historical information, however distorted. The debate between them is then over which occupies the majority of that probability-space and thus is 'more probable' than the other. But both face the competing hypothesis that the passage is as it is because Luke invented its every component to a purpose, under which umbrella there can *also* be more than one hypothesis as to Luke's actual purpose in doing that. The relative probabilities here can also be inconclusive.

For example, if the 'historical information' hypothesis turned out to be, say, 60% likely (and the 'mythical construction' hypothesis, in turn, 40% likely, by filling up the remaining space of possibilities), it could be that Bermejo-Rubio's hypothesis occupies, say, 80% of that probability-space, and Meggitt's would then occupy the remaining 20%, because his theory is a catch-all for every possible 'historical information' explanation other than Bermejo-Rubio's. In that case, Bermejo-Rubio's hypothesis would be, overall, 48% likely (60% × 80% = 0.60 × 0.80 = 0.48); Meggitt's, 12% likely (60% × 20% = 0.60 × 0.20 = 0.12); and the contrary conclusion that no historical information is in this pericope at all—it's entirely mythical—would be, simply, 40% likely (100% – 60% = 40%).

In that situation, we could not honestly express confidence *any* of these theories were true (or false). Even Bermejo-Rubio's explanation would be more probably than not *false*—there being a slightly greater 52% chance the truth is *either* Meggitt's *or* some mythological hypothesis instead (100% – 48% = 52%). But Bermejo-Rubio's explanation would still be slightly more likely than any other, including any mythological hypothesis (at 48% to 40%). And we could then honestly say that. But that still leaves us in a lot of uncertainty (a 48% chance Bermejo-Rubio is right does not confer much confidence—what in life would you hazard on a less than 50/50 chance of being right?). And it could all go the other way, with all 'historical information' hypotheses being, in sum, let's say, only 10% likely. In that case, if Bermejo-Rubio's hypothesis occupied, again, 80% of that space, then its probability would be a mere 8%, in contrast to some 'mythical construction' hypothesis or other being 90% likely (100% – 10% = 90%). Which is more than eleven times more likely (90% ÷ 8% = 11.25). Or the probabilities could be something else altogether. So how do we find out?

The first task is to determine the prior odds, on either the 'historical information' set of hypotheses or the 'mythological construct' set. And here, historicity doesn't fare well. Whether Meggitt's or Bermejo-Rubio's, as I explained in chapter four regarding Goodacre's analysis, the 'historical information' theory suffers a far lower prior probability: *usually* Gospel authors don't include pointlessly confused lore; *usually* they include things for very specific reasons, and for an allegorical or parabolic lesson they want to teach.[3] Occasionally they slip up. But 'occasionally' is just another word for 'infrequently'; and 'infrequently' is just another word for 'improbably'. The possibility Meggitt or Bermejo-Rubio are advancing is accounted for in that probability; but it's still a low probability. I thus favor the flip side of those prior odds: that this pericope is here, and in every detail explained, by Luke himself inventing it to a purpose.

Maybe the evidence can turn this around and render either Meggitt's or Bermejo-Rubio's theory more probable in the end. But they appeal to no evidence. And there isn't any. There is no evidence of this saying predating Luke. There is no evidence of Luke making some mistake by including it. There is no evidence supporting even what this pericope is supposed to preserve a notion of: that Jesus' entourage was just trivially armed for no reason relevant to Luke's narrative (Meggitt), or that Jesus even planned to arm his minions, and with a strange cloaks-for-swords procurement plan (Bermejo-Rubio). There is also no evidence Luke 'had' to include this story, so as to 'fix' it to obscure its original meaning or transform it to another. Because every other author felt free to omit it, including authors before Luke—and after Luke. So Luke would have been free to omit it, too. And neither Meggitt nor Bermejo-Rubio even has a suggestion as to what Luke thought he was transforming it into. Why did Luke choose to include this (when no other Gospel did), and

---

[3] This is the whole point of my survey of examples of this in Carrier, *Historicity*, chs. 9 and 10.

why did he change it in the specific ways he does, and why has he placed it precisely where it is, even though it seems wholly disconnected from what precedes and follows?

Hence Bermejo-Rubio's theory does not make any of the evidence probable. Nor does Meggitt's. Either theory leaves it all quite improbable. And those improbabilities stack. If we assume that Gospel authors, in their selection and adaptation of material to include, 'accidentally' let things contrary to their mission 'slip through' even as often as once in every five pericopes (surely a rather absurd over-estimate of their error-rate; I think it must be less than one in ten or even far less), then the prior odds on either Meggitt's *or* Bermejo-Rubio's theory would be 1 to 4, or 1/4 (since '1 in 5' means a ratio of 1 to 4), or even worse than the 1/9 of my own generous estimation (since '1 in 10' ratios as 1 to 9). The 1/4 prior odds must then be our *a fortiori* prior (as I explained in the previous chapter), and the 1/9 our more judicious one. Then, if we assume there are four independently weird things about this passage—such as (A) the weird command, (B) the weird answer, (C) the weird rescission of the command, and (D) the weird location in the narrative—and each is not very probable without a reason for Luke to have crafted it in just that way (and thus inventing it, contrary to Meggitt and Bermejo-Rubio), then we have four likelihood ratios multiplied together: $A \times B \times C \times D$. What, then, is the mathematical (and thus logical) effect of this fact on such theories as theirs?

Let's start with the assumption that 'no one has a better explanation' of the content and placement of this pericope than 'it's a garbled historical event' (the overall hypothesis of which Bermejo-Rubio's or Meggitt's theories are but variants). In that case their kind of explanation is no better or worse than any other. 'Luke screwed up' is, absent any specific evidence of it, just as plausible as 'Luke made all this up', absent any specific evidence of either. The evidence is then a wash: it supports neither theory over the other. And so we are left with simply the prior probability. Which, alas, does not favor anything like Meggitt's or Bermejo-Rubio's explanation, just as I explained for Goodacre before. We should sooner just assume Luke invented and positioned this entire pericope to some purpose, even though we cannot discern what it is. Because that's more usually what Luke does as an author (indeed, more usually what any Gospel author does). And that would be that. To get any other outcome, we would need specific evidence supporting 'Luke screwed up' over 'Luke made all this up', or vice versa.

And as it happens, we do. Meggitt even notes it, but oddly does not explore it and thus fails to recognize its weight, when in a footnote he mentions (but handwaves off) a pertinent study by Kevin Moore.[4] Meggitt's observation here, however, is *almost* Bayesian: "at the arrest of Jesus, the disciples managed to rustle up at least two" swords, which he says is "a number that is so devoid of symbolic potential or biblical resonances that it is a detail that probably originated in actual events, rather than the fecund imagination of those immersed in scripture." In other words, Meggitt believes that this datum (the specific number of *two* swords) is improbable on any other explanation than that there really were two. This is an argument from greater likelihood: he is claiming a historical origin makes the evidence more likely; therefore a historical origin is more likely. The logic is Bayesian. His *reasoning* is thus correct. But it is factually erroneous, missing two important details. His *premises* are false.

First, Meggitt's argument ignores the logical effect of prior probability. He is simply assuming 'we can't understand it' leaves no other explanation likely than 'therefore it's historical' (the same mistake we took Goodacre to task for in chapter four). But we have ample examples of that inference being false elsewhere, and so we should not adopt it here. The evidentiary trend is that Luke will have had some reasons for constructing every element of this story, just as he does every other. That we can't figure it out is therefore not evidence to the contrary; rather, it only evinces our ignorance of the point and context Luke meant to evoke. By analogy, 'we can't think of why the miraculous catch counted exactly 153 fishes' does not warrant the conclusion that 'therefore, historically, there really were 153 fishes'.[5] To the contrary, it warrants our admitting that we don't know the symbolic intent of there being exactly 153 of them. Which does *not* render improbable that the intent was symbolic.

The same reasoning follows for the two swords. Luke wrote 'two' for a reason. We cannot circularly *presume* to know why. And both the

---

[4] Meggitt, "Apocalyptic Jesus," 380n45, citing Kevin Moore, *Why Two Swords Were Enough: Israelite Tradition History Behind Luke 22:35–38* (University of Denver, 2009).

[5] John 21:10–11; Carrier, *Historicity*, 505–06 (cf. 450–51), where I also explain that it probably should be understood as 'fishes' (153 species) and not 'fish' (153 of the same species of fish).

Evangelical and Lukan trend indicates the reason is usually going to be symbolical. So we *cannot* conclude it was more likely historical. Meggitt has made a logical mistake here: 'neglecting the priors', as in, not correctly taking into account the actual base rate of explanations. What have we shown to be more common, whenever we can tell: symbolical reasons for weird details, or accidentally historical ones? Most often, it's been symbolical. *Most of the Gospels are myth, not history*. Ergo any single part is more likely myth than history. Which does not mean it *can't* be history, but when we don't know, we have to play the odds.

Meggitt then makes another error. Right after affirming that very point about the specificity of 'two' swords (a specificity that is peculiar and thus *is* a detail requiring an explanation), he proposes that "it is possible that the disciples had even more than that," which immediately takes away the point he just made. If they had more, then Meggitt has even more failed to explain why Luke chose to say there were two. Despite his intuition as to the logical connection between evidence and the probability of its explanation, Meggitt fails to grasp how that actually works: the evidence consists of all the weird details. *It is those details* that your explanation has to make more probable than any other. And Meggitt doesn't even attempt to explain how his theory accounts for *any* of them. Why is this story told *precisely here*? Why is the number of swords *precisely two*? Why does Jesus command that swords be *bought*—at all, much less with cloaks, a detail Meggitt himself admits is impossible (commoner's shawls, an everyday textile, could in no way cover the cost of a sword, a precision steelwork)?[6] This is the case even if a commoner's *tallit gadol* (the Jewish prayer shawl) is meant, which is more likely, and would add more symbolic resonance to this passage (selling even one's own *prayer shawl* for a means of violence).[7] And why does Jesus rescind that order as soon as he learns that they have only two swords? These are all *improbable* on the supposition of anything historical. They are therefore evidence *against* Meggitt's theory, *and* Bermejo-Rubio's. They are, rather, evidence for some symbolic intent. Because only that can likely make these details probable again.

---

[6] Meggitt, "Apocalyptic Jesus," 389–90.

[7] Both Meggitt and Bermejo-Rubio overlook this fact: Numbers 15:38 (*himation* in the LXX; *himation* in Luke 22:36). I thus hereafter translate this as 'shawl' rather than 'cloak' (a more accurate rendering of *himation* in any case).

But Meggitt's most fatal failure is his waving off the explanation of Kevin Moore, which Meggitt gives no argument or evidence against; he merely asserts that Moore's "argument is somewhat tenuous." But Meggitt never explains what is supposed to render Moore's argument so improbable. Is there evidence against it? Does any prior probability weigh against it? Does it require too many unevidenced suppositions? If you check yourself, you will find the answer in every case is 'no'. You will instead find that Moore's theory explains every strange detail of the story. By making every item here that is improbable as history *probable* again, Moore's theory is *confirmed*. That is the opposite of 'tenuous'. The likelihoods simply favor Moore as correct (and the actual priors here only amplify that conclusion).

By not recognizing how the logic of evidence works, Meggitt thought he could simultaneously say that there being two swords "is so devoid of symbolic potential or biblical resonances" that we could be certain it was history *and* that Kevin Moore *had* filled that void with symbolic potential and biblical resonances. It cannot be both. Ether it is devoid of identifiable reasons; or it is not. And there *is* an identifiable reason for the number being two.[8] So let's look at Moore's theory, and apply a correct Bayesian logic to it.

Central to Moore's thesis is a refutation of Meggitt's claim that there were no discussed traditions involving 'two' swords among Jewish thinkers of the time. He thoroughly demonstrates that in fact there was one (and indeed *only* one): the 'two swords' tradition regarding Simeon and Levi's seditious and murderous revenge for the rape of Dinah (Genesis 34). Moore shows this was widely discussed, and commonly in reference to the 'two swords' motif, and that it was usually interpreted positively.

For example, in the novel *Joseph and Aseneth*, which might even have been a hot new publication by the time Luke was composing, we read:

> Behold, have you seen these swords? With these two swords the Lord God punished the insult of the Shechemites, by which they insulted the sons of Israel, because of our sister Dinah, whom Shechem the son of Hamor had defiled.[9]

[8] I here expand on Richard Carrier, "Like, Can You Rebel Against Rome with Only Two Swords?" (31 January 2024) at richardcarrier.info/archives/27035.

[9] *Jos. Asen*. 23:14.

Here, it's "Behold, have you seen…these two swords" of "the Lord." In Luke, it's "See, Lord, here are two swords." The sense is identical. Although Genesis in fact condemns the behavior of Simeon and Levi, the common take by the time of Luke was to sell them as heroes, as we see here (making this a pro-rebellion theme, an apposite change of perspective under Roman rule). Moore argues that Luke is restoring the original take with a cryptic saying of Jesus that, when correctly understood, condemns the model of Simeon and Levi as not heroic but as reflecting a lack of understanding of God's desires and purpose. Such a cryptic approach is much the same as Luke employs everywhere else in the same chapter (and often elsewhere; as also the other Evangelists). This is thus entirely in line with Luke's methods and aims.

This would explain why the pericope is placed where it is, at the end of the Last Supper scene, which almost entirely consists of the disciples not understanding what Jesus is saying as Jesus chastises them for specific failures: betrayal of principles (through greed: Luke 22:3–6), in the case of Judas; abandonment of principles (through cowardice: Luke 22:31–34), in the case of Peter; and embracing incorrect principles, in the case of the disciples arguing about their relative social status in the world to come (not understanding that such concern with status is itself a failure to understand the gospel: Luke 22:22–30).

It is precisely at the end of this sequence that we find the 'two swords' pericope, an add-on allowing Luke to present two pairs of criticisms of the disciples (and hence of 'kinds' of failure among the faithful generally): two specific disciples being criticized (Judas and Peter); and two occasions of the disciples as a whole being criticized. Indeed, to ensure this parallelism, Luke has altered his source: Mark makes the argument over future status a specific one between James and John (Mark 10:35-45); Luke has changed this to the disciples as a whole (Luke 22:24–30). Luke has thus gone out of his way to arrange his narrative to fit in another *general* critique of the disciples (which are in some respects opposites), to parallel the two (also contrasting) ones aimed at *specific* disciples (which are also in some respects opposites).

Luke has thereby created yet another contrast: whereas the first general criticism relates to haughtiness in relation to the future world (pursuing distinctions of social status after victory, wrongly preserving the broken politics of this world into the next), the second general criticism relates to haughtiness in relation to bringing that future world about (through violence, another emblem of the broken politics of this world). The message is: don't engage in violence in jockeying for power; you are to be humble and meek, and God will reward you equally (as Luke even has Jesus say: Luke 22:25–30), in contrast to the wrong understanding, which is that (as proposed in *Joseph and Aseneth*) God will back whatever violence you righteously pursue, so indeed all you do need is just two swords.

A chiasm is thus formed, which was overlooked by Moore but supports his argument:

A Judas — **an easiness to violence for money**

{ selfishness in an absence of faith }

(Luke 22:1–6, 21–23)

B The disciples — **erroneous understanding of what's to come**

{ selfishness in the presence of faith }

(Luke 22:24–30)

B' Peter — **erroneous understanding of what's to come**

{ selfishness leading to a faith falling short }

(Luke 22:31–34)

A' The disciples — **an easiness to violence with money**

{ selfishness leading to a faith going too far }

(Luke 22:35–38)

Luke has thus covered every possible way Christians might fail their Lord. And he has had Jesus critique them and provide alternatives. The way of Judas is doomed (Luke 22:22); the way of Peter is to 'return' from his failure and 'strengthen' the brethren (Luke 22:32); the way of pursuing status is to be abandoned (Luke 22:25–30); and the way of violence must come to an end (Luke 22:37; and then as Jesus literally says in 22:49–51).

This is far too elegant to just coincidentally be historical. It is all a fiction. Central to this understanding is Moore's conclusion that this 'two swords' pericope is indeed *criticizing* the use of swords, rather than (as it paradoxically seems) promoting it. And key to grasping how it is doing that is understanding that Luke is writing in a context when the 'two swords' *traditum* (the legend of Simeon and Levi) is being widely promoted and discussed. So Luke's allusion to it will have been far more obvious to readers then than now.

But there's more.

Moore observes that Luke is thereby connecting Genesis 34 to Isaiah 53. We can extend Moore's point. Luke borrows Mark's reification of Isaiah 53:12 in Luke 23:39–43 (by having Jesus crucified with two criminals); but then Luke adds yet another allusion to it, to complete the reification of the entire verse. Isaiah 53:12 says (NIV):

a Therefore, I will give him a portion among the the great,

and he will **divide the spoils** with the strong,

b because he poured out his life **unto death**,

and was **numbered** with the transgressors.

c For he bore the sin of many,

and made **intercession** for the transgressors.

Just as Matthew 'fixes' Mark by having Jesus implausibly ride two donkeys into Jerusalem,[10] Luke 'fixes' Mark by having Jesus 'make intercession for one of the transgressors' that are crucified with him, the one who repented—and notably *not* the one who mocked Jesus by suggesting that he effect an armed escape ("Aren't you the Messiah? Save yourself and us!"). Luke thus transformed Mark's story into yet another parable denouncing militant messianism, by further reifying Isaiah 53:12. And this is material that Luke invented—it's not in his sources and has no historical plausibility.

[10] Carrier, *Historicity*, 459.

So by adding in as well the tale of two swords, Luke gets Jesus to fulfill Isaiah 53:12 three times: first in the 'two swords' pericope, where Jesus announces the fact that he fulfilled that very prophecy—where he discovers he has two armed 'soldiers' in his retinue; second when Jesus is traded for the criminal Barabbas—where we have two condemned criminals, and one is innocent (yet the innocent is the one killed: fulfilling Isaiah 53:12b); and third when Jesus interacts with his deathmates—where we have two condemned criminals, and one is forgiven (fulfilling Isaiah 53:12c). Jesus is thus 'numbered with the transgressors' three times in the playing out of his 'bearing their sin' and 'making intercession' for them. We should expect, then, for the 'two swords' pericope to contain an allusion to dividing the spoils (53:12a), thus completing the sequence of 53:12a (dividing spoils), 53:12b (dying in place of Barabbas), and 53:12c (making intercession for the one repentant criminal at his side).

So here we get more evidence than even Moore noticed. Luke's 'two swords' pericope is referring to the Genesis 34 *traditum*. Genesis 34:24–31 relates the outcome of two of Jacob's (hence, thematically, 'Israel's') sons seeking violent revenge for the rape of Dinah by Shechem the prince of the Schechemites: they deceitfully persuade the Schechemites to make penance by converting to Judaism with circumcision and sharing their lands and goods—in other words, by establishing a covenant with them, a treaty uniting their peoples. The story then proceeds to relate how 'on the third day' (Gen. 34:25) Simeon and Levi break that treaty, betray the Schechemites, murder them all with just their two swords (*machaira*, LXX Gen. 34:25; *machaira*, Luke 22:36, 38), and loot their goods as spoils. Jacob laments at this, predicting the inevitable cycle of revenge ("I and my household will be destroyed!"), while Simeon and Levi brush that off with a self-righteous justification ("Should he have treated our sister like a prostitute?"). Jewish exegetes in Luke's day praised all this as a righteous act, even though the authors of Genesis denounce it as villainous, declaring that the entire lineages of Simeon and Levi were condemned to obliteration by God for this very crime (Genesis 49:5-7). Luke is restoring that sense.

Luke might have been inspired to build this allusion by the fact that two of the disciples in his source material already have the names Simon and Levi, and share apposite qualities: in Luke, Levi is a tax agent, hence morally tainted with concern for trade and exchange, buying and selling (like, say, selling cloaks to buy swords), and 'taxing' wealth and goods, analogous to the looting of Simeon and Levi (Luke 5:27–32); and of two disciples named Simon, one is prominently 'Simon the Zealot' (Luke 6:15), a nomenclatural representative of militant messianism, and thus of murder and rebellion.

Luke does not name them here, though, perhaps to maintain his parallelism (and his messaging of *all* the disciples failing), matching his similar elision of the names of the two who debated their future rank (James and John). But careful readers might have gotten the inference. Whether he intended that or not, Luke's point by alluding to this Hebrew myth is that the way of money and war (the 'revenge' looting and killing by the two sons of Israel) only leads to doom (as Genesis relates); likewise the breaking of oaths and treaties (as they also did). Like them, Barabbas is also a 'rebel', hence a breaker of oaths and promises, and a 'murderer', hence a killer of men even for supposedly righteous reasons (Luke 23:18–19). So it builds on Moore's case that Luke adds the claim that Barabbas's rebellion took place 'in the city'. This is not in Luke's sources, Mark or Matthew, nor makes as much sense as history. Luke has thus increased his allusion to the legend of Dinah, where indeed Simeon and Levi's murderous rebellion took place 'in the city' of Schechem (*en tê polei*: LXX Gen. 34:28; *en tê polei*: Luke 23:19). So, just as the people choose Barabbas, and just as Jesus snubs the criminal who mocks him with the expectation of armed resistance, we now see Luke's critique of Simeon and Levi in clear relief: they are being compared to those guys. Two swords are all Simeon and Levi had. That was enough to sin against God; enough to choose the wrong path; enough for murder and rebellion (even if only in myth).

That Luke intends the 'two swords' pericope this way is made directly clear by Jesus's paradoxically calling his own disciples 'criminals' in fulfillment of Isaiah 53:12, merely for the crime of having the two swords he supposedly told them to get—but really, for merely *thinking like* Simeon and Levi. Luke is expanding on the Markan notion of abstaining from personal vengeance (and leaving that instead to God: Mark 6:10–12; Luke 10:10-12, 9:4-6), by criticizing it as literally 'criminal'. Hence, as Moore concludes, "Jesus' apostles and disciples are not to retaliate against those who reject their message. They are not to avenge. Instead, final judgment against" any such people "belongs to God, not to them."[11]

Moore has thus explained why it's only two swords, why that's 'enough' (Luke 22:28), and why Jesus evokes Isaiah 53:12 to condemn something he supposedly just commanded (Luke 22:37):

> The possession of two swords—and no more—is appropriate neither on legal grounds nor for any military or pragmatic considerations, but rather because the apostles believe they live in a divinely ordered realm. They will defeat their adversaries with two swords because the Lord is with them just as he was with their ancestors Simeon and Levi.[12]

Which was the very sentiment related in *Joseph and Aseneth*. Jesus is testing his disciples here, just as he has already done three times in this same chapter, with Judas, Peter, and Luke's proxies for James and John; and as in every other case in this chapter, they fail. Here they now see themselves as Simeon and Levi—and thus fail to grasp Jesus's point. Which is a standard device of paradox and incomprehension found across all the Gospels.

The case gets even stronger when we look at how this pericope is composed in Greek. Even though the grammar should suggest it, Moore opposes the idea of reading Jesus's command, contrary to the NIV, as instructing those 'with' means to take up a purse and bag and those 'without' means to instead sell their shawl and buy a blade.[13] But Moore overlooks the actual significance of this. Jesus is saying it is now time to put our money where our mouth is and invest monetarily in the evangelical mission. So, rather than instructing them to 'bring money', they are instead to take up bags and purses—for the *collection* of money. Whereas those who collect nothing to invest 'should' sell even what resources they have and take up a sword instead. This statement emphasizes the foolishness—and the doomed outcome—of his directive: those with means should *not* take up the sword; those who perceive themselves as bereft (despite, apparently, having a shawl to sell, worth enough to purchase expensive steelwork) should alone resort to swords.

In a modern guru's speech, we would recognize this proverb as dark

[11] Moore, *Two Swords*, 255.

[12] Moore, *Two Swords*, 276–77.

[13] Moore, *Two Swords*, 258–60.

sarcasm. Only the enlightened are meant to understand (as Mark explains in 4:11–13). The actual wording of the passage in Greek (which differs from most English translations) confirms this (Luke 22:36):

> ὁ ἔχων, βαλλάντιον ἀράτω ὁμοίως καὶ πήραν
> καὶ
> ὁ μὴ ἔχων, πωλησάτω τὸ ἱμάτιον αὐτοῦ καὶ ἀγορασάτω μάχαιραν.

> The one having, let him take up a bag and likewise a purse
> and
> The one not having, let him sell his shawl and buy a sword.

Having…what? Translators tend to assume this means 'having a bag' and 'having a sword', respectively. But the Greek is more ambiguous. The juxtaposition of the two prepositions, 'the one having' (*echôn*), seems in this context to be a double entendre: it appears as though Jesus is saying 'having means' (yet he never mentions actual money, just bags and purses that one could collect it in, inaugurating money-collection for the Christian mission), but really he is saying 'having sense or understanding; having listened, paid attention', a well-known sense of that verb.[14]

In other words, scholars have been mistranslating this passage as meaning exactly the opposite of what Jesus actually said—making the very same mistake Luke has had the disciples make. Instead this sentence should be understood exactly as written: "But now, one who has [understanding] should take up a bag and likewise a purse; and the one without [understanding] should sell" even "his prayer shawl and buy a weapon." And the disciples who fail to understand are the ones who fail to realize Jesus is speaking of having 'understanding' and *not* speaking of having 'material means' after all.

And indeed they will demonstrate this failure in the next scene when they draw one of these swords to attack someone—and Jesus denounces and reverses what they did (Luke 22:49–51). Here Luke has added to Mark's already cryptic tale the detail of the disciples specifically asking Jesus whether they should "strike with our swords" and then doing so before he has even answered, thus making starkly clear the message Luke intended to convey with the 'two swords' pericope just a few verses earli-

[14] §A.9 in the Liddell & Scott Lexicon (for the word *echô*).

er. Note that Mark 14:47 doesn't even say it was a disciple who attacked; and Matthew 26:51–54 elaborates on Mark with a message similar to Luke's, but Luke does not use that material. He composed his own, so as to draw a deliberate connection to his 'two swords' allusion, displaying the disciples actually again *referring* to the swords, and acting before awaiting instruction, and thus getting wrong what Jesus meant.

Which brings us back to the spoils. The true spoils are not Simeon and Levi's loot, procured by betrayal and violence, however 'righteous'. They are the humble rewards of the next world (Luke 22:24–30). And only those who *abstain* from the path of Simeon and Levi (Luke 23:13–25)—or repent of it (Luke 23:39–43)—will receive that reward. God's Kingdom is not loot. It is eternal life. Which illustrates the role of background knowledge impacting our probabilities (as I explained in the previous chapter): the content of Genesis 34 and *Joseph and Aseneth* explains and thus renders probable the contents of Luke; without which, Moore would only be speculating.

Once you see all this, it becomes obvious that this is Luke's intention. We have thus explained what this entire bizarre aside is doing here, and its every strange element. Other theories (including Meggitt's and Bemejo-Rubio's) do not, and thus have very low likelihoods (they do not make any of the content of this tale expected and thus probable). Moore's theory (especially as here extended) does, and thus it enjoys a maximal likelihood (it makes the content of this tale entirely expected and thus probable). All four oddities are fully explained: we now have a very good reason (1) why the number of swords should be specifically two; we now have a very good reason (2) why Jesus would appear to make and then (3) inexplicably rescind a command to buy swords; and we now have a very good reason (4) why this story should be placed specifically where it is. Moore's theory also explains even more evidence than this: it explains alterations Luke made to (5) the arrest narrative (having the disciples ask Jesus if they should use the swords, failing to wait for his answer, and getting wrong what he meant), (6) the Barabbas narrative (having his rebellion and murder take place 'in the city') and (7) the crucified criminals narrative (having Jesus forgive the repentant and not the militant one), among other things.

Even if we just counted the first four oddities, and even if each of those things is only twice as likely to be there if Luke designed it that way to this purpose, than that they are there by some inexplicable accident, then we get a combined likelihood ratio of 1/2 × 1/2 × 1/2 × 1/2, which is 1/16. I think it's surely at least four times as likely, not two, as each detail we are seeing is particularly weird and thus quite improbable on any other supposition than that Luke designed it that way. So in my estimation it's 1/4 × 1/4 × 1/4 × 1/4, which is 1/256. And recall from earlier, I proposed the base rate of historical information getting into verses unintentionally to be at best 1 in 5 (for thus a prior odds of 1/4) and at worst no better than 1 in 10 (for thus a prior odds of 1/9).

So we have our range of likely posterior probabilities for Meggitt's or Bermejo-Rubio's explanation: at best (being as favorable to their hypotheses as reason and evidence can allow) their theories have a combined final odds of 1/4 × 1/16 = 1/64 (prior odds × likelihood ratio = final odds), and thus a posterior probability of only 1.5% (because 1 + 64 = 65 and 1/65 is 0.015…), far less than even the hypothetical 10% that I suggested earlier; and at worst (being as skeptical of their hypotheses as reason and evidence can allow), it's 1/9 × 1/256, in which case their theories would have a final odds of 1/2304, for a posterior probability of well less than a tenth of a percent—which is effectively zero after rounding (because 1 + 2304 = 2305 and 1/2305 is 0.00043… or 0.04%; which, when rounded to the nearest whole percent, leaves us at zero). The probability of either of their theories being correct is therefore somewhere between zero and one and a half percent—a poor showing. Their theories can be dismissed as false.

By contrast, that Luke designed it all to the very purpose Moore found (and thus none of its content ever existed before Luke did that) is well nigh 100% (because 1 – 0.00043 = 0.99957 = 99.957%, which, when rounded to the nearest whole percent, leaves us at a hundred; and even going low, 1 – 0.015 = 0.985, which when rounded leaves us at ninety-nine percent). And that's just with Moore's theory's success at explaining the four central oddities of the pericope. If we added in all the other things it explains (like items (5), (6), and (7) as numbered earlier), then multiplying in *their* likelihood ratios would only make Moore's theory yet *more* probable. I don't think there can be any logically sound reason to reject it at this point. Moore has solved the riddle of this passage. Until someone comes along with a better solution, we should conclude his interpretation is indeed the one Luke probably intended.

Illustrating the Broken Paradigm of Historicity

This makes the 'two swords' pericope a good example of why the assumption of historicity is a broken paradigm. By assuming there 'must' be something historical to extract, historians go on wild benders of implausible twisting to explain why any passage exists in a Gospel, in the form we find it. Neither Meggitt's nor Bermejo-Rubio's theories explain or make likely *any* of the decisions Luke made in composing this story. Whereas if we assume the Gospels are entirely artistic myths, then we are finally looking in the right places to understand their contents.[15] Ample evidence establishes the Gospels are indeed literary art, mythologies to the core (as discussed in chapter two). So we should be approaching them that way.[16]

And here we see an example of the fruits of that approach: by understanding Luke's fable of the two swords on its own terms—every word, every point, every sentence, every component chosen by Luke *for a reason*—we get to a far more credible explanation of why Luke put this here, and why he alone thought to, and where he decided to put it, and why it has the bizarre form it does. You can't fight any band of enemies off with a mere two swords; you can't plausibly buy a sword with a commoner's shawl; no one followed this instruction to buy swords anyway; and it goes against Luke's entire agenda to even suggest (much less 'remind' anyone) that Jesus would have ordered such a thing. But it does make sense as mythic allegory, another example of the disciples misunderstanding Jesus's cryptic lessons, and pushing the Gospels' consistent agenda of anti-militarism. It then fits its context *and* Luke's particular trends in parable-composing. And all its features are explained—*especially* the weirdest—leaving nothing left to 'be historical'.

The same fate befalls every pericope in the Gospels. Beyond the countless examples I survey in ch. 10 of *Historicity* and ch. 5 of *Proving History*, one can take any attempt to squeeze historicity out of implausibly composed tales in the Gospels, and apply the same analysis I just did to Meggitt's and Bermejo-Rubio's. For example, consider a similar effort by Mark Goodacre to argue for the historicity of the names of the wom-

---

[15] Hence Carrier, *Historicity*, chs. 9 and 10.

[16] A principal benefit of the mythicist model: Carrier, *Historicity*, 616–18.

en at the cross.[17] He makes the same mistake as to priors, assuming that if we can't explain a passage in the way most passages end up explained, then the explanation is more likely something else—when the reverse is the case. The way stories usually end up explained is usually how any other will. We need *evidence* otherwise in order to conclude otherwise. Goodacre also makes the mistake of not following his own advice: he aptly critiques John Dominic Crossan's attempt to extract history from this material, by noting, in a correctly Bayesian fashion, that Crossan's theories don't make the entirety of the evidence probable; but Goodacre doesn't realize those same criticisms undermine his own proposed solution for the same material. For his explanation also does not explain *why* this information has been included, *why* each author chose to use it and place it where they did, and *how* they did.

For example, Goodacre argues that the names of the women are probably historical because we are told so little about them. But that is actually *not* likely as history. He does not attend to the background evidence that this is how fake names turn up all across the Gospels (and in myths generally)—from obviously made-up names (and people) like Bartimaeus and Nicodemus to even real names like Ananias and Simon of Cyrene.[18] The trend is in the other direction: named people appearing without explanation and doing something briefly (often something weird) and then disappearing just as suddenly, tends to signify mythology at work, not history; and in any event, there is no evidence otherwise in any particular case.

The 'three women' appear out of nowhere (in Mark they are never characters found in the ministry of Jesus), they perform obviously symbolic, indeed even numerological, functions in the narrative (three women, doing three things), their names are weirdly apposite (meaningfully drawn in context from famous Biblical characters), and then they vanish from history.[19] To be fair, one of the women is absent for the middle deed (witnessing the burial, Mark 15:47), so for the three

---

[17] Goodacre, "Prophecy Historicized," discussed in chapter four.

[18] Carrier, *Historicity*, 371–72, 490–91, 505n237 (Nicodemus), 366–67 (Ananias), 444–53 (Simon of Cyrene); and for Bartimaeus: O'Connor, "'Spiritual Blindness." See my discussion of the Argument from Names in chapter four.

[19] See my brief analysis in Carrier, *Historicity*, 421–22, 455–56n137, and in more detail in *Not the Impossible Faith*, 312–21.

deeds (witnessing the death, burial, and empty grave) the number of women present forms the structure 3:2:3. The one missing in the middle is Salomê (Wisdom), leaving only the two Marys. Which still looks like a mythical device. Just as in the case of the sons of Simon of Cyrene, there is no specific evidence for either the historicist or the mythicist explanation; the evidence is equally likely on both accounts.[20] So we have to look to what usually is the case, and there the background trend in the Gospels supports the mythical over the historical explanation. This cannot be reversed without evidence to the contrary. And there never is—not in any instance, across all the Gospels.[21]

This gets to the central point Bermejo-Rubio did not understand in our debate: you have to explain (and prove with evidence) why an author included any detail at all; and yet any reason you can come up with for why they would preserve (even if altering) a true fact transmitted to them will usually be a sufficient reason for them to invent it—if inventing things has been established as what they more usually do. It is therefore never possible to argue that a detail is authentic because it was preserved. You have to look to what the usual reason is that Gospel authors wrote things down; and the usual reason is not 'it was true'. The most usual reason is 'to make a point' (whether it was true or not). To get a different result than that in any particular case you need more than the mere possibility that it is nevertheless true. You need specific evidence that that one thing was indeed included *because* it was true, and not because it was useful in some way. If the Gospels were sober histories instead of blatant mythologies, things might be different here. But they aren't.

We must also remember that a detail's mythical utility or origin need not even originate with the author we are examining; it could have originated at any point in the transmission of the myth. For example, Bruce Metzger documented the fact that unnamed persons in myths tended to

---

[20] As concluded by William John Lyons, for example, in "The Hermeneutics of Fictional Black and Factual Red: The Markan Simon of Cyrene and the Quest for the Historical Jesus," *Journal for the Study of the Historical Jesus* 4 (June 2006), 139–54. And I add abundant evidence that this case is even more ambiguous than he concludes (*Historicity*, 444–53).

[21] See Carrier, *Proving History*, ch. 5, and *Historicity*, ch. 10.

get assigned names during a myth's transmission history.[22] Which means inventing names for mythical persons was a typical behavior, and thus not unusual enough to be 'improbable unless historical' (the misguided Bayesian logic underlying Goodacre's reasoning). The 'three women', therefore, could have acquired their names during the transmission of a legend on its way to Mark, who would not know they weren't original to the story. Although I am fairly certain Mark invented them (the function of their names in his story is too apposite to be accidental); but if you believe Mark is relating myths constructed earlier, then Mark is then not the only originator of information you have to consider.

For all these reasons, whether it's names or anything else, that it is merely *possible* some information appears in the Gospels because it is historical is not sufficient to establish that it *probably* is. You need more than that.

Second Case in Point: Historical People

This need for evidence is also missed by every historian who attempts to claim that we should believe Jesus existed 'because' we believe some other ancient person did. Because when we actually check *why* we believe that other person existed, we always find evidence that has warranted our belief, and of a kind that simply has no counterpart in the case of Jesus. It is clear that every historian making this argument has not even checked what actual evidence we have for the people they name. Nor have they reasoned out *why* certain kinds of evidence have that effect, while other kinds don't.

'There is a biography of them, therefore they existed' is a false inference because countless fictional or mythical biographies exist of nonexistent people. Countless fictional or mythical people also have named parents and siblings, even genealogies; detailed records of their deeds and sayings; even people believing they existed. So we need a different kind of evidence, evidence that is improbable on any other explanation than that the person existed. And for Jesus, there isn't any. And the fact that we lack the evidence for Jesus that we have for everyone else whose

---

22 Metzger, "Names for the Nameless."

historicity we are confident of is a major reason *why* we should question the historicity of Jesus. Already the fact that Jesus appears, right out of the gate, as a mystical being (in Paul) and then as a mythical one (in the Gospels) is reason enough to actually *doubt* the historicity of Jesus. The absence of any clear or strong evidence otherwise only confirms this.

So let's look at what historians are getting wrong here. I have taken to calling this the Argument from Spartacus, because that was the first version I encountered: 'if we trust Spartacus existed, we should trust Jesus existed'. You can keep Spartacus or replace him with anyone else, and always either of two things happens: the person you chose is someone whose historicity historians actually doubt; or the person you chose is someone whose historicity is established by clear and strong evidence that we don't have for Jesus.

Another difference breaking the analogy is that the people that get chosen for it tend *not* to be heavily mythologized revelatory beings who are more typically mythical than just any ordinary person mentioned in history (like leaders, scholars, or administrators). This is a distinction of prior probability rather than likelihoods. Which is the different question of assigning Jesus to the class of persons he is most like, and *then* determining the *prior* expectancy of his having actually existed in *that* case. I shall address that in the closing section of this chapter. In the previous section we saw, mathematically, how myth ends up a better explanation than history. Now in this section we will see the reverse: when *history* ends up a better explanation than *myth*. So again we must discuss the effect of evidence. And this will make clear what you really need in order to establish Jesus really existed like all these other people did.

Otherwise, of course, when there is no evidence for someone's historicity, their historicity can be no more expected than anyone else in their same reference class. So, if Jesus were just any other leader, scholar, or administrator, who do tend to really exist, then the prior odds would favor his existing, too—even in the absence of all other evidence. But if people as heavily mythologized as Jesus typically *didn't* exist, then Jesus probably didn't either, any more than they did—unless you can produce evidence that he is, indeed, one of the exceptions. And that means *probably* an exception; not *possibly* an exception. Because 'possibly' does not get you 'probably'. The 'possibility' is already included in the other side of the odds; it does not make those odds go away. If there is only a 1 to

2 prior odds on Jesus existing, and hence a 1 in 3 chance he existed, that he might nevertheless have existed is already covered in that one part out of three. The possibility that a historical Jesus was heavily mythologized is thus being fully recognized. But it's still *less probable*, because the possibility he *didn't* exist is covered in the other *two* parts out of three. So it remains twice as likely, no matter how 'possible' you insist it could otherwise be.

The only valid solution, of course, would be to present evidence for Jesus that was sufficient to prove him to be one of the exceptions to the trend. Rather than do that, however, historians will sometimes just insist there is 'as much' evidence for Jesus as for some other person we are all sure existed (like Spartacus); and then conclude that they have successfully presented enough evidence to prove Jesus to be, like them, an exception. But they haven't. Because the evidence we always have for their proposed analogs far outstrips what we have for Jesus. In fact we *are* so confident in their historicity *because* that evidence far outstrips the kind we have for Jesus. To illustrate this—and how Bayesian reasoning is what establishes it—I shall quickly survey the entire gallery of 'usual suspects' thrown at me in one or another version of the Argument from Spartacus.[23]

1. Socrates

We know the names of numerous eyewitnesses who wrote books about Socrates, including at least sixteen of his disciples. We know of not even one such book for Jesus. We even know the titles of some these books, and have a number of paraphrases and quotations from them. Two of them we actually have (by Xenophon and Plato). And they were written within a few years of his death, not nearly half a century later; and in his own country and language, unlike the Gospels, which were written in a foreign land and language. We have an eyewitness third-party account written during Socrates' lifetime (*The Clouds* by Aristophanes). We know of not even one such account for Jesus. We also have many contemporar-

[23] Here adapted from Carrier, *Outer Space*, ch. 5, where you'll also find citations of the scholars actually using these very examples (including Spartacus).

ies attesting to Socrates, spanning several volumes.[24] We have none for Jesus—other than as a celestial being.[25] We have quotations from many historians of Socrates, using written sources about Socrates from his own time, such as *On the Followers of Socrates* by Idomeneus and the *Metron* of Favorinus, as cited and quoted by later authors like Diogenes Laertius and Athenaeus. We have none for Jesus—only material repeated from the Gospels. Not even Eusebius could find any other sources for Jesus, beyond much later forged materials like the *Letter to Abgar*.[26] By contrast, ancient historians of Socrates were even able to quote credibly contemporary legal documents mentioning Socrates.[27]

And we have *all of those things*, even though there was no global Church of Socrates to preserve records of him.[28] Each one of those five things or sets of things is improbable—its very existence is improbable—unless Socrates did indeed exist. And all those improbabilities stack. If each one were only twice as likely to exist if Socrates existed than if he didn't (and it's surely more), the likelihood ratio favoring his existence is still 32 to 1 ($2/1 \times 2/1 \times 2/1 \times 2/1 \times 2/1 = 32/1$). And again, the actual ratio will be far larger. That's why no one doubts Socrates existed. If we had for Jesus what we have for Socrates, the same would be the case.

Notice that this would follow even if Socrates belonged to the same kind of mythical categories as Jesus (like 'worshiped savior heroes' or 'dying-and-rising gods' or 'heavily mythologized superheroes'). Then, even at my worst original estimates, the final odds on Socrates still being historical would be $1/15 \times 32/1 = 32/15$, or roughly 2 to 1 in favor; and at best, $1/2 \times 32/1 = 32/2$, or 16 to 1 in favor. And that's using the same range of prior odds I found for Jesus in my original study (in the next section I will discuss how we might need to shrink that range, but that would not affect the point here). And we should not treat Socrates like

[24] Gabriele Giannantoni, *Socratis et Socraticorum Reliquiae*, 4 vols. (Bibliopolis, 1990).

[25] Carrier, *Historicity*, chs. 8 and 11.

[26] On which see Ehrman, *Forgery and Counterforgery*, 362–66, 455–58.

[27] For example, the formal charging document bringing Socrates to trial is quoted in Diogenes Laertius, *Lives of Philosophers* 2.40.

[28] For sources on the listed evidence for Socrates see Giannantoni, *Socratis*, and Carrier, *Historicity*, 289–93; as well as Donald Robertson, "Was Socrates a Real Person?" (29 April 2018) at donaldrobertson.name/2018/04/29/was-socrates-a-real-person-and-other-questions, and John Ferguson, *Socrates: A Source Book* (Macmillan, 1970).

that anyway. Socrates is not a heavily mythologized person; he is an ordinary person. Those people tended to exist. Because when we can check, usually we find that they existed; whereas for heavily mythologized persons like Jesus, when we can check, usually we find that they didn't (a point I'll also get to later in this chapter).

The prior odds on a man like Socrates existing are thus not (as I found for Jesus) 1 to 2 but the other way around, at least to 2 to 1 or even dozens to one. For example, if we collected every member of the set of all ordinary, mundane philosophers of antiquity, surely we would find no more than one in six are mythical. And remember, 1 in 6 is 1 to 5 and thus 1/5 prior odds, because 1 + 5 = 6. If we accepted that as the prior odds on an unmiraculous man of history having actually existed, then the final odds on Socrates having existed are closer to 5/1 × 32/1 = 160/1. He's therefore over a hundred times more likely to have existed than not. Yet I have erred as far against that result here as reason could allow. So any adjustment of my numbers toward any more empirically precise frequencies would only increase those odds. So we can be more than adequately certain Socrates existed. Whereas we have none of these assurances for Jesus. The evidence for him is far worse than for Socrates; as are his prior odds.

2. Alexander the Great

We have abundant contemporary coins, inscriptions, tablets, and other physical objects from and about Alexander the Great. We even have his *de facto* death certificate, the original printed in clay, from the archives of Persia. We have many contemporary and eyewitness sources discussing him, including contemporary texts inscribed in those same clay archives that date from his actual lifetime. We have numerous credible, detailed historical accounts, referencing contemporary and even eyewitness sources. Even Arrian, who wrote five hundred years after Alexander, details to us how he used only three eyewitness historical accounts, naming and describing them as sources, and explains his method of using them.[29]

We have none of these things for Jesus. And yet these are all the very kinds of things that are extraordinarily improbable unless Alexander re-

[29] Sources and scholarship on the evidence for Alexander: Carrier, *Historicity*, 21–24.

ally existed. The tales told of him could be false or distorted; but none of this material, as we actually have it, is likely to have arisen from a mythical man. Altogether, the evidence for Alexander is easily millions to one more likely if he *existed* than if he didn't. That is so overwhelming that even if Alexander the Great belongs to a heavily mythologized reference class most of whose members didn't exist, his being an exception would be thoroughly, and arithmetically, established by the evidence. This is not the case for Jesus.[30]

As I already explained in *Historicity*, that we have all this evidence for Alexander doesn't prove Jesus didn't exist (he could have been a relative nobody, for whom evidence is not expected to survive).[31] Nor do any of the other examples here prove that. Rather, what these examples prove is that *we still don't have* this evidence for Jesus, and so we cannot make the argument being addressed right now, that doubting Jesus existed entails doubting any of these other people existed. When the priors don't favor it, *we need evidence to believe someone existed.* And *that* is what we don't have for Jesus. Especially not compared to such famed conquerers as Alexander, but even people whose impact on history is more comparable to Jesus, like Socrates or Pilate. So let's go backwards from here in a descending order of expected and surviving evidence—but then wrapping up with the seminal example of Spartacus (who is somewhere in the middle as far as impact goes).

3. Roman Emperors

Take your pick. Whether for Julius Caesar, Tiberius, Caligula, even Nerva, we have better evidence by far than we have for Jesus. We have abundant contemporary coins, inscriptions, papyri, and in some cases even inscribed personal objects from or about them. In many cases we have their own writings, and quotations of or references to yet other writings of theirs. We have many contemporary and eyewitness sources discussing them. And we have numerous credible, detailed historical accounts,

---

[30] On classing Jesus, and why changing reference class doesn't rescue him, see Carrier, *Historicity*, 245–46 ('The Alternative Class Objection'); and the next section of this chapter.

[31] The entire point of ch. 2 and the entire conclusion of ch. 8 in Carrier, *Historicity*.

even within a hundred years or so, which reference contemporary or eyewitness sources. We have none of these things for Jesus. So we do not get to believe Jesus existed because we believe Roman Emperors did. The final likelihood ratio for any of them will be thousands or even millions to one. So it won't even matter what reference class we put them in.

Just compare a single example, from a single source, on a single question of fact: the birthplace of Caligula in Suetonius, *Life of Gaius* 8.[32] He names, mentions, or even describes his sources, including the contemporary records of Gaetulicus, Pliny the Elder, the official *Acta Publica*, and the personal letters of Augustus, as well as oral tradition and a public inscription—all *in addition* to "the historians of Augustus." He lists the evidence and criticizes it. He analyzes the conflicting claims and tells us how he decided on one over the other. He gives us information about the reliability of his sources—for instance, he tells us when a source is anonymous, and he admits that's a mark against it, and he tells us what evidence any given author appealed to, and remarks on their possible motives. He quotes documents or sources verbatim. And he is openly attentive to inconsistencies. Suetonius is often regarded as a wishy-washy historian, and yet his performance here vastly outperforms *any* source we have for Jesus. And this is just one example. The evidences for Caligula are vast, including numerous authors performing as well as Suetonius, numerous eyewitnesses and contemporaries, and numerous physical artifacts. The probability that all of this was somehow faked, or somehow means something entirely other than it plainly does, is astronomically low. But it is all exactly what we expect if Caligula was a real person. Since the evidence is extraordinarily improbable otherwise (easily millions or billions to one against), the non-existence of Caligula is correspondingly just as extraordinarily improbable.

4. Hannibal

We literally have the epitaph on the grave of Quintus Fabius Maximus,

---

[32] For a full analysis see: Carrier, *Not the Impossible Faith*, 181–84. For other examples: Carrier, *Outer Space*, 94–96 (Caligula), 86–88 (Tiberius), 86–86 (Julius Caesar); and for Trajan, Hadrian, and Antoninus Pius see: Richard Carrier, "There's No Evidence for Trajan, Hadrian, or Pius?" (10 August 2019) at richardcarrier.info/archives/15665.

a man who fought Hannibal.[33] Carved in stone at his death in 205 B.C., it boasts of his victories against Hannibal ("he besieged and recaptured Tarentum and the stronghold of Hannibal," etc.). And we have the epitaph of Felsnas Larth, which explicitly mentions his service as one of Hannibal's soldiers.[34] We also have many credible, detailed accounts by later historians (like Livy) or fragments of them (like Cornelius Nepos, Diodorus, Coelius Antipater, Silenus of Caleacte, Valerius Antias, and Claudius Quadrigarius). These, we observe, cite or quote from many writings by eyewitnesses to the war, such as Cato the Elder, who served in the Roman Senate during the Hannibalic war, and the Roman historian Fabius Pictor, who lived through the war. We also have many references to Sosylus of Lacedaemon and Silenus of Caleacte, traveling companions of Hannibal who wrote extensive accounts of his wars that later historians employed as sources. Likewise the writings of Lucius Cincius Alimentus, a Roman war prisoner who dined with Hannibal during years in captivity and then wrote of his experiences after the war in his *Annals*; and the historian Gaius Acilius, who, we're told, wrote a researched account of the Hannibalic war a mere generation after.[35]

Among what we *have*, the best example of these histories is the credible and detailed account from Polybius, a contemporary to Hannibal, and personal friend of the family of Scipio Africanus who defeated Hannibal. And he explicitly relied on other documents and eyewitnesses. For example, for his history Polybius tells us he interviewed King Massinissa, a Roman ally who fought Hannibal; and Gaius Laelius, a personal friend and companion of Africanus during the war.[36] He quotes from Scipio Africanus's letter to King Philip V of Macedon regarding his personal dealings with Hannibal, and he quotes Hannibal's treaty with Rome, and even a bronze inscription erected by Hannibal himself.[37]

---

[33] *L'Année Epigraphique* 1954 (1955), 62 (§216).

[34] A.J. Pfiffig, "Eine Nennung Hannibals," *Studi Etruschi* 35 (1967), 659–63.

[35] On all these points and more see: Dexter Hoyos, *Hannibal's Dynasty: Power and Politics in the Western Mediterranean, 247–183 B.C.* (Routledge, 2005); John Prevas, *Hannibal Crosses the Alps: The Invasion of Italy and the Second Punic War* (Da Capo, 2001); Serge Lancel, *Hannibal* (Wiley-Blackwell, 1999); and J.F. Lazenby, *Hannibal's War: A Military History of the Second Punic War* (University of Oklahoma Press, 1998).

[36] Polybius, *Histories* 9.25 and 10.3.2 (respectively).

[37] Polybius, *Histories* 10.9.2–3, 3.24, and 3.33.5-18 (respectively).

Needless to say, we have nothing like any of these things for Jesus, much less all of them together, whose combined odds of existing must be at least billions if not trillions to one against the idea that Hannibal didn't exist. And again, also unlike Jesus, Hannibal doesn't begin in our sources as a revealed celestial being, nor is transformed into a mythical hero in fabulous legends—at all, much less within a generation, and those the only records of his life and deeds.

5. Pontius Pilate

We have a historical account from a contemporary, with no motive to invent him, who dealt with Pontius Pilate's actions in the political arena: Philo of Alexandria, an ambassador of the Jews to Rome.[38] Philo also wrote an entire book on Pilate, and though that doesn't survive, we know it existed, as it was read by Eusebius, and referenced by Philo himself.[39] We also have credible, detailed historical accounts from historians relying on contemporary sources, including Josephus and Tacitus. And we even have his own autograph inscription.[40] We have none of these things for Jesus. Yet it is precisely these things that confirm to us that there really was a Pilate, and he thus *wasn't* a made-up character in the Gospels. We didn't just assume that; we had very good evidence of it, evidence that is not even remotely likely to have existed if he had not, but exactly what we could expect to exist if he did. Because with all this evidence together we're looking at, again, *at least* millions to one odds favoring Pilate's existence.

6. Herod Agrippa

For either man of the name 'Herod Agrippa' (son and father, spanning the first century), we have multiple inscriptions and coins attesting to their existence; contemporary accounts from Philo of Alexandria; and

[38] Philo of Alexandria, *Embassy to Gaius* 299–305.

[39] Eusebius, *History of the Church* 2.5 and 2.7; Philo, *Embassy* 8. See Carrier, *Historicity*, 304–05. It is also suspicious that this was lost: Carrier, *Historicity*, 302–05 (304–05).

[40] Joan Taylor, "Pontius Pilate and the Imperial Cult in Roman Judaea," *New Testament Studies* 52.4 (2006), 555–82 (564–75).

credible, detailed accounts from Josephus, a historian writing a generation later, using firsthand, non-mythological sources, and who even personally knew the younger Agrippa, and clearly describes him and his father as real people—an actual father and son.[41] We have none of these things for Jesus. Yet all of this is what we expect if either Agrippa existed; none of it is likely if they didn't; and all of it together is *very* unlikely if they didn't (no doubt approaching at least a million to one). Which makes for a likelihood ratio overwhelmingly in favor of their historicity.

7. Caiaphas

For the Jewish High Priest Caiaphas we have his inscribed casket, and we have credible, researched accounts in Josephus.[42] Which combined is at least dozens to one more likely if he really existed than if he didn't, if not hundreds to one. If we didn't have these things, all we would have are later Rabbinical writings, but even they have a character that is unlikely for an invented man or a man born in myth or mysticism, and so even they would leave us with at least some positive likelihood ratio; perhaps two to one, or even five to one. Which would suffice, as he was never a revelatory superbeing, mythologized hero, or cosmic savior lord. His earliest records don't depict him as someone only met in dreams and visions. And his earliest historical accounts don't describe him in just the same respects as persons who usually didn't exist—like Moses, Osiris, or Romulus. As an 'ordinary person' whose data does not self-evidently derive from visions and mythologies, prior odds already favor his existence. Adding any favorable likelihood ratio to that only magnifies those odds, well enough into confidence.

---

[41] All surveyed in David Jacobson, *Agrippa II: The Last of the Herods* (Routledge, 2019), and Rudolf Haensch, "The Contributions of Inscriptions to our Knowledge of the Herodian Dynasty," *Scripta Classica Israelica* 33 (2014), 99–116.

[42] James VanderKam, *From Joshua to Caiaphas: High Priests after the Exile* (Fortress, 2004), 435–36; and Helen Bond, *Caiaphas: Friend of Rome and Judge of Jesus?* (Westminster/John Knox Press, 2004).

8. Spartacus

And then there is, indeed, Spartacus.[43] Let's go down the list. We have an account in Sallust's *Histories*. Sallust was born ten years before the Spartacan war and wrote thirty years after, and shared the Senate with those who fought Spartacus. We have Cicero, who served during the Spartacan war, and whose *Response to the Haruspices* and *Against Verres* mention Spartacus as a recent historical person. We have Diodorus, a contemporary of Spartacus, who covered the Spartacan war in his *Library of History*. Varro, who fought in the war against Spartacus, is also quoted on the point by Charisius.[44] We also have several later but reasonably credible (and certainly not fabulous) histories, by historians as capable as Suetonius or better, written within one to two centuries, using records and sources contemporary to Spartacus. We have none of these things for Jesus. And yet any one of these things would not likely exist if Spartacus didn't. All of them together would be very unlikely. The likelihood ratio for Spartacus is thus easily hundreds if not thousands to one. And he also did not first appear in the record as a mystical revealed being, nor was he rapidly converted into a fabulous hero in cryptic mythographies.

If we lowball the likelihood ratio for all this evidence *combined* at just 100 to 1, then bring in the previously lowballed baseline frequency of mundane persons being historical of 5 to 1 (in our discussion of Socrates), then the final odds on Spartacus being historical will be at least 500 to 1 (5/1 × 100/1 = 500/1), or as near to 100% as makes all odds. A judicious estimator would likely go higher, concluding the combined evidence is hundreds of times less likely if he didn't exist to produce it. Then the final odds on Socrates being historical are at least 1000 to 1 and maybe even 5000 to 1. If we doubled our lowballed base-rate of mundane persons being historical of 5 to 1 to 10 to 1 (a more realistic number), then that 500 or 5000 to 1 becomes 1000 to 10,000 to 1. But we wouldn't even need that. At the lowest estimate of a mere 500 to 1 Spartacus's existence is already sufficiently assured to place him in history.

---

[43] For sources and discussion see: Aldo Schiavone, *Spartacus* (tr. Jeremy Carden; Harvard University Press, 2013) and Brent Shaw, *Spartacus and the Slave Wars: A Brief History with Documents* (St. Martin's, 2001).

[44] Sosipater Charisius, *Grammatical Arts* 1.133.

So the gallery ends. I will again reiterate the following point (as critics keep pretending I don't): that we lack all this evidence for Jesus does not by itself warrant doubting Jesus existed; rather, the absence of all this evidence *does not* warrant concluding that we *should* believe Jesus existed on an analogy to persons whose existence *is* established on such evidence. Because an analogous conclusion requires analogous premises; and there aren't any here. We *don't* have this evidence for Jesus. So our confidence in these people's existence *doesn't* transfer to Jesus. We believe these people existed for reasons that don't apply to Jesus. So stop appealing to them. If you want to rescue Jesus, you'll need some other argument than that, some newfangled evidence *other* than what we have for these others. I have yet to see it.

To illustrate that point, let's look at an edge-case...

9. Apollonius of Tyana

Two scholars have completed a thorough enough study of the legendary Apollonius. The earliest, Maria Dzielska, observes the poor status of evidence for him, to the point of admitting that "a historian assuming that Apollonius of Tyana existed solely as a hero of an extensive legend... would not stray far from the truth."[45] In other words, the evidence for his historicity is sufficiently poor to render doubting it *legitimate*. The latest, Nikoletta Kanavou, is more confident, but she concurs that almost nothing reliable is to be known of the man.[46]

And yet we still have more evidence for Apollonius than we have for Jesus—evidence external to, some even prior to, the patently mythological *Life of Apollonius* written by Philostratus over a hundred years after Apollonius is supposed to have lived. Dzielska concludes nothing of that *Life* can be trusted, and Kanavou largely concurs. Like the Gospels of Jesus, all of that *Life* can be suspected of being a contrivance of

---

[45] Maria Dzielska, *Apollonius of Tyana in Legend and History* (L'Erma di Bretschneider, 1986), 9.

[46] Nikoletta Kanavou, *Philostratros' Life of Apollonios of Tyana and its Literary Context* (C.H. Beck, 2018) at books.openedition.org/chbeck/1688.

Philostratus himself. Later embellishers then relied on or merely built on the myths of Philostratus, even forging letters by Apollonius, as Philostratus himself likely did.[47]

But Dzielska and Kanavou locate some letters written in Apollonius's name in later collections, clearly intended to be by the legendary man himself, which are not only absent from Philostratus's collection, but which provide accounts that contradict Philostratus's biography, and not in ways suggesting an intentional falsification, but more credibly because they are authentic, and thus merely *unaware* of the later legends Philostratus would spin. For example, in addition to their being unfabulous and thus more realistic *as* letters, Dzielska observes that "we read" in them "that Apollonius had never been to either Italy or to the emperor's court," despite those being famous elements of Philostratus's biography. These letters thus stand a reasonable chance of being authentic, and thus as evidence of Apollonius's historicity.[48] This is far from sure; the basis for that conclusion is tenuous. But it is at least positive in value.

Dzielska also uncovers evidence of Apollonius being a historical personage before that *Life* was written, evidence that does not bear the character of worshiping a celestial or mystical being. For example, we have a casual aside from Lucian of Samosata in his eyewitness account of the fraudster Alexander of Abonuteichos, roughly mid-second-century, well before Philostratus and only a generation or two after Apollonius would have lived. In recounting this quack's pedigree, Lucian reveals two details of note: he assumes that Apollonius was so famous that every reader would know of him; and he says Alexander, a man he met and actively thwarted, was a student of one of Apollonius's disciples, "a man of Tyana by birth, one of those who had been associates [*suggenomenôn*] of the famous [*panu*] Apollonius and eyewitnesses [*eidotôn*] to all his tricks."[49]

This is more concrete than any testimony we have to Jesus. We have no objective third-party observer reporting an encounter with a student of one of Jesus's disciples; at all, much less within mere decades of the legendary man's death. Apollonius lived to the end of the first century

---

[47] Dzielska, *Apollonius*, 38–40.

[48] Dzielska, *Apollonius*, 40 (contrast the letter of Jesus to Abgar previously mentioned).

[49] Lucian of Samosata, *Alexander the False Prophet* 5; Dzielska, *Apollonius*, 38.

and possibly a decade or two beyond; Lucian wrote forty to sixty years later. Imagine if we had a non-Christian author writing before the end of the first century, discussing having met a student of a disciple of 'the famous' Jesus, a Jesus he knew all his non-Christian readers would know well enough to require no further explanation. It's not a slam dunk. This information is still dodgy. Alexander could have invented this pedigree to exploit the fame of an already-mythical sage; and Lucian is two degrees removed, so could hardly have checked—just like with later legends of apostolic pedigrees reported in Christian propaganda, which are far more dubious, to the point of useless.[50] So this would not count as particularly strong evidence. I'd give it a 2 to 1 likelihood ratio, as surely there is at least a 1 in 3 chance the pedigree is fake, and thus so could be the man. But that's still positive evidence. I'd assign the same ratio to the independent letters, being similarly unsure. So our accumulated likelihood ratio is now 2/1 × 2/1 = 4/1.

Dzielska also finds independent testimony to a contemporary recorder of Apollonius's life by a certain Soterichos of Oasis, which adds something as well. We cannot trust the 'sources' Philostratus claimed to have had; they may have been as fictional or as fabricated as the rest, as many experts have argued.[51] But Soterichos appears to be independently attested, and a *contemporary* recorder of Apollonius—and not a fabulist. Its early date, and reputedly sober character, is at least a little unlikely if Apollonius had not been real; although again we cannot be entirely confident in that, because we don't have the book, and cannot verify its authenticity or quality. I'd account this very weak indeed. The information we have on it is not very much more likely on either theory. But even if there is as much as a 40% chance it was still produced without a real Apollonius, the likelihood ratio would be 3/2 (60/40 = 6/4 = 3/2): a three parts chance that it is dependent on, and thus indicative of, a real Apollonius; and two parts, not. This updates our likelihood to 4/1 × 3/2 = 12/2 = 6/1.

I find no other evidence at all convincing. Dzielska overly trusts two alleged sources—books we don't have, but only have references to. One

[50] See Richard Carrier, "Did Polycarp Meet John the Apostle?" (31 October 2019) at richardcarrier.info/archives/15999.

[51] Alan Cameron, *Greek Mythography in the Roman World* (Oxford University Press, 2004), 124–25; Dzielska, *Apollonius*, 26.

author, Maximus of Aegaeae, Dzielska trusts on the poor reasoning that the man existed, as if a fake work could not be attributed to a real person.[52] Since we only know of his writing such a book *from* Philostratus, whose work is well established to be fiction, we cannot trust that information. The other, Moiragenes, really did write a previous book on Apollonius sometime in the early second century.[53] But we cannot actually ascertain that it was itself anything but fiction; it appears to have been as fabulous as the *Life* of Philostratus. Dzielska is also over-trusting of the 3rd (or possibly 4th) century Adana inscription.[54] As a fawning, and centuries late, religious homage, it could be derivative of the same propaganda campaign Philostratus began (Kanavou doesn't even deem it worth mentioning).[55] And, finally, Dio only mentions the existence of (and reverence for) this later legend of the man, which does nothing to corroborate its reality.[56] As there is no particular evidence that any of these data are any more likely to exist if Apollonius existed than if he didn't, I would not count them. Their likelihoods are all equal and thus a wash.

But that still leaves us with that 6/1 likelihood—whereby the possibly independent letters, the mention by Lucian, and the existence of a possibly sober and contemporary account by Soterichos is, all together, six times more likely if Apollonius existed than if he didn't. If we judged that Apollonius, like Jesus, belongs to a set of heavily mythologized people of whom only 1 in 3 likely existed, for a prior odds against of 1/2, the final odds on Apollonius being historical would be $1/2 \times 6/1$, and thus 3/1 (from 6/2), or in other words, three to one odds he was a real person. That's a probability of 75% (because $3 + 1 = 4$, and $3/4 = 0.75$), and that's on just those three rather weak items of evidence.

The uncertainty this entails (75% isn't a high confidence; it admits a solid 1 in 4 chance Apollonius didn't exist after all) is accurately reflected in Dzielska's admission that, indeed, we can't be all that confident. Her

---

[52] Dzielska, *Apollonius*, 34–35.

[53] Dzielska, *Apollonius*, 46, 97; it is attested in Origen, *Against Celsus* 6.41.

[54] Dzielska, *Apollonius*, 64–70.

[55] See Miroslav Marcovich, "The Epigram on Apollonius of Tyana," *Zeitschrift für Papyrologie und Epigraphik* 45 (1982), 263–65.

[56] Dio Cassius, *Roman History* 78.18.4.

judgment thus matches the logical analysis of her case. Nevertheless, overall, it is still more likely he existed than didn't. And this is because we do not have the evidence calling his existence into question that we have for Jesus; and because we do have evidence Apollonius existed that we do not have for Jesus. The shakiness of this conclusion is reflected in the upper probability being well below 90% (what we would usually call a minimum of certainty), but still well above 50% (what we would usually call a minimum of doubt). Probably Apollonius existed. But we can't be entirely sure.

Such would also be reflected in a completed margin of error. We should estimate the probability (the likelihood) of each item of evidence (and the prior odds) from a position of the greatest reasonable skepticism *as well* as a position of the greatest reasonable trust (emphasis in both cases on the word *reasonable*). The one calculation would give us our *a judicantiori* margin of error (the least likely we can reasonably think it is that Apollonius existed); the other, our *a fortiori* margin of error (the most likely we can reasonably think it is that Apollonius existed).[57] Our certainty would be limited to that range: we would not be able to say with confidence which end, or where between, the actual probability is, and so we would have to reasonably accept both as possible.[58]

In my original study I would have put the lower bound probably somewhere around 1/15 × 6/1, or roughly 1/4 final odds on Apollonius existing. To be exact, the odds are 6/15, which is 1/2.5 or a probability of 29% (because $6/(6 + 15) = 6/21 \approx 0.286$), and really, less, if I also lowballed the likelihoods (to *as low* as I can reasonably believe). But even at that we have a final range of 29% to 75%. Such a result spans both sides of the midline, a lower bound in 'didn't exist' and an upper bound in 'did exist'. In such a case, we have to conclude that, on balance, most probably Apollonius existed, but we should not rest confident in that. We gain only a little confidence if we adjust my lower bound (see below) to about 1/5 × 6/1, which gets us 6 to 5 odds, and my upper bound (see below) to about 1/4 × 6/1, which gets us 6/4 and thus 3 to 2 odds. Because (after rounding) that then leaves us with a chance Apollonius

[57] On the margins of error and the terms here used see Carrier, *Proving History*, index, 'margin of error' and '*a fortiori*, method of'.

[58] This is a standard principle of probabilistic reasoning explained further in the Appendix.

existed of still only 54% to 60%, which is barely better than just saying it's 50/50. You might even weigh all this evidence more than I do, but I doubt so much more as to warrant certainty.

And yet we lack even *this* evidence for Jesus. Which is why those insisting he nevertheless existed have had to dig to the bottom of the barrel for arguments to get their conclusion (as we just surveyed in chapters three and four), and why they cling to entirely dubious evidence, overselling it as clearer than it is (as we will survey in chapters eight, nine, and ten). The case for Jesus is simply much weaker than it is for Apollonius, as well as met with more countermanding evidence (as I recount in chs. 8, 9, and 11 of *Historicity*). That now might even include evidence of Christians who didn't think Jesus was an earthly person at all, and of a propaganda war between them and Christians insisting otherwise—an insistence that should not be necessary for a real man (as we'll see in the next chapter). I only don't score that because the evidence for it is too late and unclear to be certain; but it does exist, knocking down any attempt to argue the contrary point that it should exist but doesn't. Thus both arguments balance each other out, leaving us at a wash. But even that result remains important.

In the end, even with all the evidence we have for him, it is not unreasonable to doubt the historicity of Apollonius. It must therefore be even more reasonable to doubt the historicity of Jesus.

Third Case in Point: Mythical People

As already mentioned, heavily mythologized people are different from just anyone claimed to exist in history. Ancient writers will mention all sorts of named people, of all ranks and roles, as historical. Those people usually turn out to exist. When we are given enough data to check, they usually check out. So we are warranted in assuming they existed, even from just a casual unsourced mention of them, because absent specific evidence either way, the prior odds favor them being nevertheless real, and indeed well enough for reasonable confidence. They are simply unlikely to have been made up. But people who are heavily mythologized, worshiped as celestials, communicated with mystically—when we get to check them, they *don't* usually check out. Their historicity is therefore *dubious* without specific evidence.

Jesus is a heavily mythologized person.[59] His first mentions are as a celestial, with whom people communicated mystically, as someone they met in visions or dreams (Phil. 2:6–11, Gal. 1:11–16, Rom. 16:25–26, 2 Cor. 12:1–10, 1 Cor. 8:6 and 15:3–8); and his first narratives are patent mythographies, by anonymous persons who cite no identifiable sources (Mark, Matthew, Luke, and John)—and even their *hypothesized* sources (like Q) are anonymous mythographies. There is no objective third-party confirmation of even his existence, much less anything about him. Outsiders later assumed he existed, but solely on the basis of those mythographies (or informants trusting them), which were written after the generation of any prospective witnesses had largely passed on, in a land and language foreign to any there would still have been. Jesus is thus not like other historical persons. He is more like heroes of yore—Abraham, Moses, Daniel, Hercules, Romulus, Dionysus, Osiris, even Homer, Odysseus, or Aesop; or, from later eras, King Arthur, Moroni, Ned Ludd, John Frum, or Tom Navy.[60]

So we cannot take the prior odds of just anyone existing and apply them to Jesus. That would be as logically invalid as doing the same for any of those other people. Jesus instead belongs to a class of people who usually didn't exist. And we cannot ignore that datum and pretend Jesus does *not* belong to that class. All attempts to date to change Jesus' reference class so as to make this one go away are apologetical and not logically sound (we'll survey some examples shortly).[61] So the fact of it must

[59] Yes, even in the Gospel of Mark: Carrier, *Outer Space*, ch. 6. And beyond: Carrier, *Historicity*, chs. 6, 8, 9, 10 and 11. For a complete list now see: Richard Carrier, "All the Fantastical Things in the Gospel according to Mark" (30 July 2024) at richardcarrier.info/archives/29744.

[60] For all of these, see the indexes to Carrier, *Historicity* and *Outer Space*. Except for Moroni, see David Persuitte, *Joseph Smith and the Origins of The Book of Mormon*, 2d ed. (McFarland, 2000); although his status as a historicized myth is clear even in the devotional studies of Alan Miner, "A Chronological Setting for the Epistles of Mormon to Moroni," *Journal of Book of Mormon Studies* 3.2 (1994), 94–113; John Sorenson, "Mormon's Sources," *Journal of the Book of Mormon and Other Restoration Scripture* 20.2 (2011), 2–15, and Brent Lee Metcalfe, "Apologetic and Critical Assumptions about Book of Mormon Historicity," *Dialogue: A Journal of Mormon Thought* 26.3 (1993), 153–184.

[61] See Carrier, *Historicity*, ch. 6: there, §4 shows that it does not matter to this equation *how* Jesus became mythologized; §5 shows that any other class he belongs to does not remove him from this class and thus its effects; §6 shows that his being mythical entails

be logically accounted for; and that means, accounted for *mathematically*. So the first question we have to answer is: *how often* are people *like Jesus* real people? Because we well know sometimes they are.[62] But they *also* turn out not to be *more frequently* than just any other people recorded in history.[63] But how often is that? That is the only question critics should be engaging. It took ten years for anyone to do that, and that one attempt (a project led by Kamil Gregor) will be addressed here.[64]

This means we need to find and analyze a reference class; and that means, the most *pertinent* reference class, not a fraudulent one.[65] We could just add up all mythologized people claimed to exist. But there are too many for that project to be practical. And moreover, we are not interested in people merely assigned myths or inserted into myths; we are only interested in people whose narratives originate in myths and who were heavily, and not merely, mythologized. In *that* set of people, there are far fewer historical persons. Those people tend not to exist. And Jesus is one of them.

So the prior odds on Jesus existing—meaning, the odds *before* we consider any evidence specific to Jesus—must logically be the same as anyone else in that set. Because he *starts* no more likely to exist than any of them do. We then need specific evidence to turn that expectation

---

no more complex a theory than any specific theory of historicity does; §7 shows that the amount of time that has passed between a set-member's alleged existence and the formulation of their myth has no effect on the probability of their historicity—unless their narrative myth formed contemporary to their existence, which is not the case for Jesus, but was for Haile Selassie (Carrier, *Historicity*, 53–55 vs. 18–20).

[62] Example of Haile Selassie: Carrier, *Historicity*, 18–20. Gullotta ("Doubts," 344; see chapter three) cites the examples of "Alexander the Great, Augustus Caesar, and Apollonius of Tyana," which we will take up shortly.

[63] Carrier, *Historicity* 239–44, 252–53; cf. 229–32.

[64] Such engagement is only forthcoming as of this writing: Kamil Gregor and Christopher Hansen, "Mytho-Historical Heroes: The Raglan Archetype in Application to Ancient Mediterranean Persons," in *Literature & Aesthetics* (with my forthcoming response, "John Wick vs. Jesus and the Logical Significance of the Tragic Hero-King Genre: A Response to Gregor and Hansen," here summarized); and Kamil Gregor, Christopher Hansen, and Brian Blais, "The Prior Probability of Jesus Mythicism Re-evaluated in Light of the Gospels' Dramatic Date" in the *Journal of Early Christian History* (with my forthcoming response, "On the Causal Irrelevance of Dramatic Date to the Likelihood of a Story's Historicity: A Reply to Gregor, Hansen, and Blais").

[65] Carrier, *Historicity*, ch. 6; and Richard Carrier, "Jesus and the Problem of the Fraudulent Reference Class" (20 August 2021) at richardcarrier.info/archives/18711.

around, like we just surveyed for Alexander or Apollonius. But we will account for the effect of that evidence separately, in the likelihood ratio. Here we are only assessing the prior odds. And for that, Jesus must be treated the same as anyone else sufficiently like him. Just as we would do with 'resurrected heroes' (to carry over the analogy I began in chapter one): the prior odds Jesus was really resurrected cannot start any higher than the prior odds that *any* resurrected hero really was. We *then* can examine the evidence particular to Jesus and see if it does make Jesus special; but if it doesn't, then he isn't.

In *Historicity* I surveyed several reference classes Jesus belongs to, all of which have high frequencies of their members not being historical.[66] Jesus belongs to a specific class of counter-cultural martyred sages (like Socrates and Aesop); to celestially translated superheroes (like Romulus and Osiris); and to Rank-Raglan tragic-ruler myths (like Hercules and Moses). He also belongs to several other sets of people whose members tend not to be historical:

- Conveniently named godmen ('Jesus' is 'Yahweh Saves').[67]
- Legendary cult founders.[68]
- Miracle-working sages.[69]
- Incarnated preexistent beings.[70]
- Worshiped savior-Lords.[71]
- Revelatory space aliens.[72]
- Heroes of sacred literature.[73]
- Dying-and-rising superheroes.[74]

[66] Carrier, *Historicity*, 222–34 (cf. 214–22), corresponding to 'elements' 46, 47, and 48 (with 44 and 45); likewise, *Historicity*, 168–73 ('element' 31) and 159–63 ('element' 29), and 430–31; and as discussed in Carrier, *Outer Space*, ch. 6, and *Proving History*, 131–32.

[67] Carrier, *Historicity*, 239–42.

[68] Carrier, *Historicity*, 8–11, 114–24, 159–63, 557–63.

[69] Carrier, *Historicity*, 230.

[70] Carrier, *Historicity*, 56–58, 230.

[71] Carrier, *Historicity*, 96–108, 114–24.

[72] Carrier, *Historicity*, 137–41, 146, 197–206; and ch. 11. On the designation 'space alien' here, see discussion in chapter two.

[73] Carrier, *Historicity*, 214–22.

[74] Carrier, *Historicity*, 168–73, 225–29, 239. See also chapter two.

- Improbable fulfillers of innumerable prophecies.[75]

And:

- Subjects of biographies that model their protagonist on mythical heroes they are meant to supersede (like Moses, Elijah, Odysseus, Romulus, and Dionysus), and are rife with fabulous and improbable events, and which name no sources, discuss no sources, and have no established sources.[76]

Revelatory gods. Preexistent incarnated supermen. Legendary kings and culture heroes. Worshiped savior deities. Mystery-cult sky-lords. Dying-and-rising demigods. Ancient heavenly founders. Literarily constructed religious heroes. Conveniently named godmen. Are these people *usually* historical? The answer is obviously 'no'. So how often, then, *are* they historical? Some, surely. But it's not going to be a very high frequency. These kinds of people usually don't exist. And yet Jesus is *all* these kinds of people. So the fact that Jesus belongs to so many sets whose members tend not to really exist (but all of whose members received biographies or other tales placing them in Earth history, just like Jesus) is already a clue that the prior odds on him existing are not going to be the same as for ordinary persons, like everyday leaders, administrators, or scholars; or even the same as for somewhat mythologized persons like Caesar Augustus.

The problem with all these sets, however, is that their memberships are small, or their data minimal, or both. So though they evoke suspicion—particularly when someone belongs to so many of them—they are still inadequate *by themselves* to mathematically determine the frequency of historicity within them. For example, in the Socrates-Aesop set, we have only two members, half of whom historical. But with so few members we cannot answer the question of whether the base rate of historicity for that set *is* the observed 50% or something else, because statistical anomalies are highly likely when you only get to see two instances.

For example, if the base rate of historicity for that set were actual-

[75] Carrier, *Historicity*, 141–43, 230; and ch. 10.

[76] Carrier, *Historicity*, ch. 10 (see also chapter two here).

ly 33%, the probability that selecting two members would get us one historical and one not is near 33% × 67% = 22% (rounded). That's the chance of drawing one historical person out of the hat, combined with the chance of then drawing one mythical person out of that hat.[77] That our observed result will then happen between one in four and one in five times of repeating the procedure leaves us unable to say that that hasn't happened in this case. Particularly because the same exact result holds if the base rate of historicity for that set were actually *twice* that, at 67%. The math is identical (you just swap terms: 67% × 33% = 22%). So observing a frequency of 50/50 after only two members have been selected is *just as likely* whether the base rate is 33% *or* 67%. And likewise many other probabilities. As the true base rates approach zero or one, eventually we can expect a 50/50 showing after only two draws to be too unlikely to consider; but that still leaves a very wide range of possible priors left over, which we cannot rule out. A set of such a small size is therefore of no use to us. You may as well just say the prior is 50% (the average of all possible priors, when each prior is equally likely), which is the same as starting with an uninformed prior (see chapter five).

This is why I ended up using the Rank-Raglan set as the proxy for all highly mythologized persons generally.[78] It has fifteen members, fourteen besides Jesus; and because so many features must be present to qualify as a member of that set, 'accidental' membership in the set is highly improbable. It's *hard* to be a member. And yet so many are. Which demonstrates the set is a real phenomenon. With so many members, any high rate of accidental membership should produce in it a high rate of historical persons—unless membership in that set was indeed indicative of usually being mythical. Hence I did not choose this set to trick anyone or game the calculations. And I did not invent the set. It clearly is not accidental, but a real microgenre, indeed one very popular at the time, and one that really does show a peculiarly high rate of non-historicity in

---

[77] The actual probability calculation is more complicated when we are drawing items from a hat with finite items, which is selection without replacement; the equation I am using assumes replacement, and thus that the hat has infinite members. But the difference in outcome, when rounded to a whole percent, is too negligible to concern us. A precise equation would depend on how many members are in the hat. For example, if there are twenty one, and thus seven are historical, to sequentially draw two members, one historical and one not, would be: 7/21 × 14/20 = 98/420 = 23% (rounded).

[78] Carrier, *Historicity*, 229–34 and 239–44.

its members.[79]

I thus chose the Rank-Raglan set because it allows us mathematical access to how often persons *that* mythologized tend to be historical. It merely proxies to the wider set of heavily mythologized persons generally. So we can count on the results being the same if we were to assemble in one hat a hodgepodge of all just-as-heavily mythologized heroes generally (all members of all the myth-heavy sets Jesus belongs to, and all comparable sets to those). The only way to disprove that would be to actually do the work: empirically assemble all the heavily (and not merely) mythical persons in Greco-Roman antiquity, and assess their likely historicity, and thus determine an average base rate across them all. I predict you will end up with no different result.

The reason that in such a procedure you need to limit your set to 'heavily' (and not merely) mythologized persons is that Jesus was not merely mythologized; and it is *heavily* mythologized persons who strongly tend not to exist. Since Jesus belongs to *that* set, we must not hide the effect of that fact by pretending he belongs to a less mythologized set *instead*. And the reason you need to limit your set to 'Greco-Roman antiquity' (at least inclusive of all peoples and cultures under the Roman Empire) is that other regions and eras are too culturally and causally different to be pertinent.[80] The base rates in them may be different for reasons not applicable when Christianity arose, and thus anachronistic to the region and era we are examining. And historians must avoid anachronism.

For example, once Christendom dominated the West, a trend toward making kings and heroes out to be like Christ flourished, a causal situation that did not exist when Christianity arose; likewise, after the printing press (and hence the rise of newspapers, globalism, and widespread literacy), the ability to get away with inventing historical people declined. Although it did not vanish—for it still happened in the cases of Mormon and Moroni, John Frum and Tom Navy, Ned Ludd, and other

[79] I had taken it for granted that scholars would already know this, but if not, they might need to read up on how literary genres are identified to understand my procedure: see Simon Evnine, "'But Is It Science Fiction?': Science Fiction and a Theory of Genre," *Midwest Studies in Philosophy* 39 (2015), 1-28; David Duff (ed), *Modern Genre Theory* (Routledge, 2000); and (most relevantly) Anne Stevens and Molly O'Donnell (eds), *The Microgenre: A Quick Look at Small Culture* (Bloomsbury Academic, 2020).

[80] Gregor and Hansen agree with this point in "Mytho-Historical Heroes."

inventions, like the Roswell saucer and alien autopsies—we still cannot say the rate of success *then* will have been *the same* as in antiquity when facts were far harder to check. So whatever those later trends produced is no longer wholly informative for antiquity. We have to look at the rate of success in antiquity: how often *then* (and in the cultural complex Christianity arose in) did highly mythical people get historicized—*and* how often did real people get just as mythologized as them, because it is the ratio between those two that determines the prior odds on any new example being one or the other, like Jesus.

We cannot object to this by appealing to the *possibility* of a heavily mythologized person being a real person. That possibility is already accounted for in the *probability*. Which derives from the *usual frequency* of that being the case, then and there. So if you wish to object to that *probability*, you are going to have to present evidence against it, which means evidence for the frequency being different than I found—a different frequency of heavily mythologized persons being historical. If you do not have adequate and genuine evidence that that frequency differs from what I calculated, you simply must accept that what I calculated from the data *are* the prior odds on someone like Jesus having nevertheless been historical. In the case of the Rank-Raglan class, I found those prior odds to be somewhere between 1 to 15 and 1 to 2, which equates to a member of that set (like Jesus) being expected to be real of, at most, 1 in 3 times (a roughly 33% chance), and at worst, 1 in 16 times (a roughly 6% chance).

I believe we can now narrow these error margins, as I'll explain shortly. But the range I arrived at was so wide because of all the uncertainties produced by the set still being small and the historicity of its members being in varying degrees uncertain. The two problems are mathematically related. Consider the small size of the set: though we only have fifteen members (we'd prefer at least a hundred, and ideally a thousand, for statistical precision), we can account for that by assigning a corresponding imprecision to our results (a wide margin of error).

For example, suppose for a moment that the *actual* base rate of someone really existing among 'all' Rank-Raglan members (including, say, dozens more we don't know about) was 80% (such that, really, '8 out of 10' persons in the Rank-Raglan class were historical), but we just *accidentally* ended up with a surviving record of fourteen non-historical ones (besides Jesus). The probability of that being the case is worked out the same way as for the two-member set earlier: we take 20% (the chance of drawing a non-historical person out of that hat in that case, which is 100% – 80%) and multiply it again by 20%, and so on, for every instance, which is in total fourteen times. Which you can enter into a calculator as 0.20^{14} (using the x^y function), which you'll then find equals 0.00000000016384, a figure ten decimal places below one, which is tens of billions to one against. So we can be pretty sure the base rate of being historical in the Rank-Raglan set was *not* 80%, given the data we have. Suppose, instead, that the real base rate were 50%. Then it's 0.50^{14} and thus 0.00006103515625, which is tens of thousands to one against. And so on down the line.

This all assumes random selection, of course; but to argue our selection isn't random (when it is complete: all possible members of the set in extant records have been accounted for) you would have to show that, somehow, the surviving record is *biased* towards preserving mythical examples of Rank-Raglan heroes and suppressing historical ones—which is neither in evidence nor plausible; and thus, unless you have evidence proving it, simply presuming it is a gerrymander (see chapter five). Far more likely what survives has been selected by the *random* happenstances of history; and what we have may even be complete, or close to complete—given what we know, it is not likely there are many 'lost' Rank-Raglan heroes. So we can safely assume random selection.

With that, you will find that when you repeat all this for every possible base rate (and there is advanced calculus that can figure that for you, but you'll see shortly why it won't be necessary here), the most probable base rate on what we observe is simply 1 in 16—the one I figured. Because I used Laplace's Rule of Succession to derive it.[81] Which is a formula developed for exactly this purpose: to determine the most likely base rate, given the observed rate, after averaging for all possible base rates. So that simply is what the evidence entails. And you can't argue against the evidence.

However, though that frequency is the most likely (compared to all others), there is *still* a decent chance of it being something else. The probability of getting our observed result if 1 in 16 is the true base rate is 0.9375^{14} (15/16 multiplied fourteen times), or about 40.5%. And it

[81] Carrier, *Historicity*, 243; *Proving History*, 337.

will be higher for lower base rates (obviously: for example, if the rate of historical persons is zero, the probability of drawing from that hat fourteen nonhistorical persons is then a full 100%). But if we factor in the prior probability of lower (and thus increasingly less likely) rates, the best-performing rate is simply 1 in 16. However, we can add up the probabilities of every possible base rate from 1 in 16 on up to, say, 1 in 3, and the probability that the base rate falls somewhere in-between *those* two values will be high enough to be confident it falls in that range and not outside it (and remember, falling outside it includes *both* all higher base rates *and* all lower ones, including zero).

To run that calculation requires integral calculus, which it is unreasonable to expect a historian to know. It is enough to know that the probability of our observation (fourteen straight selections from the hat, every one mythical), on an assumed 'true' frequency of 1 in 3 being historical, is only *a third of one percent* (2/3 multiplied fourteen times, which is 0.6667^{14} for 0.0034 or 0.34%). So if we summed the probabilities of each possible base rate all the way between 1 in 16 and 1 in 3, the total will be close enough to 100% that you can be confident it does fall somewhere in there, and not beyond. 1 in 3 is, after all, over three times higher a rate than the rate most likely, and the intervening span of 1 in 16 to 1 in 3 consumes almost a third of the entire space of possibilities. The true frequency is simply not likely to be higher.

Rather than use calculus, I arrived at that upper-end frequency by wildly over-estimating the number of historical persons in the set, which functionally is the same thing as assuming the base rate is higher than the data seem to indicate. Hence I assumed, contrary to the evidence, that four of its fourteen documented members were historical, for an expected base rate near 1 in 3. Which addressed the second problem: our uncertainty as to the historicity of its members. They all appear mythical. But maybe some aren't? By literally *inventing* historicity for a third of the set, on a basis of no evidence whatsoever, I have undeniably far *over*-estimated the rate of historicity in that set. So it cannot be argued that the frequency must be *yet higher than that*. It is therefore not reasonable to disagree with my estimated range of prior odds: given what I had shown by then, it's at worst 1 to 15 and at best 1 to 2—and thus at best a 1 in 3 chance. There is simply no factually informed way to argue the frequency is higher than 1 in 3. And that simply entails prior odds on any member existing of 1 to 2. And Jesus is a member. Logically, he must share the same prior odds as anyone else in the set.

If you want to argue Jesus is 'special' and therefore should have a higher final odds of existing than other members of this set, then you will have to present evidence *specific to Jesus*, showing that he is in fact special and not just any usual member of this set (or any other set he is in). And that is the role played by the next step in Bayesian reasoning: figuring the likelihood ratios for all the evidence specific to Jesus, and multiplying those by the prior odds, to get the final odds. But it is logically invalid to double-count that evidence. So when figuring the *prior* odds on Jesus existing, you *cannot* assume he is special. You must assume he is just like everyone else he is like. Only *evidence* can change that.

With this explained, it should be clear now how critics have simply been evading this—my actual point—and pretending I said something else instead. What they are supposed to be doing is either accepting that the empirical data entail that persons as heavily mythologized as Jesus tend not to exist, indeed no more than once in every three instances; or presenting *actual empirical data* demonstrating that persons as heavily mythologized as Jesus turn out to be historical *more often* than once in every three instances. But no one has ever succeeded at this; or even attempted it—not even Kamil Gregor's team, who only built 'merely' mythologized sets, which is simply not relevant to the heavily mythologized set. As my original study said: we are only supposed to be counting persons subject to "massive, rapid legendary development," not minor or trivial legendary development.[82] Instead, critics always handwave around these facts by either complaining about the trivia of the Rank-Raglan set (such as trying to get it to 'not be true' that Jesus belongs to that set, or putting him in some larger set, more of whose members are histor-

[82] Carrier, *Historicity*, 245. As we'll see, all Gregor and Hansen do in "Mytho-Historical Heroes" is build a larger set of 'merely' mythologized persons, which does not remove Jesus from the set of 'heavily' mythologized persons and its consequences (as I explain in "John Wick vs. Jesus" and already warned against as an inapplicable approach in Carrier, *Historicity*, 245–46). That also renders irrelevant the results in Gregor, Hansen, and Blais, "Prior Probability," which is entirely dependent on the results of "Mytho-Historical Heroes." But "Prior Probability" is additionally flawed by erroneously counting dramatic date over degree of mythologization when determining the prior probability of historicity, an error I explain in Carrier, "Causal Irrelevance," but had already warned against in my original study (Carrier, *Historicity*, 244–45).

ical), which misses the entire point of using that set (which is to proxy to the superset of all persons as heavily mythologized as Jesus, so as to ascertain *how often* such persons usually turn out to be historical), or else complaining that I did not allow the possibility that Jesus could be that heavily mythologized and still be historical, like Apollonius of Tyana—when I *did* allow for that; in fact, I allowed an impressive one in three chance of it.[83]

In answer to that second complaint, all that membership in the Rank-Raglan set entails is a certain *probability* of someone in that set being mythical; it does not 'negate their historicity' (as Gullotta ineptly claims).[84] In *Historicity* I was repeatedly clear: the question is not whether there are historical Rank-Raglan heroes; the question is *how often* Rank-Raglan heroes are historical. To get a different result than mine simply requires rolling up your sleeves and doing the work, of collecting empirical data and counting results: by that means (and that means alone) you could get a different frequency out of the Rank-Raglan set. Or maybe you can get a different frequency from some other pertinent set, like the superset of all heavily mythologized people. But if you aren't even endeavoring to find out, then you can have no valid criticism of my results. My results are factual. So if you want a different result, you're going to need some facts.

That leaves the first complaint. This ranges from trying to claim the Rank-Raglan set doesn't exist (but as demonstrated in chapter three, *all* the folklore and mythology literature agrees that it does) to trying to claim that Jesus isn't in it (which can only be accomplished by denying plain facts of similarity in generic features between the Gospels, even just Mark, and the Rank-Raglan microgenre). But neither of those approaches is factually valid, either.

First of all, it is extraordinarily improbable by chance accident that we could gerrymander *fourteen* ancient persons into a set requiring *a dozen* peculiar features to belong. The only credible explanation for this is that the set exists: it represents a real microgenre replicated across ancient mythology. It is not the only mythic genre (nor even the only

---

[83] All the critics mentioned in chapter three who even mention my use of the Rank-Raglan set do one or both: Gullotta, "Doubts," 340–44; Litwa, *Gospels*, 35–38; Hansen, "Raglan's Hero"; and even Gregor and Hansen, "Mytho-Historical Heroes," as just noted.

[84] Gullotta, "Doubts," 344.

one I looked at); it's just one so popular then that it was more replicated than any other, allowing us to see how often that scale of mythologization happened to real people. We can expect any other 'high myth' genre will share the same frequency of historical persons drawn in. We certainly have no basis for believing that that will be a higher frequency, as if somehow the Rank-Raglan genre was unusually more predictive of non-historicity than any other high-myth genre. But even if by some unevidenced mechanism it was, Jesus is in the set. So it predicts he was mythical just as much as anyone else in that set.

Which is why the next tactic is to try and get Jesus out of the set. But that can't factually be done. (1) Can we honestly say the Gospels never declare Jesus the heir of a king (Mark 10:47–48, 12:35–37)? (2) Or the son of a god (Mark 1:1, 1:9–11, 3:11, 5:7, 15:39)? (3) Or as being hailed king of his people (Mark 11; 15:2, 18, 26)? (4) Or as forsaken by his god and people just before his death (Mark 15:9–14, 34)? (5) Or as then driven from his city and reign (Mark 15:12–22)? (6) Or that the Gospels never described his death and its circumstances as surprising (Mark 15:33–34, 37–39, 44)? (7) Or never locate it on a hill or high place (Mark 15:22)? (8) Or never say he had a tomb (9) or that his body went missing from it (Mark 16)? (10) Or never narrate him defeating a great adversary before coming into his kingdom—even though 'Satan' literally means 'Adversary' and is a considerable monster to overcome (Mark 1:13; Matthew 4:1–11)? (11) Can we honestly say the Gospels never say Jesus was raised by someone who was not his father (Matthew 1; Luke 1–2, 3:23–38)? (12) Or never mention his mother being a virgin (Matthew 2; Luke 1)? (13) Or never describe the circumstances of his conception as unusual (Matthew 2; Luke 1)? (14) Or never narrate an attempt on his life as a baby (15) or his thus being smuggled out of the country to escape it (Matthew 2)? (16) Or never narrate Jesus coming into his kingdom after being away (Mark 11)? (17) Or never have Jesus then promulgate laws (Mark 12; Matthew 5)? (18) Can we honestly say they narrated wars or natural catastrophes befalling his reign? (19) Or describe Jesus as having children to succeed him? (20) Can we honestly say that any Gospel narrates his childhood? Matthew skips it entirely. Mark skips even the birth. Luke 2:40–42 is the only account that comes close, and even that basically skips over it until near or at Jesus's bar mitzvah—and allowing *that* to nevertheless count here would only drop

Jesus by one point, not enough to matter.[85]

In Mark's story alone, Jesus satisfies fourteen of these features, out of what we know to be twenty-two in all, every one of them unusual. Matthew brings the count to twenty; almost every feature known to the genre.[86] Most people are not royal scions, nor get buried in tombs, nor promulgate laws; nor any of the rest. Most are not targeted with assassination as a baby, for example, much less smuggled away and raised in a foreign land to avoid it. And almost none are attended by miracles and wonders, like bizarre conceptions and deaths, or win a battle-of-wits with the Devil. Most people aren't even born to women who were virgins at their conception (only a firstborn can ever claim such, and only if their mother had no prior husbands or partners; while only half of firstborn children are even sons in the first place, and most ancient mothers had more than two children), and yet that's all that's required for the genre to be satisfied—the authors of the Gospels after Mark went one better than this requirement of the genre by even making their hero's mother a virgin *at his birth*, which certainly no historical person can claim. A person who has this many mythical features attached to them—and features derived from a singular genre typical of mythical people, no less—certainly qualifies as heavily mythologized. The more so as so many more myth-indicating features are attached to Jesus than even these (such as miracle working, fulfilling prophecy, and emulating prior mythical heroes).

Those who can't stomach denying these facts try to solve the problem the other way around: by trying to nitpick how these criteria are semantically defined, so as to get *everyone else* out of the set. But these tactics are always purely rhetorical, like trying to 'change' or 'apply' the criteria so narrowly that no one qualifies anymore, such as insisting that because Jesus never literally sat on a physical throne, that he therefore

[85] As I already noted: Carrier, *Historicity*, 234. Some might also argue that Golgotha is not identified as a hill in Mark 15:22, but Roman crucifixions were meant to be visible, thus implying an elevated place, and Mark translates the Aramaic as the place of 'a' skull (not of *skulls*, plural), which would have suggested to ancient readers its appearance as a mound (the Greek word he uses is *kranion*, which literally refers to the skullcap).

[86] Jesus might even allegorically fit all twenty-two, but I did not consider that in my scoring because the last two matches are debatable: Carrier, *History*, 233–34.

can never have been 'driven from his throne'.[87] But 'throne' has always been a metaphor for a king's reign, not a literal technicality requiring an actual throne to be mentioned. Likewise the reign itself: the story does not require Jesus to have been literally, politically, crowned as a king; it only requires that he be hailed and recognized as one, a major feature of every Gospel. This tactic is like insisting that because *Hamlet* features a knife, no play can be classified as a tragedy unless a knife is involved in the story. Genres do not work that way. Once a scholar has discovered a genre and factually described the generic features shared across instantiations of that genre, you cannot make that genre 'go away' by redefining the features so that no story belongs to that genre anymore. All you are really then doing is defining *a different genre*, one that doesn't exist. That does not make the other genre disappear from the historical record.

Semantics cannot get you out of facts. Otto Rank and Lord Raglan both gave slightly different lists of criteria with different wording, and their wording was always more allusive than precise. For example, Rank described one criterion as being the 'child of distinguished parents', whereas Raglan more specifically says the hero's father is a king and his mother of the same royal family. In truth, neither wording precisely matches how they applied the criterion. When we look at heroes that score above half their criteria, the feature they all share (if they score this feature at all) is that they are the scion of a king (or the equivalent of a king, like a tribal chieftain or *de facto* monarch), regardless of whether through their father or an ancestor, and thus they are the *heir* of a king. Likewise that their mother is related to their father by blood (a feature Jesus does not score—until apocryphal Gospels later added it, by which time Infancy Gospels also appeared relating Jesus' childhood, the two criteria then canceling each other out). Hence I correctly reworded these genre features as 'his father is a king or the heir of a king' and 'his parents are related to each other'. This more accurately describes the microgenre that Rank and Raglan each identified, and from their own examples of it. Alan Dundes concurred, exemplified by his own application of this genre to Jesus; hence I cited and employed his findings (this was not any innovation of mine).[88]

---

[87] Hansen, "Lord Raglan's Hero," 144 (see other examples in chapter three).

[88] It should also be self-evident that I did not adopt either Rank or Raglan's ordering

One might still quibble over the scores we all assigned (perhaps in one case or another they should go up or down by one or two features), but in no case yet has anyone shown that any member of the Rank-Raglan set does not belong in it. Even the most skeptical (but still honest) scoring leaves no one on the list with a feature-count less than twelve. For example, Hercules never 'literally' is a king (in fact one of the features of his story is that he was supposed to be but fates always conspire to prevent it). I still allow him to score the trope because he does *effectively* reign (in much the way Jesus or Moses do), and thus I rated him the 17 points that Raglan and Dundes did. But even if we allowed this not to count, Hercules still scores 16. More than enough. By contrast, I do think Hercules should not have been scored on the 'reigns uneventfully' feature because none of his would-be reigns lacked wars to prosecute or catastrophes to avert (however much one might quibble about that). But dropping that feature, too, still leaves him with a score of 15. Well above the 12 needed to qualify as 'heavily mythologized' into that set.[89]

The closest one might get to knocking someone out of the genre is the fact that the biblical hero Joseph scores 12, yet the attempt made on his life occurs when he is "seventeen years old" (Genesis 37:2), not as a baby.[90] And this is thwarted by his would-be killers—unable to go through with it—selling him off into slavery in a foreign land instead (Genesis 37). The latter still counts, as it matters not to the genre *how* the youngling is "spirited away from those trying to kill him," nor that his foster 'parents' are actually his 'owners' (just as it matters not whether a tragedy involves a knife): Joseph is still spirited away from his would-be killers, still ends up in a foreign land, and without his parents (but with custodians in their place). But one might ask whether we should down-score Joseph because the attempt on his life occurs at the age of seventeen, which would leave his score at 11, just below the cut-off.

By the same logic we would have to down-score Jesus by the fact that Luke tells one story of him at age twelve. Which is the last year of

of criteria (Carrier, *Historicity*, 229–30). The order has no effect on the outcome; I chose mine only to simplify my ensuing discussion and analysis.

[89] Gregor and Hansen, in "Mytho-Historical Heroes," offer various re-scoring of the heroes I listed which might be preferable to the Rank-Raglan-Dundes scoring, but, as we'll see shortly, none end up below 12, thus having no effect on my results.

[90] As suggested in Gregor and Hansen, "Mytho-Historical Heroes."

childhood and could have been imagined occurring at the conclusion of it (Jewish boys were declared men upon their thirteenth birthday), but one could still count that as "a story of his childhood."[91] That would hardly matter, because Jesus going from 20 to 19 makes no difference to the conclusion that he is in the set; as anyone scoring over half the full 22 (and hence more than 11) is. He still scores 20 in Matthew's version of the myth as well, which is earlier than Luke's. But for Joseph it *would* matter whether we should count "an attempt is made to kill him as a baby" that is actually narrated of the hero in his teen years.

I believe this signals another poor description of his own criteria by Lord Raglan, one I failed to correct. The story of the attempt on Joseph's life is too apposite to consider accidental, as if it were not an intentional emulation of the genre. The attempt is based on the killers' desire to prevent the youngling coming to rule over them (Gen. 37:8), based on a prophecy thereof (Gen. 37:7), and involved creating a belief that the hero has indeed been done away with (Gen. 37:31–35); while his murder is avoided by circumstances almost comical (Gen. 37:21–29) and someone ultimately having pity on the abandoned youngling (Gen. 37:21–22, 29). These are all features shared by many of the infancy narratives that score the 'attempt on life' criterion elsewhere (such as Moses and Romulus). And Raglan himself scored it. So he clearly understood his own designation ('at birth') as only *typical*, not *definitive* of the genre. So I think we should (and I now would) revise the criterion to say, "An attempt is made to kill him in his youth (usually an infant)." Which would also raise my score for Mithradates.[92] The rest comes out the same. For example, Gregor's team correctly point out that Joseph should also be down-scored owing to a famine under his reign (as related in Genesis 47, thus discounting him on my criterion 11 measuring an uneventful reign, just like Hercules), but if we also up-score Mithradates for merely having a sepulcher (my criterion 19), as they also argue, then we must do so for Joseph, too, leaving him within the genre at a score of 12.[93] So Joseph should remain scored at 12. Which marks no change to my results.

---

[91] Carrier, *Historicity*, 234n199 ("counting this as a story of his childhood anyway would still only reduce his score from 20 to 19").

[92] Reversing Carrier, *Historicity*, 232n193.

[93] Genesis 50:22–26; Exodus 13:19; Joshua 24:32.

That leaves only one other evasion to attempt: trying to claim more historical people are in the 'heavily mythologized' side of the Rank-Raglan set than I counted. Only one serious attempt at this has been made, and it has born at least some fruit. Gregor's group have convinced me that Alexander the Great belongs in the set, as do Mithradates of Pontus and Apollonius of Tyana.[94] This has no major effect on my results, since I already granted four historical members, and even rounded up; so to get a higher prior probability than I did, one needs to not only get historical people into the set (by *legitimately* scoring more than half of the genre's twenty-two features), but *more than four*. So adding Apollonius, Mithradates, and Alexander in makes little difference. You need twice that. So Gregor's team tries to get some thirty more persons into the set, but only by describing a larger set of 'merely' mythologized persons (broadening the Rank-Raglan criteria to include almost anyone), not the set I was describing, which is of 'heavily' mythologized persons (or "massively" mythologized, as my original study put it). I maintained that necessary feature by keeping all the criteria narrowly genre-specific.[95] Only Apollonius, Mithradates, and Alexander actually enter the set by *those* criteria.

This means the only substantial effect the Gregor team's findings have on my results is that they narrow my margins of error when estimating the prior probability of historicity for members of my high-scoring Rank-Raglan set. As I mentioned earlier, I used Laplace's Law, $(s + 1)/(n + 2)$, which entails the number of historical persons in that set (plus one) is to be divided by the number of total persons in the set (plus two) to derive the expected base rate of historical members in the set.[96] As we are determining the rate applicable to Jesus, we exclude him from the count, leaving 14 total members. Gregor and Hansen's results can reckon that now as 17 members. So we should update the Laplacean equation for the base rate of historicity in the high-scoring Rank-Raglan set from $(0 + 1)/(14 + 2) = 1/16$ (approximately 6%) on the lower bound and $(4 + 1)/(14 + 2) = 5/16$ (approximately 31%, which I generously rounded to 33% to make an even one third chance) on the upper bound, now to

[94] Gregor and Hansen, "Mytho-Historical Heroes."

[95] For a more detailed explanation see Carrier, "John Wick vs. Jesus."

[96] Carrier, *Historicity*, 243.

(3 + 1)/(17 + 2) = 4/19 (approximately 21%) on the lower bound and (4 + 1)/(17 + 2) = 5/19 (approximately 26%) on the upper bound (see the Appendix for an updated table of probabilities).

Ironically, this means Gregor and Hansen have actually *reduced* the maximum prior probability that Jesus was historical (from 33% to 26%). However, their result substantially increases the *minimum* prior (from 6% to 21%). Which demonstrates that the prior probability for Jesus was indeed closer to my upper margin of error. But this is all within my study's allowed tolerances. I predicted the prior would fall between 6% and 33%, and they have simply confirmed that. If we went a step further and allowed that Moses and Joseph were historical (despite there being no principled reason to), we would have five historical persons out of the seventeen, and the upper bound would be (5 + 1)/(17 + 2) = 6/19 or about 32%, which I would then generously round again to my originally estimated 33%. And so we would be right back where I started, at 2 to 1 prior odds Jesus didn't exist. So there is simply no way to get the prior probability that Jesus existed above what I already concluded it to be.

Which leaves only one tactic left: to pad a bunch of historical persons' credentials to shoehorn them into the genre, when in fact they don't fit. This is what Gregor and Hansen did, absurdly counting waging wars as 'uneventful reigns', and 'having tutors' as 'having foster parents', and 'idle threats' as 'assassination attempts', and 'schoolmasters' as 'kings', and 'omens of a hero's impending death' as 'mysterious events at their death', and so on, thereby filling up a set with non-fabulous members. Their procedure is logically invalid. They are ignoring that this is a *genre* (more precisely, a micro-genre), and the generic features we are examining must fit the genre. And they are ignoring the fact that building a larger set to which Jesus belongs does not remove him from other sets to which he still also belongs. Jesus simply belongs to both sets; while the effect of belonging to the 'heavily mythologized' set remains. I thus already refuted the argument of Gregor's team in my original study, devoting an entire section there to the error they are committing.[97] But evidently

[97] Carrier, *Historicity*, 245–46 (§6.5, 'The Alternative Class Objection'). I then anticipated and refuted several other arguments bearing on the prior (including §6.6, 'The Complexity Objection', 246–48, and §6.7, the 'Rapid Legendary Development' objection, 248–52).

more needs to be said.[98]

Consider a modern analogy. Modern cinema is rife now with the 'righteous mass killer' mythotype. Lately the most popular member of this reference class is the entire *John Wick* franchise. But the micro-genre—the hero-type—goes back decades. *Magnum Force*, *Death Wish*, *Commando*, *A Better Tomorrow*, *Raw Deal*, *Die Hard*, *El Mariachi*, *Leon the Professional*, *Shoot 'Em Up*, *Man on Fire*, *Taken*, *The Man from Nowhere*, *Nobody* (and that's just the short list; there are easily dozens of instantiations of this myth in cinema spanning the last fifty years), all evolved from the Western genre, with early examples like *Navajo Joe* and *Shane,* and later examples like *The Outlaw Josey Wales*, and early 'blaxploitation' cinema, with examples like *Shaft* and *Hit Man*. These are clearly distinctive and related—they clearly demarcate a genre—even though they do not each share *all* of the typical characteristics of that genre, and even though they instantiate those characteristics in different ways. Yet the genre is clearly real.

The characteristics of this micro-genre principally include these: (1) a lone hero (2) somehow ends up in such a narratively convoluted set of circumstances that, despite their not being in an actual war, they are morally justified in murdering (3) a large number of people (4) who are always violent criminals or conspiring with such, and the hero is (5) typically motivated by rescuing a loved one, or avenging one who was murdered. Often (6) the hero is a man (7) with a violent past attempting to escape it (they might be fleeing that life, for example, or a retired or weary assassin); (8) the villains represent a larger threat to society an audience will be happy to see killed off (such as a criminal syndicate, terrorist cell, evil government, or sex-slave operation) and (9) who are led by a principal villain, whether the worst of them or the cause of their vile enterprise, (10) who must ultimately be killed as well. And typically (11) the hero will suffer some set-back that seems surely to spell their doom (such as becoming trapped, captured, cornered, or injured), (12) from which they will escape and triumph.

Any film meeting more than half of these criteria (seven or more) could still be describing historical people on occasion (maybe?). But if we look at the narrower subset of that superset (films that meet at

[98] I say more in Carrier, "John Wick vs. Jesus." Here I only summarize the key points.

least eight criteria, for example, or even ten), we still find a large number of films (at least twelve), in which the number of historical persons depicted plummets. And yet by that measure no real person ever qualifies for the genre. There are *zero* historical instantiations of this hero-type. Which is because the convoluted, hyper-specific arrangement of circumstances needed to justify a lone mass shooter are too extraordinarily improbable to ever actually happen (just like even half of a Rank-Raglan tale).

You could do what Gregor's team did, and 'expand' the criteria so broadly as to allow any mass shooter to qualify—for example, we could count a mass murderer's claim to be defending their nation or race as somehow 'protecting' or 'avenging' a loved one, and count any challenge they faced as a 'setback' from which they 'triumphed'—but then we wouldn't be looking at an instantiation of the genre. Certainly, John Wick belongs to a set of all mass shooters, most of whom are historical; but John Wick also belongs to a narrower set of *fantastical* mass shooters, most of whom are *not* historical. We cannot introduce the former fact as an excuse to ignore the latter fact. The latter fact does not go away—and in result, the prior probability of a Wick-style hero being historical remains low.

Which is why these films have such specific and complex narratives. The sequence of events needed to get the audience to agree that the protagonist in *Die Hard*, John McClane, needs to kill everyone he does is bizarrely convoluted: for reasons, the authorities can't take care of it; for reasons, the villains are numerous and all bloodthirsty killers with infinite morale; for reasons, they are all easily identified as bloodthirsty killers; for reasons, the villains actually think they can get away with whatever they are doing, even though their operation is so exposed and vulnerable a single person can completely dismantle it; plus, it just so happens, someone the killer loves has been kidnapped and threatened with death, or actually killed; and, for reasons, there is no way to rescue or avenge them through legitimate means. Also, for reasons, the hero's murder rampage never puts innocent bystanders in danger. There somehow isn't even risk of stray bullets killing children in their sleep down the street.

It is thus safe to say that if you ever encountered a 'biography' of someone who meets in it at least eight, much less even ten, of the twelve criteria for the 'righteous mass murderer' myth, you would agree almost certainly that person did not exist—no matter how much any religious group believes they did. You surely would require a lot of really good (*not* ambiguous) evidence that they existed before you would grant they were an exception to the rule that such persons typically don't exist. You would not accept arguments against this stance like 'the genre doesn't exist, therefore you cannot infer members of it are probably fictional' or 'we can get a lot of historical people in if we manipulate the descriptive criteria for the genre' or 'John Wick doesn't belong to the genre, because a dog can't be a loved one and thus Wick doesn't score on point five, therefore he is probably a historical person' (that argument isn't even logical, much less correct: Wick's beloved dog was *intentionally* included in the script to play precisely that narrative role).

When there is no personal, institutional, or cultural pressure to insist John Wick is a historical person, you are easily able to recognize that he probably isn't, and you get that just from his belonging to a micro-genre well-known to be populated with mythical people. You also easily understand that it would take more than ambiguous or questionable evidence to convince you he was the rare exception, and John Wick really did exist after all. You would have no difficulty admitting both that 'the prior odds on John Wick existing are low, because most members of his mythotype don't exist' and that 'I can be convinced John Wick nevertheless existed if I am presented enough evidence to overcome those prior odds against it'. Only when it's Jesus do we suddenly forget all this.

That must end. We need to treat Jesus just like every other legendary hero he resembles, and not as some unique exception to every rule in the world.

Conclusion

Jesus looks like a mythical person. By every possible genre analysis, set of criteria, or feature-list you could ever legitimately bring to bear, there is simply no way to say this is not the case. And the Gospels are unmistakably mythographies—even as biographies, they are self-evidently *mythic* biographies, as long established in the field, from the first to the twenty-fifth anniversary edition of Richard Burridge's *What Are the Gospels?* (see chapter two). Their content and construction resemble no other classification of storytelling. Any other figure as heavily mythologized as Jesus would be classified as a mythical person. And we would admit the prior odds on their existing are therefore low. Indeed we would readily accept an upper estimate on those odds of 2 to 1 against; we might even think that too generous.

We would also admit that we need more than ambiguous or questionable evidence to convince us any other such person existed. We would not treat Jesus differently than anyone else like him, whether Ned Ludd or John Frum, or the Roswell flying saucer and the bodies of its extraterrestrial pilots, or the angels Moroni or Gabriel, or the heroes Hercules or Dionysus, or the patriarchs Moses or Abraham. And we know what it takes, because we can see the kind of evidence that convinces us anyone else existed. It is far better evidence than we have for Jesus. Indeed, we have more and better evidence even for personages whose historicity we are not entirely certain of (like Apollonius). But clear-cut cases are even worse. Jesus is not like Hannibal or Spartacus. He is like Moroni and John Frum. So not only do the prior odds favor him being mythical, but even the evidence particular to him leaves no other conclusion.

If anyone resisting that realization has at least accepted this much, they will fall back to the last rampart of defense: attempting to maintain that, yes, prior odds favor Jesus being made-up, but we really do have enough, and good enough, evidence to turn that around and assure us that he did, nevertheless, really exist—that he wasn't just a revelatory being given an earthly mythography a generation or more later, like so many other ancient savior heroes. Those final ramparts may be some attempt to recover history from outside the Bible (but alas, no external references can be established to be independent of Bible), or from the Gospels (but as we have seen in this and previous chapters, none of those efforts are sound; myth-making always ends up just as good or better an explanation for all of their contents). So really only one rampart has any chance of holding: trying to extract some historical Jesus from the Epistles. But that will inevitably also falter. For no evidence there rises beyond the status of 'ambiguous or questionable', which is simply not sufficient to warrant any confidence Jesus existed.

I will demonstrate that in the closing chapters of this book. But first I'll take a brief detour into the overlooked evidence of some early Christians who might have been trying to tell us that the earthly sojourn of Jesus was indeed a myth.

7

The Mistaken Invention of Docetism

Docetism is entirely a modern construct, invented by scholars of the last two centuries, possibly based on some orthodox polemics of late antiquity. But no such thing actually existed in early antiquity. And that false paradigm has led to numerous errors in understanding early Christianity, missing the actual point and context of a lot of early Christian literature. And among those errors is overlooking the possibility that some of this misinterpreted evidence makes better sense when understood as a response to Christians denying the earthly historicity of Jesus Christ. Which would then be an example of how adopting mythicism as a paradigm opens up new understandings of history, beyond merely questions relating to Jesus.

But to illustrate this point, I must first digress on another.

The Mistaken Invention of Gnosticism

As I was completing my postdoctoral research program on the historicity of Jesus I started to suspect that the modern construct of 'Gnosticism' didn't really exist. I had so little confidence in it that I never even mention it in *Historicity*. Gnosticism plays no part in my understanding of the origin or early development of Christianity. This is surprising to the uninformed, who often think 'mythicism' depends on Gnosticism as part of its explanatory model. It does not. I had no use for it. It describes nothing. It explains nothing. I think it was never actually a thing.

My conclusion was confirmed when, to my surprise, the Westar Institute (of which I have since become a fellow), in the very year I published *Historicity*, published its official report on the subject, and it came to the same result: Gnosticism did not exist; it is entirely a construct of modern scholarship.[1] That two dozen eminent scholars unanimously reached the same decision I did, quite independently, pretty well confirms that our conclusion is correct. Gnosticism is on the junk heap. It has no value anymore as an interpretive category. It either refers to no actual thing that existed in antiquity, or when defined vaguely enough to actually encompass anything that did, it then refers to practically every sect of Christianity, 'orthodox' or not, and thus distinguishes none. The word is therefore useless and ought to be abandoned.

Which illustrates a general methodological point I have made in earlier chapters. It turns out that when you stop repeating the dogmas of the field built on the shoulders of mere prestige, and stop seeing everything through that lens, and instead just look at the evidence as it actually is, things start to look quite different. Doubting Jesus becomes more credible, just like doubting there was a Q source; and now, doubting Gnosticism.[2] No ancient author ever discussed any sect or grouping of sects as 'Gnostics' as if that were a title or even distinguished anyone from anyone else. And there was no ancient group that possessed all of the modernly-attributed features supposed to signify 'Gnosticism'; while every Christian group possessed one or more of those features, or

---

[1] Hal Taussig, "Christianity Seminar: A Report on the 2014 Fall Meeting," *The Fourth R* 28.2 (2015), 21–24, briefed the report that was released by committee the previous year. Then Maia Kotrosits (ed.), "Reflections on the Category Gnosticism," special issue of *Forum: Foundations and Facts* 5.1 (2016), covered the results in more detail. All of which led to a chapter in the final seminar publication: Erin Vearncombe, Brandon Scott, and Hal Taussig, *After Jesus Before Christianity: A Historical Exploration of the First Two Centuries of Jesus Movements* (HarperOne, 2021), 216–231 ('Demolishing Gnosticism'). See also Einar Thomassen, "There Is No Such Thing as Gnosticism: But What Have We Got Instead?" in *Nag Hammadi a 70 Ans. Qu'avons-Nous Appris? Nag Hammadi at 70: What Have We Learned?* (ed. Eric Crégheur, Louis Painchaud, and Tuomas Rasimus; Peeters Publishers, 2019), 3–16.

[2] On the increasing dubiousness of the Q-hypothesis, see note 24 in chapter two.

some version of them.

For instance, before the contrivances of the Nicene Council,[3] every sect of Christianity on which we have information on the point believed in a distinct Entity who created the universe at God's behest, and in some kind of secret knowledge ('gnosis') that was essential to ensuring one's salvation, and a dualist view of the cosmos in which the lower world of flesh was corrupted by meddling (usually fallen) divine beings while the upper world's God and his hosts were awaiting a chance to destroy it all and start over, and to help us escape our corrupt bodies and locations by fleeing into superior celestial ones. Indeed, all of these beliefs are affirmed repeatedly by Paul.[4]

Hence the paradigmatic 'Gnostic' sect is a fiction. Marcionism, for example, did credit Creation to a bumbling Demiurge from whom Jesus had to save us, contrary to Paul who credited it to Jesus (and its ruination to Satan). But Marcion's sect was otherwise no different from Paul's in any other respect supposedly distinctive of Gnosticism. Paul's sect, meanwhile, credited all the evils of the world to that world's corruption by Satan and his fallen legion and their progeny, the demons. The difference from Marcion's Demiurge theory is almost trivial. Either way, the idea that this Creation is corrupt and evil and we have to escape it is not only entirely orthodox, it's canonical.[5] When ancient authors used the word *gnôstikos*, they did not intend it as a proper noun, but as a mere nominal adjective. It simply meant 'those who claimed to know things'; while their critics claimed to know things, too—just different things. Hence they weren't attacking other sects for claiming *gnôsis*. They were attacking them for claiming *the wrong gnôsos*.

The scholarship I cited in the first note of this chapter covers all the ins and outs of this revelation. But I will close my point here with a paradigmatic example. Someone might object to all this by pointing out that (supposedly) Irenaeus titled his entire anti-heretical masterwork

---

[3] On which see Bart Ehrman's survey of what led up to that, and why it created a Frankenstein's monster of a creed that never existed before, in *How Jesus Became God: The Exaltation of a Jewish Preacher from Galilee* (HarperOne, 2014).

[4] Carrier, *Historicity*, 92–96, 108–14, 180–93; for example: 1 Cor. 8:6 and 15:34–58, 2 Cor. 4–5, Gal. 4–5, Rom. 7–8 and 12:2, etc.

[5] 2 Peter 2–3; 1 Thess. 4; Jude; Romans 7–8; Galatians 4; 1 John 2 and 5; Ephesians 6; Colossians 2; 1 Corinthians 15; 2 Corinthians 4-5.

"On the Detection and Overthrow of the Gnostics." Surely, then, Gnostics existed, and were even described as such in antiquity? But that's a false translation—a product of that false modern paradigm. The actual Greek reads *Elegchos kai Anatropê tês Pseudônymou Gnôseôs*, "Refuting and Overthrowing False Knowledge." Those last two words, forming a phrase from 1 Timothy 6:20, are *pseudônymos* and *gnôsis*, 'false knowledge'—not 'Gnostics'. There is no proper noun here at all. Nor is *gnôsis* the target, but 'false' *gnôsis*.

So our modern dogma has corrupted even the translation of this text; but also, in result, its interpretation. For if that work is not about 'Gnostics', then its contents cannot be related to that paradigm, either. In reality the title simply refers to everyone Irenaeus disagrees with—all people who 'claim to know' but, really, what they claim is false. It's just a synonym for heresy. All of which consists of what Irenaeus believed to be *false* claims to special knowledge; not *claims to* special knowledge, which even Ireneaeus affirms. Because all across his refutations of his opponents he fills his text with the special knowledge he claims is correct and thus refutes them.

Hence when Irenaeus says "Valentinus adapted the principles" of "the so-called 'gnostic' heresy" (*apo tês legomenês gnôstikês haireseôs*), he did not actually mean what modern translations do. Rather, he simply meant "the heresy called 'knowing'," as in, any heresy based on false knowledge rather than true knowledge (as Irenaeus saw it). Hence my noting that *gnôstikos*, the word usually translated 'Gnostic', really just meant 'one who claims to know', or in other words, 'one who claims to know *better*.' What Irenaeus is accusing Valentinus of is not of 'being a Gnostic', but of knowing things, secret things about the cosmos, that are false. Irenaeus is not saying anyone claiming to know secret things about the cosmos is a heretic. Irenaeus himself believed he knew secret things about the cosmos too—they were just different things than Valentinus. That is his point. The *gnôsis* Valentinus claimed to have was wrong—only orthodox *gnôsis* was correct.

Hence the phrases *pseudônymos gnôsis* and *legomenos gnostikos* designate no set of beliefs at all. They simply mean 'people I disagree with'.

Et Tu, Docetism?

I long suspected this was also true of Docetism. Although unlike Gnosticism, ancient heresiologists *did* name a sect 'the Docetists', but that sect had nothing to do with the modern concept. What ancient heresiologists meant by that term does not correspond to what modern scholars reinvented that word to mean at all. 'Docetism' as now and commonly understood is a modern construct, not an ancient one. It is like Gnosticism. It simply did not exist.

I am not alone. Such doubts have already been brewing across academia for a while now.[6] The category of 'docetism' is now called 'defunct' by M. David Litwa,[7] while in a preface to a recent volume entirely devoted to the subject we find the bold declaration that "it is far from certain that there really existed anything like a docetic movement or tendency in earliest Christianity," and "it is not certain that Ignatius," usually cited as attesting it, "was aiming at a particular group, nor that he used the label appropriately" (in fact, as we'll see, he didn't use it at all). Because "the origins of the concept and the phenomena that hide behind it or are referred to with this term are diverse and often not easy to grasp," with the result that "some scholars have argued that there never existed such a thing as Docetism and that it is all a modern construct."[8] As T.C. Hoklotubbe observes, "many early Christian teachers and texts have been mischaracterized as docetic" to the point that "docetism, just as Karen L. King has argued about the term Gnosticism, is 'a rhetorical term [that]

---

[6] T. Christopher Hoklotubbe, "What is Docetism?," in *Re-Making the World: Christianity and Categories: Essays in Honor of Karen L. King* (ed. Taylor Petrey: Siebeck 2019), 49–71; Karen King, "Reconsidering Docetism," in *Nag Hammadi a 70*, 17–30; Joseph Verheyden, Reimund Bieringer, Jens Schröter, and Ines Jäger (eds.), *Docetism in the Early Church: The Quest for an Elusive Phenomenon* (Mohr Siebeck, 2018); Heike Omerzu, "'My Power, Power, You Have Left Me': Christology in the Gospel of Peter," in *Connecting Gospels: Beyond the Canonical/Non-Canonical Divide* (ed. Francis Watson and Sarah Parkhouse; Oxford University Press, 2018), 163–88; David Wilhite, "Was Marcion a Docetist? The Body of Evidence vs. Tertullian's Argument," *Vigiliae Christianae* 71.1 (2017), 1–36; Jean-Daniel Dubois, "Le Docétisme des Christologies Gnostiques Revisité," *New Testament Studies* 63.2 (2017), 279–304; P.M. Head, "On the Christology of the Gospel of Peter," *Vigiliae Christianae* 46.3 (1992), 209–24; Jerry McCant, "The Gospel of Peter: Docetism Reconsidered," *New Testament Studies* 30.2 (1984), 258–73.

[7] M. David Litwa in *Found Christianities: Remaking the World of the Second Century CE* (T&T Clark, 2022), 262n31.

[8] Verheyden et al., *Docetism*, 1.

has been confused with a historical entity'," and so we should "set aside our modern category of docetism" and move on.[9] I agree.

What is this anachronistic modern construct? The entry on Docetism in the *Oxford Dictionary of the Christian Church* offers a vague summary: "In the early Church," we are told, Docetism was "a tendency, rather than a formulated and unified doctrine, which considered the humanity and sufferings of the earthly Christ as apparent rather than real." This would make even Paul a Docetist (who says Christ was "made in human *likeness*" and "being *in appearance* as a man," Philippians 2:6–8), so it is largely useless as a distinguishing description.[10] We should look to the more ambitious entry in *Eerdmans Dictionary of the Bible*: Docetism is "a designation for various views regarding the humanity of Christ that began to manifest themselves in the late 1st century" that was "a by-product of the Hellenistic environment of early Christianity," which, "philosophically, made a radical distinction between the material and the spiritual, and thus denied that the spiritual Christ actually assumed human form," which thus amounted to "a denial of the Incarnation" and thus even Christ's "Resurrection." *That* is the modern concept. But no ancient person believed that. Nor was anyone attacked for believing it—besides (maybe) a single person, Marcion (and, in a completely different sense, Basilides), and even then, probably falsely. So the notion that an *array* of sects did this wasn't even an *ancient* fabrication. It's entirely modern. Moreover, the ancient word for Docetism was never used of these men, or any such sect; it applied to a completely unrelated doctrine.

Since, like Gnosticism, the modern construct of Docetism struggles for coherence, under its banner has been placed wildly disparate doctrines, such as claiming Jesus escaped the crucifixion by switcheroo (perhaps Simon of Cyrene ended up on the cross!), or by sending a mere illusion of himself to minister to Earth (perhaps he thus merely appeared to be killed there!). But these were never any Christian's beliefs. *That notion is a modern invention.*

To demonstrate this, I must walk us through every supposed example.

---

[9] Quoting Hoklotubbe, "What is Docetism?," 54 and 51, respectively.

[10] For an expansion of this point, see Francis Watson, "Pauline Reception and the Problem of Docetism," in Verheyden et al., *Docetism*, 51–66.

1. Second Peter

Sometimes cited as referencing Docetism is 2 Peter, well-known as a second century forgery. But it never refers to that concept, nor describes anything like it. 2 Peter never concerns itself with whether Jesus escaped the crucifixion or was an illusion. The author never references physically touching Jesus to confirm otherwise, for example, nor asserts the 'reality' of his appearance, but only the fact of it. Which means, to the contrary, what 2 Peter actually says gives us what may be the clearest expression of there having been Christians denying the (terrestrial) historicity of Jesus—Christians who were interpreting the Gospels as "cleverly devised myths" (*sesophismenois mythois*, 2 Peter 1:16) and not historical accounts. And thus, to rebut them, this author forged an eye-witness testimony to the actual historicity of Jesus (*not* to his Incarnation or Resurrection, 2 Peter 1:16–18), insisting this stood in contrast to other Christians to be shunned (2 Peter 2:1–3, 10–12, 17–22), who were saying those kinds of stories (and thus the Gospels as a whole) were all just a smartly constructed mythology, not something that actually happened so as to have been witnessed as 2 Peter claims.[11]

This becomes obvious when you read the text as actually written, without dogmatic assumptions like Docetism skewing what you see. 2 Peter declares:

> I will also make every effort so that you are able to recall these things at any time after my departure. For we did not follow cleverly contrived myths [*sesophismenois mythois*] when we made known to you the power and coming of our Lord Jesus Christ; instead, we were eyewitnesses of his majesty. For he received honor and glory from God the Father when the voice came to him from the Majestic Glory, saying 'This is my beloved Son, with whom I am well-pleased!' We ourselves heard this voice when it came from heaven while we were with him on the holy mountain. We also have the prophetic word strongly confirmed, and you will do well to pay attention to it.
>
> —2 Peter 1:15–19 (NIV)

[11] Carrier, *Historicity*, 351 (349–56 for context).

The author then digresses on the power and reliability of prophecy, leading to the conclusion of his argument for the historicity of Jesus:

> But there were also false prophets among the people, just as there will be false teachers among you. They will secretly introduce destructive heresies, even denying the sovereign Lord who bought them—bringing swift destruction on themselves. Many will follow their depraved conduct and will bring the way of truth into disrepute. In their greed these teachers will exploit you with fabricated stories [πλαστοῖς λόγοις]. Their condemnation has long been hanging over them, and their destruction has not been sleeping.
>
> —2 Peter 2:1–3 (NIV)

The author then digresses with a litany of pompous moral polemics (none of which we have any warrant to believe is true), insisting his targets—the ones "making up stories" about the "cleverly constructed myths" that thus "deny" the literal Jesus of the Gospel tales that this author is defending—are the most immoral and evil people imaginable, the greatest and vilest threats, blasphemers and sinners; and thus, we are to conclude, must be condemned and avoided, not listened to.

His targets are Christians, "false" prophets and teachers "among you," 2 Peter 2:1, who can therefore "sneak in destructive heresies," *pareisazousin hairesis apôleias*; and they can do this *because* they are in the Christian fold, which is worse, this author says, than if they were outsiders (2 Peter 2:20–21). And yet these are the people who deny the historicity of tales like the Transfiguration (2 Peter 1:16–18). They claim those stories are "cleverly devised myths" (2 Peter 1:16) that require "interpretation" (2 Peter 2:3), though their explanations are "made up" (2 Peter 2:3), and thus not "true" (2 Peter 1:12, 2:2) in the sense of events actually having happened (hence 2 Peter 1:16–18).

This is not Docetism being attacked here. It is Christians denying the historicity of the Gospels—and thus Jesus (that is, in our *terrestrial* sense; they probably believed in the *celestial* historicity of Jesus, exactly as we propose). 2 Peter 1:16 establishes the battle-lines, while the rest of the text aims to persuade its readers which side to stand on: good Christians do not follow a mythical understanding of the stories in the Gospels (*exakolouthêsantes*, meaning 'follow' in the sense here of 'repeat, rely on') but believe in the "coming of Jesus Christ in power" (*parousian*, in the sense here of 'presence, arrival'). The author explicitly juxtaposes *that* in opposition to the 'cleverly devised myths' position (*ou gar … egnôrisamen … all' epoptai*). So the actual pre-apocalyptic arrival of Jesus on Earth is at issue here; not whether he assumed flesh, died, and rose. Those questions are never addressed in this letter; they therefore were not being disputed.

Even at worst, there is no way to extract Docetism from this passage. To get a different reading of the text, you have to assume that it is there first; indeed, awkwardly force it in, against the evidence. There is no evidence supporting that assumption at all. So even if you wish to remain skeptical as to what this passage is about, you still cannot declare there is no evidence of Christians doubting the historicity of Jesus—because you cannot remove this from possibly being just that.

2. First John

A similar example often touted is the preface to the Epistle that came to be attributed to a certain John the Elder (the actual name 'John' never appears in this or any of the Johannine Epistles; it's a later ascription):

> That which was from the beginning, which we have heard, which we have seen with our eyes, which we have looked at and our hands have touched—this we proclaim concerning the Word of Life. The Life appeared; we have seen it and testify to it, and we proclaim to you the eternal Life, which was with the Father and has appeared to us. We proclaim to you what we have seen and heard, so that you also may have fellowship with us.
>
> —1 John 1:1–3 (NIV)

This gives the impression of being jointly authored by the apostles, though it avoids ever saying that. The authors never identify themselves as apostles, and even the word for 'appeared' is ambiguous, *ephanerôthê* more literally meaning 'revealed, made manifest', common terminology for the epiphanies of gods or angels. But this is surely a deliberate riff on the conclusion of our final redaction of the Gospel of John (complete with the same pose of a first-person plural authorship: 'we' are writing and saying all this, a device also used in 2 Peter 1:16, 18, 19).[12]

[12] On this being a deliberate post-Gospel forgery: Ehrman, *Forgery and Counterforgery*, 418–25 (Johannines); Tom Thatcher, "Johannine Epistles," in *The Reception of Jesus in the*

And like that Gospel, this Epistle protests too much. This author is so desperate to emphasize that what he is selling was 'seen, heard, and touched' that he repeats it three times in the space of three sentences. This passage seems contrived to invent and assert an apostolic pedigree for confirming the actual physical, historical visitation of Jesus in the Gospels, just as 2 Peter was. It thus opposes anyone who would deny that. But who was denying it? And what, exactly, were they denying?

If we do not 'assume' this is referring to Docetists, is there any evidence that it is? No. And several scholars agree, as we'll see when we get to discussing the later part of this letter (where we learn those denying these things are not unbelievers but fellow Christians). But already here, without assumptions, what we actually have to judge by are prior texts like the Epistles of Paul and their repeated assertions that the gospel was learned, and the risen Christ met, only in dreams and visions: "in me" (Gal. 1:16); not "from any man" of "flesh and blood" but a "revelation from Jesus" (Gal. 1:11–12, 16, cf. 1 Cor. 15:1–8); hence the *kerygma* and *gospel* of Jesus are learned only by being "revealed" as concealed in "scripture" (Rom. 16:25–26; see chapter four). The most immediately obvious interpretation of 1 John 1:1–3 is therefore in light of this, our actual background knowledge: its authors are reacting to *this*.

So the Christians that 1 John is rebutting here appear to be those who deny any meeting with Jesus ever physically occurred—that Jesus 'appeared' (*ephanerôthê*) but only in visions and dreams. We cannot rule this out. And it requires no constructed assumptions about some nebulous Docetism never here described or mentioned. The simplest and most direct meaning of this text is to deny, and override, mythicist Christians. It is saying the mission of Jesus was not a myth, but actually happened. It was not learned of in a vision, but the man was literally seen and touched and heard—exactly as the Gospels relate. This text is thus a defense of a literal reading of the Gospels over any strictly allegorical one. Like 2 Peter, it was designed to dictate how the Gospels are to be understood—without too hamfistedly just saying so.

It cannot be argued that the underlying text of John 20 (and its inspiring text, Luke 24) were anti-Docetic, either. Because they do not address any claim about Jesus not having been incarnated or having ac-

---

First Three Centuries, Volume 1: From Paul to Josephus (ed. Helen Bond; T&T Clark, 2019), 297–307. Hence I exclude it from the relevant evidence in Carrier, *Historicity*, 263, 528. On the editorial use of the first person plural as a rhetorical device, see Trobisch, *Origin of Christian Scripture*.

tually died—they are concerned solely with different conceptions of the resurrection body, whether it should be the same body of flesh that died, or a new body altogether ("you do not plant the body that will be, but just a seed" and then "God gives it a body as he has determined," 1 Cor. 15:37–38), leaving the old one in the grave like a discarded shell (because "flesh and blood cannot inherit the kingdom of God," 1 Cor. 15:50).[13] So 1 John 1:1–3 could be referencing that dispute. But the universality of this passage suggests otherwise. It does not limit its remarks to the resurrection or the resurrection body and does not emphasize the role of 'flesh' at all. It appears, rather, that *that* idea, contrived by the authors of John and Luke, is here being expanded to combat a denial of the entire historicity of Jesus, and thus is no longer limited to only a dispute over the nature of the resurrection body, but to the entire idea of Jesus having already come (rather than revealing that he *would* come, in the rapture, per 1 Thessalonians 4:16 and 1 Corinthians 11:26).

Either way, there is no reference to Docetism here. One can *imagine* it, but that does not establish it. This is just as likely targeting mythicists—Christians who denied the terrestrial historicity of Jesus altogether. And in the context of 2 Peter, that seems even the more credible interpretation; it is certainly no less so. Which in turn affects how we interpret another passage in this letter, in 1 John 4 (echoed in 2 John 7). But before we examine that, we should tour the rest and come back around to it, by then suitably reinforced with the pertinent background knowledge.

3. Ignatius

Often the Epistles of Ignatius are presented as containing evidence of Docetism.[14] But once again, just as with supposed evidence of Gnosti-

[13] Which is how some may have interpreted 1 Cor. 15:34–58, particularly in light of Paul's assertion that the risen Jesus was only seen in visions, and thus not 'physically' encountered in any more reassuring way (Gal. 1:11–16; cf. 1 Cor. 15:5–8). On this very dispute see Dale Martin, *The Corinthian Body* (Yale University Press, 1999); Caroline Bynum, *The Resurrection of the Body in Western Christianity, 200-1336* (Columbia University Press, 1995); and Richard Carrier, "The Spiritual Body of Christ and the Legend of the Empty Tomb" in *The Empty Tomb: Jesus beyond the Grave* (ed. Robert M. Price and Jeffery Lowder; Prometheus Books, 2005), 105–232.

[14] For example: Paul Foster, "Ignatius," in *The Reception of Jesus in the First Three Centuries, Volume 2: From Thomas to Tertullian* (ed. Jens Schröter and Christine Jabobi; T&T Clark, 2019), 41–57. Otherwise, on the dating and interpretation of Ignatius see: Carrier, *His-*

cism, this is always by circular argument: one has to presume everything he says has a Docetic purpose to get the conclusion that that is the purpose it has. But when you read the text as written, it cannot bear this interpretation at all.

I've made this point before.[15] But to really see it, consider how the creed evolved from Paul to Ignatius. In the early first century, it looks like this:

> I want to remind you . . . By this gospel you are saved, if you hold firmly to the word I preached to you. Otherwise, you have believed in vain. For what I received I passed on to you as of greatest importance: that Christ died for our sins according to the Scriptures, that he was buried, that he was raised on the third day according to the Scriptures, and that he appeared . . . [by revelation to a select few].
>
> —1 Corinthians 15:1–8 (NIV)

But a hundred years later, it has changed into this:

> Stop your ears when anyone speaks to you at variance with the Jesus Christ who was descended from David, and came through Mary; who really was born and ate and drank; who really was persecuted under Pontius Pilate; who really was crucified and died in the sight of witnesses in heaven, and on Earth, and even under the Earth; who really was raised from the dead, too, His Father resurrecting Him, in the same way His Father will resurrect those of us, who believe in Him by Jesus Christ, apart from whom we do not truly have life.
>
> —Ignatius, *Trallians* 9

How did the creed change so radically, into so conspicuous an assertion of historicism? Why have all these new details—historical details, found only in the Gospels, not in Paul—become essential components of the creed one must affirm, such that all who deny any of them are damned and to be shunned? Both Paul and Ignatius are saying you must believe *exactly* what they list, else your faith is pointless; yet what they each say you must thus believe has completely transformed.

---

toricity, 315–23.

[15] Carrier, *Historicity*, 318–20; supplemented with context in *Outer Space*, 160–63, further developed here.

The same sentiments are repeated so often across the Ignatian letters to almost signal a panic.[16] Ignatius is disturbed by Christians who were denying all of these things: in some sense or other (he avoids explaining) they are teaching that Jesus was not 'descended from David', did not 'come through' Mary, wasn't 'really' crucified by Pontius Pilate—nor was he 'really' born, or anyone's dinner guest (never seen 'eating and drinking'). Elsewhere Ignatius thinks to add that Jesus 'really was' baptized by John.[17] And among his concerns is the need that these things not only really happened, but "in the sight of witnesses ... on Earth." Hence Ignatius emphasizes the importance of eyewitnesses to Jesus's physical arrival and presence on Earth, just like 2 Peter and 1 John; indeed, by appealing to similar examples and authorities.

Hence, in another passage, where Ignatius is clearly concerned more with debates over the resurrection body than historicity, he says this (in apparent reference to the scene in Luke 24:36–45):

> For I know that *even after* his resurrection [Jesus] was in flesh. And I believe that he is so now. When, for instance, he came to those who were with Peter, he said to them, 'Lay hold, handle me, and see that I am not a bodiless demon'. And immediately they touched him, and believed, being convinced both by his flesh and by the spirit. And this is why they thought nothing of dying, and were found to be above death. After his resurrection he even ate and drank with them, as one of flesh, although spiritually he was united to the Father.
>
> —Ignatius, *Smyrnaeans* 3

The reference to eating and drinking, and earthly witnesses, and confirming he is not an ethereal being all overlaps the credal declaration in *Trallians* 9, but here his concern relates solely to the nature of the *risen* body ("even *after* his resurrection he was flesh," *kai meta tên anastasin en sarki auton*). Again as Hoklotubbe observes, this tells us nothing of "what these opponents held about Jesus' body during his earthly ministry."[18] Whereas in *Trallians* 9, Ignatius's concern is no longer with the nature of the resurrection body, but now with the entire historicity of Jesus—birth, life, and death (elsewhere even baptism). Something far

---

[16] See Ignatius, *Magnesians* 11, 18 and 20; and *Smyrnaeans* 1–3.

[17] Ignatius, *Smyrnaeans* 1.

[18] Hoklotubbe, "What is Docetism?," 53.

more sweeping is at issue there.

Consider the differences between Paul's Corinthian creed and Ignatius's Trallian creed:

- **Paul said Jesus "came into being from David's sperm" (*genomenou ek spermatos Dauid*, Romans 1:3; see chapter eight).**
- Ignatius now insists we have to say Jesus came 'from the descendants of David' (*ek genous Dauid*)—conspicuously, precisely the thing Paul never said (as I document in chapter eight). The concern is historicizing: from God creating an appropriate body for Jesus to die in that fulfilled prophecy, to now being a historical descendant.

- **Paul said Jesus "came into being from a woman," implying that that woman is "Hagar . . . an allegory" (Galatians 4:4, 24–26; see chapter nine).**
- Ignatius now insists we must say Jesus came from an actual woman named 'Mary', not some generic or allegorical 'woman'. Paul never mentions a Mary. That's not in any creed he attests. So why is her name now important to affirm in the creed? The trend is, again, historicizing: it is now necessary to insist Jesus historically existed on Earth, mother and all. *So someone was denying that.*

- **In both places ("from David's seed" and "from a woman") Paul says Jesus was 'made' or 'came into being' (*ginomai*), not was 'born' or 'begotten' (*gennaô*).**
- With *hos alêthôs egennêthê*, "who was truly born" (*Trallians* 9.1), Ignatius conspicuously reverses this vocabulary, insisting we now must say Jesus was 'born' (*gennaô*), not 'made' (*ginomai*). Later scribes tried doctoring both passages of Paul in this very same way, signaling awareness of the same problem Ignatius was also trying to solve (see chapter eight). Which means they *understood* the problem. The trend is again historicizing: from the ambiguous ('came into existence') to the precise ('was actually born'). Why is that *now* so important to insist upon? Why were any Christians denying it?

- **Paul said Jesus ate and drank in a vision (1 Corinthians 11:23; see discussion in chapter two).**
- Ignatius now insists we must say Jesus ate and drank *for real* (*hos*

alêthôs...ephagen te kai epien). Why is that important? Why must Christians affirm this to not be shunned? The adverb *alêthôs* means 'truly', 'really', 'in reality'; the opposite of, say, 'in a vision' or 'in a cleverly devised myth'. The trend is again historicizing. We must now affirm this actually happened. Why?

- **Paul said, "the archons of this eon ... crucified" Jesus (*archontôn tou aiônos toutou...estaurôsan*, 1 Corinthians 2:8), language evocative of celestial demonic powers (see discussion in chapter two).**
- Ignatius now insists we must say Pontius Pilate crucified Jesus—and shun any Christian who says otherwise. So who was saying otherwise? Why has the name of the crucifier become important to the creed? And why does that only happen after the Gospels chose to insert Pilate into the story? The trend is again historicizing: it is now necessary to remove any suggestion that Jesus was killed *by some other entity.* Lest we be outcast, we must now insist that he was killed by a known historical man. Indeed, to the Smyrnaeans Ignatius even insists you must say this happened "under Pontius Pilate and Herod the Tetrarch," historicizing even further (*Smyrnaeans* 1, following Luke 23).

- **Paul implies there were no earthly witnesses to Jesus until after his resurrection, and even then only in ethereal visions (e.g. 1 Cor. 15:3–8; Gal. 1:11–16; Rom. 10:14–18 and 16:25–26).[19]**
- Ignatius now says we must say there *were* earthly witnesses. Why did that become necessary? Why did that enter the creed? What were the Christians this new creed was designed to exclude saying instead? The trend is again historicizing: the notion that we now need witnesses to *earthly events* implies Ignatius's opponents were preaching the crucifixion (and everything else) as a cosmic event whom no historical person could have been witness to, being learned only by revelation and secret messages in scripture. In other words, it sounds like his opponents were mythicists.

None of this fits the theory that Ignatius's opponents were Docetists. It certainly does not apply to any 'switcheroo' version of that concept, because Ignatius is worried about Christians denying the entire Gos-

[19] Translations conceal the relevance of Romans 10 here: see Carrier, *Historicity*, 554, 572.

pel narrative. But it also doesn't fit the 'illusionist' version. For example, 'Docetism' does not explain why the names are necessary. Why emphasize *historical details* as essential, like Mary and Pontius Pilate, and Herod Antipas and John the Baptist? That is explained if the historicity of Jesus is being denied; for then Jesus must be anchored to history. But these details do nothing to combat the Docetist claim that Jesus did all these things illusorily. For then he still did them in some sense, and it is only 'in what sense' that is supposed to be the point of argument. But at no point does Ignatius attack the notion that Jesus merely 'seemed' or 'pretended' to be killed by Pilate or born to Mary or baptized by John. It appears, rather, that the opposition was saying it didn't happen at all. Because the antonym of *alêthôs*, 'truly', is *pseudôs*, 'falsely'. The dispute appears to be over whether it even happened (rather than only in 'cleverly devised myths') and not 'in what way' it happened.

Likewise, the way Ignatius is rewriting the vocabulary of Paul indicates the dispute is not over whether Jesus 'pretended' to be of Davidic flesh, but *how* he came to be of Davidic flesh—for Paul affirms his Incarnation; but Ignatius does not like *how* he does. All his changes indicate a need to make the Incarnation more anchored to history ('descended' from David; 'born' to Mary). This does not appear to be combating illusionism. Likewise the need for earthly witnesses. That would not argue against illusionism at all. Witnesses would see an illusion entirely the same way as the real thing; so their being witnesses would not combat the notion of it being an illusion. What it combats is the claim that it didn't happen at all. Ignatius appears to be arguing with mythicists, not Docetists.

Again, one can take a more skeptical stance and say it is not clear. But that very ambiguity completes my point. The one thing that is not present here is any clear statement of the existence of Docetism or a description of its tenets. If we were not impelled to make this material fit that mold, we would not see it here at all. On a plain reading, Ignatius is worried about Christians saying these events did not happen; not that they happened and were witnessed but that they were accomplished by some illusory device or other. At every turn, his concern is to anchor Jesus to history, not to some particular metaphysics. So we have here again (1) no evidence for Docetism (you have to circularly presume it is here, and against the grain of the evidence, to get it to be) but (2) a possible attestation of mythicist Christians instead that cannot be ruled out, such that it cannot be claimed no such evidence exists. It may well exist here. And there is no way to 'remove' it as such evidence without a circular argument.

Ignatius simply does not say his opponents claimed Jesus only 'appeared' to descend from David, be born to Mary, eat and drink, get baptized by John and crucified by Pilate, and rise from the dead. He says his opponents denied *anyone witnessed* these things—implying they must be something like allegorical myths. If the concern had been 'it wasn't Jesus' who did these things, then Ignatius would say 'Jesus did these things', not that he 'really' did them. And if the concern was 'it was an illusion', then he'd say 'this was not an illusion', and not that 'there were witnesses', a retort that would be wholly impotent against a charge of illusion. Ignatius clearly had never heard of the claim that the witnesses were deceived by an illusion. Because he doesn't argue against it. He simply presumes *there being witnesses* resolves the dispute—which means it was not a dispute about 'illusions'. Read simply as written, it looks rather like Ignatius's opponents are saying the same thing 2 Peter's opponents are saying: that none of these things happened as the Gospels relate; that they are all 'cleverly devised myths'—allegory, not history (and if history, not earthly).

Nevertheless, the modern construct of Docetism partly derives from one remark in Ignatius in the next paragraph, even though it should never have signaled such a notion. From the standard *Ante-Nicene Fathers* translation:

> But if, as some that are without God, that is, the unbelieving, say, that He only seemed to suffer (they themselves only seeming to exist), then why am I in bonds? Why do I long to be exposed to the wild beasts? Do I therefore die in vain? Am I not then guilty of falsehood against the Lord?
>
> —Ignatius, *Trallians* 10 (ANF)

Here we see the same concern seen in 1 John and 2 Peter that these Christians, who say none of this stuff 'really' happened, would thereby be guilty of 'falsehood against the Lord' and hence of denying him—or even blaspheming him.

And here we at least have a connection to a pertinent word, the verb *dokein*, 'to seem'. But the ANF translation of this is hardly intelligible. If Jesus only 'appeared' to suffer but didn't really, then (Ignatius is being made to say) those claiming this themselves only 'appear' to exist but don't really? But they do exist. So what is his point? This cannot be the sense. Nor can this be a reference to their not existing after death (not receiving the resurrection), as we find suggested in *Smyrnaeans* 2, when Ignatius speaks of the resurrection and what 'will happen' to them instead if they are right, using *symbêsetai*, future tense. Because the participle and infinitive *here* are both in the present, *not* the future tense. Once again, a text has been misread by looking at it through a modern dogmatic lens, rather than setting that lens aside and simply reading the text as written, in its actual context.

The actual text reads:

> Εἰ δέ, ὥσπερ τινὲς ἄθεοι ὄντες, τουτέστιν ἄπιστοι, λέγουσιν τὸ δοκεῖν πεπονθέναι αὐτόν αὐτοὶ ὄντες τὸ δοκεῖν ἐγὼ τί δέδεμαι τί δὲ καὶ εὔχομαι θηριομαχῆσαι; Δωρεὰν οὖν ἀποθνήσκω. Ἄρα οὖν καταψεύδομαι τοῦ κυρίου.[20]

Which we can organize as:

Εἰ δέ ὥσπερ τινὲς	If some, for instance
ἄθεοι ὄντες	being atheists
(τουτέστιν ἄπιστοι)	(i.e. unbelievers)
λέγουσιν	say
τὸ δοκεῖν πεπονθέναι αὐτόν	he seems to suffer
αὐτοὶ ὄντες	themselves being
τὸ δοκεῖν	to seem
ἐγὼ τί δέδεμαι …	Why am I in bonds? …

The Greek has no plural infinitive, and *dokein* is here given in the present (not past) infinitive, and as an articular infinitive (it's not *dokein*

[20] The key line is repeated almost identically in Ignatius, *Smyrnaeans* 2 (τὸ δοκεῖν αὐτὸν πεπονθέναι αὐτοὶ τὸ δοκεῖν ὄντες), but is structurally more at place here in *Trallians* 10, suggesting he is quoting himself there, but originally composed it here.

but *to dokein*). So it is not speaking of the past (Jesus's ministry and crucifixion), but the present (what these targets of his polemics believe or teach). The infinitives are also not in parallel. The first is an infinitive of indirect discourse, while the second is an infinitive of description: *legousin to dokein peponthenai auton*, lit. "saying that he seems to suffer" and *autoi ontes to dokein*, lit. "they themselves being to seem"—*not* 'seem to be', as this is no longer indirect discourse but a continuation of the participles of description (*atheoi ontes*... *autoi ontes*). Even if we break the parallelism and read that participial clause as still in (nominative) indirect discourse (as something they say about themselves, and not something Ignatius is saying about them), the order of sense is still 'being to seem' or 'they are seeming' or 'because they seem' etc.

The first use of *to dokein* is a thing Ignatius claims they said: that Jesus 'seems to suffer / endure', which is in the present, not past tense, and thus does not seem likely to refer to a past event like the crucifixion. The second use of *to dokein* is most likely a thing Ignatius is saying about them: 'given that / because they are *to dokein*.' But because there is no plural infinitive, we cannot be sure the subject (rather than the object) of that first instance is Jesus (*auton*). It could be *them* (whether implied or also derivative of the *autoi*), and Jesus is then the *object* of the verb *dokein*, not the subject. Which would make more sense given that the primary meaning of *dokein* is not 'seem' but 'think, suppose, imagine', and indeed 'frequently in relating a dream or vision'.[21] Unlike the English word 'to seem' the Greek word *dokein* does not connect to vision as its primary metaphor, but thought. It is a word about thinking, imagining, supposing, having an opinion, or being wrong or self-deceived. So we should not allow the anachronistic valence of our English word to infect how we read the ancient word—like going directly to 'visual illusions' as what it refers to, when it might not. Something like 'intellectual supposition' would be closer to the Greek reader's mind. The closest overlap with 'vision' we find is with the active sense of the verb *dokein* to mean someone 'pretending' to be or do something, and thus only 'seeming' to be or do it.[22] But even that is through the metaphor of thinking: to be *thought* to be or do a thing more than being *seen* to be or do a thing.[23]

So the phrase *to dokein peponthenai auton* could simply mean "they

---

[21] §I.1 in the Liddell & Scott Lexicon.

[22] §I.4 in the Liddell & Scott Lexicon.

[23] See §II.1 in the Liddell & Scott Lexicon.

think / suppose / imagine that he suffers."[24] In which case what Ignatius is saying is, in effect, "if someone says they imagine he suffers." Then the second infinitive makes more sense: "because they think / suppose / imagine" things; i.e., thinking or supposing or imagining things *is what they do*. So the sentence should be translated, "But if some that are without God ... say that they 'imagine' he suffers (given that they 'imagine'), why am I in bonds?"

This would explain both infinitives and why they are in the present tense (even though the suffering of Jesus is in the past). And it would make the sentence intelligible. This also makes more sense of a line Ignatius delivers elsewhere: *Ei gar to dokein tauta eprachthê hypo tou kyriou hêmôn, kagô to dokein dedemai*, "But if these things were done by our Lord only in appearance, then am I also only in appearance bound" (ANF), following his discussion of the resurrection scene in Luke (quoted earlier).[25] It might be, rather, "But if these things were done by our Lord only in the imagination, then I am in chains only in the imagination," i.e. "If Jesus was only imagined / supposed / thought to have done these things, then I only imagine / suppose / think I am in chains," or, expressed less awkwardly in English grammar, "If these things were only imaginarily done by our Lord, then I am only imaginarily in chains."

If someone thinks the Gospel stories only imaginatively *represent* (not depict) what happened to Jesus, while the real things that happened were learned through visions and scriptural secrets, then for them the Gospels aren't historical records. This would fit what Ignatius says: he is describing people who think the Gospels are (as 2 Peter says) 'cleverly devised myths' and that the sufferings of Jesus can only really have been learned through visions or interpretations of scripture—hence, in the imagination. "They say they imagine Jesus suffered, because they are imaginers" is then the sense (or even, "They say they suppose or pretend Jesus suffered, because they are supposers or pretenders").

Ignatius is being polemical, as all heresy-hunters were (just as we saw 2 Peter was). So he is not being fair to what his opponents actually say and think—he is mocking them. But they might be saying the Gospels are myths and the Incarnation and Crucifixion are known mystically, by revelation. Which allows their version of events to be polemically

---

[24] See Smyth §2018, 2022.

[25] Ignatius, *Smyrnaeans* 4, where he is likewise calling for Christians who say these things to be rejected and shunned.

described as 'just imagined', and thus as only 'seeming' to have happened, ergo *to dokein*. This is not how those Christians would describe themselves and their beliefs. But it is how a disingenuous polemicist would. Hence Ignatius feels free to call these Christians unbelievers ('faithless'), even atheists ('godless'), even though clearly they are neither—rather, they are denying a historical reality that Ignatius deems essential to affirm. Because, Ignatius concludes, if he follows them, then "I give a false account of the Lord." Which looks like his worry is that the stories he believes in, and suffers for, *are false*; that they are *imaginary*—not that they have a different metaphysical interpretation, but that they didn't happen as told. And I'm not alone in this. Paul Hartog notes several historians now suspect that Ignatius seems particularly occupied with affirming the historicity of these things, and not just their metaphysical nature.[26]

Since, again, this is just as likely to be what Ignatius means, we can't rule it out. Which means we can't 'rule in' the Docetist alternative. We would need some evidence leaning toward that. But the evidence so far appears to be leaning against it. It is thus not gaining ground as the correct reading here, but losing ground—all because we abandoned assumptions, and just asked what the evidence actually is, and what the words can actually mean, *without* assumption—but in the light of established background knowledge instead, like that the primary use of the verb *dokein* is *to imagine*, not to seem; and particularly in the active when taking an infinitive predicate, when it 'frequently' related to describing visions and suppositions.[27]

This would concur exactly with what we read in Irenaeus:

> He shall also judge those who describe Christ as only in opinion [*putativum*]. For how can they imagine [*putant*] that they do themselves carry on a real [*vere*] discussion [*disputare*], when their Master was a mere imaginary being [*putativus*]? Or how can they receive anything steadfast from Him, if He was a merely imagined being [*putativus*],

---

[26] Paul Hartog, "The Impact of the Christological Controversies: Comparing the Ignatian Kerygma and Romans 1," in Verheyden et al., *Docetism in the Early Church*, 175–95 (185–90).

[27] For an example of straining to make this evidence fit Docetism yet with an awareness of its difficulties (and a recourse to weak analogies nevertheless), see the Hermeneia Commentary of William Schoedel, *Ignatius of Antioch: A Commentary on the Letters of Ignatius of Antioch* (Fortress, 1985), 155–56.

> and not a verity [*veritas*]? And how can these men really be partaken of salvation, if He in whom they profess to believe, manifested Himself [*ostendebat*] as a merely imaginary being [*putativum*]? Everything, therefore, connected with these men is unreal [*putativum*], and nothing truth [*veritas*]; and, in these circumstances, it may be made a question whether (since, perchance, they themselves in like manner are not men [*homines*], but mere dumb animals) they do not present [*perferant*], in most cases, simply a shadow of humanity [*hominum umbras*].[28]
>
> —Irenaeus, *Against Heresies* 4.33.5 (ANF)

The Greek here is lost; we only have a Medieval Latin translation. But the key word is *putativum*, which would correlate with the Greek *to dokein*, yet more clearly translates as 'imagine, impute' and not 'seem, appear'. So this Latin translator understood what I am talking about. They did not see in that Greek word a reference to visual illusions, but suppositions of the mind.[29] The translator even preserved the expected pun, when he says they 'imagine' (*putant*, which would render into Latin the Greek word δοκοῦσιν) that they are carrying on a true discourse, just as we can take Ignatius as saying—and likewise 2 Peter 2:3 also, which condemns the same thing as *plastois logois*, 'fabricated discourse'. So Irenaeus thinks these Christians claim Jesus *putativum ostendebant*, 'presented' himself as 'imaginary' (or even a 'supposition'), not as an *illusion*.[30]

There is no concern here about the incarnation (the 'flesh' of Jesus) or whether Jesus did anything (like die), but *how it is known* that he did. The question is thus not illusionism, but historicity: the Christians being condemned here are saying we can only know Christ became incarnate and died for our sins through our imagination, which means either by

[28] Latin text from J.-P. Migne, *Patrologiae cursus completus: Series graeca*, vol. 7 (Paris: Garnier Fratres, 1882), 1075.

[29] Lewis & Short, *A Latin Dictionary* (Oxford University Press, 1995), 1495, s.v. 'putativus', "imaginary, presumptive, putative," adv. "by supposition, putatively," from the secondary sense of the verb *puto* as to think or ponder: 1495–96, 'puto', §II.A and esp. B (extending into thought the primary sense of 'to clean, prune').

[30] Likewise at Irenaeus, *Against Heresies* 3.16.1: *putative eum passum naturaliter impassibilem exsistentem* (Migne 7.920), that some say "he putatively suffered, being naturally incapable of suffering" or in other words, "he was imagined [or thought or supposed] to have suffered, being naturally incapable of suffering." This does not refer to the same point, as here Jesus is still incarnated, crucified, and dying; the claim being denounced here is, rather, that he doesn't feel pain; likewise at Irenaeus, *Against Heresies* 3.18.6. That is not Docetism either.

supposition (such as reading it out of prophetic scripture) or in the theatre of the mind (such as learning of it by a revelation), and not through it being a witnessed historical event. Which is exactly what we have seen in 2 Peter, 1 John, and now Ignatius.

So, back to Ignatius, if we don't *presume* he means 'Docetists' but had never heard of that concept (especially as it appears he didn't) and if we only translate what he wrote directly, and in a way that makes both his uses of the word *dokein* sensible, we'd sooner choose the *primary* meaning of that verb. Then we'd render Ignatius as saying "if they say they imagine [or suppose] he suffered, because they imagine [or suppose]" things. He'd then be talking about people who are preaching that the Gospel crucifixion narratives (and Baptism and Nativity narratives and everything else) are imaginary ('putative'), not historical ('real')—in other words, that they represent something symbolically—or to put it pejoratively: that they have the gall to claim the Gospels are 'cleverly devised myths' (2 Peter 1:16), not historical events as related.

Docetism seems much less likely an interpretation of the text of Ignatius. It makes less sense of Ignatius's chosen words in Greek. It makes less sense of his argument. It makes less sense of the specific things he's worried about. It makes less sense of the specific things he needs his fellow Christian's to affirm. And even at our most forgiving we still cannot say with any certainty that 'Docetism' is what Ignatius is talking about. It is just as likely he's talking about mythicist Christians—Christians who taught that the Gospels are mythologies, and not historical records of their Lord; and that the Incarnation and Crucifixion are events only known by revelation (hence 'in the imagination'), and not events anyone witnessed in the ordinary way.

4. Clement of Alexandria

So there is no particular evidence for Docetism in the Bible or Ignatius (or Irenaeus). You have to import that as an assumption to get it back out of those sources; and even that approach strains against the evidence as it is. Neither source fits that interpretation very well. But there also isn't any evidence of the Docetism we want to import. Because apocryphal and apologetical texts that are used by modern scholars to argue for it (such as the writings of Clement of Alexandria) attest no such thing at all.

The only occasions in antiquity when we hear of a sect or grouping of sects called the Docetists are in a turn-of-the-3rd century letter by Serapion, Bishop of Antioch from 197 to 203, who merely mentions them but does not describe their beliefs (so we will visit that later)—and then in the later 3rd century anti-heretical works of Clement and Hippolytus (or Pseudo-Hippolytus).

Clement tells us (emphasis mine):

> Of the heresies, some receive their appellation from a name, as that which is called after Valentinus, and that after Marcion, and that after Basilides, although they boast of adducing the opinion of Matthew ... Some take their designation from a place, as the Peratici; some from a nation, as that of the Phrygians; some from an action, as that of the Encratites; **and some from peculiar dogmas, as that of the Docetae**, and that of the Haermatites; and some from suppositions, and from individuals they have honored, as those called Cainists and the Ophians; and some from nefarious practices and enormities, as those of the Simonians called Entychites.
>
> —Clement of Alexandria, *Stromata* 7.17 (ANF)

Clement never goes much into what he thinks the 'peculiar doctrines' are that define the Docetists as a sect. But already *he distinguishes it* from Marcionism and Basilidinism and Valentinianism—so he is *not* including their teachings as Docetic. This is a serious problem for the modern conception.

Indeed, the only time Clement says anything as to what distinguishes the Docetists, it's nothing to do with the modern conception at all. Clement says: *Toioutois epicheirei kai ho tês dokêseôs exarchôn Ioulios Kassianos* (in the ANF Latin translation: *talibus argumentis utitur quoque Julius Cassianus, qui fixit princeps sectae Docetarum*) "Such arguments are also employed by Julius Cassian, who first created [the sect of] the Docetists."[31] What arguments? Those concerning solely gender and sexuality, such as Cassian's warning to "let no one say that because we have these parts, that the female body is shaped this way and the male that way, the one to receive, the other to give seed, therefore sexual intercourse is allowed by God." In other words, we should not infer function *from appearance*. The term 'Docetist' is here intended in a completely unrelated sense to anything modernly conceived or referenced in any of

[31] Clement of Alexandria, *Stromata* 3.13.

the texts we've discussed. And Cassian post-dates Marcion and Valentinus (and Ignatius!), as Hoklotubbe observes, yet is described by Clement as 'originating' Docetism, which rules out any attribution of the ancient term to them.[32]

Earlier, Clement had placed the likes of Marcion under the same umbrella as Cassian only in respect to the Pauline view that the flesh is *psychic* and the risen body *pneumatic*.[33] But this refers to that dispute about the nature of the resurrection body I mentioned earlier, which does not pertain to the Incarnation or death of Jesus or anything else. So that is not Docetism either. Clement otherwise distinguishes them when he goes on to say that by declaring birth an evil, "on this" basis "Cassian formed the Docetists" but on that same basis "Marcion and Valentinus" formed the view that "the flesh is an animal." Here Clement is saying the Docetist doctrine is wholly different from Marcionism and Valentinianism, and that they share only the view that birth is an evil. He is also saying that the entire distinctive notion of Docetism was constructed on *this* view—a view about sex and reproduction; not illusionism, or anything else the modern concept imagines.

And yet we are not told here that the Docetists denied the birth of Jesus (or his being given a body of flesh *without* a birth, which is still an Incarnation), or his death or anything else, only that they held to what we might today call the 'corruption of the flesh' (i.e., Original Sin), which is compatible with the Incarnation—in all the ways it has been ever since: the Immaculate Conception was invented by Catholics to solve this problem; Protestants solved it by appealing to divine grace. Clement implies the Docetists may have solved the problem in a manner similar to modern Protestants, if their approach resembled that of the Valentinians he pairs them with, who said that though Jesus had flesh, it was in some fashion miraculously bestowed by God to work differently, even processing food differently to ensure Jesus never had to defecate—and on this point Clement provides, indeed, a direct quote from Valentinus to that very effect.[34] Otherwise, Clement says Cassian interpreted bodies to be just 'suits' that people wear (and wear in their fallen state, citing an allegorical reading of Genesis 3:21), and thus not indicative of our real nature—and *therefore* inferences about whether sex

[32] Hoklotubbe, "What Is Docetism?," 62–63.

[33] Clement of Alexandria, *Stromata* 3.17.

[34] Clement of Alexandria, *Stromata* 3.7.

is good or intended by God cannot be drawn therefrom.[35] But this entails nothing as to the Incarnation or death of Jesus. This is not Docetism in the modern sense at all, as confirmed by the detailed analysis of M. David Litwa.[36] Clement's Docetists were so-named by entirely the opposite application of *dokein*: that the body 'seems' to indicate God endorsed human sexuality is to be *rejected* as mere seeming, and *not* accepted as the truth of the matter.

5. *(Pseudo-)Hippolytus*

We get a different view from Hippolytus (or whoever the author was of the third-century *Refutation of All Heresies*), who tells us the most of any ancient author about the Docetists as a sect. They are introduced at the end of his seventh volume with the line, "let us see what also has been invented by the Docetae." He then elaborates in the introduction of his eighth volume: "Having adequately and sufficiently explained the doctrines of the majority" of heretical sects "in the seven books before this," including Marcionism and others (so Hippolytus, too, is *distinguishing* Docetists *from* the Marcionites, not equating them), "we shall not now be silent as regards the opinions that follow," and thus he "shall refute those" who suppose "that they have acquired" a purported "steadfastness of doctrine, when it is only in appearance," i.e. only imagined (using the same pun intended by Ignatius and Irenaeus), and "these have styled themselves *Docetae*, and propound the following opinions." He then relates a long variety of doctrines—none of which relate to the modern conception. In fact, they exclude it.

For example, Pseudo-Hippolytus explains:

> In order, therefore, say the Docetae, that [Jesus] may be clad in the darkness that is prevalent in more distant quarters of creation,[37] an angel journeyed with Him from above, and announced the glad tidings to Mary, says [the Docetist], as it has been written.

[35] Clement of Alexandria, *Stromata* 3.14.

[36] M. David Litwa, "Deification and Defecation: Valentinus Fragment 3 and the Physiology of Jesus's Digestion," *Journal of Early Christian Studies* 31 (2023), 1–18. See also Litwa, *Found Christianities*, 259–66.

[37] A marginal gloss here says "they say flesh," i.e. this is a doctrine about all flesh. See: Miroslav Marcovich, *Refutatio omnium haeresium* (De Gruyter, 1986), 328. I am relying entirely on his critical edition of the Greek for my discussion of Hippolytus here.

> And the [child] from her was born [*gennêthen*], as it has been written. And He who came from above put on [*enedusato*, as of clothes] that which was born; and so did He all things, as it has been written [of Him] in the Gospels. He washed in Jordan, ... was baptized ... [and] the Ruler condemned his own peculiar figment [*plasma*, lit. 'anything formed or moulded, image, figure'] to a death of the cross ... (etc.)
>
> —Hippolytus, *Refutation of All Heresies* 8.10.6–8 (8.3 ANF)

He goes on to describe a variant of Paul's *pneumatic* two-body resurrection doctrine, whereupon "that soul which had been nourished in the body born of the Virgin" then "stripped off that body and nailed it to the accursed tree," and in that way "triumphed by means of this" discarded body "over principalities and powers," but he "would not be found naked, but would, instead of that flesh [*anti tês sarkos ekeinês*], assume that [other] body, which had been represented" to him at his baptism (the "prefigured body," *ektetupômenon sôma*). This is just a version of Pauline Incarnationism, not Docetism in the modern sense. For here Jesus really did come down, really was born to Mary, really did wear a real body of flesh, really did die in it, and really did rise from the dead—in a newer supernatural body. This cannot have any connection, then, to what Ignatius was concerned with, or 1 John or 2 Peter.

Hippolytus never mentions the doctrines about sex that Clement regarded as fundamental to their name, but he does cross near to it by mentioning they regarded the body of flesh as a kind of discardable 'environment suit', and thus it was not fundamental to Christ's nature, but just a tool he used to accomplish his ends. Hence the common thread we find in Clement and Hippolytus is that 'how things seem' cannot dictate 'how things are'. Hence, for example, that a penis fits into a vagina cannot dictate that sex was intended by God and therefore good. Likewise the properties of a man's suit cannot tell us anything about the properties of the man himself. We're to look past appearances to see the truth. Hence the play on words throughout Hippolytus's closing summary of what defines Docetism as a sect plays on the idea of 'seeming' and 'supposing' repeatedly enough to suggest that this is, indeed, why the adherents of this sect took that name for themselves.

As Hippolytus explains (emphasis mine):

> Each [Christian, they say] is so constituted as to **discern** [*noein*]

> Jesus, who is of a nature similar to their own. And it was the nature of this Jesus which that only-begotten and eternal One assumed from everlasting places. These places, however, are diverse. Consequently, a proportionate number of heresies, with the utmost emulation, seek Jesus. But all these heresies have their own peculiar Jesus; so **he is seen** [*orômenos*] differently according as the place is different towards which, he says, each soul is borne and hastens.
>
> Now, each soul **supposes** [*dokousa*, a conjugation of *dokein*] that the Jesus seen from its particular place is alone that Jesus who is its own peculiar kinsman and fellow-citizen. And on first **beholding** [*idousa*] this Jesus, that soul **recognises** [*egnôrise*] Him as its own peculiar brother, but the rest as bastards. Those, then, that derive their nature from the places below, are not able to **see** [*idein*] the forms of the Saviour which are above them. Those, however, he says, who are from above, from the intermediate decad and the most excellent ogdoad—whence, say the Docetae, we are—have themselves **known** [*isasi*] not in part, but entirely, Jesus the Saviour. And those, who are from above, are alone perfect, but all the rest are only partially so.
>
> —Hippolytus, *Refutation of All Heresies* 8.10.9–10 (8.3 ANF)

The Docetists thus called themselves that *because* their entire salvific system hinged on distinguishing what *seems* to be the case from what you can correctly imagine or *suppose* to be the case. Those who become obsessed with the flesh of Jesus are those most confused, being obsessed with how things seem rather than how they really are. Those who realize Jesus now lives in a superior body different from the body of flesh (and thus, we can conclude, lacking such things as sexual organs or stomachs or anuses), and then who see through even that to his true spiritual nature, are *the perfected* and thus the most blessed. Something similar (ascending ranks of Christians according to increasing esoteric knowledge) is positively referenced in Clement of Alexandria.[38]

Nowhere in this is there a denial of the humanity, Incarnation, death, or Resurrection of Jesus. Nowhere is Jesus 'not really' eating and drinking and being born and beaten and killed when he was on Earth, or not wearing a body of flesh for the purpose, much less not witnessed

[38] Carrier, *Historicity*, 112–13.

doing these things. As Hippolytus plainly says, the Docetists admit "that all the occurrences took place with Him as it has been written in the Gospels."[39] This simply has nothing to do with the modern notion of Docetism, or any text alleged to be Docetic by that conception—only, at best, in this *original* conception, which is not Illusionism, but Paulinism, a doctrine really only about *the resurrection* body, not the body Jesus once lived and died in. Hence as Hippolytus goes on to explain, it is the resurrection body that Jesus assumes that "could not be seen by any, on account of the excessive magnitude of his glory," other than by the eye of faith, and hence only to believers (a notion found likewise in Origen).[40]

The ancient Docetists were thus using the term in the opposite way to the modern conception. They were calling for a *rejection* of how things seemed, and to look beyond the seeming to what things really were. They were not denying anything about the Incarnation or death or Resurrection or the birth or life of Jesus at all. Nor were they claiming he only 'seemed' to do those things. They were not saying he 'seemed' to be flesh but wasn't; they were saying that anyone focused on the reality of his actual flesh is overly focused on how things seem, and not looking beyond to greater and more important truths. Their application of *dokein* referred to defects in the believer, not to Jesus. This is in no way what Ignatius or 2 Peter or 1 John are talking about. They are not being challenged with this view at all, and thus are not responding to it. They are reacting to something else entirely.

The only passage in Hippolytus that reflects something like the modern notion of Docetism regards Marcion and his sect, not 'the Docetae'. And it suffers from being both probably false and still not what Ignatius, 2 Peter, and 1 John could have been talking about. But we will get to that when we discuss Tertullian, whose argument Pseudo-Hippolytus appears simply to be repeating. We must first complete our survey of who the ancient 'Docetae' actually were.

6. Serapion and the Gospel of Peter

Now that we have a correct read on what ancient Docetists were about—the only actual Docetists—we can go back and examine a major point where this modern error started: a misreading of Serapion's letter, partly

[39] Hippolytus, *Refutation of All Heresies* 10.12 (ANF).

[40] Hippolytus, *Refutation* 10.12; cf. Origen, *Contra Celsum* 2.64–67.

preserved in Eusebius, discussing the Gospel of Peter. Which reads:

> For we, brethren, receive both Peter and the other apostles as Christ; but we reject intelligently the writings falsely ascribed to them, knowing that such were not handed down to us. When I visited you I supposed that all of you held the true faith, and as I had not read the Gospel which they put forward under the name of Peter, I said, 'If this is the only thing which occasions dispute among you, let it be read'. But now having learned, from what has been told me, that their mind was involved in some heresy, I will hasten to come to you again. Therefore, brethren, expect me shortly.
>
> But you will learn, brethren, from what has been written to you, that we perceived the nature of the heresy of Marcion, and that, not understanding what he was saying, he contradicted himself. For having obtained this Gospel from others who had studied it diligently, namely, from the successors of those who first used it, whom we call Docetists (for most of their opinions are connected with the teaching of that school) we have been able to read it through, and we find many things in accordance with the true doctrine of the Savior, but some things added to that doctrine, which we have pointed out for you farther on.[41]

The section of his letter Serapion refers to that listed these Docetic 'additions' is not preserved. But there is still nothing here relating to the modern concept of Docetism. As T.C. Hoklotubbe and Allen Brent demonstrate, neither Serapion's remarks nor the Gospel of Peter itself relate to the modern concept of Docetism.[42] There is nothing about 'seeming', or denying anything about Christ, much less the Incarnation or Resurrection. Surviving fragments of the Gospel of Peter affirm both—they even affirm that Jesus rose from the grave in the same body that died.[43] And Origen confirms the actual 'Docetae' only deny Jesus felt pain, not that he inhabited flesh and died (I'll revisit Origen's observations later).[44] Serapion does not himself describe what the Docetists

[41] From Eusebius, *History of the Church* 6.12.3-6 (ANF).

[42] Hoklotubbe, "What Is Docetism?," 61–61; Allen Brent, "Can There Be Degrees of Docetism?," in Verheyden et al., *Docetism in the Early Church*, 5–26 (18–19).

[43] For this and following observations see: McCant, "Gospel of Peter"; Head, "Christology"; and Omerzu, "My Power."

[44] Origen, *Commentary on John* 10.21–24.

believe (or what in the Gospel of Peter suggested them) in the portion of his letter that Eusebius quotes. But whatever Serapion saw in that Gospel that aligned with what 'the Docetists' say he says are 'additions' to orthodox teaching, *not subtractions*. So he's talking about something else. We can reasonably assume he is speaking of the same sect as Clement and Hippolytus were, and thus he means something to the effect of adding 'teachings' from Jesus himself (perhaps in lost sections of that Gospel; as we only have part of its passion narrative) about disregarding the body as unimportant (and thus, for example, denying that sex is good or a function intended by God).

Hence modern scholars are wrong to think Serapion is talking about what *they* mean by 'Docetism'. He isn't. There is no evidence for that modern conception here; while any correct interpretation of Serapion must follow from our actual background knowledge (like what his contemporaries Clement and Hippolytus say these Docetists taught, and what is actually in the surviving sections of the Gospel of Peter), not modern anachronistic assumptions. That the Gospel of Peter is in any way 'Docetic' has already been refuted by Jerry McCant, P.M. Head, and Heike Omerzu, who, among other things, demonstrate all its same features are in the supposedly *anti*-Docetic Gospel of John, and don't relate to the modern conception anyway—which is not about whether Jesus could feel pain or where his soul was when he was dead. Which are also not disputes Ignatius or 2 Peter or 1 John are concerned with.

7. *The Apocalypse of Peter*

Another text often cited as somehow demonstrating the modern concept of Docetism is the *Apocalypse of Peter*, the notion being that it depicts a 'double-Jesus' version of Docetism—one Jesus on earth and another (simultaneously) in heaven. It does not. The word 'apocalypse' means 'revelation', and accordingly this text makes clear the entire thing *is a vision* Peter is having, while sitting with Jesus chatting in the temple square *before* his arrest—it is not being represented as an actual historical event anyone witnessed. It is thus not an account of the crucifixion, but a purely symbolic scene, such as litters the canonical book of Revelation, or as Peter experiences in Acts 10.

Moreover, the text of this vision says the *same* person is present in both places: there is not 'one' Jesus in heaven and 'another' on Earth, but the real Jesus is the same person the villains seize and crucify as occupies the fleshly body they drive nails into.[45] This is explicit in the text, which has Jesus say to Peter *after* his vision (emphasis mine):

> Be strong, for you are the one to whom these mysteries have been given, to know them through revelation, that **he whom they crucified is the first-born**, and the home of demons, and the stony vessel in which they dwell, of Elohim, of the cross, which is under the Law. **But he who stands near him is the living Savior**, the first in him, **whom they seized and released**, who stands joyfully looking at those who **did him** violence, while they are divided among themselves. Therefore he laughs at their lack of perception, knowing that they are born blind. So then the one susceptible to suffering shall come, since **the body is the substitute**. But what they **released** was **my incorporeal body**.[46]

This is not Docetism. It is simply saying the mortal body is worthless offal that Jesus left behind, escaping at its death as an incorporeal soul, which could hover outside its body and laugh at those who think they can harm him by harming his body. This is basically the same thing as the Stoic doctrine of the sage, whose soul is above the body, serene, even as it occupies it, even in the midst of that body being tormented. That's not Docetism. It's just dualism. Otherwise the text makes clear these are not different people: the one crucified *is* Jesus's body, occupied by Jesus's soul until death, only *figuratively* looking on himself as he dies—like an 'out of body experience'—and still only in Peter's mystical vision (this is not being described as objectively happening).

The teaching that Jesus wore a human body to suffer and die in—in other words, the Incarnation, Jesus' doctrinally necessary (and ritually temporary) humanity—is not being denied here. Nor is the Resurrection. That subject does not come up in this text, which might even be a lost fragment of the Gospel of Peter, as it takes place earlier in its narrative than the fragment we have. And indeed, what is actually Docetic about it in the ancient (and not modern) sense is having Jesus teach the doctrine that how things *seem* (his flesh is killed) is not how they *are* (he lives eternal, unharmed). This accords with what Clement and Hippolytus said Docetists teach. It does not accord with any modern conception of Docetism.

---

[45] Hoklotubbe, "What Is Docetism?," 57–58.

[46] Translation of James Brashler and Roger Bullard, "The Coptic Apocalypse of Peter," in *Nag Hammadi Codex VII* (ed. Birger Pearson; Brill, 1996), 78–79.

8. The Treatise of Seth

Often cited as well is the *Second Treatise of the Great Seth*, probably of the 3rd century. This is the text that some modern scholars think says Simon of Cyrene was crucified on Earth in Jesus's place. Which of course would be a post-Gospel doctrine, as it embellishes ideas and characters invented by the Gospels. And it cannot be what Ignatius or 2 Peter or 1 John are talking about; or Hippolytus or Clement or even Irenaeus. But the *Treatise of Seth* doesn't even say that anyway. This is, again, a modern fabrication.[47] You can scour the text. At no point does it ever say Simon is the one crucified. It merely repeats the canonical Gospel tradition that Simon carried the cross.

Seth does speak in the third person of the crucifixion, but only to illustrate what the *Apocalypse of Peter* did: that the body is merely a suit occupied by the soul. That is not denying the Incarnation; it is affirming it. *Seth* even affirms the belief that "we shall die with Christ" (thus it does not deny he died), and says Jesus "visited a bodily dwelling" and "cast out the one who was in it first" and "went in" (in other words, he became incarnate by possessing someone else's body of flesh), and this is the body that died, the soul escaping upon death to laugh at those who thought they could kill the soul by killing the body it occupied. Like the *Apocalypse of Peter*, this text never gets into the subject of the Resurrection. But it is not denying the Incarnation at all.

The pertinent section reads as follows (emphasis mine):

> Those who were there **punished me**. And I did not die in reality but in appearance, lest I be put to shame by them because these are my kinsfolk. I removed the shame from me and **I did not become fainthearted in the face of what happened to me at their hands**. I was about to succumb to fear, and I <suffered> according to their sight and thought, in order that they may never find any word to speak about them. For **my death**, which they think happened, (happened) to them in their error and blindness, since **they nailed their man unto their death**.
>
> For their Ennoias did not see me, for they were deaf and blind. But in doing these things, they condemn themselves. **Yes, they saw**

[47] Hoklotubbe, "What Is Docetism?," 56–57. The similar idea that Judas was crucified in place of Jesus comes from a Medieval forgery, the Gospel of Barnabas, and is therefore irrelevant to antiquity: Jan Joosten, "The Date and Provenance of the 'Gospel of Barnabas'," *Journal of Theological Studies* 61.1 (2010), 200–15.

> **me; they punished me.** [But] **it was another**, their father, who drank the gall and the vinegar; it was not I. They **struck me** with the reed; [but] **it was another**, Simon, who bore the cross on his shoulder. **I was another** upon whom they placed the crown of thorns. **But I was rejoicing in the height** over all the wealth of the Archons and the offspring of their error, of their empty glory. And I was laughing at their ignorance.[48]

This text is indeed vague as to where this is happening, and who the Archons are who are abusing and killing him. This could even be a mythicist text, though oblique references (such as to Simon) might imply not. Either way, this appears related to the *Apocalypse of Peter*, and we can infer it is describing the same concepts: body-soul dualism; the body is just a house, an environment-suit, a temporary abode; killing it doesn't kill *the person*, who is a soul. While there are things said that one might link to Docetism here ("I did not die in reality but in appearance"), they do not describe what the modern notion imagines. This is still Jesus becoming incarnate and dying (he "went in" to that body; "my death"; "punished me"; "struck me"; "what happened to me"). But it isn't a 'real' death because souls are immortal—dualism, not Docetism.

Seth indeed describes a possessionist doctrine of the Incarnation (emphasis again mine):

> And I subjected all their powers. For as I came downward, no one saw me. For I was altering **my shapes**, changing from form to form. And therefore, when I was at their gates, **I assumed** their likeness. For I passed them by quietly, and I was viewing the places, and I was not afraid nor ashamed, for I was undefiled. And I was speaking with them, mingling with them through those who are mine, and trampling on those who are harsh to them with zeal, and quenching the flame. And I was doing all these things because of my desire to accomplish what I desired by the will of the Father above.

And then, "after we went forth from our home, and came down to this world, and came into being in the world in bodies, we were hated and persecuted." Jesus is clearly describing here exactly what Paul does

[48] Gregory Riley, "Second Treatise of the Great Seth," in Pearson (ed.), *Nag Hammadi Codex VII*, 129–99.

in Philippians 2—apart from having the mortal body already available to occupy (by angelic possession), rather than (as Paul describes) it being manufactured for him.

Here at least we have something *close* to modern Docetism. But there is still no denial of the Incarnation, but an affirmation of it. Jesus "came into being in the world in bodies" and thus "I assumed their likeness" and "I was speaking with them, mingling with them" and again this was "my death," they "punished me," they "struck me," this is "what happened to me." This is not what the New Testament anywhere, or Ignatius in particular, was talking about.

9. The Ascension of Isaiah

Another text sometimes claimed to be Docetic is the last extant redaction of the *Ascension of Isaiah*. But this contains nothing Docetic at all. There is no celestial crucifixion being copied by an earthly one—whichever version of the text you are looking at, there is only ever one crucifixion in it, and one can only debate where it was located in any given recension.[49] But every version represents the Incarnation and death and resurrection of Jesus as real historical events. There is no illusion; no Jesus escaping execution.

The only thing in the *Ascension of Isaiah* remotely near to the modern notion is that it depicts the Incarnate baby Jesus miraculously teleporting out of Mary's womb (so as to avoid the ignominy of touching a vagina). But that only coheres with what Clement said the Docetist Cassian taught: that birth is an evil; which could motivate something like the idea that the baby Jesus had to teleport out of a womb. But this in no way correlates with the modern concept of Docetism, as it in no way denies the Incarnation. It merely quibbles over the trivia of *how* Jesus was born; not whether he was, or in what kind of body. There is no illusion; no switcheroo; no denial of his being in a body of flesh. It is doubtful even Ignatius would see this as undermining his belief that Mary 'begat' Jesus, as if a magical Caesarean section removed one's status as begotten by their mother. That's still 'from Mary' and 'begotten' (not 'made'), as his body, a real body of flesh, gestated in a historical human womb like any other. Teleporting bodies are not Docetism (Luke 24:31, 36; John 20:19,

[49] Hence: Carrier, *Historicity*, 36–48; that attempts to read *Asc. Is.* as Docetic are strained and implausible, 36–37n1.

26). Nor is a pre-existent Jesus descending into a fetus (as historicists must presume Paul means in Philippians 2:6–8).

10. Irenaeus and Basilides

Though switcheroos aren't what any of the authors we have discussed in this chapter were ever talking about, the modern notion does subsume that idea as well, and there is one accusation of such a doctrine to address. This won't help us interpret Ignatius or 2 Peter, for example, or any of the others, as this is clearly not what they were concerned with. But for completeness I should address it: Irenaeus accuses Basilides of teaching Simon of Cyrene did, indeed, get switched in to be crucified in place of Jesus.[50] But Irenaeus is probably lying.[51]

Independently of Irenaeus no one else writing about Basilides repeats this claim, despite authors like Clement or Hippolytus writing at some length about what he taught. So we have grounds to doubt Irenaeus's honesty on this point—or his intelligence, if he was duped by a parody. To the contrary, after a lengthy and detailed description of his teachings, Pseudo-Hippolytus says Basilides taught that "all the events of the Savior's life occurred …wholly as is written in the Gospels," including his death and resurrection.[52] Hoklotubbe suspects the *Apocalypse of Peter* and *The Treatise of Seth* might more accurately represent teachings of Basilides, adding that "it should be noted how unhelpful it is to describe any of these Basilidean-like Christologies as docetic in so far as each affirms that Jesus possessed a physical body capable of suffering."[53]

It is inconceivable that an author like Hippolytus, writing so much on Basilides, had never heard of this teaching about Simon. But ancient Christian heresiologies are notoriously untrustworthy in their polemical accounts of their opponents, and what Irenaeus says sounds very much like he is riffing on material like the *Treatise of Seth* and the *Apocalypse of Peter*—which we just examined and found said no such thing. Instead, when Irenaeus complains that Basilides taught that "salvation belongs to the soul alone, for the body is by nature subject to corruption," that sounds more like a polemical misrepresentation of what was actually

[50] Irenaeus, *Against Heresies* 1.24.4.

[51] So Litwa, *Found Christianities*, 120–21.

[52] (Ps.-)Hippolytus, *Refutation of All Heresies* 7.15 (ANF).

[53] Hoklotubbe, "What Is Docetism?," 54–58 (57).

no different than the pneumatist teaching of Paul—that same debate about the nature of the resurrection body I already mentioned—and not Docetism.[54]

This is also a teaching uniquely attributed to Basilides (and solely by Irenaeus), which we know for a fact cannot be what Serapion was discussing (as we have the relevant portion of the Gospel of Peter and it contains no such story), or what any ancient Docetist believed (as Clement and Hippolytus do not include Basilides among their Docetists), or what Ignatius or 2 Peter or 1 John where talking about (as they say nothing about this, but are concerned with entirely different matters). And no other passage in Irenaeus attests to this or any other kind of Docetism.

For example, Irenaeus's description of a heresy about Simon Magus 'pretending' to be the celestial Son of God and suffering for it isn't about Jesus.[55] And what Irenaeus says Saturninus taught, that "the savior was without birth, without body, and without figure, but was, by supposition [*putative*], a visible man," is vague as to what Saturninus actually taught.[56] Many a Christian believed the Logos was 'without birth, body, or figure' and *later* became 'in appearance a man'. That's literally canonical. Besides finding this very teaching in Philippians (2:6-11) and the Gospel of John (1:1–3, 14), Hebrews says Jesus is like Melchizedek, "without father or mother, without genealogy, without beginning of days or end of life; resembling the Son of God, he remains a priest forever" (7:3, 15–24). Mythicist Christianity would *also* have taught Jesus was 'without birth' and, but for the brief cosmic event of his incarnation, 'without a body' of flesh, and that his brief sojourn as a man would indeed only be known 'by supposition', through scripture and revelation.

So it is not possible to extract Docetism from these remarks, either. Especially since, again, polemicists like Irenaeus cannot be trusted to accurately represent what their opponents actually said. Other discussions in Irenaeus are similarly not at all clear whether he is even talking about heretical opinions *on* the Incarnation, rather than the cosmology of Jesus *pre*-Incarnation.[57] Only by importing Docetic assumptions not

---

[54] Irenaeus, *Against Heresies* 1.24.5.

[55] Irenaeus, *Against Heresies* 1.23.

[56] Irenaeus, *Against Heresies* 1.24.2. See Hoklotubbe, "What Is Docetism?," 64–65, which also addresses more obscure passages even less reliable, like Pseudo-Tertullian, *Against All Heresies* 1.4 and 6.1, or less relevant, like the *Acts of John*.

[57] For example, Irenaeus, *Against Heresies* 1.12.

in these texts can we get to any other conclusion. It is therefore not possible to recover Docetism from Irenaeus (as has already been argued by David Wilhite).[58]

11. Tertullian

Finally, we know Tertullian accuses Marcion of advancing something like what is now called Docetism—that Marcion supposedly taught Jesus was only a phantom—but he never calls this Docetism, nor links the notion with any other sect (much less 'the Docetae'), and we already saw how everyone else distinguishes Marcion *from* the Docetae. So we can entirely doubt the honesty and reliability of Tertullian on this point, too. He is a particularly dubious narrator of his opponents' views, and everything we know of Marcion's teachings (even from Tertullian) does not support his interpretation.[59] So as David Wilhite bluntly put it: "there is no credible evidence that Marcion was a docetist."[60]

To begin with, Marcion's preferred Gospel, even as modified, was in fact *anti*-Docetic—not only emphasizing the death and Resurrection (and thus Incarnation) of Jesus, but that the risen Jesus was *not* a phantom.[61] Even Tertullian attests this fact with the specious question, "if" Jesus "were altogether a phantom, why did" Marcion's Gospel have Jesus himself "upbraid" his Disciples "for supposing Him to be a phantom?"[62] Which suggests Tertullian is not being honest with us as to what Marcion actually taught. So when Tertullian elaborately accuses Marcion of "alleging Christ to be a phantom" we have good cause to doubt he is telling us the truth.[63] Indeed, in volumes three and four of his po-

---

[58] Wilhite, "Marcion a Docetist?"

[59] Hoklotubbe, "What Is Docetism?," 58–59; likewise Judith Lieu, *Marcion and the Making of a Heretic: God and Scripture in the Second Century* (Cambridge University Press, 2016), 378. Hoklotubbe, "What Is Docetism?," 60–61, also debunks attributions of Docetism to Valentinus by producing Valentinian texts explicitly saying otherwise, a conclusion also arrived at by Allen Brent, "Can There Be Degrees of Docetism?," in Verheyden et al., *Docetism in the Early Church*, 5–26 (12–15).

[60] Wilhite, "Marcion a Docetist?," 2.

[61] Marcion preserved Luke 24:37–39: Jason BeDuhn, *The First Edition of the New Testament: Marcion's Scriptural Canon* (Polebridge, 2013), 196–97; Dieter Roth, *The Text of Marcion's Gospel* (Brill, 2015), 435.

[62] Tertullian, *Against Marcion* 4.43.6.

[63] Tertullian, *Against Marcion* 3.8; likewise in Tertullian, *On the Flesh of Christ*.

lemical attack it looks like Tertullian is inventing this belief and *attributing* it to Marcion, through a convoluted bad-faith inference from what Marcion otherwise did teach: that the flesh is inferior and ultimately to be discarded; a teaching identical to Paul's (1 Cor. 15:34–58).[64] In other words, that same debate over the nature of the resurrection body; not Jesus's body before death.

At no point does Tertullian ever *quote* Marcion saying any of the things Tertullian attributes to him on this point, even though he readily can on others. No one else quotes Marcion on this point, either, other than simply replicating Tertullian.[65] Indeed this seems to have been a rhetorical tactic originating with Tertullian. He starts by inferring Marcion taught that the resurrection body is composed of some supernatural material (either narratively, from its ability to teleport, perhaps: Luke 24:31, 36; or doctrinally, from Marcion's teachings regarding Creation and the Resurrection; or both); then equates that by false equivalence to the resurrection body being phantasmal; and then he conflates the resurrection with the entire life of Jesus; all to make Marcion look foolish. Tertullian's critique is thus entirely disingenuous.

Tertullian's bad-faith reasoning becomes almost transparent when he says Marcion must "reject the bodily substance of Christ, since he had introduced his very god to our notice as neither the author nor the restorer of the flesh."[66] In other words, when Tertullian says Marcion 'taught' that Jesus was never made flesh, really what he means is that Marcion *must* have taught this or that it was an unnoticed consequence (a *reductio ad absurdum*) of what he did teach, disingenuously disregarding the fact that having Jesus briefly assume a body of flesh to sacrifice it is perfectly coherent with Marcion's teaching that bodies of flesh derive only from the corrupted world order.

We find this same disingenuous method of inference almost spelled out by Irenaeus, too, who describes these notions more as *consequences* of things Marcion taught; not things he actually taught.[67] Irenaeus thus starts with their teachings about Creation (whereby Jesus does not create

[64] Tertullian, *Against Marcion* 4.43.

[65] For example, Hippolytus, *Refutation of All Heresies* 10.15 (ANF) appears to be nothing more than a paraphrase of Tertullian, *Against Marcion* 3.8 (ANF).

[66] Tertullian, *Against Marcion* 3.8 (ANF).

[67] Irenaeus, *Against Heresies* 3.11.2–3. Wilhite, "Marcion a Docetist?," 11, doubts this passage even refers to Marcion; but on that account, it probably still refers to Marcionites.

the corrupt flesh of the world; his antagonist, the Demiurge, does), then conflates descriptions of the soul of Christ with his occupation of a body of flesh, to 'derive' a teaching not actually part of Marcion's theology: that 'the Logos' was never 'made flesh', a semantic game as to the referent of the words 'Logos' and 'made'. To Marcion (and others of a similar bent), the Logos *occupied* a body of flesh. Irenaeus is implying that that doesn't count as actually *changing* the Logos *into* flesh, a distinction of little actual relevance. His obfuscation is indicative of dishonesty: he does not want to explain to us what Marcion actually taught. He is concealing it under hyperbole.[68]

Tertullian appears to be following the same polemical mode, and thus he, too, is not actually finding this idea that 'Jesus was not enfleshed' in Marcion; he's manufacturing it, as also well demonstrated by Wilhite.[69] And yet Marcion, even by Tertullian's dubious account, never claimed Jesus didn't occupy a body of flesh, or didn't eat or drink, or that he evaded being crucified by Pontius Pilate or baptized by John, or that he wasn't witnessed doing these things on Earth—so Ignatius cannot have been speaking of any such doctrine as Marcion's, even if Tertullian and Irenaeus *were* describing it accurately. Nor, likewise, 2 Peter or 1 John. Indeed, though Marcion removed the Nativity narrative from Luke (and thus his genealogy and the name of his mother), he retained its references to Jesus being, historically and physically, born to a human mother, such that his critics (like Tertullian) struggled against this evidence to claim he denied it.[70]

This understanding is confirmed by a remark from Origen (emphasis mine):

> Thus it is true to call [Jesus] man and to call Him not man; man, because He was capable of death; not man, on account of His being diviner than man. Marcion, I suppose, took sound words in a wrong

[68] See Brent, "Degrees of Docetism?," 20–22. Brent calls these errors 'confusions', but such charity is not warranted.

[69] Wilhite, "Marcion a Docetist?" ("a critical reading of the primary sources finds docetism to be a possible implication of Marcion's thinking, but not an explicit teaching of Marcion himself," 2). Which is why BeDuhn, *First Edition*, 214–18 (214), observes that the 'redaction' of the New Testament that "Marcion supposedly carried out to … bring the text into harmony with his doctrines fails to materialize."

[70] Roth, *Text*, 417, 422, and BeDuhn, *First Edition*, 105, 110 (Luke 8:20–21, 11:27–28); cf. Roth, *Text*, 118–20, 297–98, and BeDuhn, *First Edition*, 145–46.

> sense, when he rejected His birth from Mary, and declared that **as to His divine nature** He was not born of Mary, and hence made bold to delete from the Gospel the passages which have this effect. And a like fate seems to have overtaken **those who make away with His humanity** and receive His deity alone; and also those opposites of these who cancel His deity and confess Him as a man to be a holy man, and the most righteous of all men. **And those who hold the doctrine of Dokesis,** not remembering that He humbled Himself even unto death and became obedient even to the cross, but **only imagining in Him the absence of suffering**...do what they can to deprive us of the man who is more just than all men.
>
> —Origen, *Commentary on John* 10 (ANF)

Here we see Origen did not understand Marcion to be a Docetist or as denying the humanity of Jesus—he refers to those as 'other' people than him, distinct from him. Indeed, Origen even distinguishes the Docetists from those denying the humanity of Jesus, thus refuting the modern conception of Docetism altogether. He also does not identify those 'other' people or explain what they instead teach; so we cannot confidently peg them into the modern Docetist mold, either.

Otherwise, Origen says the only thing his Docetists deny is that Jesus felt pain on the cross (just as the Gospels of John and Peter depict); and Origen's critique of them is thus simply that this makes Jesus's sacrifice less heroic and thus less salvific. But it is clear here that these Docetists did not deny Jesus assumed flesh and died. They are not denying the Incarnation or Resurrection or the metaphysical humanity of Jesus, but only reimagine the character of his soul. We also get here a more honest account of Marcion's view as to Jesus's birth: Origen's wording entails Marcion did not deny Jesus was born to a human mother, only that *his divine nature* was not (having been made by God at the dawn of Creation), and *that* is why he excluded the Nativity—hence not for the reasons Tertullian alleged. Origen is thus attesting Marcion agreed Jesus really inhabited a body of flesh—we can infer, by possession (such as we saw in the *Treatise of Seth*). So Marcion also was not advocating the modern notion of Docetism.

12. Revisiting the Bible

Now that we've seen that modern Docetism didn't exist outside the Bible, we can look anew at the claims it can be found inside the Bible. The *Oxford Dictionary* and other standard references will still cite as purported evidence of it several passages in the Bible, most of which we've already seen do not in fact attest it. The only one actually relevant I have left for now, when we can view it in the light of all the background knowledge we have just surveyed:

> Dear friends, do not believe every spirit, but test the spirits to see whether they are from God, because many false prophets have gone out into the world. This is how you can recognize the Spirit of God: Every spirit that **acknowledges that Jesus Christ has come in the flesh** is from God, but every spirit that does not acknowledge Jesus [came in the flesh] is not from God. This is the spirit of **the antichrist**, which you have heard is coming and even now is already in the world.
>
> —1 John 4:1–3 (NIV)

Clearly this is not referring to Jesus escaping the crucifixion with a switcheroo, in which belief Jesus obviously *has* come, *and* in the flesh (hence the supposed need to dodge that very flesh getting killed). Yet this *is* referring to some Christian sectarian belief: 'antichrist' here means the opposite of, yet pretending to be, the Christ; and the problem being addressed here is some intra-church prophetic declarations unliked by this author. On this much scholars rightly agree. But does this refer to some kind of 'Docetic' Christian illusionists when it says there are Christians who "do not acknowledge Jesus came in the flesh"?

All this text actually says is that anyone claiming Jesus did not "come in the flesh" is not preaching the 'real' Jesus. This was much like—and indeed is probably deliberately emulating—how Paul warns that there are 'other' Jesuses being preached in 2 Corinthians 11:4; a problem likewise referenced in Galatians 1:6–12. Though in neither case does Paul spell out what these alternative gospels said, the context in Paul implies it was the (original) Torah-observant gospel that he was competing with, wherein Gentiles had to convert to Judaism to be Christian, the only thing Paul reveals in Galatians 2 that his conception of the gospel uniquely rejected, and with which Galatians 3–5 is solely concerned (and his argument being that whether Torah adherence was or was not required by 'the gospel' is an interpretation and not actually a revealed component of it—see chapter four). But to the author(s) of John it clearly intends some other kind of dispute than any we find in Paul.

By viewing this text through the lens of the modern invention of Docetism, the evident assumption scholars are making is that the key part in dispute was 'in the flesh', and hence, 'denying the Incarnation'. But if we didn't look at the text through that lens, we might conclude instead that the key dispute was over 'having come', *elêluthota*, in Greek a pun on the previous line about false prophets 'having gone out', *exelêluthasin*. It's the same word only with the addition of 'out', to describe their spreading around their notions from church to church. So perhaps what this author is attacking are Christians denying a Jesus in the flesh *had already come*—as in, came *here*, to Earth.

A similar pun appears in 2 John 7, there again calling the "antichrist" those "who do not acknowledge Jesus Christ as coming [*erchomenon*] in the flesh" yet "have gone out [*exêlthon*] into the world [*kosmon*]," i.e. the world of flesh. Here the participle is in the present tense ('coming') but in relation to the aorist ('have gone out') and thus is still represented as having happened in the past. This verse thus preserves the same concern as to whether Jesus *has already come* (and hence come when he was in flesh). It thus appears they are not saying their opponents deny 'Jesus had flesh' but that he came to Earth when he did. And my previous analysis of the first chapter of this letter reinforces that possibility.

Daniel Streett comes to nearly the same conclusion.[71] Though he assumes Jesus existed and thus he defends a different interpretation of this letter than mine (suggesting the dispute must therefore have pertained to the salvific *importance* of Jesus's 'coming in the flesh'), he nevertheless adequately dispatches the notion that 1 John's targets are Docetists in any sense—and he concurs that "the emphasis" in these passages "was not on 'flesh', but on the fact that the Messiah had come into the world."[72] I think once we concede that—*and* allow doubting the historicity of Jesus—an entirely different interpretation comes to the fore: 1 John's opponents were denying Jesus *had come* (just as in 2 Peter 1:16); not that he had once ritually worn flesh.

In other words, we are here looking at two sects, one claiming that

[71] Daniel Streett, *They Went Out From Us: The Identity of the Opponents in First John* (De Gruyter, 2011).

[72] Streett, *They Went Out*, 227.

when Jesus became flesh he came here, to Earth, already (a 'first coming'); the other claiming that when Jesus became flesh, that happened somewhere else (probably somewhere cosmic), and he *hadn't* come to Earth yet—that would only happen in the final apocalypse (per 1 Thessalonians 4:16). Hence, for example, in 1 Corinthians 11:26 Paul says Christians shall take the Lord's supper until Christ *comes*—not *comes again*.[73] Hebrews appears to say the same.[74] As does 1 Corinthians 15:23 and 1 Thessalonians 2:19.[75] At the very least, we cannot rule this out. This is as likely a reading of 1 John 4 as any other. So we cannot simply 'assume' it's the Incarnation being denied by these 'false prophets', rather than the Earthly sojourn. We need evidence to conclude that. And there isn't any.

No other passage cited from the Bible even pertains. The *Oxford Dictionary* lists Colossians 2 (a known forgery, by someone later pretending to be Paul) as evincing a Docetist target, but you can read all through that and you'll find no such thing. That can only be read out of the text by assuming it's there. Without that assumption, any plain reading of that chapter gets us only to a target identical to the ones the real Paul was dealing with (such as in Galatians 4): Torah-observant Christians insisting Gentiles get circumcised and live kosher. There is nothing actually there about denying the Incarnation (or even the coming) of Christ. Paul's imitator is simply explaining how Christ's Incarnation relieves his readers of having to become Jews (otherwise this chapter does look like a mythicist text: see my discussion in chapter two).

When we instead look across the New Testament for passages actually similar to 1 John 4 (and 2 John 7), we find, instead, 1 Timothy 1 (condemning Christians who "hold to myths and endless genealogies," *prosechein mythois kai genealogiais aperantois* and thereby "turn aside to fruitless discussion," *exetrapêsan eis mataiologian*), 1 Timothy 4 (insisting Christians shun "profane and cronish myths," *bebêlos kai graôdeis*

---

[73] Carrier, *Historicity*, p. 560.

[74] Carrier, *Historicity*, 538–57 (544: "Jesus 'once and for all, at the end of the ages, appeared [*phaneroô*] in order to put away sin by sacrificing himself' (Heb. 9.26), the verb here being a common term for divine revelations and manifestations (it actually means 'make known, make clear, reveal')" and "then he 'shall appear [*optanomai*] a second time' (9.28), this time a verb of more concrete seeing—so we will observe his next arrival with our eyes.").

[75] Where (just as in 1 Cor. 11:26) Paul says Jesus "becomes present" or "visits" (*en tê parousia*) only after his resurrection; rather than saying that would be his *second* visit or presence.

mythous), 2 Timothy 4 (condemning Christians who "turn their ears away from the truth and turn aside to myths," *epi de tous mythous ektrapêsontai*)—and 1 John 1 and 2 Peter, which, as we already saw, appear to aim at a similar target. These all repeat concerns never found in Paul: now there is "fruitless discussion" of "myths" or "old wives' tales" that include "genealogies" that these "false" Christians are becoming obsessed with; Christians whom 2 Peter even condemns for *calling* these things "cleverly-devised myths," as opposed to recognizing them as "true" historical accounts—a truth which 2 Peter and 1 John were forged to reassert.

Across all these texts there is some dispute going on over how to interpret and understand the Gospels—which are texts that did not exist in Paul's day, nor did any of the stories comprising them, which is why there were no 'myths' for Paul to be concerned about. What we seem to see here are, rather, attacks not on Docetists, but on mythicist Christians, who were claiming Christ became flesh (and died and rose) but had not come into *our* midst yet, and who thus were claiming that the Gospels merely *mythologically* represent this, the actual truth—and therefore are not *actually* historical records of Jesus visiting Earth. We thus might suspect the genealogies being condemned then are not the biological ones appended to Matthew and Luke (otherwise, why collect these letters into an edition containing the very thing they condemned?), but ideological ones, like the pedigree of stories told about Jesus (if not something even more esoteric, like the complex theories of celestial emanation we hear about in the heresiological literature). This is why 2 Peter seeks to reestablish that pedigree as the eyewitness of Peter—and not, say, the original apostolic revelations and the creative parabolic writing of subsequent movement leaders.

At the very least, again, we cannot rule this out. It is not at all clear that these texts are targeting Docetists. It is just as likely they are targeting mythicist Christians. There is no evidence making either interpretation more likely than the other—apart from the evidence making a discussion of Docetism at all simply unlikely, which we have already surveyed. Which tends then to leave the mythicist interpretation more likely: there were Christians teaching that the Gospels were mere myths, contrived to a parabolic meaning and not a literal one, and one should therefore discuss their symbolical meaning instead, and even appeal to interpretive pedigrees for the purpose; and historicists condemned them as treating these texts in the manner of myths and old-wive's tales, to be interpreted rather than simply believed; and then their opponents are 'refuted' by fabricating eyewitnesses confirming their literal truth (the function of 1 John and 2 Peter, for example), thus negating any alternative pedigree governing their interpretation. In other words, one is to regard these tales as *the truth* (1 Tim. 2:4, 2:7, 3:9, 3:15, 4:3, 4:6, 6:5; 2 Tim. 2:15, 2:18, 2:25, 3:7–8, 4:4); *not* as myths.

And we can infer this because we never get to hear from their targets. We have been allowed to see no texts from them, nor any descriptions of what they believed or were teaching; all of it was left to rot or destroyed.[76] So we cannot resolve the question of what exactly they were saying and these texts are condemning. But it is not credibly 'Docetist'. It is more credibly mythicist. One might reserve judgment about that. But even then you must admit these could yet be fossils of that lost original understanding of the Christian myth. It therefore cannot be said that none has survived.

Conclusion

We've learned three things here.

- First, the sect the ancients identified as the Docetists did not teach anything like what modern scholars call Docetism. They did not deny the Incarnation or Resurrection or the death or humanity of Christ, but only had particular views regarding the low value of a body of flesh, such that they reimagined *how* Jesus became incarnate, and what kind of body he rose from the dead in, or whether he felt pain, concerns not addressed in Ignatius, 2 Peter, or 1 John, and thus not in view there.

- Second, 'switcheroo' Christologies are also not their concern—

[76] Unless some innocuously survive, e.g., in 1 Peter, 1 Clement, Hebrews, Colossians and Ephesians (see chapter two); or the earliest redaction layer of the Ascension of Isaiah; and perhaps the surviving fragments of Heracleon's commentary on the Gospel of John (preserved in quotation by Origen). Carl Berglund, in *Origen's References to Heracleon: A Quotation-Analytical Study of the Earliest Known Commentary on the Gospel of John* (Mohr Siebrek, 2020), analyzes those fragments on an assumption of historicity; but abandon that assumption, and Heracleon's text appears to be denying historicity (Heracleon was thus reversing the rhetorical purpose of the Gospel of John). This warrants a new look.

and, besides, are only incoherently folded under the modern label of Docetism anyway, and probably didn't even exist (Basilides alone was accused of teaching such a thing, and not credibly).

- Third, by name, Marcion alone was accused of denying the Incarnation, but that accusation is demonstrably false. The data establish that he actually maintained the reality of Christ's Incarnation, death, and Resurrection—and that Jesus had a human mother, and really ate and drank, and really was executed by Pontius Pilate; and that these all had earthly witnesses to testify to the fact. So Ignatius, 2 Peter, or 1 John cannot have been responding to Marcion.

The evidence is thus more probable on a more direct explanation rooted in real, actual background knowledge: Ignatius, 2 Peter, and 1 John are all responding to a sect of Christians who were claiming Jesus never visited Earth, that the Gospels are mere myths allegorizing something else. And for that 'something else' the most credible alternative is the one I and Lataster have argued for: that Jesus began as a revealed being, and his incarnation, death, burial, and resurrection were believed to have all taken place in another realm of the cosmos, most likely the sky realms of Satan and his celestially fallen and demonic minions, just as Paul appears to say in 1 Corinthians 2:6–8 (see chapter two), and is said in Ephesians 2:2, and thus could only be known to have happened mystically—through inspired readings of secret messages in scripture, and through direct revelations from on high, after the fact, exactly as Paul says (Romans 16:25–26).

This is the only theory that perfectly fits the evidence of Ignatius, 2 Peter, and 1 John without strain. They were not writing against Docetists (modern or ancient). They were writing against mythicists. And these polemical replies are all that survives for us to know of them. Later Christians heeded their request that these people and their doctrines be shunned and not heard; and so they preserved nothing of them, not even in quotation or refutation, apart from these few and early denunciations. This is all relatively late (all these authors are early-to-mid-second century), and so it cannot argue for these shunned Christians preserving the original faith. They certainly might have been. But they could just as likely have been an evolved 'heresy' against the original creed. Without more or better evidence, we cannot ascertain which it was from what we have.

But this evidence does remove a common objection from play: the argument that surely we would have some reference to this belief, *had it been* the original belief. That argument is fallacious on its own terms. Because we know (it's in our background knowledge, after all) that Christians preserved almost nothing they opposed. The evidence of this behavior, and its results, is extensive.[77] The Nag Hammadi discovery alone proves the point: the quantity of information we never had before its accidental recovery reflects the far greater quantity of information that remains entirely lost—so thorough was Christian destruction of opposition literature. Which required no conspiracy; only a shared belief as to what to shun or destroy. This argument is likewise falsified by the example of the resurrection appearance myth (from inner revelations to dinner parties, as discussed in chapter one), which also left no traces—apart from the evidence in the earliest Epistles, just as with mythicism. So we really have no reason to *expect* any evidence to survive of this belief; just as we have no reason to regarding the original revelatory nature of Jesus's post-resurrection appearances. And yet some slipped through, and in the way it usually does: by our seeing early polemics against it (but still not getting to hear from the targets of those polemics themselves).

Ignatius, 2 Peter, and 1 John thus all represent evidence of Christians clinging to the original mythology, of a cosmic passion rather than an earthly one. Indeed, they evince the fact that these other Christians were actively trying to argue against the new historicizing faith built on the Gospels, thus requiring them and their arguments to be condemned as evil and shunned entirely (being 'false' prophets and teachers, even 'atheists'). Success at that was fairly complete: we hear no more of it after the mid-second century. The historicists (which included even heretics like Marcion) prevailed. Yet as Arthur Droge argues, we have direct evidence of this cosmic passion being a Christian belief in (what Droge regards as) an interpolation in Paul's first letter to the Corinthians.[78] Droge argues

[77] Carrier, *Historicity*, 148–52, 275–78, 301–08, 349–56, 608.

[78] Arthur Droge, "Whodunnit? Paul's Peculiar Passion and Its Implications," in *Recovering an Undomesticated Apostle: Essays on the Legacy of Paul* (ed. C.B. Zeichmann and J.A. Egger; Montreal: McGill-Queen's University Press, 2023), 305–33.

for further support in the historicist Christian doctoring of the *Ascension of Isaiah*, also evincing an effort to conceal a mythicist view among early Christians, as I also suspected.[79] And (as I noted in chapter three) Justin Martyr also suggests an awareness of this belief among Christianity's critics, with his charge (in *Dialogue with Trypho* 9.1) of "empty fables… without any proof" echoing the same concern in 2 Peter and Ignatius.

It is notable how close historians are coming to this realization even as they fall just short of it. Consider the analysis of Tom Thatcher.[80] He establishes that the Johannine Epistles appear to have been created to serve the same function as the related Epistles of Ignatius: to identify mystics in the Christian ranks, who did not countenance an earthly historical Jesus as relevant to their movement, and denounce and shun them. He finds this to be the intent of such passages as 2 John 10–11, 3 John 9–10, and the others we've examined.[81] In his own words:

> Those whom the Elder calls the Antichrists received and represented Jesus through the lens of their immediate experience of his living words as communicated by the Spirit, an approach that left the corpus and shape of Jesus tradition fluid and open.

Which was a view that had to be quashed to maintain any kind of central authority or control, and therefore:

> The Elder, and presumably others like him, responded to this approach by portraying Jesus as a figure from the past, an historical individual who could and must be 'remembered' in the narrow sense simply because the corpus of his teachings and deeds was closed by the fact of his death.

Thatcher references his own more extensive demonstration of this conclusion, and another by Urban von Wahlde, and we can now add

---

[79] Carrier, *Historicity*, 36–48, 320–23, 356–57.

[80] Tom Thatcher, "Johannine Epistles," in *The Reception of Jesus in the First Three Centuries, Volume 1: From Paul to Josephus* (ed. Helen Bond; London: T&T Clark, 2019), 298–307 (300–02 for his survey of the relative dating of the Johannine Epistles).

[81] Thatcher, "Johannine Epistles," 298–300.

Maarten Menken.[82] And we already saw this kind of reasoning is supported by Daniel Streett. They are all still caught up in the assumptions of historicity, maintaining the premise that real memories of Jesus can be found somewhere in the mix of traditions about him—and still maintaining what I now believe to be a dubious understanding of 'Docetism'. But take away those assumptions, and their case remains, and then actually advances mine: the Johannine Epistles, like the Johannine Gospel (and, as well, 2 Peter), is *inventing* an eyewitness tradition, not preserving one, and they are doing so to combat a wing of their own movement that imagined no such Jesus *at all*. The 'Antichrists' as Thatcher labels them appear in fact to be *mythicists*. Their Jesus only underwent his historical drama in the heavens; he was never a historical person on Earth, whom one could 'see with our eyes' and 'touch with our hands' (1 John 1:1–3; John 20–21). This comports as well with the findings of von Wahlde and Menken, who concur that the Jonannines *cannot* be understood as addressing Docetism.[83]

I don't agree with all of their theories or conclusions, but Thatcher, von Wahlde, and Menken all well argue that the Johannine literature was all constructed to condemn and expel competing Christians with affirmations of historical factuality; hence, I would say, it was to get rid of mythicists as heretics and elevate historicism as orthodoxy. Thatcher and von Wahlde agree with almost as much, and for much the same reason I myself suspected: that Jesus had to be historicized precisely to lock down dogma and authority, and thus put an end to 'democratic' Christianity based on revelations (and thus on an imaginary, rather than a historical Jesus), which continually usurped authority and thus undermined the increasingly hierarchical and competitive church industry.[84] Thatcher, von Wahlde, and Menken see this as a competition between mystics and traditionalists, and thus the mystics as shedding, downplaying, or

[82] Tom Thatcher, *Why John Wrote a Gospel: Jesus—Memory—History* (Westminster John Knox, 2006); Urban von Wahlde, *The Johannine Commandments: 1 John and the Struggle for the Johannine Tradition* (Paulist, 1990). See also Urban von Wahlde, *Gnosticism, Docetism, and the Judaisms of the First Century: The Search for the Wider Context of the Johannine Literature and Why It Matters* (T&T Clark, 2015), and Maarten Menken, "The Secessionists of the Jonannine Epistles and Docetism," in Verheyden et al., *Docetism in the Early Church*, 125–42.

[83] Von Wahlde, *Gnosticism, Docetism*, 61–81; Menken, "Secessionists."

[84] Carrier, *Historicity*, 351–53 (cf. 331, 521).

deviating from historical traditions. But all their evidence coheres just as well with those mystics being preservers of the *original* tradition, and the 'traditionalists' the innovators and usurpers, who built their traditions—of specifically a 'historical' Jesus—on myths and lies.[85]

We should heed that possibility. Because the earliest evidence—from Paul, Hebrews, 1 Clement, possibly even 1 Peter (as discussed in chapter two)—all aligns more closely to that being the case, than the other way around.[86] The only bastion left to oppose this conclusion is the attempt to establish that Paul knew Jesus's historical family. So to that question we now turn, the subject of the next three chapters: did Paul say Jesus had a real father, mother, and brothers?

[85] I don't consider it necessary to defend here, but for scholars who still believe the prevailing Christian sect(s) did *not* argue the Gospels were to be read as literal history, see my detailed treatment in Richard Carrier, "Establishing the Biblical Literalism of Early Christians" (26 September 2020) at richardcarrier.info/archives/17150.

[86] Carrier, *Historicity*, 308–15 (1 Clement), 528–31 (1 Peter etc.), 538–53 (Hebrews), 510–28, 531–38, 553–92 (Paul).

8

Why Romans 1:3 Cannot Demonstrate a Historical Jesus

After losing all the other ground there is, anyone still keen on rescuing a historical Jesus will appeal to passages that devotional readings imagine refer to a historical family of Jesus. But this requires straining against the evidence, again, to force a sense that is not actually in the text as written.

The first of these passages is Romans 1:1–3, purportedly attesting Paul's knowledge of Jesus's father.[1] Though neither here nor anywhere in Paul's letters does he describe Jesus having a father, or clearly reference a genealogy, too many translations attempt to invent these by inserting a doctrine of faith here instead of faithfully rendering Paul's actual words. His actual words are more cryptic and unusual, and indeed even conspicuously avoid saying what modern interpreters would have him say. The key verse here is Romans 1:3, whose sense spans Romans 1:2–3. Here is a representative sample of its variant translations:

[1] Addressed in Carrier, *Historicity*, 575–77, and *Outer Space*, 171–90. Which already refute every argument posed to the contrary in Chris Hansen, "Romans 1:3 and the Celestial Jesus: A Rebuttal to Revisionist Interpretations of Jesus's Descendance from David in Paul," *McMaster Journal of Theology and Ministry* 22 (2020–2021), 31–60, and likewise in other critics (as surveyed in chapter three), all of whom entirely evaded the arguments they were supposed to critique, which this chapter shall expand. Also compare Lataster, *Questioning*, 267, 422–24.

> God promised this Good News long ago through his prophets in the holy Scriptures. The Good News is about his Son. In his earthly life he was born into King David's family line. (NLT)

> The gospel he promised beforehand through his prophets in the Holy Scriptures regarding his Son, who as to his earthly life was a descendant of David. (NIV)

> [The gospel] which He promised beforehand through His prophets in the Holy Scriptures, concerning His Son, having come of the seed of David according to flesh. (BLB)

> [The gospel] which he had promised afore by his prophets in the holy scriptures, concerning his Son Jesus Christ our Lord, which was made of the seed of David according to the flesh. (KJV)

The actual sentence in Greek is:

> *Euaggelion theou proepêggeilato dia tôn prophêtôn autou en graphais hagiais peri tou Huiou autou tou genomenou ek spermatos David kata sarka.*

Which literally reads:

> The gospel of God, preannounced by his prophets in the holy writings, concerning his Son having come to be out of the sperm of David according to flesh.

There is nothing here about 'his earthly life' (there is no mention of Earth), or his being 'born into King David's family line' (the words 'born', 'into', 'King', 'family', *and* 'line' are all absent from the words of Paul), or even being a 'descendant' of David (no such word or phrase appears here, either; so contrast this with how Ignatius changes the wording to *actually* say that, as we saw in the last chapter). So what, then, is Paul saying?

Unusual Wording Signals Unusual Meaning

Whether the language here is Paul's or comes from a prior formula composed by someone else, the same conclusions follow. We can say Paul's Greek could mean 'having come of [or from] the seed of David', but even that can mislead in English, for the sense is not of movement (it is not describing Jesus traveling or arriving somewhere, so there is no 'passing through a genealogical line' entailed here), but of coming into existence, 'having come' in the sense of 'having come to be'. Indeed an entirely credible translation is exactly what the original KJV says (and even its rival, the Catholic DRV): Jesus 'was made' of the seed of David. The participle *genomenou*, from *ginomai*, always indicates coming into existence, and as such it can be used to refer to birth (so it could mean 'born'), but it can also be used to refer to manufacture—including of people and their bodies.

That is a common lexical meaning of this verb.[2] And applicable examples abound. Josephus, another first century Jewish author writing in Greek, uses the same word to describe God's manufacture of the world, as well as God's manufacture of Eve and her body.[3] In fact, Josephus uses an expression similar to Paul's there: Adam acknowledges *autên...ex autou genomenên*, that "she was made out of himself."[4] This can be translated as "she came from" Adam (indeed, literally, from his body) but that is the same meaning in context: God *made* her. She was not born. Similarly, *genomenou ek spermatos David* can mean "made out of David's sperm." That is in fact the simplest and most direct translation of Paul's words. This is why both the King James translators and the original Douay-Rheims translators of the Vulgate (and the Vulgate itself) chose to render it exactly that way.

This is, after all, what Paul literally says. Indeed, not just here, but as well in Galatians 4:4 (which we'll discuss more in the next chapter)—and Philippians 2:7, which more evidently refers to Jesus's body being manufactured rather than born: *heauton ekenôsen morphên doulou labôn en homoiômati anthrôpôn genomenos*, lit. "emptying himself, he took the

---

[2] §I.2 in the Liddell and Scott Lexicon: 'to be produced' (hence 'made' or 'manufactured').

[3] Josephus, *Jewish Antiquities* 1.1.1 (§27–28, §36).

[4] Likewise: Josephus, *Jewish Antiquities* 2.16.4 (§342): "the Egyptians entered a road made [*gegenêmenên*] especially for the Hebrews"; 3.7.5 (§162): a Jewish temple priest's garment "was made [*ginetai*] in this way"; 8.5.1 (§5): "God, for whom" Solomon's temple "was made [*egineto*], cooperated" in its construction; etc. Pertinent examples from the NT include: Matthew 4:3; Mark 2:27; John 1:10, 14; Hebrews 11:3.

form of a slave, being made in the likeness of men," just like in Hebrews 2:17, where Jesus had to be "made like" humans (*homoiôthênai*) to redeem them. Even the NIV admits "being made" is the sense in Philippians, and the KJV and DRV render all three verses that way (Romans 1:3, Galatians 4:4, and Philippians 2:7); likewise the ancient Vulgate itself (*factus est ei ex semine*, Rom. 1:3; *factum ex muliere, factum sub lege*, Gal. 4:4; *in similitudinem hominum factus*, Phil. 2:7). Even Tertullian, our earliest interpreter of this text, explicitly confirms this distinction was understood, declaring that Paul peculiarly chose to say "made" rather than "born."[5]

Some translators today will import their faith doctrine even into Philippians 2:7, and render the sentence as "born in the likeness of men," but that is awkward. One is born *as* a man, not "in the likeness of men." The sense seems more clearly to be 'made, produced' (as the Vulgate translators well understood). You can make someone into the likeness of men; you don't usually *beget* them 'into' the likeness of men. Moreover, the context is speaking of a change of state (Philippians 2:6–8), not merely a relocation of abode. For example, Paul does not say Jesus 'went into' a human body in a womb to be born therefrom; he says Jesus was made into a facsimile of a man. Once we stop anachronistically reading the Gospels into Paul, we find here no clear reference to any Nativity, but to Jesus being given a manufactured body just like Eve (per Josephus), and the original Adam (per Paul), who also was not born, but manufactured by God.

Hence Paul says Adam "was made" into a living being, making a particular point of this with exactly the same vocabulary: *egeneto…eis psychên zôsan* (1 Corinthians 15:45). That Paul is referencing the manufacture of Adam's body is clear in context: "the first man Adam was made into a living being" (*psychên zôsan*) in direct apposition to Jesus, "the last Adam" who was made "into a life-giving spirit" (*pneuma zôopoioun*), referencing the two bodies of Paul's entire discourse: the *psychikon sôma* and the *pneumatikon sôma* (as stated in the immediately preceding verse 44, and the immediately following verses 46–47). That this is describing a change of state (for Adam, from inanimate to animate; for Jesus, from carnal to supernatural) makes no difference to what this change of state

[5] Tertullian, *On the Flesh of Christ* 20.3 (*quod factum potius dicit quam natum, simplicius enim enuntiasset natum*), speaking on Gal. 4:4, though the same point would follow for Rom. 1:3.

consists of: God's production of a body. Paul does this again with the future resurrected dead: as Paul says, the body that dies is not "the body that will be made," *genêsomenon* (1 Cor. 15:37); rather, the future body will be "given" by God, *didôsin*, not born (1 Cor. 15:38); literally "made" by God—just like a house, only "without hands" (*acheiropoiêton*: 2 Cor. 5:1–3).

In fact Paul consistently never uses the verb *ginomai* for human birth; not once in any of the some twenty thousand words we have from him. When he means human birth, he always uses instead the verb "to beget," *gennaô* (e.g. Romans 9:11, and Gallatians 4:23 and 29). Indeed, most New Testament authors did. This is confirmed even by the devotional analysis of Matthew Bates: "using the NT as the database, it is roughly fifty times more likely that the author" here "would have used *gennaô* rather than *ginomai* if the author's intention was to signal merely 'natural human birth', which the author emphatically did not do."[6]

Which makes Paul's usage even more conspicuous in both Romans 1:3 and Galatians 4:4, where in both places Paul emulates a common phrase for human birth or ancestry, yet in defiance of the actual convention, he swaps out the verbs—a decision that would strike anyone then as odd, and thus significant, even if he wasn't the author who made this choice. This was so obvious to ancient readers that Tertullian even remarked on it (as we just saw), and independent efforts were made to cover it up: in his reformulation of the creed, Ignatius conspicuously switches the verbs back (as we saw in the previous chapter); and after him, scribes attempted switching them out in the manuscripts of *both* Romans 1:3 *and* Galatians 4:4, demonstrating conscious knowledge of a problem that needed to be 'solved' by correcting the vocabulary.[7] So Paul's choice was well recognized even then as unusual. And an unusual choice of words implies an unusual intent or meaning.

For example, everywhere else that the idiom "born of a woman" appears as a metonym for a mortal human it employs 'beget', not 'come to be'. For example, while in Galatians 4:4 Paul says *genomenon ek gynaikos*,

---

[6] Matthew Bates, "A Christology of Incarnation and Enthronment: Romans 1:3–4 as as Unified, Nonadoptionist, and Nonconciliatory," *Catholic Biblical Quarterly* 77 (2015), 107–27 (115–17).

[7] Bart Ehrman, *The Orthodox Corruption of Scripture: The Effect of Early Christological Controversies on the Text of the New Testament* (Oxford University Press, 1993), 239.

in the Septuagint text of Job 14:1 we find, instead, *gennêtos gynaikos*.[8] Not only has Paul (or his source) changed the verb, he has added *ek* (producing a more conspicuous parallel to what must be his intended sense in Romans 1:3), "out of, from," which he repeats when explaining the mothers he is talking about are allegories for metaphysical states of being (Gal. 4:22–24; see next chapter). There he speaks of Sarah and Hagar's children as 'begotten' (indeed, *kata sarka gegennêtai*, "begotten according to flesh"), thus recognizing he is describing a tale of real human births. Yet Paul switched the term out when connecting Jesus to this allegory. That has to be intentional. And as Bates pointed out, the intention has to be that Paul did not want us to understand Jesus as having been begotten—or, at least, did not consider that relevant to his point—but rather is intentionally drawing attention, instead, to Jesus's change of state: from pre-existent archangel to enfleshed 'slave' to the carnal world (as per Philippians 2:6–11, and per the overall point of Galatians 4).

Likewise the idiom for ancestry, where one would say *ek spermatos* followed by an ancestor's name: that does indeed mean 'descent', yet Paul has gone against that convention, too. On no occasion in Greek literature prior to Late Antiquity is that idiom employed with *ginomai*—or even, in fact, *gennaô*, as the idiom does not reference birth at all, but merely describes lineage (and thus it sometimes might be attached, instead, to the verb *êlthen*, 'to come' from, as in movement or travel, referring to the entire implied sequence of births).[9] Paul has conspicuously—and odd-

---

[8] Likewise Job 11:2, 15:14, and 25:14; similarly, Sirach 10:18, Matthew 11:11, and Luke 7:28. The closest we might find is a clause in Josephus, *Antiquities of the Jews* 16.11.5 (§382), *ek basilidos gynaikos gegomenous*, but that isn't an example of the idiom (this is not referring to someone's mortality or status as a human), but a description of being the legitimate sons of "a king's wife" (thus referencing not the fact of being born, but having a specific kind of mother).

[9] My own comprehensive proximity search of the Thesaurus Linguae Graecae produced no such results prior to Eusebius. Yet the idiom *ek spermatos* [ancestor] is established—indeed, even in Rom. 11:1 (*ek spermatos Abraam*), and, notably, in the second century forgery 2 Tim. 2:8 (*ek spermatos David*), which has removed Paul's unusual phrasing, restoring the original idiom (a change also performed by Ignatius, *Ephesians* 18:2 and *Romans* 7:2). Other examples include 1 Maccabees 7:14 (*ek spermatos Aarôn êlthen*); *Testaments of the Twelve Patriarchs* 3.8.15 (*ek spermatos Abraam*); and *Testament of Job* 1.5 (*ek spermatos Iakôb*). The first instance of attaching *ginomai* is effected by Eusebius, in emulation of Paul: *ho Christos tou theou ek spermatos Isaak gegone to kata sarka* (*Proof of the*

ly—broken this convention by connecting this phrase to *ginomai*, 'come to be, made'. This reflects a conscious decision to *alter* what the idiom intends. Paul (or, again, his source) has thus made clear that he does not mean, simply, ancestry, but something importantly different from that—and the clue to ascertaining *what* lies in what he has changed: his choice of verb.

Here again Paul did not choose to attach (or even reattach) the idiom to 'beget' (*gennaô*), but chose instead to select (or preserve) what is Paul's own preferred word for 'manufacturing' people and their bodies, thus *refusing* to employ his own preferred word for 'human birth'. The consistency of Paul's practice everywhere else leaves no other likely interpretation than that Paul means to make clear that Jesus was not 'born of' the seed of David; he was 'made from' it (just as Bates and I argue). What exactly that means may now be hard to extract. But his readers surely knew—that's why Paul did not have to explain it. His unusual modification of this idiom is the same as his unusual modification of the other (in Galatians); and that connects directly with his credal assertion (in Philippians) of a pre-existent Jesus coming into the world by being given a body, not arriving there as the output of a biological lineage.

At the very worst, *we cannot rule this out*. Which is the most important point here. However much you might want this verse to reference descendance (and thus biological birth, begotten by a human father), from Paul's actual, and indeed unusual, choice of words (even if preserved from a source), you cannot establish that that is any more likely what Paul means than that he means, instead, that Jesus was given a body of flesh to inhabit (per Philippians 2:7), just like God gives bodies to Adam, Eve, and the future resurrected. Yes, it was important that that body come from David's semen (*ek spermatos David*). But that, we shall see, is because scripture required that it be. But by God's unlimited might, such a prophecy could be fulfilled in any number of ways without a questionable lineage of biological vessels. In fact, when we read the prophecy in question, it can *only* have been fulfilled, as worded, by a far more direct device than that.

Gospel 2.1.11; cf. 2.3.109, 3.2.32, etc.).

Fulfilling Nathan's Prophecy

As explained in chapter five, when estimating the probabilities of things we must attend to our background knowledge, because that determines what was common or likely or expected (or not) in the time and place (or even author) we are concerned with; and *how* common or likely or expected (or not). Paul is writing in the context of first century apocalyptic Judaism, as an apocalyptic Jew. Extensive background evidence, therefore, establishes two facts about him to an effective certainty:

- **First:** Jews like Paul, and Christians like him, routinely expected the Messiah (their 'Christ') to fulfill prophecies in the Scriptures—*especially* those that were explicitly about that Messiah (typically a future triumphant Davidic king), but even many more passages than that, which were variously by then believed to be about that Messiah.[10] To qualify as a Messiah, one had to meet at least a minimum of these prophecies; and *all* that were explicit.

- **Second:** it is beyond doubt that one such prophecy was that of the Holy Prophet Nathan, which every Messiah had to fulfill. This predicted that the future eternal king, God's chosen, would in some sense come from the famed King David himself. And this appears explicitly as prophecy, in a standard volume of scripture: 2 Samuel.

That prophecy was spoken by Nathan in the voice of God himself:

> When your days are fulfilled and you lie down with your fathers, I will raise up [LXX, *anastêsô*] your offspring [LXX, *to sperma sou*] after you, who shall come forth from your body [LXX, *ek tês koilias sou*], and I will establish his kingdom.
>
> He shall build a house for my name, and I will establish the throne of his kingdom for ever [LXX, *heôs eis ton aiôna*]. I will be his father, and he shall be my son.
>
> When he commits iniquity [LXX, *ean elthê hê adikia autou*], I will

[10] Carrier, *Historicity*, 66–92, 137–46.

> chasten him with the rod of men, with the stripes of the sons of men. But I will not take my steadfast love from him, as I took it from Saul, whom I put away from before you.
>
> And your house and your kingdom shall be made sure for ever [LXX, *heôs aiônos*] before me; your throne shall be established for ever [LXX, *heôs aiônos*].
>
> —2 Samuel 7:12–16 (RSV)

This is the text as most faithfully translated from the Hebrew. But we also know Paul often employed Greek translations (like the LXX) and treated them as exegetically valid interpretations of the original. So I have noted above where that Greek text has significance.

When Nathan says God will 'raise up' the eternal king, the same word is used that Christians employed of resurrection (*anastêsô*), so Christians could easily see here a prediction of the messiah's resurrection. And the penalty clause ("when his injustice comes") is more ambiguous in the Greek as to whether this son might *do* injustice or *receive* it, allowing room to interpret the prophecy as predicting the messiah's *unjust* suffering, also making it attractive to Christian exegetes—it could thus be tied into the Suffering Servant material of Isaiah 53 and the Dying Messiah material of Daniel 9, passages we saw in chapter two many exegetes also strove to connect to the messiah. David's offspring is also described as 'sperm' (*to sperma*, singular; likewise in the original Hebrew), which both the Greek and Hebrew say will come directly from David's 'insides' (*koilias*, 'belly, intestines, any internal organ or cavity'). And in both versions Nathan says that this son's 'throne' itself (twice), not just the kingdom (three times), will endure forever (twice again: until the end of time, *heôs eis ton aiôna* and *heôs aiônos*). This messianic figure is also prefigured in both editions as the Son of God, also ideal for a Christian reading (hence Acts 2:30).

This prophecy was not obscure; it was one of the most fundamental predictions of the messiah. As echoed in the Psalms, "he shows unfailing love to his anointed [Hebrew: *mashiach*; Greek: *christô*], to David and to his descendants [Greek: *kai tô spermati*, which is again in the singular; likewise in the Hebrew] forever [*heôs aiônos* in the Greek; matching expression in the Hebrew]" (18:50 NIV; similarly: Psalms 89:3–4, 28–37; 132:10–12; etc.). And as demonstrated by Christopher Whitsett (among others), it is without doubt one of the passages Paul is referring to in Romans 1:3.[11] Nathan's prophecy is the only passage explicitly from a prophet (as opposed to merely a psalm), and the only passage in standard scripture altogether, rendering such a promise specifically to "a sperm" that is at the same time declared "God's son" and sourced "from" David (the LXX using, indeed, *ek*). Paul thus references a "promise" coming from a "holy writing" of "the prophets" that was written "concerning **[God's] son**, having come **from** the **seed** of **David**." That's this prophecy. There is no other that fits so closely. But even echoes of this prophecy in the Psalms repeat the same salient elements: a singular seed must come from David and rule forever. For example, Psalms 18:50, 89:3–4 and 89:28–37, and 132:10–12 all simply paraphrase Nathan's prophecy, reminding readers of (1) a promise from God (2) that David's (3) singular seed (4) will sit an eternal throne. It's unmistakable that this is what Romans 1:3 means.

The original intent of this prophecy was almost certainly to describe Solomon (David's son) as favored by God; and it is his throne that will last forever (not Solomon himself). The word 'seed' is in the singular, and it comes directly from David's belly, not someone else's. So it is Solomon who would establish this eternal throne. Occasionally, God warns, he might have to chasten these future kings, but his love will never depart them, and so their throne will last forever (literally to the end of time). God even uses a counterexample to make his point clear: he specifically points out that Saul's line did not inherit the throne (David is the son of Jesse); but *David's* line always will. Every echo of this prophecy in the Psalms repeats that point: the throne will be eternal; it will never cease; it will always be sat by seed of David.

The problem is that this prophecy, as written, was falsified: that throne did not last. It came to an end with the death of Zedekiah and the Babylonian destruction of the last kingdom of the Hebrews some six centuries before the time of Paul. It was never restored. The restoration of a 'kingdom' of sorts occurred almost two centuries before the time of Paul, ruled by the Hasmoneans, but they had no claim to Davidic ancestry (or even to the tribe of Judah); and even their kingdom hardly

[11] Christopher Whitsett, "Son of God, Seed of David: Paul's Messianic Exegesis in Romans 2:3-4," *Journal of Biblical Literature* 119.4 (Winter 2000), 661–81 (the title of which is misprinted; the article is about Rom. 1:3–4).

survived in any relevant sense by the time of Jesus, as more and more of it was acceded into the Roman province of Syria (and thus to Roman, hence even outright foreign, rule). But even if one counted the Hasmonean dynasty as nevertheless sitting David's 'throne', the prophecy still failed: that throne sat vacant for centuries *before* the Hasmoneans.

There are only two ways to deal with this conundrum: either declare Nathan's prophecy false—and thus Nathan a false prophet and the entire book of 2 Samuel not an inspired scripture—or commit to 'reinterpreting' it in some way that it could be imagined still not to have failed. The background evidence firmly establishes that no Jews selected option one. They all maintained Nathan's prophecies, and 2 Samuel altogether, as the true and inspired word of God. For actual messianic pretenders or prospects, the most obvious recourse would have been to say that Nathan spoke obscurely and that his words (which were God's own words) should be taken non-literally, but in some fashion figuratively. And the most obvious way to do that would be to claim some hidden scion of David still survived every generation, merely 'holding the throne' figuratively as a birthright. It's an awkward solution. Because this isn't what Nathan says. His words plainly say the *throne and kingdom* would be eternal from David onward. So this solution is strained. But we well know apocalyptic Jewish exegetes were used to straining the sense of scripture to rescue it from being false. So there would be nothing improbable about that. And we can cite many examples like it.[12]

But what might a messianic pretender or prospect do who couldn't convincingly claim to be this scion of David? Since the scripture is already being strained, it would be no trouble to strain it an inch more, and propose that God spoke *entirely* figuratively, and one need merely be *declared by God* to be the seed of David, 'anointed' as it were into that role. Ancestry need then not matter. But even if it did, since ancestral claims could also not be *disproved*, one could attempt to *claim* that they happened to be of that line, and then use traditional superstitious methods of proving it—performing 'miracles' or impressing the masses with their charisma or genius, demonstrating God's endorsement of their claim—or political ones—like convincing respected authorities to endorse your

[12] Gerbern Oegema, *The Anointed and his People: Messianic Expectations from the Maccabees to Bar Kochba* (T&T Clark 1998).

claim, perhaps even forging genealogical records to the point.[13] Either way, any messianic claimant always had to establish that they fulfilled this prophecy *somehow*. They need not have done that in any empirically valid way; they just had to accomplish it by some device, any device that would convince what were usually nonrational and superstitious (or even just politically pragmatic) followers.

So with all this background knowledge in place, what can we predict would happen if someone were convinced by a dream or vision that they had met a *celestial* messiah? This imaginary figure still has to satisfy that same prophecy, just as a real one would. There are again only two ways to deal with this conundrum: either declare the vision false, a Satanic or demonic deceit or otherwise merely unreal; or commit to 'reinterpreting' the prophecy in some way that it could be imagined as still, nevertheless, fulfilled. The background evidence firmly establishes that almost no one—then or ever—has been convinced they met a genuine deity in a dream or vision, and then upon confronting some easily-evaded technicality, decided they were deceived and abandoned their faith. This is, in fact, behavior entirely contrary to the usual order of human nature.[14]

Abandoning a firmly held faith usually takes years of study and consideration, in a cultural atmosphere normalizing critical questioning and freedom of belief; while any strong faith is highly resistant to trivial contradictions that are easily rationalized away, succumbing only to extended and cumulative refutations instead. And that is true even of merely cultural or reasoned belief; when it comes to people who actually believe they have spoken to the gods, and who can thus appeal to a powerful emotional and veridical experience, such faith is even more resistant to

---

[13] On charismatic epistemology driving the Christian movement, for example, see: Richard Carrier, *The Scientist in the Early Roman Empire* (Pitchstone, 2017), 500–26.

[14] Carrier, *Historicity*, 124–37. The seminal study on this point remains Leon Festinger, Henry Riecken, and Stanley Schachter, *When Prophecy Fails: A Social and Psychological Study of a Modern Group That Predicted the Destruction of the World* (University of Minnesota Press, 1956), which led to the formal development of cognitive dissonance theory, in Leon Festinger, *A Theory of Cognitive Dissonance* (Stanford University Press, 1957). For a review of developments in the science since: Eddie Harmon-Jones (ed.), *Cognitive Dissonance: Reexamining a Pivotal Theory in Psychology*, 2nd ed. (American Psychological Association, 2019). For its effects in respect to prophecy: Suzanne Newcombe and Sarah Harvey (eds.), *Prophecy in the New Millennium: When Prophecies Persist* (Routledge, 2013).

abandonment. It is not possible to override that with a minor technicality.

This means we can predict with effective certainty that once the apostles were convinced by their visions or dreams of an *imagined* messianic Lord confirming to them everything they dearly wanted to believe, they would no more 'abandon' their resulting faith over Nathan's prophecy than anyone inspired by a historical messianic claimant would. Just as the latter would 'reinterpret' that prophecy to fit the actual facts of their situation, rather than abandon their claim or belief, so would the former. And since we know this is what would happen *with effective certainty*, the probability that it would not happen is functionally zero. These apostles would simply have devised a way to read Nathan's prophecy as fulfilled by their believed messiah.

And both politically and culturally, we know such cognitive dissonance need not require an actually killed (hence actually 'failed') claimant. I already demonstrated in *Historicity* that a slain cosmic messiah solved many other desperate problems, and inspiration for such a solution then abounded.[15] And Jewish exegetes were already toying with the anticipated need of a dying messiah, believing they were seeing it predicted in scripture already (as discussed in chapter two). So the idea was already in the air or ripe for invention.

A Necessary Digression on Logic

Returning to the point of chapter five, let's apply here the rule of priors and likelihoods. On priors, we know figurative and creative fulfillments of prophecy were routine in that time, and therefore no less likely than literal ones. On likelihoods, this evidence is entirely expected even if Jesus didn't exist; therefore, it cannot be 'more' expected if he did. Romans 1:3 therefore evinces nothing. It cannot tell us whether Jesus existed or not, because it would appear in Paul's discourses whether Jesus existed or not—and indeed, in exactly the weird way we find it.

The logic here is unassailable:

---

[15] See pp. 70–72 here; and Carrier, *Historicity*, 153–63 and 164–214, respectively.

- We know from abundant background knowledge that a messianic Jew who did become convinced of a celestial messiah (in the very manner Paul describes they were: 1 Cor. 15:3–8; Gal. 1:11–16; Rom. 16:25–26) would have, to a certainty, devised a way to read Nathan's prophecy as still, nevertheless, thereby fulfilled. So we cannot say that is improbable. It is not even *measurably* improbable.

- We further know from abundant background knowledge that a messianic Jew of that time and place readily believed God had unlimited supernatural power and thus was not 'constrained' by any laws of physics or biology, and in fact routinely defied both in awesome miraculous fashion. This is a God who parts seas, stores the world's rains and snows in vaults in outer space, manufactures fetuses *in situ*, teleports babies out of wombs, resurrects the world's dead, and levitates mighty halls and thrones thousands of miles above the Earth. This is the same God whom Paul casually believed was already storing our future resurrection bodies for us in outer space (2 Cor. 5), or even stored the buried corpses of Adam and Eve there (2 Cor. 12; referencing the *Life of Adam and Eve*, which documents those graves as in 'the third heaven'—see my discussion in chapter two).

- We also know from abundant background knowledge that a messianic Jew of that time and place readily believed God could fulfill prophecy figuratively. The very same Jews who believed that a non-eternal 'throne and kingdom' can somehow still have been eternal since the time of David (so as to get Nathan's prophecy still to be true), would be equally ready to devise a figurative way a *celestial* messiah could not fail that prophecy, too. After all, all historical claimants failed it (the throne was not eternal); yet were believed nevertheless not to have. Some excuse was always devised by which its 'eternality' could still be maintained against the evidence; so, too, for any imagined celestial claimant.

So, again, 'that is improbable' is not a true statement of the facts here. To the contrary, the probability is effectively 100% that Paul and the apostles adopted a figurative or miraculous way by which Jesus fulfilled Nathan's prophecy *even if* they imagined he never visited Earth and had no human parents. Which means the probability that we would find the words "his Son Jesus Christ our Lord...was made of the seed of David according to the flesh" in the writings of Paul *if* Paul did not believe in an earthly sojourn of Christ is, simply, 100% (or as near to as makes all odds). Likewise all derivative statements in the Epistles, which are just different ways of saying this same ambiguous thing.[16] That sentence therefore can never be evidence *against* his having believed that. All messiahs had to satisfy Nathan's prophecy. The apostles firmly believed their Jesus was the messiah. Ergo, they would have solved Nathan's prophecy for Jesus. And this is the case no matter what kind of Jesus they believed in. Therefore, Romans 1:3 can never be evidence for historicity; because it can never be evidence against minimal mythicism, as that predicts this same belief (and the same sentence) to virtual 100% certainty.

This would not be the case had Paul not been so weird in how he says this, though. So the reason this verse does not evince anything is precisely its strange ambiguity. It is Paul's unusual choices of wording that eliminate this as evidence for historicity. If Paul had simply said what the NLT translators falsely *claim* he said, that "in his earthly life Jesus was born into King David's family line," then we'd be assured of historicity—as *then* it *would* be improbable that Paul would say this, if he *didn't* know Jesus to have been a recent earthly historical man. Which is why the NLT translators faked up what Paul said—just as medieval scribes did by doctoring his vocabulary to cover up the same thing: that Paul was actually *too ambiguous* to sustain this as evidence of historicity. But alas, Paul *was* 'too ambiguous' to sustain this as evidence of historicity. And so it isn't.

I could end this chapter and its argument here. We do not need to know how they solved this prophecy for Jesus—after all, they never say, not even to say that Jesus solved it by, say, presenting from his father's records a genealogy confirming his Davidic ancestry, or anything comparable. Because we already know, with certainty, that if the apostles

[16] For example: Heb. 7:11-17 (Jesus "arose from the tribe Judah"); Rom. 15:8 (Jesus "came from the circumcision," i.e. the Jews), 9:5 (Jesus came "from the forefathers"), and 15:12 (Jesus was the "root of Jesse"); and Gal. 3:16 (Jesus is "Abraham's seed"). None of these say *how* he fulfilled these things; and all are just repetitions of the same prophecy of Nathan (as anyone who comes 'from David' satisfies all these other propositions, no matter how): Carrier, *Historicity*, 575.

believed Jesus recently underwent his incarnation and death in the firmament above (or any other location beyond human witness), then they would also have believed Jesus fulfilled Nathan's prophecy. And thus we already know, with certainty, that they would have believed "Jesus Christ our Lord…was made of the seed of David according to the flesh"—no matter in what way they thought God worked that out, just as it would not matter in what way they worked that out if they believed in a real earthly Jesus.

Nevertheless, someone who cannot follow this logic might still attempt to object at this point, arguing something to the effect of 'there is no way they could have solved this problem in that case, therefore it is still improbable' (in the way it would be if Paul had said what the NLT does), which in principle is the only way to get Romans 1:3 back in as evidence for historicity. On this reasoning, there is just no way any Jewish exegete of that time could imagine Nathan's prophecy as fulfilled *but by* ordinary, literal human ancestry. In my original study I refuted this argument by presenting ways that, in fact, they could imagine just such a thing. Therefore, the claim that they could not imagine such a thing is false, and therefore no longer operates as a logically sound objection to my conclusion that this passage affords us no evidence either way.

So here one must understand some basic principles of logic. There is a logical difference between empirical and modal arguments.[17] Modal arguments are so named from the fact that they are governed by 'modal logic', which is the logic of 'modalities' of truth, like 'possibility' or 'capability'. Empirical arguments, by contrast, are arguments to fact, and thus rely on standard logic (usually inductive; I demonstrated in chapter five that Bayesian logic is what governs claims as to what is most probable in history). Unlike a modal argument, empirical arguments require evidence that their conclusion is probably true. Modal arguments, however, do not require this. All modal arguments might require is evidence of a possibility or impossibility; they do not usually require the conclusion be proved probable or improbable.

Consider an example. If you say 'that your car was stolen is impossible', all I need to disprove what you just said is evidence that it is *possible*

[17] For a primer: Rod Girle, *Modal Logics and Philosophy*, 2nd ed. (Routledge, 2010), esp. 1–27.

my car was stolen. I do not have to present evidence that it is *probable* my car was stolen. Because all you asserted was its impossibility; which its mere possibility already sufficiently disproves. 'It's impossible because I was home the whole time your car was parked outside my house' is defeated by 'A thief can steal a car without someone in an adjacent building noticing'. Note that I do not have to present evidence that an actual thief actually did effect stealth to steal the car; the mere fact that we both recognize one *could* have is sufficient to eliminate the argument. And if someone were to refuse to recognize that, we could present evidence of it—but that evidence would not be evidence of what happened to my car, but evidence of what often happens to cars generally. Which is evidence of a possibility; not evidence of a probability. But such evidence would suffice to disprove your charge.

If, by contrast, you said 'that your car was stolen is improbable', two distinct burdens arise that don't arise for modal arguments: first, to sustain your claim, you must prove with evidence that your claim is true—namely, that my car being stolen *is actually improbable*; second, to refute your claim, I must prove with evidence that my claim is true—namely, that my car being stolen is probable after all. If neither of us can meet this burden, then the question of whether my car was most likely stolen remains unanswered—it is then as likely stolen as not, unless some background evidence established that theft wasn't (or was) commonly the cause of missing cars in this case, and therefore the claim of its being stolen bore a low prior probability (or, conversely, a high one). But that isn't usually the case. Usually, if a car is missing, it's as likely stolen as not. It could have been towed or misplaced, but you need evidence to establish that any of these three explanations (stolen, towed, or misplaced) is more likely than the other. And that argument would be empirical, not merely modal (you'd have to look at actual evidence of actual frequencies in that actual context).

The significance of all this is that the only way to object to a standard claim to fact (that something is *probable*) is with an argument *to a probability*, for which you need evidence that what you are saying is in fact what more probably happened; but to object to a claim of impossibility, all you need is to respond with evidence of what's possible—you do not have to prove that it is probable at all. That the apostles would say a purely cosmic messiah fulfilled Nathan's prophecy has already been proved probable. It's as probable as anything can be. There is no evidence to the contrary. So you cannot object with an empirical argument. There simply is no evidence that it is improbable that they would do this. What might then be substituted is, rather, a modal argument: that it *must* be improbable *because it is impossible* (hence again: 'your car can't have been stolen because I was home the whole time your car was parked outside my house'). Which can be refuted with mere evidence of its being possible (hence again: 'abundant background evidence attests that a thief can steal a car without someone in an adjacent building noticing'). Which then forces the arguer to revert to making an empirical argument, attempting to prove (with evidence) that the proposed scenario was still improbable. But since they won't have any such evidence, that conclusion isn't sound. They simply have no logically sound argument. The car could have been stolen without their noticing. They have no evidence it wasn't. And that's that.

This is the situation we are in with regard to the evidence of Romans 1:3. I have proved that it's being fitted to Jesus is 100% expected regardless of the metaphysics of Jesus. It therefore can never be evidence for a historical Jesus. Nor is it evidence against it, either. Like the car, which is as likely stolen as towed or misplaced, this passage is as likely signifying normal human ancestry as miraculous or figurative ancestry. There is no evidence that either is more probable than the other. Given the text as written, it is just as likely to have been generated by either point of view. So it distinguishes neither. And this is why that passage is of no use to historicists. Indeed all the unusual things about it even make that interpretation less probable. But that still does not mean Jesus didn't exist. Paul could well have believed Jesus (a real historical Jesus) was in fact made in the womb of his mother by God, directly from the semen of David, regardless of ancestry. That is, after all, what the authors of the Gospels of Matthew and Luke must have imagined as having happened.

If, nevertheless, you wish to resort to the modal argument, that there is 'no way' a first century apocalyptic Jew could get the Nathan prophecy to fit a celestial Christ, then all I need to refute you is to present evidence of possible ways they nevertheless could. And so I shall. I shall argue that Paul understood Nathan's prophecy to be true *exactly as written*: God took semen from David's belly and used it to build a mortal body for Jesus when the appropriate time came. But it is crucial to recognize that

I am not arguing that this is 'surely' what Paul meant when writing this verse. My sole and only point is that this is a 'possible' way he could have meant it—as in, it is a solution that was entirely available to him given the tools and methods Jewish exegetes of his time regularly employed. It is, in other words, like evidence that thieves can stealthily steal cars near you: not in any way evidence that that is what happened; but solely evidence that you cannot claim it *couldn't be* what happened.

As to the question of probability, that has already been resolved: that the apostles would come up with *some* way to interpret a celestial Christ as fulfilling Nathan's prophecy is already, effectively, 100% certain. And that's that. No further objections are valid. If there were only one 'possible' way to do that, then that would be 100% certain to be how they did it. But if there is more than one way they could, it could be any of them—but even then that it would be *one* of them is 100% assured. Hence I will aver that what follows *is* the *most* likely way they then would have explained Nathan's prophecy as fulfilled—because it requires the fewest and smallest leaps of reasoning for them, and best fits the available precedents in our background knowledge. But that should not be confused for saying that that is most likely what Paul understood himself to be saying in Romans 1:3. That depends on how probable it is that Jesus did not exist, which depends on other evidence than this.

For example, if it is only 67% likely Paul believed in a solely celestial Christ, and it is 60% likely he *then* understood Christ as fulfilling the prophecy in the way I describe, then the total probability that that is what Romans 1:3 refers to is only 67% × 60% ≈ 40%, and thus more probably than not Paul meant something else. But that is only *after* we have resolved how likely it is that Jesus existed; it therefore can no longer affect the probability that he did. Conversely, if it is 67% likely Paul believed in a solely celestial Christ, and it is 90% likely he then understood Christ as fulfilling the prophecy in the way I describe, then the total probability that that is what Romans 1:3 refers to is 67% × 90% = 60% (rounding to the nearest whole percent), and thus more probably than not Paul did indeed mean what I suggest—albeit not to anything near a certainty that he did. Because 60% leaves a 40% chance he was imagining something else, like a figurative interpretation of Nathan's prophecy—or even an ordinary biological one, because there is on this account still a 33% chance Paul knew Jesus to be a real historical man.

And notice, as well, that I could be right about this *even if that were the case*. The probability that Paul *both* knew Jesus existed (33%) *and* understood Jesus to have been magically Davidic in the very manner I shall describe (90%) is then 33% × 90% = 30% (rounded). So Paul could well have believed God made Jesus literally the immediate son of David, *and* believed this of a historical Jesus. Which is why what I shall argue next is also not evidence *against* the historicity of Jesus. It is equally compatible with Jesus existing and not existing.

How Christ Can Be Nathan's Messiah

There is actually a very obvious way that a messiah could then have been imagined to rescue Nathan's prophecy from being false: simply reading the prophecy *literally*, exactly as written. Which invokes no improbabilities: reading prophecies literally was commonplace; as was imagining God metaphysically capable of anything, particularly things he or other divinities were readily believed to have done. When Nathan says a singular seed will be physically taken from David's 'insides' and that *this* seed will be declared 'God's Son' and God will allow this seed to be abused but resurrected, and sit upon an eternal, uninterrupted throne of God's Kingdom, all of that can easily be what the apostles thought actually happened: God took semen from David, and then manufactured with it a body for an eternal Lord, Jesus Christ. That body would be abused and killed; but Jesus would rise from the dead, and then sit upon the promised eternal throne.[18]

Being an immortal superpower, Jesus would never die and never be overthrown; therefore, he really would sit eternally on the throne of God's kingdom (at least until the prophesied 'end of time' as described in 1 Corinthians 15:20–28). And he would do that being no mere descendent but, literally and directly, an actual son of David. Then Nathan's prophecy is no longer falsified by the failure of the earthly throne: since God promised the eternal kingdom to this future son of David, its clock only begins when this son comes into the promised inheritance—when

[18] The role of the incarnation was therefore to *both* fulfill prophecy *and* effect the final atoning power believed to be required by yet other prophecies: 1 Cor. 2:7–8, 15:3; Phil. 2:8–9; Heb. 9; per Dan. 9 and Is. 53. See Carrier, *Historicity*, 83–87, 143–46, 156–59.

that seed from David's belly is used to produce a body of flesh for Christ to occupy and die in, and *then* by his resurrection he begins that eternal kingdom. Hence Romans 1:4 outright says Jesus will *then* be "through the Spirit of holiness appointed the Son of God in power by his resurrection from the dead" and *thereupon* be "Jesus Christ our Lord" (cf. Philippians 2:9–11).

So on that reading, Nathan's prophecy did not refer to Solomon or his throne or line (because then it would be literally false). It referred to a different son of David—biologically, Solomon's yet-unborn brother—and thus to a different throne and kingdom, a future one that *would* last forever. Nathan and God then can no longer be accused of false prophecy. The earthly throne failed. But, to deceive the Satanic powers (Rom. 16:25–26 and 1 Cor. 2:7–8), that *wasn't* the throne God was referring to. This is in fact a simpler and more obvious and direct solution to the failure of this prophecy, more elegant than the usual recourse of fudging a 'hidden scion' into somehow being the same thing as an 'eternal throne and kingdom'. And yet messianic Jews readily embraced that more awkward solution. Some therefore will have even *more* readily embraced a far *less* awkward one, particularly those who believe in God's mystical, magical activity in the cosmos—as well as his need to 'hide' the real meaning of his prophecies from the celestial powers who would oppose them (per 1 Cor. 2:6–10), thus *already implying* unusual plans.

We cannot balk at this by snickering at the fact that this entails God maintaining, in essence, a 'cosmic sperm bank', storing the semen of David in hiding (just like the snow hidden in the vaults of heaven) until the day he needed it to construct the promised body to effect his plan of an eternal kingdom. That God stored things in the heavens (corpses, snow, rain, hail, unborn and thus 'stored' souls, even never-decaying books, and trees and bodies per 2 Cor. 5 and 1 Cor. 12), in ways only today realized by advanced technologies, was a routine belief of Jewish exegetes at the time.[19] Indeed, there was a Jewish belief then (attested in 4 Ezra 12:32–34) that God 'stored' (as in magically preserved) the messiah himself, for centuries, just to satisfy Nathan's prophecy in the very way I have suggested: being, literally, the direct son of David (thus Solomon's lost brother), secretly awaiting the moment he would assume the promised

[19] Carrier, *Historicity*, 179–80, 194–97.

kingdom (in the meantime subsisting as a wandering beggar), *thereby* keeping Nathan's prophecy literally true.[20]

If God could accomplish this with a whole human man, he certainly could for a mere drop of semen. And, indeed, pre-modern belief already encompassed the idea of magically transporting and storing human semen.[21] The Talmud records the legend that God even assigned an angel for the purpose: named Laylah ('Night').

> The angel that is appointed over conception is called Night. And that angel takes the drop of semen from which a person will be formed and presents it before the Holy One, Blessed be He, and says before Him: Master of the Universe, what will be of this drop? Will the person fashioned from it be mighty or weak? Will he be clever or stupid? Will he be wealthy or poor?[22]

This legend cannot be dated. Only the first attester to it can be placed a couple centuries after Christianity began; it could well long predate that. But the relevance of the legend here is not to establish that this belief existed when the apostles began their exegesis, but to establish how readily the entire Rabbinate adopted the idea, and thus so could the Apostolate. It demonstrates how easy it was to arrive at bizarre conclusions about the operations of the world and the capacities and interests of God. If an angel could magically preserve and transport semen from a body, all the way to God for review, and back again into the womb in (or the testicles from) which it would produce a child (and no one in the Talmud balked at this; they accepted it and discuss it as if it were obviously true) then we cannot balk at any similar thinking arising earlier in the same era. If the rabbis could come up with this, the apostles could come up with any belief like it. (Which is another example of modal logic.)

The same reasoning follows for the still-attested fact of a pre-Chris-

[20] Abraham Berger, "Captive at the Gate of Rome: The Story of a Messianic Motif," *Proceedings of the American Academy of Jewish Research* 44 (1977), 1–17; John Reeves, *Trajectories in Near Eastern Apocalyptic: A Postrabbinic Jewish Apocalypse Reader* (Society of Biblical Literature, 2005), 53–55; Alexei Sivertsev, *Judaism and Imperial Ideology in Late Antiquity* (Cambridge University Press, 2011), 137–53.

[21] Carrier, *Historicity*, 576 (esp. in the 2023 rev. ed.).

[22] *b.Niddah* 16b (translation from sefaria.org), mystically interpreting Job 3:3; attributed to Rabbi Ḥanina bar Pappa (3rd/4th century).

tian belief within Persian Zoroastrianism that the semen of its own messiah would be preserved in a magical lake for a thousand years until each prophesied virgin would bathe within to be impregnated with his child.[23] And this was a religion whose eschatology and angelology considerably influenced the Judaism of Christian times; so it was not some isolated belief system no one knew about.[24] The same reasoning that helped move the Jews to adopt into their faith a foreign Zoroastrian belief in the eschatological resurrection of the dead (no doubt by the simple reasoning that "if their God could do that, then so could ours") would likewise merit embracing the notion that its god could magically preserve semen for a thousand years, indeed specifically to fulfill its own messianic scheme—particularly as soon as such a belief became useful.

The result is always the same: this was an idea easily arrived at in that era; it therefore cannot be claimed to have been impossible or even 'too improbable' for the apostles to conceive. They wouldn't even need these inspiring precedents—the same ease with which each of these precedents was itself arrived at would apply to the apostles coming up with it even on their own. Its utility all but assures it, lest a better idea came to them (in which case they will have satisfied Nathan's prophecy regardless). But the multiply attested possibility of *this* idea already circulating only bolsters the point. As does its entirely apposite fit to the notion of interpreting Nathan's prophecy literally as written, so as to entirely repair it from having historically failed. There is therefore no argument possible that this idea would have been 'impossible' or 'inconceivable' to the apos-

---

[23] Edwin Yamauchi, "Religions: Persia," in *The International Standard Bible Encyclopedia*, vol. 4 (ed. Geoffrey Bromiley; Eerdmans, 1979), 127 (future saviors "were to be born of virgins from the seed of Zoroaster preserved in Lake Kasaoya"); and Mark Muesse, *The Age of the Sages: The Axial Age in Asia and the Near East* (Fortress, 2013), 29.

[24] Werner Sundermann, "Zoroastrian Motifs in Non-Zoroastrian Traditions," *Journal of the Royal Asiatic Society* 18.2 (2008), 155–65; Alan Segal, "Iranian Views of the Afterlife and Ascent to the Heavens," *Life after Death: A History of the Afterlife in Western Religion* (Doubleday, 2004), 173–203; Lloyd Applegate, "Zoroastrianism and Its Probable Influence on Judaism and Christianity," *Journal of Religion and Psychical Research* 23.4 (2000), 184–96; John Hinnells, *Zoroastrian and Parsi Studies: Selected Works of John R. Hinnells* (Routledge, 2017; orig. 2000), 29–92; Albert De Jong, *Traditions of the Magi: Zoroastrianism in Greek and Latin Literature* (Brill, 1997); and Mary Boyce, *Zoroastrians: Their Religious Beliefs and Practices*, 2nd ed. (Routledge, 2000). For a summary: Richard Carrier, *Not the Impossible Faith: Why Christianity Didn't Need a Miracle to Succeed* (Lulu, 2009), 90–99.

tles—or indeed, anyone of the time. The modal argument is defeated. And the empirical argument has already been won without it.

If God could just 'make' bodies—and the apostles believed he could (of Adam and Eve; of the faithful's future resurrection bodies), and the evangelists, too (as Matthew and Luke both have God manufacture a Davidic fetus for Jesus to descend into, bypassing any impartation of David's seed by sexual contact with Joseph)—then Nathan's prophecy required no historical biology to fulfill. God could simply take the semen from David, hold onto it, and then use it to form a body for Jesus to occupy in his sojourn of flesh. There is no evidence supporting the conclusion that the apostles would 'never' think of this. And there is ample evidence it was the sort of thing readily thought of.

It's still possible they realized Nathan's prophecy some other way. Romans 1:3 could be the product of any number of solutions. As I already demonstrated, we know for a certainty that they would have come up with a way, even if not this. So it does not matter what way they came up with. But all the evidence we do have entails that if they did come up with a celestial solution, as they had to do to fit a celestial messiah, this is the most likely. Because it requires the fewest and shortest steps of reasoning—it reads the text of 2 Samuel literally as-is, with no fudging. And it requires the least innovation—simply imagining God working his miraculous magic, as he was commonly believed to do. And in the end, this is an entirely viable solution wholly fitting the thought of their time. The modal argument thus fails. It simply is not the case that they would not have thought of this when required. And so the empirical argument stands: something akin was in fact required, and thus assured. This verse therefore is not unexpected either way—they'd have said it regardless—and therefore this verse is of no use establishing whether Jesus really existed.

The mathematical point here is crucial (and I know difficult) for historians to understand. But remember my discussion of how the probability of evidence actually works in chapter five, where I quoted my original study explaining:

> The question you should ask here is not 'Is that likely what Paul would have meant by that?' but rather, 'If Paul was in fact a mythicist, *is that likely what he would write*?' (and then 'If Paul was in fact a historicist,

is that likely what he would write?', for the comparative probability).[25]

The value of the evidence being considered (its strength in either direction) is then a direct function of the difference between those two probabilities (if any). The usual mistake historians make will be to say "usually when people say 'came from the seed' of someone they mean in the ordinary way," and then conclude "therefore it is more probable that's what Paul meant here." *But that is logically fallacious.* Because the probability we are looking for here is the probability Paul would say this *if he was a mythicist*, in which context it would *not* be usual for him to say exactly this and mean the usual thing. So "what is usual" for *most people* is not applicable here.

In other words, to assume "it would be usual" for Paul to mean an ordinary thing here is *to assume he is a historicist*, which makes your reasoning circular. Which is a fallacy. You cannot start with your conclusion as a premise to argue for that same conclusion. As I said in chapter five (and *Historicity*), "that is simply a measure of the strength of your bias." *Was* Paul a 'usual' person, or not? *Is* he talking about a historical person or a cosmic one? We can assume neither about Paul when evaluating each item of evidence, because determining which it is *is why we are looking at that evidence.* So here, we only want to know, "Is Paul's wording weirder if he was a mythicist *than if* he was a historicist?" and it's not (as explained up to now). If Paul had actually said, for example, "Descended from David" (as Ignatius did), then that *would* be weird (and hence "unusual") for Paul to say if he was a mythicist, and then that *would* be evidence for historicity (it would be more likely that he would choose those words on historicity than on mythicism, and so the likelihood ratio would favor historicity—and one need then merely assess how much). But what Paul chose to say is instead ambiguous. It therefore isn't weird enough to tell us whether Paul is or is not a mythicist. *It is mathematically not useful as evidence for determining that.*

The question of how likely it is that Paul is a mythicist in the first place (and thus not going to be using language in the "usual" way) is a product of all the other evidence (see chapter six). Whereas the probability that he would say what he does in Romans 1:3 (and not what

[25] Carrier, *Historicity*, 513 (512–14).

Ignatius and later editors tried changing him to say) if he was a mythicist is basically 100%. Scripture entailed he had to say it; and his wording fits any such metaphysics (likewise for anyone before him who may have originated it). So then we must ask, "Is it weird of Paul to say this (and in this way) if he was a historicist?" We could say it is, a little (his deviation from idiom indicates he is doing *something* unusual, *not* something usual), but that can be fully accommodated by, say, a historicist miraculism (as mythified in the Gospels). So at best we can say it's also 100% expected that this is what Paul would say (and how he would say it) if he was (instead) a historicist—it being among the countless ways he could have chosen to express a terrestrial birth, particularly a miraculous one.[26] But if it's 100% expected on mythicism, and 100% expected on historicity, then it's likelihood ratio is 1:1, and it thus has no effect either way (as explained in chapter five). It evinces nothing. We simply can't tell. And that is why this passage has no value as evidence in this debate.

Conclusion

For all that, it 'could' be that Paul is just being weird, and describing an ordinary birth and genealogical pedigree in vague and unusual language. But we cannot establish that to be any more likely. In fact, it is less so. The awkward fit between theory and evidence here is not entirely probable. We have to force that theory to fit the evidence; whereas no such force is required if Paul is talking about metaphysics rather than biology, and hence a magical fulfillment of prophecy—a perfectly common thing for him, and other Christians and apocalyptic Jews, to do. Which is equally likely on either theory of Christian origins (both a historicist Paul and a mythicist Paul can have imagined a miraculous genesis for Jesus, indeed even exactly the same one).

An allegorical sense is also possible. In Galatians 3 Paul understands Christians to be capable of becoming the 'seed of Abraham' (*tou Abraam sperma*, Gal. 3:29) metaphorically—spiritually, not biologically—and if that was so easy to conceive (as evidently it was), a similar approach

[26] On the mathematical reduction of an array of options to a 100% expectancy see Carrier, *Proving History*, index, 'coefficient of contingency' (with examples in Carrier, *Historicity*, 288–89, 323, 357, 606).

could have been used for fulfilling Nathan's prophecy. Which need not be developed by the same argument; any exegetical 'solution by metaphor' would do. Paul often references allegorical, figurative, and 'mysterious' ways of understanding what deceptively seem like plain statements of fact.[27] So the Christian's options were aplenty.

We have an obvious example: the authors of Matthew and Luke clearly did not believe Joseph imparted the seed of David to Mary and thence to Jesus—they conspicuously deny this.[28] So how did they think Jesus became the son (and hence 'seed') of David?[29] There are only two possible ways they could: either they believed God (whether directly or by an angel acting at his command) magically extracted the semen from David—*or* Joseph—and used it to manufacture a fetus inside Mary's womb (which, either way, is exactly the same concept of sperm manipulation I just described); or they believed God somehow 'made' that fetus into Davidic flesh by divine fiat (or some other device).

The same way God could make Gentiles 'Abraham's seed' by intervention of the Spirit, he could make Jesus 'David's seed' by similar transformative magic. All he need do is declare it so. He is, after all, God. That would be fully in accord with thinking accepted by Paul (as we see in Gal. 3), and so could easily be what Paul (and his fellow Christians) were thinking in Romans 1:3. We cannot rule this out, either, except by presenting more evidence for an alternative (either from Paul himself or other authors of his time, such as 1 Clement or Hebrews). But there is no such evidence for any alternative, other than for direct sperm magic, for which, we have seen, there *is* some evidence—in external precedent, in Paul's wording, and in the literal reading of Nathan's prophecy, which explicitly describes God taking semen directly from David's belly and using it to manufacture for him an eternal son. This is therefore the most likely way Paul and his fellows, even the authors of Matthew and Luke, would have imagined it.

Since there is no evidence against this understanding, yet there is evidence for it (particularly in the exact wording of the prophecy and

---

27 For example: Gal. 4 (e.g. 4:24); Rom. 16:25–26, 1 Cor. 2:7–8, 1 Cor. 4:1; Rom. 11:25; 1 Cor. 15:51–52.

28 Mt. 1:16–25; Lk. 1:26–38, 3:23.

29 Mt. 1:1, 9:27, 15:22, 20:30–31, 21:9, 21:15; Luke 18:38–39.

Paul's peculiar semantics at every turn), it prevails on Bayesian logic. Its prior probability is equal to every competing alternative—for this or any other prophecy, there is as much evidence establishing ordinary as magical or even metaphorical fulfillments of scripture. Whereas the likelihoods all skew towards sperm magic: the wording of Paul (in Rom. 1:3 and elsewhere) is not that expected on a biological reading, but is, rather, somewhat unexpected and odd; whereas the spermatic magic hypothesis exactly predicts everything we have from Paul on the point. A metaphorical interpretation sits somewhere in between—making the peculiarities of the evidence more likely than on a biological reading, but not as likely as on the metaphysical one. That is the only theory that has a perfect fit to the evidence, explaining entirely how Paul could believe Nathan's prophecy was fulfilled (when, on an ordinary reading, it was decisively falsified by the biblical death of David's son and the historical cessation of David's throne), and why Paul would choose to describe Jesus's coming into a Davidic inheritance with words denoting the manufacture and bestowing of bodies, rather than words denoting a vetted genealogy and ordinary human birth.

And yet for all that, in *Historicity* I concluded as much against myself as reasonably possible when formulating my upper margin of error. I thus concluded that *nevertheless* Paul's remark in Romans 1:3 (that 'according to the flesh' Jesus 'came from the sperm of David') might be twice as likely to be there, and in the form we find it, if Jesus *did* exist after all, and Paul was speaking of a believed genealogy of Jesus's earthly father or some kind of miraculous conception in Jesus's mother, than if he meant something else (like celestial sperm magic or a figuratively or spiritually bestowed ancestry). Hence I gave it a likelihood ratio favoring the historicity of Jesus of 2 to 1 (or 2/1).[30] Which therefore accounts for the possibility that I am wrong, and that this passage is, after all, *not* 100% expected on either theory, and thus *is* less likely to be found in Paul's opus if Jesus didn't exist than if he did—even though that's implausible, as explained in the bulk of this chapter.

But even that decision reflects the empirical fact that Paul is too vague for this evidence to count any more than that. Because Paul never says anything *clearly* indicating that he knew Jesus had an ordinary hu-

[30] Carrier, *Historicity*, 594 (cf. 581).

man father. And that *being* a fact *must* be represented logically, and thus mathematically, in our reasoning. Paul never even mentions Jesus having a father (the word is absent from Romans 1:3 and everywhere else his Davidic derivation is alluded to). Paul never specifically says Jesus 'descended' from anyone (as Ignatius later would, as we saw in chapter seven). Neither does Paul say anything more concrete, like "Jesus' father according to the flesh," or "Jesus's father, who is no longer with us," or "his earthly father was named Joseph," or "I visited his family and met his father Joseph" (or even "I never met his father"), or "his father according to the flesh was of the line of David," or "in life Jesus had renounced his earthly family" (as reported in Mark 3:31–35) or "but his father remained loyal to the church" (or "died before his son in the flesh came into his glory"), or "I learned that Jesus's father had received a revelation announcing his child would be the savior," or even "Jesus was as a baby circumcised on the eighth day in the presence of his father in accordance with the law" (and thus ritually entered the covenant of the Hebrews); or any of a thousand things Paul could have said that, *had* he said them, would clinch the conclusion that he thereby knew Jesus to be a historical man.[31] If Paul had said anything—anything at all—like this, then the likelihood of *that* if Jesus did not exist would easily be hundreds if not thousands to one against. That he did exist would then be assured to us (as explained in chapter six). But, for whatever reason, Paul didn't do that. So there is no such evidence left to cite. Therefore we cannot count and weigh Romans 1:3 as if it said any of these things; that it *didn't* is precisely the problem.

Conversely, on the other side of my error margin, I did not weigh this passage as evidence against historicity, either. Because even if Paul plainly said Jesus was the seed of David by mere feat of metaphysics, he could as likely have said that of a sainted historical man as a non-existent one. So even if everything I have argued in this chapter is true, it would not affect the probability of a historical Jesus *either way*.

So at the very least what I have established is that the evidence of Romans 1:3 is ambiguous and not as clear-cut as often made out. So its existence in Paul's letters is not *as improbable* if there was no real Jesus as historicists claim. Because, for all the reasons here given, Paul's

---

[31] Any one of which or more he could have said: Carrier, *Historicity*, 518–19n13.

unexpected obscurity and vagueness on the point leaves us with a more than trivial chance that this text could as well derive from the theology surrounding an imaginary Jesus, and thus represent purely metaphysical *beliefs* rather than historical *facts*. That is why, on my more judicious margin of error, I think we should take Paul as meaning exactly what he said, and not try to invent mountains of implausible or unattested claims to get him to have said something else. God made Jesus directly from the sperm of David to sit a then-eternal throne, exactly as Nathan prophesied. Since there is no way to get any other meaning to be more assured, and since what Paul says is equally expected whether Jesus existed or not, Romans 1:3 should be removed from the table. It cannot argue for a historical Jesus, any more than it can argue against it.

So for Paul's scripturally required declaration of Jesus acquiring a Davidic body my original study's conclusion remains: at worst this tells us nothing about whether Paul thought Jesus was born or made (which is as likely either way, and thus has no effect either way) or it doesn't securely evince he understood this to be a human birth (ordinary or miraculous), and so at best it indicates only that he *might* have believed that (counting weakly 2:1 for historicity).

9

Why Galatians 4:4 Cannot Demonstrate a Historical Jesus

Not only did Paul never say anything clearly indicating he knew Jesus had an ordinary human father, he also never says anything clearly indicating he knew Jesus had an ordinary human mother. He never says anything like "Jesus's mother Mary," or "Jesus's mother, who is no longer with us," or "I visited his family and met his mother" (or even "I was never able to meet his mother"), or "in life Jesus had renounced his earthly family, but his mother remained loyal to the church," or "Jesus's mother Mary handed on to us that she received a revelation announcing her child would be the savior," or "take up a collection for the support of Jesus's blessed mother," or "born to Mary, and circumcised on the eighth day," or any of a thousand things Paul could have said that, *had* he said them,[1] would clinch the conclusion that he thereby knew Jesus to be a historical man.

All we have is one vague statement in Galatians 4:4, where Paul says Jesus "came to be from a woman, came to be under the law" (*genomenon ek gynaikos genomenon hypo nomon*). Which is terribly unspecific. Paul doesn't even say here that the woman Jesus was supposedly born to (or 'came from') was Jewish; and yet even so simple an addition as that would secure this as good evidence for a historical Jesus. Which

[1] Any one of which or more he could have said: Carrier, *Historicity*, 518–19n13.

also forestalls any argument to the effect that Paul is here trying to give Jesus's credentials as a Jew: for Paul never says this 'woman' was Jewish.[2] If Paul had said anything—anything at all—like this or any of those other more specific things, then, again, the likelihood of *that* if Jesus did not exist would easily be hundreds or thousands to one against. And that he did exist would then be mathematically assured. But, for whatever reason, Paul didn't do that. And we simply must take this into account in our calculations of probability.

Again, we need not *expect* Paul to have clearly mentioned Jesus's historical mother (or father)—in such ways, or any other. Paul's silence on this point isn't evidence *against* the historicity of Jesus. But neither can we use an imagined Pauline mention of his mother that doesn't exist as if it were evidence Jesus did exist. And this is why scholars must stop citing Galatians 4:4 as if it were such a thing. It is not. Because that passage is part of an extended allegorical argument that never relates to real mothers as all.[3] When Paul says "God sent out his son, coming from a woman, coming under the law," Paul is referring to an 'allegory' (*allêgoroumena*, Galatians 4:24), not to real mothers, and thus he is not interested in whether Jesus had an actual mother here, even if he knew Jesus had one. Paul's use of the word 'mother' in this case is a figurative (not literal) expression for entering and occupying the realm of flesh. That, Paul explains to us, constitutes 'being born' from 'Hagar'—a mytho-symbolic mother, not an actual one.

This is made all the clearer by Paul choosing to alter the popular idiom 'born of a woman' (a metonym for 'mortal') into 'made from a woman'.[4] He is thus deliberately removing that idiom's consistent reference to begetting (*gennaô*) a child (the thing that makes men mortal), and replacing it with a more ambiguous verb (*ginomai*) that allows coming into existence some other way, a choice that seems intended to echo that

---

[2] Of course only patrimony or circumcision (Exod. 12:48) could make someone a Jew anyway: Shaye Cohen, *The Beginnings of Jewishness: Boundaries, Varieties, Uncertainties* (University of California Press, 1999), 305–06.

[3] Addressed in Carrier, *Historicity*, 577–82, and *Outer Space*, 46, 161–62, 173, 180, 189. See also Lataster, *Questioning*, 265–70, 312–20.

[4] For comparative examples of the actual idiom, see Job 11:2, 15:14, and 25:14; similarly, Sirach 10:18, Matthew 11:11, and Luke 7:28 (and note 8 in chapter eight). Only centuries later do Christian authors pick up or modify Paul's construction.

same unusual choice in Romans 1:3—*and* Philippians 2:7, which even more clearly appears to describe Jesus being given a body by God ("made to resemble a man") and not natural parturition.

Paul also does not use the standard idiom's construction ('begotten of a woman', *gennêtos gynaikos*, verb with simple genitive).[5] He imports the preposition *ek* ('out of'), in agreement with his practice elsewhere for Adam and Eve being made by God rather than born (in 1 Corinthians 11:12). And though he also keeps that deviation from the usual idiom for mortality when discussing human births in Galatians 4:22–23, he is explicitly speaking allegorically there, too (4:24), even about those 'literal' births. So Paul is making deliberate choices, in light of his allegory, to deviate from the usual idiom. We therefore cannot infer he means it in the usual way. Which means he has actually *not* used that idiom; he has chosen to say a different thing *on purpose*.

The change of verb is the most telling. As we saw in the last chapter, Paul never otherwise uses *ginomai* of human birth, only of manufactured bodies (like Adam or the bodies of the resurrected). Whenever he speaks of human birth, he always uses *gennaô* (even here in this chapter of Galatians). So his own consistent practice indicates the significance of his choice. All of which I explained already in the previous chapter—including notice that ancient readers clearly understood this, as Tertullian explicitly tells us so, while both Ignatius and later anonymous 'emenders' of Galatians 4:4 and Romans 1:3 tried to fix the problem, reversing Paul's choice by swapping back in the more appropriate word (*gennaô*, 'beget'). Thus, although *ginomai* can mean 'born', Tertullian, and the choices of both Paul and his concerned revisers, tell us it was not understood that way here.

Only one critic, Daniel Gullotta, has even attempted to address this observation.[6] But he simply ignores my every argument and deploys arguments wholly irrelevant to it, or unsupported by any evidence, reflecting the same censurable and unproductive behavior I documented in chapter three. For example, Gullotta argues that Paul cannot have meant Galatians 4:4 allegorically because Paul believed Jesus was a mortal hu-

---

[5] Per the examples in the previous note. And this observation and its analysis I owe to Aaron Adair (by personal correspondence).

[6] Gullotta, "Doubts," 328–30.

man (even Jewish, indeed Davidic) man.[7] But we actually *agree* Paul believed that. So it is no argument against our minimal mythicist model of Christian origins that the first Christians believed Jesus to have been given a mortal human body of Davidic flesh to die in. I already covered this in detail in the last chapter. Since on our theory they learned of this by revelation and scripture (indeed it was outright required by it), rather than by meeting Jesus in life, their belief in it is entirely expected—in fact entirely predicted—by our theory. Therefore their mentioning it can never be evidence against our theory; and therefore it can never be evidence for the historicity of Jesus.

Likewise, Gullotta argues that "Paul claims that Jesus was 'descended from David according to the flesh' (Rom. 1.3), and thus, contra Carrier, this would mean that Jesus, for Paul, was a descendant of Sarah, and not Hagar," and therefore Paul can't have meant Jesus was a descendant of Hagar.[8] But my argument is that Paul is not attributing a genealogy *to anyone* here, much less Jesus. Hagar is not an ancestor. She symbolizes the world of flesh. As Gullotta even admits, Paul is not discussing a literal biological descent from Hagar; Hagar here is only a symbol, not a person (Galatians 4:8–9, 22–26); likewise Sarah, who symbolizes the world of the spirit, an escape from the world of flesh, and thus, escape from death (and the law that leads to death). So Paul is saying Jesus has been *both* a son of Hagar like everyone else (during his brief mortal sojourn in the world of flesh) *and* a son of Sarah (upon his resurrection) like every baptized Christian now is. Hence he became "the son born by the power of the spirit,"[9] just like every Christian who follows in his steps: we are all 'born of Hagar' until we are baptized into eternal life and become 'born of Sarah'. Gullotta's argument is thus irrelevant. It not only ignores what we actually said, it only rebuts something we never said.

Gullotta had no other arguments against my point, other than to gainsay the conclusion that Paul's argument is allegorical from Galatians 3 through 4, by claiming that the point in his speech in which Paul explains this is towards the end (Galatians 4:24), and that is 'too far away'

[7] Gullotta, "Doubts," 330.

[8] Gullotta, "Doubts," 329.

[9] Gal. 4:29; cf. 1 Cor. 15:42–49 and Rom. 1:4. See discussion of Gal. 4:29 in chapter two.

from Galatians 4:4 to be referring thereto.[10] Which is not a sensible point. By this logic, Lincoln's Gettysburg Address is at no point about slavery because it never gets around to mentioning that until the end, and then only by allusion (when he says the Civil War procured "a new birth of freedom"). Nevertheless, since Gullotta is gaslighting us, the only way to move the debate forward now is with a thorough analysis of the rhetoric of Paul's argument, from start to finish.

The Rhetorical Flow of Galatians

So let's walk through Paul's argument. Paul preludes his argument in Galatians 1–2 by establishing his authority in the matter he wishes to argue for (his revelation of Jesus; his later securing endorsement from the apostles before him; and his standing up to them). His argument then begins with Galatians 3. There, he first introduces the thesis he must defend (Gal. 3:1–5), which is, in essence, that the Galatians were saved by the grace of Christ's substitutionary sacrifice in the flesh, bringing them safely into the world of the spirit (Gal. 3:2–5, 14; cf. Gal. 4:6–7, 29), and therefore they need not return to the world of flesh (by returning to worldly religious practices, Gal. 3:23–24, 4:8–11; particularly Judaic ones, Gal. 4:21, 25, 29–41). This is why he challenges them, "Are you so foolish? After beginning by means of the spirit, are you now trying to finish by means of the flesh?" (Gal. 3:3, NIV). This is the context and thesis of Paul's entire argument.

To ground his argument in Scripture (and, we can expect, to rebut his intended opponents with a display of deeper mastery of Scripture), Paul inserts at this point an exegesis of the Abraham narrative (Gal. 3:6–20), then uses that to argue his point that the spirit has superseded the flesh (Gal. 3:21–29), because Abraham represents an allegorical father to all who believe ("those who have faith are children of Abraham," Gal. 3:7). He then immediately tells us he is going to make the same argument again, only in different terms ("What I am saying is…," Gal. 4:1), switching from the father in the story (Abraham) to the mothers in that story (Sarah and her slave Hagar), continuing his allegorical

[10] Gullotta, "Doubts," 329.

mode of reasoning: from Abraham as allegorical father, to Sarah and Hagar as allegorical mothers. And there he develops the same point, but from an exegesis of Sarah and Hagar instead of Abraham (beginning with a discussion of inheritance, Gal. 4:1–4, which is the entire theme of the Sarah-Hagar narrative, as he goes on to explain, Gal. 4:22–31). Paul thus ends this continuous argument (which began at Gal. 3:1) with his conclusion: "It is for freedom that Christ has set us free," so "stand firm, then, and do not let yourselves be burdened again by a yoke of slavery" to worldly religious rules or rituals (Gal. 5:1).

Paul then applies this conclusion to circumcision specifically (5:2–12), and builds on that to segue into consequent moral advice (5:13–26, this time on how to live), particularly in those respects needed to quell the heated disputes and thus divisions that he has been aiming to resolve since verse 3:1. He then ends his argument with a chiastic inversion of those last two points: first, again, moral advice (6:1–10, this time on how to judge); *then* a concluding renunciation of circumcision (6:11–18).

The overall structure looks like this:

Gal. 3:1–5 **Thesis** (General)

  Gal. 3:6–20 **Exegesis of Abraham**

    Gal. 3:21–29 **Thesis** (from Abraham)

    Gal. 4:1–7 **Thesis** (from Sarah & Hagar)

    Gal. 4:8–20 **Application** (to Paul's opponents)

  Gal. 4:21–31 **Exegesis of Sarah & Hagar**

Gal. 5:1 **Conclusion**

Gal. 5:1–12 **Application** (to circumcision)

  Gal. 5:13–16 **Moral Advice** (how to live)

  Gal. 6:1–10 **Moral Advice** (how to judge)

Gal. 6:11–18 **Application** (to circumcision)

The section that concerns us is the first half of this, Galatians 3–5:1. It is a coherent argument from start to finish, and operates chiastically: from an exegesis of Abraham (the father of Israel) to his thesis in light of it; then from his thesis in light of Sarah and Hagar (the mothers of the same Abraham story) to his exegesis of that. Throughout this section, from top to bottom, Paul is speaking allegorically.

Allegory, All the Way Down

In Galatians 3:16, Paul says "The promises were spoken to Abraham and to his seed," but "Scripture does not say 'and to seeds', meaning many people, but 'and to your seed', meaning one person, who is Christ" (remember from the last chapter how this singular reading of the word 'seed' also explains Paul's understanding of the prophecy of Nathan in Romans 1:3). And therefore, Paul argues, by becoming the Sons of God by spiritual (hence allegorical) adoption (Gal. 3:26–29), now "*you* are Abraham's seed" (Gal. 3:29). Thus the Scriptures, and the word 'seed', are both to be understood allegorically; therefore the Galatians are being told they can allegorically *be* the seed of Abraham. Paul is explicitly not speaking of literal biology. He is speaking figuratively, and specifically doing so to render 'literal biology' irrelevant. So Paul is not making a biological argument here at all. He is not referring to birth or ancestry. He is explaining that one should *disregard* that.

Likewise, when Paul says "we were imprisoned and guarded under the law" until Christ, "therefore the law was our disciplinarian until Christ came" (Gal. 3:23–25, NRSV), he does not mean literal guards, literal disciplinarians, or literal prison; when Paul says "you are all children of God through faith" and have thus "clothed yourselves with Christ" (Gal. 3:26–27), he does not mean literal children or literal clothing. He is speaking allegorically. His entire mode of argument is allegorical. When Paul says "there is no longer Jew or Greek, there is no longer slave or free, there is no longer male and female" (Gal. 3:28–29), he does not mean this literally, as if somehow people's biology or legal status has actually been changed. He is speaking allegorically.

Paul then segues without pause into a continuation of this allegorical mode: "heirs, as long as they are minors, are no better than slaves, though they are the owners of all the property" but "they remain under guardians and trustees until the date set by the father," and therefore "so with us: while we were minors, we were enslaved to the elemental spirits of the world" (Gal. 4:1–4). Paul does not mean literal heirs, literal slaves, literal owners, literal property, literal guardians, literal trustees, literal fathers, literal minors—or even literal 'elements'. The phrase *ta stoicheia* is indeed here correctly translated (because it actually here means) 'elemental spirits', but that translation conceals the allegorical mode of Paul's discourse by converting the word back into what Paul *literally* meant (per Gal. 4:8–9), even though he actually used an allegorical expression (simply 'the elements'). Which is another example of Paul explicating his intended meaning many verses *after* he started the allegorical usage (the allegorical intention of 'elements' in Gal. 4:3 only gets identified in Gal. 4:8, when he says he meant "those who by nature are not gods"). So we can expect this is how he will manage the next allegorical explication.

And indeed it is precisely here that we find Paul say:

> But when the fullness of time had come, God sent his Son, born of a woman, born under the law, in order to redeem those who were under the law, so that we might receive adoption as children. And because you are children, God has sent the Spirit of his Son into our hearts, crying, 'Abba! Father!' So you are no longer a slave but a child, and if a child then also an heir, through God.
>
> —Gal. 4:4–7 (NRSV)

Paul's entire argument has been allegorical across every single line from Gal. 3:23 to now. So why would he suddenly change his mode of discourse into the literal here? That is contrary to the expected sense and its context. Indeed, the contended line (verse 4:4) is crucially referencing key allegorical lines he segued here from (again, many passages away, in verses 3:7 and 3:29): that we are 'sons' of Abraham and thus heirs to his estate—and thus to any promises made to Abraham, such as God's promise of the eternal salvation of his descendants. So why would anything *else* in this same verse not be referencing the *same* allegory? Why would we assume Paul means a literal woman here? Because he doesn't mean literal children or literal father, or literal heir to a literal estate, or even literal slave (in the sense of being the legal property of a human owner). It's all allegory. So why would Paul suddenly switch out of allegory *only* when referencing a mother? And why do that, and then immediately go back into allegory with a statement ("so we might receive adoption as children," Gal. 4:5) that also does not refer to biology, despite again using biology as a metaphor? A switch to literal biology here would make no sense, or even undermine his point; it certainly would do no work toward making his point.

This becomes even clearer when we follow the argument of Galatians 4, which begins with "My point is this: heirs, as long as they are minors, are no better than slaves, though they are the owners of all the property" (Gal. 4:1) and ends with "Now you, my friends, are children of the promise, like Isaac" (the son of Sarah and Abraham) and therefore "we are children, not of the slave but of the free woman" (Gal. 4:28, 31). Paul's allegory extends from beginning to end. It is in the midst of this that he utters the line in Gal. 4:4. So the fact that Paul gets around to *explaining* that he is using allegory only in verse 24 has no relevance to determining whether he means the 'allegory' is only in verses 24–29, or the whole argument of the entire chapter. He clearly means the entire chapter.

In fact Paul only explains the relevance of saying Jesus was "born of a woman, born under the law, in order to redeem those who were under the law, so that we might receive adoption as children" (Gal. 4:4–5) in his subsequent allegorical analysis (here in my own literal word-for-word translation):

> The [son, from v. 22] from [*ek*] the slave [woman], was **born [*gennaô*] according to the flesh** [*kata sarka*]; the other, from [*ek*] the free [woman], **through the promise** [*dia epangelias*]. Now **this is an allegory** [*allêgoroumena*]: these are two covenants.
>
> —Gal. 4:23–24

There is no other explanation for why Paul even bothers to say Jesus was 'born of a woman' earlier in this argument. It explicates nothing (she is not said to be Jewish, so it cannot be establishing that he was Jewish; he is not said to have been circumcised, so it cannot be establishing that he entered the covenant; etc.). It doesn't even make sense as a mere synecdoche for mortality, because Paul changed the idiom to *remove* the implication of being begotten and replaced it with his being 'made' (per Philippians 2:7, as I discussed in the previous chapter). So even if Paul chose this idiom to say Jesus was mortal, we still cannot know that he meant that idiom literally ('Jesus passed through a vagina') or figuratively ('Jesus submitted to being born of Hagar like us').

Instead, when Paul tells us his reasons for bringing up Jesus 'being born of a woman' at all, he says he is using an allegory: the women of which he speaks are symbolical, not literal. Being 'born of a woman' means entering either realm: of flesh and death (as Jesus submitted to endure); or of spirit and immortality (as Jesus then received and now bestows). This ties in Paul's discourse on our being either slaves or free men.[11] Being born 'under the law' (Gal. 4:4, 5, 21) to Paul means simply entering the corrupted world of flesh (Gal. 4:3, 23, 29), and thereby becoming enslaved to its physics, and hence to an inevitable death (Gal. 4:3, 8–9), just as the Philippians creed said Jesus did: when becoming human, Jesus thereby became a *doulos*, 'slave' (Phil. 2:7)—once again, obviously not meant literally, just as Paul does not mean it literally of the Galatians. It is meant in the same cosmic sense in both places, as submitting to the world of flesh. This is why Paul brings up 'women' and being 'born from' them and says these are allegories for entering the world of flesh or spirit. He does not mean 'those now' (the Christians and their Jewish harassers, Gal. 4:29) are literally, biologically the 'sons' of Sarah and Hagar. He means this allegorically. And that entails he meant the same of Jesus, as that is the whole point of Paul's argument across all of Galatians 4.

For example, Paul says the applicable scripture declaring that "the children of the desolate woman [Hagar] are more numerous than the children of the one who is married [Sarah]" (Gal. 4:27) is not about real women. He declares that it is, instead, saying the *Jews* are (allegorically) the sons of Hagar (meaning "Mount Sinai, [who] bears children who are to be slaves," Gal. 4:25), even though *biologically* they claim to be the sons of Sarah; while the *Christians* are (allegorically) the sons of Sarah ("the Jerusalem that is above is free, and she is our mother," Gal. 4:36), *regardless* of their biology. And this is because, through baptism, Chris-

[11] By using *doulos* or cognates: Gal. 4:1, 3, 7, 8, 9, 22, 23, 24, 25, 30, 31; and using *eleutheros*, 'free man', or *klêronomos*, a grown-up 'heir': Gal. 4:1, 7, 22, 23, 26, 30, 31; and in messaging about becoming one or the other: Gal. 4:1–4, 5–7, 9, 28–31.

tians emulate and attach themselves to the same transition accomplished by Jesus, from death of the flesh into eternal life (Gal. 3:26–29, 4:5–7; cf. Rom. 6:3–5, 8:12–17)—from sons of Hagar into sons of Sarah. The argument is therefore that Jesus, too, became a son of Hagar in order to produce this very outcome; which entails he now is a son of Sarah, just as all Christians are who are baptized into his name. So being a son of Hagar, in Paul's argument, does not require Jesus to have had a real mother; it only requires him at some point to have been mortal, and thus 'under the law' (and its condemnation to death) rather than 'free' (which he became only after the death of his mortal body).

This is why Paul parallels our being 'under' (*hypo*) the sway of the elemental spirits (Gal. 4:3; Gal. 4:8–9) with Jesus being put 'under' (*hypo*) the sway of the law (Gal. 4:4), so that we *all* could be rescued from being 'under' (*hypo*) the sway of that law, and thus of the elemental spirits, ourselves (Gal. 4:5, 4:21). That's why, Paul says, God 'sent' his son (*exapesteilen*, hence a preexistent being) and 'made' him (using *ginomai*) 'from' (*ek*) a woman and thus made him 'under' the law, just as we are 'born' (using, instead, *gennaô*, Gal. 4:23, 29) 'from' (*ek*) a woman (Gal. 4:22–24)—either the slave woman or the free, but either way, not a literal woman. And as for us, so for Jesus—because Paul's entire point is: as for Jesus, *so for us*. Jesus became a son of Hagar, in order to become a son of Sarah, all so we could do the same thing.

Therefore, we cannot conclude Paul meant the 'son' of God (Gal. 4:4) was literally, biologically, the 'son' of a woman. Paul's argument requires him here to mean Jesus was figuratively born of Hagar—and thence, after death, born of Sarah, and therefore so shall the Galatians be, as long as they do not re-enslave themselves to 'the law' (Gal. 4:3, 4, 9; hence Paul's conclusion of the entire argument of Gal. 3–4 in verse 5:1: "For freedom Christ has set us free; stand firm, therefore, and do not submit again to a yoke of slavery"). This is confirmed by the fact that Paul's discourse is allegorical all through these verses (indeed in every line from at least Gal. 3:23 to Gal. 4:8), and the fact that Paul explicitly links his discourse about inheritance, slavery, and freedom (Gal. 4:1–11) to his exegesis of Sarah and Hagar (Gal. 4:22–31), which means that that is not a change of subject, but a continuation of the same subject. That Paul separates those two sections of his argument with a personal digression on his and his opponents' relationship to the Galatians (Gal.

4:12–20) is therefore not evidence that verse 24 does not refer to verses 1–11. They are clearly about the same thing; and indeed the second section is completing and making sense of the first. Paul's 'women' in this ring-structured argument are therefore all allegorical. There are *no* literal women here. To think otherwise misses the entire point of Paul's exegesis, and of his argument all the way from verse 4:1.

We could still reason that 'maybe' Paul believes this about Jesus *because* he knows Jesus was biologically born to a human mother; but we have no evidence that that is the case. So we cannot argue from it being the case. We simply don't know. It's 50/50 either way. He could just as well be saying this because of his allegorical reasoning (the expression simply references 'being born to Hagar' as 'being made and subject to flesh'); or it could be because of his historical knowledge of a real mother. Paul simply isn't specific enough to allow us to *know* it was the latter. And that is why we cannot use this as evidence for a historical Jesus. In context, it's simply too vague. Which we might also reason is weird. Why is Paul only ever weirdly vague about things like this? Why does he never make *any* clear statement as to the earthly history of Jesus, across all 20,000 or so words across his six or so authentic letters? But that's the result of stepping back and looking at the whole picture.[12] Zeroing in on this single passage in Galatians gets us no usable data either way.[13]

Conclusion

Philo of Alexandria similarly allegorizes Sarah and Hagar, concluding that Sarah (whom he says was a perpetual virgin) symbolically gave birth to 'wisdom' (Sophia).[14] So if we pursue wisdom, he argues, we "receive a share of her seed" (*spermata*, thereby also using 'sperm' allegorically). Knowing this, we would not read a line anywhere else in Philo saying Sophia (wisdom) was 'born of a woman' and then argue that therefore he must be talking about a historical person named 'Sophia'. Because we

---

[12] Carrier, *Historicity*, 510–28, 531–38, 553–92.

[13] Carrier, *Historicity*, 592–95.

[14] Philo, *On Mating with the Preliminary Studies* 6–7. Compare, for Jesus: Aaron Adair, "The Morning Star and the Womb of Dawn," *Biblica* 105 (2024), 420–43.

know Philo can say that and mean something else. So we would be forestalled from grasping at that phrase to argue Sophia existed as a historical person. The same conclusion follows for Paul, and therefore for his declaration that Jesus came from 'a woman'. The very context in which he says that—the very way, even, that he says it—forestalls us from grasping at that phrase to argue it was meant literally.

And yet, for all that, in *Historicity* I still allowed the possibility that this sentence remains strange if Jesus didn't exist, and thus I still counted it as evidence Jesus existed—I simply counted it as weak owing to its undeniable vagueness, and the readiness of other explanations for it that are not mere conjecture but empirically supported by the very context in which it appears, and the odd way in which it is said. So, at a stretch, I concluded that this passage could yet be twice as expected to be written by Paul here if Jesus existed than if he didn't. Which is the farthest I could reasonably go.

And even that was farther than logic should allow. As I have just shown here, there is really no basis for seeing this line as weird and thus unexpected at all if Jesus didn't exist. It is strange precisely in the opposite sense: its vagueness, its context (the specific 'argument from women' that it is a part of, as well as the general argument's entire allegorical mode from start to finish), and even its peculiar vocabulary (switching out the idiomatically expected *gennaô* for *ginomai*, Paul's preferred word for people who are manufactured rather than born), all suggest Paul is *not* talking about biological birth here, and therefore we *cannot* conclude he slipped into a reference to literal biology only in this one vague moment, serving no necessary purpose in his argument. So counting it as twice as likely if Jesus existed than if he didn't is already stretching its weight too far. In context, it looks pretty much entirely *expected* if Jesus didn't exist. When we combine the predictions of our theory (that Paul would believe God gave Jesus a mortal, human body to die in) and the facts of the given context (that Paul is making an allegorical argument about allegorical mothers in Galatians 4—and explicitly even says so, so we aren't even conjecturing it), it is entirely expected that Paul would *there* say Jesus 'came to be from a woman' allegorically. To be evidence for historicity, this behavior would need to be improbable here; it's not.

So, once again, I think we should read Paul at exactly what he said, and not try to invent stacks of implausible or unevidenced claims to get him to have said something else. He plainly says the 'women' of which he is speaking across the entire chapter of Galatians 4 are allegories for one's metaphysical status; and accordingly, he continues to emphasize Jesus was 'made' rather than 'born' (per, again, Phil. 2:7 and Rom. 1:3), unlike the Galatians to whom he writes and their harassers among the Jews, which he describes consistently as 'born' rather than 'made' (Gal. 4:23, 24, 28). Jesus is clearly for Paul somehow different or special in how he entered the world; and is 'like us' only in the singular fact of having still thereby entered the realm of flesh subject to the law, and thus having joined 'the children of Hagar' thereby, so as to represent them in his death, and thence in his rebirth among 'the children of Sarah' by his resurrection (Gal. 4:22–31; cf. Rom. 1:3–4), hence becoming "the firstborn of many brethren" (Rom. 8:29), who are the true "children of God" (Gal. 3:26, 4:6–7; cf. Rom. 8:14–21, 9:8, 9:26; Phil. 2:15).

Which does not, of course, argue the converse point. That Paul just happened to not be talking about real mothers in Galatians 4 does not afford any evidence that he knew Jesus *lacked* an ordinary human mother. His belief that God 'sent' a preexistent son into the world is still compatible with the same belief evinced (and exaggerated) in the later Gospels, that somehow Jesus entered a fetus manufactured for him in Mary's womb. We have no evidence of this (Paul never says anything affirming or implying this). But we have no evidence against it, either. So the fact that we really should not be counting this as evidence for a historical Jesus does not argue that we should be counting it as evidence *against* a historical Jesus either. It is simply useless data either way.

Which means for Paul's allegory about metaphysical mothers my original study's conclusion remains: at worst this tells us nothing about whether Paul thought Jesus had an ordinary human mother (which is as likely either way, and thus has no effect either way) or it doesn't securely evince he did, and so at best it indicates only that he *might* have known Jesus had a human mother (counting weakly 2:1 for historicity).

Meanwhile, the fact that by becoming a son of Sarah Jesus became the firstborn of many brethren—the Christians whom Paul's argument across Galatians 4 establishes are now sons of Sarah—also leads us to the next and last item of proposed evidence to consider. In Galatians 3 Paul avers all Christians are the 'seed' of Abraham, regardless of biology (cf. Rom. 4:13–16, 9:6–8), just as Jesus and his brethren are all 'of a woman' regardless of biology (hence "therefore, brothers and sisters, we are not children of the slave woman, but of the free woman," Gal. 4:31). Then, right in the midst of all that, Paul specifically says this transpires through becoming the brothers of Christ (Gal. 3:13–18). Which brings us to the last possible evidence to consider, the only evidence left: what Paul could have meant when he refers to Brothers of the Lord.

10

All Baptized Christians Were the Brothers of the Lord

Not only did Paul never say anything clearly indicating he knew Jesus had an ordinary human father or mother (as we saw in chapters eight and nine), he also never says anything clearly indicating he knew Jesus had ordinary human brothers. In this case, Paul outright tells us that all baptized Christians are 'Brothers of the Lord' by spiritual adoption, being all the 'sons of God', while he exhibits no knowledge of the Lord having any other kind of brother than that.[1]

The mere oddity of this fact is alone evidence. On all occasions when Paul could be referencing these family relations (father, mother, and brothers), Paul always chooses an oblique and unusual way of doing it, one that leaves considerable doubt as to what he means. That is not expected if there was an ordinary historical Jesus; but it is expected to be what would survive for us to read if there wasn't. Any more *direct* discussion of this—such as an explanation from Paul, had he ever written it down, that Jesus's father was *literally* King David, or that Jesus was *only* to be described as 'come from a mother' allegorically or as manufactured in outer space, or that the 'Brothers of the Lord' he referred to in certain

[1] Addressed in Carrier, *Historicity*, 108 and 582–92 (including all evidence outside Paul:, 310, 326–31, 337–42, 371–75, 453–55, 528–29). The present chapter expands on that with new information and argument.

passages were *only* the children of God, not the literal biological relations of Jesus—will have been among the pieces of Paul's letters left on the cutting-room floor. Because our editions of these texts passed through the editorial hands of stalwart historicists—from Marcion to his opponents—so what we have is what we expect if Jesus was imaginary, but less so if he was real. Because in *that* case we'd get clearer statements of *that*, which would *not* be cut but eagerly preserved. So what *was* preserved is more unexpected if Jesus existed than if he didn't.

Any ancient deniers of historicity (as discussed in chapter seven) we get to hear nothing from—all their writings were suppressed, even in quotation or paraphrase. So we have no reason to expect the edition of Paul's letters we have to give any clearer a clue than has survived. But had Jesus been a real person, we should expect many a clearer a clue than that. It need not involve references to his family; there are many other things that could have evinced this in Paul's letters. I won't develop that point here, as I've already throughly treated it in chapter 11 of *On the Historicity of Jesus*. But even with respect to this one issue, it is strange enough that the family relations of Jesus are all missing from *every other* early Epistle, including 1 Clement, and the Epistle of James—and even the book of Acts, once it begins recounting the public history of the church in Acts 2. But, that, too, I've already covered in *Historicity*: in chapter 11.3 for the other Epistles in the canon; chapter 9.3 for Acts; chapter 8.5 for Clement; and indeed, as well, chapter 8.8 for Hegesippus in the late 2nd century, the first author to mention 'real' brothers of Jesus apart from the Gospels and repetitions thereof (such as Acts 1). But that leaves the last piece of evidence anyone can really offer for there having been a real Jesus (as opposed to a mystically imagined one): whether *Paul* actually knew his biological brothers—which would indeed establish Jesus existed, to an effective certainty. The problem is that Paul never actually *says* that. So like the supposed evidence for Paul knowing Jesus had a father or a mother, this evidence, too, doesn't actually exist.

The fact is, Paul never says anything *clearly* indicating that he knew Jesus had ordinary human brothers. The only two times scholars even allege that he did (in Galatians 1:19 and 1 Corinthians 9:5), Paul does not specify that that is what he means, rather than fictive brothers. So we can't tell. It could be either. And that being a fact must again be represented logically, and thus mathematically, in our reasoning. Paul clearly mentions Jesus having fictive brothers (we'll survey the evidence for that shortly). But he never mentions Jesus having real brothers. He never clarifies that, for example, some of the brothers he mentions are brothers of the Lord "according to the flesh" or by any other designation indicating they were his brothers in some sense different from all the other brothers of the Lord Paul and his readers knew. Paul also never specifically says Jesus and these brothers shared a literal mother (or father), or discusses how other Christians defer to them because they are his surviving kin, or that they even were his surviving kin.

Neither does Paul say anything more concrete, like that Jesus' "brothers in life" were divided amongst each other as to whether to become his brothers in death through adoption by God; or that "James his brother" gained a prominent place in the movement because of his being Jesus' kin by blood; or "I visited his family and met his brothers" or "in life Jesus had renounced his earthly family" (as claimed in Mark 3:31–35); or "his own brother James had a revelation that brought him into the church"; or any of a thousand things Paul could have said that, *had* he said them,[2] would clinch the conclusion that he thereby knew Jesus to be a historical man. If Paul had said anything—anything at all—like this, then the likelihood of *that* if Jesus did not exist would easily be yet more hundreds or thousands to one against. That he did exist would then be assured to us.

But, for whatever reason, Paul didn't do that. So there is no such evidence left to cite. And therefore, honestly, we shouldn't count and weigh any passage about 'Brothers of the Lord' in Paul. They are all too ambiguous.

What Paul Says He Knew

The usual argument is that 'Paul says he knew the brothers of Jesus', and since only a real person can have those, Paul himself proves to us Jesus existed. But that is not what Paul says. What he actually says is quite different.

Paul's most detailed explanations of what he actually knew appear in Romans 8:15–19 through 9:26, and Galatians 3:26–4:7. The "Son of

---

[2] Any one of which or more he could have said: Carrier, *Historicity*, 518–19n13.

God… Jesus Christ our Lord" (Romans 1:4), Paul says, is "the firstborn of many brethren" (*prôtotokon en pollois adelphois*, Romans 8:29), because all who are baptized into Christ "are the sons of God" (*huioi eisin theou*, Romans 8:14). And they are so because they have been "adopted as sons" (*huiothesias*) and thus cry out to God, "Abba! Father!" (Romans 8:15). And since, Paul tells his fellow Christians, "the Spirit now testifies" that we have become "the children of God" (*tekna theou*, Romans 8:16), that is the reason we are now "the heirs" (*klêronomoi*) to God's kingdom, "indeed, we are co-heirs with Christ" (*synklêronomoi de Christou*, Romans 8:17). Thus, elsewhere, Paul says of all who are "baptized" (*ebaptisthête*) into Christ that "you are all the sons of God" (*pantes gar huioi theou este*) and therefore all "heirs" to his kingdom (*klêronomoi*, Galatians 3:26–29). Paul thus makes clear that baptism was the adoption ceremony (Gal. 3:27), for this is how we share in Christ's suffering and inheritance (Rom. 8:17, referencing Rom. 6:2–10; and Rom. 8:15, referencing Gal. 4:6; cf. Col. 2:11–14).

We're even told Christ chose to become incarnate and die precisely "so that we might receive adoption to sonship" (*hina tên huiothesian apolabômen*, Galatians 4:5) in order to give us a share in the Kingdom of God (Gal. 4:1, 7). How? Paul answers:

> Because you are His sons, God sent the Spirit of His Son into our hearts, the Spirit who calls out, 'Abba! Father!' So you are no longer a slave, but God's child. And since you are His child, God has made you also an heir.
>
> —Galatians 4:6–7 (NIV)

And for this reason scripture even predicted, Paul says, that all his fellow Christians "shall be called Sons of the Living God" (*klêthêsontai huioi theou zôntos*, Romans 9:26, quoting Hosea 1:10, even verbatim from the LXX).

Note what this means. Paul repeatedly makes very clear that all baptized Christians are the brothers of Jesus, and *therefore* coequal heirs to God's Kingdom, because Jesus is *the first* Son of God and thus *the* Heir. It is thus by being the Lord's brother that we get to claim eternal life and power with him. It's very clear that this was a fundamental and pervasive understanding in the Christian sect. It is what they believed made them special, what singled them out as following the right path, what made them a distinct sect among the Jews. They were the Sons of the Living God. And so they share in the inheritance of the *firstborn* Son of God, the Lord Jesus—being also, like him, the adopted sons of God, and thus the brethren of Christ their Lord. Which means Paul's Christians all understood themselves to be Brothers of the Lord. Paul says this so explicitly, so often, that it's quite beyond any reasonable dispute.

Paul and all his congregations thus understood all baptized Christians to be the 'brothers' of Christ (who was only "the firstborn among many brethren," per Romans 8:29; which of course means brothers and sisters). And not only Paul. This is repeated, with additional prooftexts, in Hebrews 2:10–18, where Jesus himself is made to proclaim Christians to be his "brothers" (*adelphous autous kalein*, Heb. 2:11; cf. Heb. 12:4–9), and Ephesians 1:5 and 14, where we are told that God "predestined us for adoption to sonship through Jesus Christ" (*proorisas hêmas eis huiothesian dia Iêsou Christou*) thereby "guaranteeing our inheritance" (*arrabôn tês klêronomias hêmôn*). It also appears in 1 John 5:1–5, acknowledging we are all "born of God" (*ek tou theou gegennêtai*) and thus "the children of God" (*tekna tou theou*) like Jesus (1 Jn. 1:5; cf. 1 Jn. 5:18–21). Likewise 1 John 2:28–3:10 (e.g., "what great love the Father has lavished on us, that we should be called children of God!" 1 Jn. 3:1, NIV). The concept is accepted and elaborated even as late as Irenaeus.[3] And it has precedent in the Psalms of Solomon ("He shall gather a holy people" such that "all are their God's sons," Ps. Sol. 17:26–27).

Literally every study on this subject in the last thirty years (at least ten independent studies) agrees with this conclusion: the Christians of Paul's generation regarded themselves as brothers of each other *because* they believed they were the adopted sons of God and therefore the brothers of Jesus—who was merely the *firstborn* of them.[4] They nevertheless

[3] Irenaeus, *Demonstration of the Apostolic Preaching* 3 (through "baptism" we become the "sons" of God) and 8 (God opened up the "covenant of adoption").

[4] James Scott, *Adoption as Sons of God: An Exegetical Investigation into the Background of υἱοθεσία in the Pauline Corpus* (Mohr Siebeck, 1992), esp. 221–44; D.M. Bossman, "Paul's Fictive Kinship Movement," *Biblical Theology Bulletin* 26.4 (1996), 163–71; J.C. Walters, "Paul, Adoption, and Inheritance," in *Paul in the Greco-Roman World. A Handbook* (ed. J. P. Sampley; T&T Clark, 2003), 42–76; Reidar Aasgaard, *My Beloved Brothers and Sisters: Christian Siblingship in Paul* (T&T Clark 2004); T.J. Burke, *Adopted into God's Family: Exploring a Pauline Metaphor* (Apollos/IVC, 2006); Caroline Johnson Hodge, *If Sons,*

avoid the obvious conclusion: that we should doubt Paul means anything else in Galatians 1:19 or 1 Corinthians 9:5. Indeed, Reidar Aasgaard points out that Paul mentions brothers "122" times in his letters, and yet "natural siblings account for only two," 1 Cor. 9:5 and Gal. 1:19. "The rest, 120 instances, are used in a metaphorical sense." Which should cause us to doubt that those two are exceptions at all—for Aasgaard simply assumes they are; he adduces no evidence of it. Because there is none. Rather, all his own evidence suggests the contrary.

Since Paul makes clear all baptized Christians were proud to understand themselves as the Brothers of the Lord, it is not possible to get a different conclusion. For example, Paul never evinces any notion that they were forbidden to call themselves that or that the phrase had any other special meaning than that. To the contrary, Paul repeatedly says, without qualification, that all baptized Christians are the children of God and therefore the brothers of all his sons, including his firstborn son. Which is why Paul says they qualify as co-heirs with him to God's Kingdom. There is no indication of the phrase 'Brothers of the Lord' being policed to mean otherwise. Hence there is no way to make this evidence 'go away' by inventing some excuse, such as that 'maybe' only biological kin were 'allowed' to be called 'brothers of the Lord' even though all baptized Christians *were* 'brothers of the Lord'. That is a modern apologetic contrivance, for which there is no evidence. And we must follow the evidence, not our fantasies. And the evidence simply and unmistakably establishes that when Paul says 'brothers of the Lord' without qualification, his readers would understand him to mean a baptized Christian. We have no evidence that he or they ever understood it in any other sense.

Paul's use of the phrase therefore is of no use to us as evidence. Except to the extent that it can be evidence *against* historicity. It's entirely

---

Then Heirs: A Study of Kinship and Ethnicity in the Letters of Paul (Oxford University Press, 2007); Michael Peppard, "Adopted and Begotten Sons of God: Paul and John on Divine Sonship," *The Catholic Biblical Quarterly* 73.1 (January 2011), 92-110; Jeremy Punt, "He Is Heavy...He's My Brother: Unravelling Fraternity in Paul (Galatians)," *Neotestamentica* 46.1 (2012), 153–171; Paul Trebilco, *Self-designations and Group Identity in the New Testament* (Cambridge University Press, 2012), esp. 45; Amy Peeler, *You Are My Son: The Family of God in the Epistle to the Hebrews* (T&T Clark 2014). See also: Harold Attridge, "Hebrews," in *The Reception of Jesus in the First Three Centuries, Volume 1: From Paul to Josephus* (ed. Helen Bond; T&T Clark, 2019), 243–58 (253–54).

possible that Jesus existed and had no brothers, or he had brothers and they did not join the church, or they died soon after, or just never had occasion to be mentioned in the earliest literature. Although the fact that we would have to posit those things to get this evidence to be expected again—yet we have no evidence any of those things are true, and they are each inherently less likely than not—entails we must mathematically account for the unexpected nature of this evidence. Because what all the earliest literature does establish, to a reasonable probability, is that no one in the first generation had ever heard of any such kin of Jesus.

They do not appear in 1 Clement. Indeed real brothers of Jesus are unexpectedly missing there.[5] For example, the death of "James" gets no mention in its list of examples of important martyrs, nor do any kin get mentioned as authorities (in a letter entirely about reestablishing ecclesial authorities). They do not appear in Hebrews, either, or any of the apostolic Epistles in the canon.[6] The author of James does not identify himself as the brother of Jesus but of his fellow Christians.[7] And Jude describes himself as only a brother of James (in Jude 1). No other Epistles in the canon mention biological brothers of Jesus, either; not even the forgeries. And they had no evident place in the public Christian history related in Acts.[8] As an appendix to the Gospel, the brothers of Jesus are mentioned generically among the family of Jesus in the private history of Acts 1 (verse 14; the fictive brethren of the congregation are referenced separately in verse 16). But as soon as the public history of the Church begins in Acts 2, they vanish from all its recorded history. No James mentioned in Acts is described as a brother of Jesus. And the two men it does name James are listed separately as apostles in Acts 1:13. It is thus only "James, the brother of John" who is "put to death with the sword" in Acts 12:2; while the later "James" of Acts 12:17, 15:13, and 21:18 is only described as among the Christian brethren. So the Gospels appear to have fabricated brothers for Jesus as a literary device. Hence Mark only knows them as family Jesus renounced, evidently unaware that any of them became leaders or even members of the church. Mark

[5] Carrier, *Historicity*, 310.

[6] Carrier, *Historicity*, 528–29, 538–53.

[7] James 1:1–2, 16, 19, etc.

[8] Carrier, *Historicity*, 371–75.

also gives them generic names, and has them appear only in two scenes, where they serve only as props for teaching a lesson.[9] Indeed we only *ever* hear of them in fiction. Besides the patently fictional Gospels, the next they ever show up in the record is in apocryphal mythology of the late second century.[10]

And, of course, Paul never mentions them. When he discusses brothers of the Lord at all, so far as all the evidence indicates, it is always and only the Christian brethren he means. So the fact that it doesn't occur to Paul that he needed to make clear what he did or did not mean in Galatians 1:19 and 1 Corinthians 9:5 suggests that he had no knowledge of it even being *possible* that Jesus had living brothers. This is not a very strong evidence (the various ways he could overlook this are not *wholly* improbable, along with all the ways a real Jesus might have had no surviving brothers worth thinking about). But it should weigh something. And that means it should weigh in the other direction: not *for* Jesus existing, but against. Because we would more expect Paul to know he has to specify he means *a different kind* of brother in those two verses than he usually does. And even at best, it's a wash: we can't tell which he means.

So the conclusion is inescapable. Paul is quite elaborate in repeatedly explaining across multiple letters this notion that all baptized Christians are the sons of God and therefore brothers of the Lord and hence 'co-heirs' with him to God's coming Kingdom. By contrast, never once does Paul even articulate the notion that there were any biological brothers of Jesus, much less elaborately and repeatedly across multiple letters. Paul never exhibits any knowledge of that, or of any need to specify when he meant that. The only brothers of the Lord Paul ever describes knowing about are baptized Christians.

Is there any way to challenge this conclusion?

Did Paul Know Any *Other* Kind of Brother of the Lord?

Paul references Christians as 'brothers' (and 'sisters') over a hundred

---

[9] Carrier, *Historicity*, 453–55.

[10] As first attested (even somewhat ambiguously) in Hegesippus: Carrier, *Historicity*, 326–31.

times across his letters. But the information we just surveyed entails this was merely an abbreviation for brothers *of the Lord*. Contrary to apologetics, it is not the case that Paul distinguishes anyone as a brother only 'in' Christ. People are often described as 'in' Christ but never called 'brothers in Christ'. That phrase exists nowhere in the Epistles; not even in Philippians 1:14, as correctly translated by the NIV.[11] It is also not the case that Paul distinguishes kinds of brothers by selective use of the definite article; to the contrary, he frequently refers to Christian's as 'the' brother(s).[12] The same evidence shows that Paul does not choose personalizing pronouns (like 'our brother' or 'my brother') for this purpose either. Nor does stating the relationship in the genitive signal this.[13] Indeed, by counterexample, Romans 9:3 shows Paul knew he had to specify when a phrase like 'brother of' *was* meant biologically. So there is no way to get those two verses to be grammatically or intentionally 'different' than all the rest. Paul's idioms are consistent across all his letters.

The only distinction is between abbreviation and pleonasm. And there are only two passages where Paul uses the pleonasm (the full expression) 'Brother(s) of the Lord'. In Galatians 1:19, he says that on his first visit to Jerusalem he "saw none of the other apostles—only James, the Lord's brother" (NIV). And in 1 Corinthians 9:5, he says "Don't we have the right to take a believing wife along with us, as do the other apostles and the Lord's brothers and Cephas?" (NIV). So is there any evidence that he nevertheless somehow meant, just in these two verses, biological kin?

1. Galatians 1:19

In Galatians 1, Paul doesn't say it but we can infer that he is responding to some argument against him to the effect of, "You aren't a real apostle; you just cribbed everything from other apostles," and this was then a rider to another argument, to the effect of, "Someone told us there is a

---

[11] Carrier, *Historicity*, 584n94.

[12] Carrier, *Historicity*, 589–90n99.

[13] A genitive of fraternal relationship often indicates *fictive* kinship in the NT, e.g. Matt. 25:40; Rom. 14:10, 15, 21; 1 Cor. 6:5; 2 Cor. 8:22; 1 Thess. 3:2, 4:6; Heb. 2:12; Rev. 12:10, 19:10, 22:9.

different gospel than yours, so why should we trust yours over theirs?" This whole letter was written to rebut that second accusation. But to do that he had to rebut the first accusation.

So Paul spends the entire first chapter of Galatians arguing for his credentials as a real apostle and his gospel as authentic. His first argument is to insist that he did not learn the gospel from any person at all, but most definitely received it by revelation directly from Jesus (Galatians 1:11–12), thus electing him as an apostle (1 Corinthians 9:1, 15:5–8; Galatians 1:13–18). His second argument is to insist that he was an enemy of the church until that happened, and so he must be telling the truth now (Galatians 1:13–18, 23–24). His third argument is to insist that he never even met an apostle until years after he was converted and already preaching the gospel (Galatians 1:16–20). And even then, he emphasizes, this barely counted, for on that occasion he met just two Christians, and for only a fortnight.

Paul literally goes out of his way at this point to insist to the Galatians, "I assure you before God that what I am writing you is no lie" (Galatians 1:20). So this was clearly a very important point to him, and to the Galatians. One might suspect he is trying to whitewash the truth here by protesting too much; one might wonder, for example, how he persecuted the church (Galatians 1:13, 23) without meeting any Christians he could learn its gospel from (or why he would be persecuting it without even knowing what its gospel was). But that is not relevant to understanding what Paul's argument *is*. And what he is arguing is that he learned the gospel from no human being, and only met anyone who could have taught it to him years after. Paul then goes on to say he did not tarry in Judea, either, but was away in "Syria and Cilicia" after that, until fourteen years later, when the Lord told him to go present his gospel for examination by the leading apostles in Jerusalem (Galatians 1:21–2:2). At which event they confirmed both his gospel and his apostleship (Galatians 2:3–10); and any continued claim to there being 'two' gospels was only a consequence of their hypocrisies (Galatians 2:11–21). I already covered the point in chapter four that Paul and (or so Paul says) the other apostles confirmed 'his' gospel was the same as theirs and not a different one.

It is in the context of all this that Paul has to identify whoever he did meet on that one two-week occasion years before, and swear by it:

> After three years, I went up to Jerusalem to get acquainted with Cephas and stayed with him fifteen days. I saw none of the other apostles—only James, the Lord's brother. I assure you before God that what I am writing you is no lie.
>
> —Galatians 1:18–20 (NIV)

Less informed translations here read "I saw none of the other apostles except James, the Lord's brother," but that is not a credible translation of Paul's Greek. Once this was pointed out, more careful translations started to render this as the NIV does, replacing 'except' with 'only'.

The reason for this is that it cannot be that Paul meant to say "I met two apostles, Cephas and James" or "I stayed with Cephas and met another apostle, James" or anything the like, as then he would just say that. Instead Paul went out of his way to choose a rare, convoluted, and distinct grammatical construction (*heteron de tôn apostolôn ouk eidon ei mê Iakôbon ton adelphon tou Kyriou*) that we now know meant the opposite of this: that that other person he met was *not* an apostle, as demonstrated decades ago by L.P. Trudinger.[14] So Paul chose specifically to say he saw only *one* apostle, Cephas, counting that as his only meeting with any 'apostles' at all, and that he happened to meet only one other Christian *who was not an apostle*. This entails the James in this passage (Galatians 1:19) was not an apostle; which further entails he was not the same person as the James mentioned in the next chapter (Galatians 2:9–12), who *was* an apostle—indeed, no mere apostle, but one of the three of highest rank in the church, the so-called 'pillars' (Galatians 2:9). Who all had to be apostles because there was no higher rank in the church than that (1 Corinthians 12:28); so no one listed among them could not have been one.

This correlates with the earliest Gospel, which reports that the 'pillars' Paul lists with Cephas—James and John—were brothers of each other, not of Jesus (Mark 1:19, 3:17), and those three men indeed comprised the Lord's top three men (Mark 3:16–17, 5:37, 9:2, 10:41, 14:33). Mark 10:35, 41, even has this "James and John" ask to sit at their leader's right and left in his glory; and Paul lists them in just this fashion, now

[14] L. Paul Trudinger, "[*Heteron de tōn apostolōn ouk eidon, ei mē iakōbon*]: A Note on Galatians I 19," *Novum Testamentum* 17 (July 1975), 200–02. Agreed by Hans Dieter Betz, *Galatians: A Commentary on Paul's Letter to the Churches in Galatia* (Fortress, 1979), 78, and the translation committees of the NIV, NAB, and BLB.

with Cephas in place of Jesus: "James, Cephas, and John," with James to the left and John to the right, and their leader in the middle (placing Cephas at the apex of the chiasmus). The author of Mark clearly understood this (and the fact that Mark employed the Epistles of Paul for material like this was already discussed here in chapter two). Which is why Mark has Jesus completely renounce his biological brothers, evidently unaware that any would be high ranking leaders in his church (Mark 3:31–35); and why the author of Acts had never heard of such a thing either; nor 1 Clement or anyone else of the first generation.

It is thus plain to anyone not reading this text with a prejudiced eye that Paul is distinguishing these two men: in Galatians 1:19 he identifies the James there as merely "the brother of the Lord," a Christian of *no* rank—hence Paul specifically emphasizes this was a James *not* of apostolic rank; then in Galatians 2:9 he identifies the James there as one of the "the pillars," a Christian of *superlative* rank—one of the top three apostles. This is unlikely to be coincidental. Paul has gone out of his way to signal these are not the same men. The James of 1:19 is not the pillar; the James of 2:9 is. The James of 1:19 is not an apostle; the James of 2:9 is. The Galatians don't need this spelled out beyond that, because these identifiers were for them sufficient. They knew the pillars were apostles. And they knew apostles were also 'Brothers of the Lord'. But they also knew that the Greek formula of *heteron* plus the genitive meant 'other than' and not 'another of'.[15] And so Paul's convoluted expression "other than the apostles I saw none but James the brother" would have clearly demarcated this James as *merely* of the brethren, that this James is being excluded from the category of the apostles, yet still considered essential to mention. As Paul's argument is that he hardly met any human who could teach him the gospel at this point (Galatians 1:11–12, 16–17; and again, whether his claim is true or false does not matter to this point), he was obligated to list any Christian he met then, not just apostles. That is why he swears these are the only two Christians he met; and that still no one else in all the churches of Judea "knew" his "face" yet (Galatians 1:22–23).

It is thus significant that Paul does not just say James was a Brother of the Lord; he first says he is not an apostle (*heteron de tôn apostolōn*

[15] Smyth §1433 and §1434; Liddell & Scott (1996), 'heteros' §A.III.1 (c. gen.); and Trudinger, "A Note on Galatians."

ouk), and *then* identifies him as a Brother of the Lord (*ei mê Iakōbon ton adelphon tou Kyriou*). If Paul had said anything like "I met two apostles, Cephas and James the Brother of the Lord," or, "I stayed with Cephas, and met the apostle James the Brother of the Lord," *then* we would have to infer that this James was a Brother of the Lord in some sense Cephas was not. And *that* would be evidence for the conclusion that this James was distinctively a *biological* brother of Jesus and no *mere* brother of Jesus. But Paul chose not to say that. So he is not excluding Peter (lit. Cephas) from the category of Brothers of the Lord; he is excluding James (lit. Jacob) from the category of apostles.

That is what his chosen grammar entails. Hence the only substantive objection ever raised to Trudinger's point was that of George Howard, who claimed all the examples Trudinger adduced of this grammatical formula entailed the things being compared nevertheless still belonged to the same category of things.[16] To "make friends other than the ones they already have" (Thucydides, *Peloponnesian War* 1.28) only made sense to the Greek ear because both friends belong to the same category: different kinds of friends (the ones that are new, and the ones that are not). The fifth element, "being an element other than the four, is indestructible" (Ps.-Aristotle, *De Mundo* 392a9) only made sense to the Greek ear because all five elements belong to the same category: different kinds of elements (the one that is indestructible, and the others that are not).

Howard is correct—and yet he did not notice that this is exactly the case here: Paul is listing Christians. "Other than the apostles I saw no one but James the brother" would make sense to the Greek ear because both apostolic and non-apostolic Christians belong to the same category: different kinds of brethren (the ones that are of apostolic rank, and the ones that are not). This is also the case even if we read the verse as referring to a biological brother of Jesus, for even then Paul is still saying these two people belonged to a common category: Christians ('believers'). So Howard's objection does not rebut but actually confirms Trudinger's finding: this is what that phrase meant in ancient Greek, and thus what Paul was deliberately choosing to say. Howard's point thus *confirms* that Paul was excluding James from the category of apos-

[16] George Howard, "Was James an Apostle? A Reflection on a New Proposal for Gal. I 19," *Novum Testamentum* 19 (January 1977), 63–64.

tles; just as (Pseudo-)Aristotle was excluding the fifth element from the category of destructible elements, and Thucydides was excluding new friends from the category of old friends. But all are following Howard's rule: both kinds of friends are still friends; both kinds of elements are still elements; and both kinds of brethren (apostolic and non-apostolic) are still brethren.

This is why it matters that we know 'the believers' repeatedly called themselves 'the brethren'.[17] Indeed, they understood themselves specifically to be the Brethren of the Lord (as previously demonstrated). This would have been, in effect, a name for themselves—the word 'Christian' not yet widely enough in use (per Acts 11:26), and 'Nazorian' (per Acts 24:5) never used by Paul. Paul is therefore plainly saying "I met two Christians, the apostle Cephas and the congregant James," hence "besides Cephas, I met no other apostle; only James the Brother of the Lord" was analogous then to saying today, "Other than Peter, I met no other priest; only James the Christian." This would never be taken to mean Peter was not a Christian; that he is a priest, everyone knows, already means he is a Christian, so it does not have to be additionally specified. Only James has to be specified as a Christian. The same is true of calling Cephas an apostle: the Galatians already knew that meant a brother of rank, and so Paul would have no reason to redundantly say that. And indeed Paul's chosen grammatical construction *requires* Cephas to have also been a Christian—and hence, also, a Brother of the Lord. Whereas to say James was not an apostle but *was*, at least, a Brother of the Lord, would *not* be redundant: for Paul has to make clear this person was a Christian, and just not one of rank. And in ancient Greek, this was a well known way Paul would say that. That's how the Galatians would have understood this sentence. For them to take it in any other sense would have required Paul to formulate it in another way. But he didn't.

2. 1 Corinthians 9:5

Paul would not (and does not) use the prolix expression 'Brothers of the Lord' most of the time because that would be tedious and unnecessary;

[17] For example: Rom. 1:13, 8:29, 16:14; 1 Cor. 6:8, 8:12, 15:6, 16:11; 2 Cor. 8:23, 9:3, 9:5, 11:9, 11:26; Gal. 1:2, 2:4, 5:13, 6:18; Phil. 1:14, 4:1, 4:21; 1 Thess. 4:10, 5:26, 5:27.

he simply truncates it to 'brother' (over a hundred times). His readers know in what sense they are brothers; and the affectional brevity makes for more readable letters.

There are only two occasions when Paul uses the full expression, and they share a common feature: on both occasions Paul needs to make a distinction between apostolic and non-apostolic Christians. Then he uses the full phrase to signify what he means: a fellow Christian other than an apostle (and not, for example, any apostle's *literal* brother). If in Galatians 1:19 Paul had merely said 'Peter' and 'James the brother', one could mistake that as meaning *Peter's* brother, a common connotation in ancient Greek when supplying only the definite article, which can imply a possessive. Such a misunderstanding would be particularly at risk in an account of Paul having 'stayed with' Peter two weeks, and thus having potentially met his family. That family's absence from Paul's list means he intended the Galatians to understand that he did *not* meet Peter's family; which would suggest Peter did not normally reside in Jerusalem, or had no family there at that time. But we can only conclude this because Paul made clear that this James was not *Peter's* brother but *a* brother, a fellow Christian. Hence Paul had to employ the full phrase here. This emphasis also aided his cause—to relate all the Christians (all the 'flesh and blood' who were teaching the gospel) that he met then.

The only other time Paul does this served a similar purpose: in 1 Corinthians 9:5. Here Paul makes the following argument:

> Don't we have the right to food and drink? Don't we have the right to take a believing wife along with us, as do the other apostles and the Lord's brothers and Cephas? Or is it only I and Barnabas who lack the right to not work for a living?
>
> —1 Corinthians 9:4–6 (NIV)

We lack the argument Paul is responding to—something has been removed between the end of chapter eight and the beginning of chapter nine (resulting in an abrupt change of subject). But it's clear from how the argument of chapter nine proceeds that Paul and his companion Barnabas were being criticized for expecting the churches they visited to pay for their keep. Indeed, Paul's letters are rife with his need to defend himself against charges of graft.[18] And here, this concern intersected with the subject of mooching. This expectation of being taken care of evidently included any wives or maids they brought with them. The Greek literally says "sister woman" (*adelphên gynaika*) meaning a Sister of the Lord who was also someone's female companion or helpmeet. The word *gynê* can mean just 'woman' and not necessarily a wife, so it is unclear whether the argument pertained, for example, to Barnabas's wife or Paul's maid or something else. Indeed, Paul says they hadn't even taken advantage of this right (9:12). He argues only that they *have* this right. So with the missing introductory material it is unclear what exactly he was accused of or what he is attempting to establish now, or why he even has to argue for a right he says he never used (is he responding to a kerfuffle over him or Barnabas seeking this right for an upcoming occasion?). All we can tell for sure is that Paul wants to argue that he (and, evidently, Barnabas) should have this right, the same as everyone else who receives it.

It is no accident that this involved more intimations that Paul wasn't a 'real' apostle (1 Cor. 9:1–4), just as in Galatians 1. We are thus looking at a similar context: Paul needs to establish his credentials as an apostle, and part of that is establishing the rights he can claim on his mission. And in this case his argument *requires* that he list both apostles *and* non-apostolic Christians claiming that right. So once again Paul has to make a distinction between those two classes of Christian. The only other time he has to do this is in Galatians 1:19. So just as in that case, here as well he employs the pleonasm: Brothers of the Lord. And as there, here he means non-apostolic Christians—'ordinary' or 'mere' brethren. He does not mean—and in fact here *cannot* mean—the biological kin of Jesus. Because it would ruin Paul's entire argument to insist that he could claim the rights of *the actual family of Jesus*. Obviously they could claim a level of honor he could not. To the contrary, Paul's argument requires that the examples he lists be his peers or inferiors.

The 'brothers of the Lord' here must, therefore, be a group of *inferior rank* to apostles; Paul's point being that if even ordinary Christians traveling on church business were taken care of, then surely he, an actual

---

[18] See my discussion and examples in Richard Carrier, *The Probabilistic Argument for Interpolation in 1 Thessalonians 2:14–16*. Besides 1 Cor. 9, examples include: 1 Cor. 16; 2 Cor. 8–9 and 12:11–21; Phil. 4:11–19; Rom. 15:25–29; and 1 Thess. 1:5–2:10.

apostle, should as well. And indeed, that ordinary Christians traveling on church business (not just apostles) were expected to be taken care of this way is addressed (and thus attested) in the *Didachê* (11–13). While apostles were supposed to be equals, as Paul many times said.[19] So, just as obviously, any right Cephas and 'the other apostles' claimed should be owed to Paul, too; but all the more so any right extended even to mere brethren. This is why he centers that example, with his list forming the apex structure [other apostles] : [mere Christians] : [the apostle], drawing attention to the centerpiece of this argument, his *coup de grâce*: that even *non*-apostolic Christians are getting this right.

The overall structure of Paul's sentence is even clearer on this point. Because Paul has to be assuming this is understood when he says he and his companions have a right to take with them on church business 'a sister woman', *adelphên gunaika*, 'a woman or wife [who is a] sister', meaning a *fictive* sister, not a biological one. So when in the same sentence we hear about similarly generic 'brothers' (*adelphoi*) we already have cause to wonder *what kind*. And lo, Paul says: he means the brethren *of the Lord*. Christians. The subtle chiastic structure in 1 Corinthians 9:5 reinforces this suspicion:

we have

A the authority [*exousian*]

B a sister woman [*adelphên gynaika*]

C to lead around [*periagein*]

D as also

C the other apostles [*apostoloi*, 'those sent out']

B and the brethren [*adelphoi*, masc.] of the Lord

A and Cephas.

[19] 1 Cor. 4 (and 1:11–14, 3:19–23, and 12:28); 2 Cor. 11 (and 12:11); 1 Thess. 2:6; and Gal. 2.

Paul starts with 'we' meaning, literally, Paul and his companions (particularly Barnabas, 1 Cor. 9:6), but meaning, *arguendo*, the entire Christian community. But this verb also subtly relates logically (rather than grammatically) to 'our' having the examples he lists: we have the authority (*exousia*) of Peter (*Kephas*); we have the example of the sisters (*adelphai*) and brothers (*adelphoi*); and we have the example of the apostles (*apostoloi*) and their mission (*periagein*).

Paul's ensuing chiasm thus encompasses the entire Christian community: (A) the font of all their authority (Peter, the first revelator, per 1 Corinthians 15:5–8), (B) fictive kin (sisters and brothers of the Lord; hence, *all* Christians on church business), and (C) apostles—for in both places Paul references apostolic activity with 'to be sent out' and 'to lead around', where in both Paul is including himself and his companions: he says the 'other' apostles (reminding his readers that he is one); and he says he and his companions are thereby 'going about' with a 'sister' (defending which was his entire point).

The structure of Paul's argument thus implies all of these 'brothers' and 'sisters' are fictive, the adopted children of God. There is no evidence here of Paul being aware of any other kind of sibling—as he is in Romans 9:3, when listing fellow Jews as his brothers, he knows he has to specify "according to the flesh," yet here he does not.[20] He does not specify in *any* way that the 'brothers' he mentions here are biological but the 'sisters' he mentions are not. He is assuming his readers know. Which means he had no idea of there even being biological brethren. Because, again, Paul tells us he and his congregations knew all about fictive Brothers of the Lord, but mentions no other kind. So that he does not specify any other kind here signals he *meant* no other kind here—a fact that bothered later Christian's enough to try and 'edit' this passage to make it more explicitly mean biological kin of Jesus.[21] So they under-

[20] Paul thus did not then need to repeat this qualifier in Romans 16:7 ("Andronicus and Junia, my kinsmen," *syggeneis mou*), which most scholars agree refers to the same thing (his fellow Christians who were Jewish, not his actual family), e.g. Thomas Schreiner, *Romans* (Baker, 2018), 769; Robert Jewett, *Romans: A Commentary* (Fortress, 2006), 962; Grant Osborne, *Romans* (InterVarsity, 2004) 406.

[21] By including the names of Jesus's brothers as lifted from the Gospels (in 1 Cor. 9:6, ms. 1874, 10th century): Reuben Swanson, *New Testament Greek Manuscripts: Variant Readings Arranged in Horizontal Lines against Codex Vaticanus: 1 Corinthians* (Sheffield

stood the ambiguity. We therefore cannot establish from this verse that Paul himself knew about biological brothers of the Lord. Fictive brethren fit the wording and even better fit the argument Paul is making. Just as with Galatians 1:19.

The Evidence of Origen and Josephus

That leaves only one last piece of evidence. As noted, there is no evidence that Jesus had real brothers in the New Testament or beyond, outside fiction (only the Gospels, Acts 1, and late second century legends). In anything even resembling history, they always vanish (such as in Acts 2–28). The one exception some might appeal to is a reference in Josephus to a certain "brother of Jesus (the one called Christ), whose name was James" who gets executed by the Sanhedrin, for reasons never specifically described, shortly before the Jewish War.[22]

The evidence that this was never originally a passage about our Jesus at all (and hence the phrase "the [one] called Christ" was a late third century interpolation, probably accidental) is quite extensive. But as I noted in chapter two, even if Josephus actually wrote this line (which is incredible), "it still can't help us establish a historical Jesus because we cannot establish that Josephus knew (or even would or could have known—or even cared) what sort of 'brother' James was to Jesus." Given that Christians were then routinely describing themselves as 'Brothers of the Lord', any story that reached Josephus about a James 'the brother of their Lord' could easily have been mistaken as a story about biological kin. There is no evidence Josephus knew about their theology of adoption and thus their fictive kinship monikers. So we cannot establish to any probability that Josephus had reliable information that James was, exceptionally, the *biological* brother of Jesus, and not a cultic one. And it would be too easy for him not to know the difference, or even not to care. So this passage is not something we can rely on as evidence, *even if* it was unaltered.

Academic Press, 2003), 125. Conversely, another manuscript drops the definite article, forming the phrase "the other apostles and brethren of the Lord" as if *aware* of Paul's original meaning and thus trying to preserve *rather* than conceal it (ms. K, 9th century).

[22] Josephus, *Antiquities of the Jews* 20.200.

Nevertheless, that it was altered is assured. This has been multiply demonstrated.[23] The list of evidence is long:

- This passage was unknown to Origen. Despite his explicit search of Josephus for material about Jesus in his answer to Celsus, he was never able to find this actual passage. For he never quotes any distinctive material from it, nor correctly describes its content.

- It is objectively evident that when Origen *claims* he found a passage like it, he actually mistook a story about James from the writings of Hegesippus as being in Josephus—a kind of mistake I documented that Origen sometimes made.[24] We can be sure of this because Origen's description of the passage's content matches several peculiar details in Hegesippus, and none in Josephus.[25]

- Before Eusebius in the fourth century, all other accounts of the death of James 'the brother of Jesus' (such as in Hegesippus) do not match this one in Josephus; therefore, they *also* had no knowledge of this passage being about the Christian James.

- We know Acts used this same work of Josephus as a source for historical color.[26] Yet the author of Acts never noticed this passage as

---

[23] Carrier, "Origen" (reproduced in *Hitler Homer*, 337–68, and summarized in *Historicity*, 337–42); now supported by: Nicholas Allen, "Josephus on James the Just? A Re-Evaluation of *Antiquitates Judaicae* 20.9.1," *Journal of Early Christian History* 7.1 (2017), 1–27; Chris Hansen, "Jesus' Historicity and Sources: The Misuse of Extrabiblical Sources for Jesus and a Suggestion," *American Journal of Biblical Theology* 22.6 (2021), 1–21 (6); Margaret Williams, *Early Classical Authors on Jesus* (T&T Clark, 2022), 54; and Nicholas List, "The Death of James the Just Revisited," *Journal of Early Christian Studies* 32 (2024), 17–44.

[24] For example, Origen confused the *Protevangelium of James* §23 as having been in Josephus, and thus incorrectly cited Josephus as his source for it in *Commentary on Matthew* (frg. 25); see Carrier, "Origen," 509–10n33.

[25] This mistake is replicated three times: Origen, *Against Celsus* 1.47 and 2.13, and *Commentary on Matthew* 10.17.

[26] Carrier, *Historicity*, 267, referencing: Richard Pervo, *Dating Acts: Between the Evangelists and the Apologists* (Polebridge, 2006); Barbara Shellard, *New Light on Luke: Its Purpose, Sources, and Literary Context* (Sheffield Academic, 2002), 31-34; Steve Mason, "Josephus and Luke–Acts," in *Josephus and the New Testament* (Hendrickson Publishers, 1992),

being about his Jesus. Which is inexplicable, given that if it was, it shows Jews being punished for persecuting Christians, exactly the kind of thing the author of Acts strove to include; instead, Acts never mentions this James even being martyred, while the only James who dies in Acts is the brother of John, not Jesus, and is beheaded by a king, not stoned by the Sanhedrin court. This is inexplicable even if the author of Acts did not employ Josephus, for it is not likely that Josephus would know this story but the Christian author of Acts would not.

- The phrase *tou legomenou christou* ("the [one] called Christ") was a common Christian idiom, found in the Gospels (Mt. 1:16, 27:17, 27:22; Jn. 4:25) and later Christian literature, especially the works of Origen.

- Yet the key term in that phrase is wholly alien in Josephus, who always avoided using the word 'Christ' as messiah, even when repeatedly describing messianic pretenders (see discussion here in chapter two), and who didn't think to provide or cross-reference any explanation of the term here. Yet he always does that when using obscure terms—as exemplified in this very same passage, where he *both* refers readers to his prior discussion of the Sadducees *and* provides an explanation of its relevance here. And that was far less obscure a term.

- If Josephus had written this passage as about the persecution of Christians, he would have explained a great deal more, as is his style consistently in all his historical writing; only a Christian would just assume all those things were already known to the reader—like what a 'Christ' was; that James was a Christian; that Jews sought to kill Christians (and why); and why the Jewish elite *and* Roman author-

---

185–229; Gregory Sterling, *Historiography and Self-Definition: Josephos, Luke–Acts and Apologetic Historiography* (Brill, 1992); Heinz Schreckenberg, "Flavius Josephus und die lukanischen Schriften," in *Wort in der Zeit: Neutestamentliche Studien* (ed. Karl Rengstorf and Wilfrid Haubeck; Brill, 1980), 179-209; and Max Krenkel, *Josephus und Lucas: Der schriftstellerische Einfluss des jüdischen Geschichtschreibers auf den Christlichen* (H. Haessel, 1894). To these can now be added: Steve Mason, "Did the Author of Luke-Acts Know the Works of Josephus?" in *Jews and Christians in the Roman World: From Historical Method to Cases* (Brill, 2023), 445–88.

ities *opposed* the killing of James if he was a Christian (as they could adduce legendary examples of that from Acts).

- Not even the Testimonium Flavianum explains any of these things. It never mentions Jesus having family; it never mentions Jews trying to kill Christians (at all, much less why); and it never explains why the Jewish and Roman elite would *oppose* that treatment of them. That was almost certainly not written by Josephus anyway (as discussed in chapter two), but if it or anything like it had been, Josephus would still have referenced it here and explained its relevance.

- The first time anyone reports finding these passages in Josephus is in the 4th century writings of Eusebius, who makes abundant rhetorical use of them.[27] This has led several scholars to suspect Eusebius forged them. But the culprit could as likely have been his tutor and predecessor at the same library, Pamphilus, in turn Origen's successor at that same library.

For these and other reasons, the words *tou legomenou christou*, "the [one] called Christ," most likely originated as a Christian marginal note (by Origen or his successor, Pamphilus, or *his* successor, Eusebius; or another scribe or scholar in the same Library of Caesarea), expressing a belief rather than a fact—possibly from trying to find the passage Origen claimed he'd seen here but mistakenly saw in Hegesippus instead. It was then interpolated accidentally (being mistaken as omitted text by a later scribe), a very common (and widely documented) error.

This may even have been accomplished by replacing the *original* words here, *ton tou damnaiou*, "the son of Damneus." That same phrase is repeated at the end of the story, and repetition of an identical phrase a few lines after may have led a scribe to suspect that the marginal note was instead correcting a dittograph—an accidental duplication caused by a previous scribe skipping some lines by mistake (thus starting at the 'wrong' Jesus in the story). More likely, that duplication was not an error but exactly what Josephus meant: Ananus is punished for killing the

---

[27] Eusebius, *Evangelical Demonstration* 3.5, *Ecclesiastical History* 1.11, and *Theophania* 5.44.

brother of Jesus ben Damneus by being deposed and replaced *by* Jesus ben Damneus. This is the only account that makes any sense of the story as told, for it is the only reason given for why Jesus ben Damneus succeeds Ananus—and the only reason the Jewish and Roman elite would be outraged by, and actually avenge, the killing of his brother. James being a Christian makes no sense of these elements of the story at all.

So the case for this being interpolated is already conclusive. And I am excluding from this evidence the fact that Origen also says he did not believe the James that Paul mentions in Gal. 1:19 was the actual brother of Jesus (declaring that "Paul…says that he regarded this James as a brother of the Lord, not so much on account of their relationship by blood, or of their being brought up together, as because of his virtue and doctrine") because that appears to be theologically motivated and not based on any real knowledge of the matter.[28]

However I *could* have added another reason we can be sure Josephus never wrote the words "called Christ" in this passage: had Origen known of the James passage that *we* have, then he would have written completely different things than he did, rather than mistakenly describing a narrative of James found only in Hegesippus. Origen would *not* have said Josephus connected the fall of Jerusalem to the killing of James. Because he would not have read that in Josephus's account of James (or anywhere in the works of Josephus). Origen would *not* have said Josephus called him James 'the Just', and he would *not* have said Josephus related that the people dubbed him that for being superlatively just. Because those details are in Hegesippus, not Josephus. But not only would Origen not have said any of those things, he would instead have said entirely *different* things. For Origen would have used the actual material in the Josephan passage to bolster his apologetic against Celsus. The fact that he didn't is therefore *additional* evidence that Origen never knew any passage actually in Josephus connected to Jesus Christ—because it wasn't yet there.

Observe how Origen milked the passage in Josephus regarding John the Baptist for his apologetic against Celsus.[29] And observe how Origen milked the passage in Hegesippus for his apologetic against Celsus (he

[28] Origen, *Against Celsus* 1.47.

[29] Origen, *Against Celsus* 1.47, in reference to Josephus, *Antiquities of the Jews* 18.109–19.

merely mistakenly cited it as in Josephus).[30] So we know that Origen desired to milk passages in Josephus for all their apologetic value, when he finds any that have any such value. And our version of the James passage in Josephus would have had so much such value that Origen could not have neglected to milk it, too.[31] If Origen had known such a passage, he would have seen that it shows the Roman and Jewish elite opposing the persecution of Christians; and that Ananus only killed Christians because he was particularly cruel and adhered to an obsolete Jewish sect; and that Josephus agreed with this assessment and thus did not deem Christians worthy of such animus. So, had Origen seen *this* passage, rather than all that business about James being dubbed the Just and his death being connected to the fall of Jerusalem, Origen would have described Ananus and his peculiar cruelty, and Josephus's criticism of it, and the Roman and Jewish opposition to it.

In Bayesian terms, all of that—the things Origen would not have said, and the things he would have said, had he found this passage in Josephus as we have it—is quite unlikely, unless Origen never knew this passage as we have it; and that is unlikely unless it never said what our text says. The suspect phrase must be an interpolation, post-dating Origen's time at the Library of Caesarea.

The point here is not that these things are 'impossible'. We can invent 'excuses' for why Origen would do everything completely contrary to every expectation. But none of those excuses will be *probable*. That is why all this evidence counts against the phrase "the one called Christ" being authentic to Josephus: it is not that Origen *necessarily* would have omitted some things and said other things, but that it is very *probable* that he would. These details are therefore unexpected—unless that phrase wasn't yet in the text of Josephus. This entails a likelihood ratio favoring interpolation (see chapters five and six). Indeed, I would have to assign it a ratio of considerable weight. It must be at least ten times more likely Origen would say what he did say (and not something else) if this phrase wasn't yet in his text of Josephus (and he simply mistook a scroll of Hegesippus for Josephus) than if it was there and Origen was ineptly describing it.

---

[30] Twice even: Origen, *Against Celsus* 1.47 and 2.13.

[31] Josephus, *Antiquities of the Jews* 20.199–203.

We can add to that all the remaining evidence. If those words *were* in the original text of Josephus, then several things become unlikely, which otherwise are entirely expected: (1) it becomes unlikely that before Eusebius no Christian accounts of the death of James would agree with this passage in any indicative way; (2) it also becomes unlikely that the author of Acts would never have heard of it (or its content from any prior source) and used none of it, even though it hands that author a rhetorical coup of particular interest to his agenda, and we have ample evidence that that author knew the *Antiquities* of Josephus and mined it as a source; (3) it becomes unlikely that we would find here the mere unexplained phrase *tou legomenou christou*, an idiom common to Christians (and readily understood by Christians), using a word everywhere else actively avoided by Josephus (outside the forgery of the Testimonium Flavianum, which this passage also does not cite); (4) it becomes unlikely that Josephus would simply have added this phrase and not provided any cross-reference or explanation of it or its relevance (like he does with the term 'Saduccees' in the same narrative); (5) it also becomes unlikely that Josephus would have felt no need to explain any of the unusual things happening in his story—why all the elite are against persecuting Christians, why Christians are being persecuted at all, that James even was a Christian (since merely being the brother of Jesus 'the Christ' does not establish that), or what even a 'Christ' was, or why James being the brother of one had anything to do with what was happening in the story, or why it even needed to be mentioned (what use is that information to his readers?); and (6) it becomes unlikely that the Testimonium Flavianum would exhibit no knowledge of any of the information in this passage—why it never mentions the family of Jesus, or that James his brother in particular became a Christian, or that anyone sought to persecute the Christians for any reason, or that anyone opposed their persecution for any reason.

And again, in each case here, 'unlikely' does not mean 'impossible'. The point is that each and every one of these things is not at all what we expect if Josephus wrote "the one called Christ" but is exactly what we expect if he didn't. You must logically account for this discrepancy. You cannot ignore it, as if it had no effect. Indeed, there are so many of these unexpected details that their weight stacks toward only one conclusion: those words weren't there, and Josephus was not writing about any Christian James at all. Even if each of those six details were only five times as likely to be as we find them if Josephus didn't write "the one called Christ" than if he did (even though I aver each and every one is then surely even more likely than that), with the unexpected material in Origin added to that, we have a combined likelihood ratio of 10/1 × 5/1 × 5/1 × 5/1 × 5/1 × 5/1 × 5/1 = 156,250/1 in favor of interpolation, well over a hundred thousand to one. Even if we assume a base rate of interpolation for any passage of value to Christians across extant ancient literature of 1000 to 1 against,[32] the final odds that this has indeed been interpolated will be at least 1/1000 × 156,250/1 = 15,625/1, or over ten thousand to one. Which is as near to 100% as makes for a sufficient certainty.[33]

So this evidence is of no value. And as we've seen so far, neither is anything else. There simply is no credible evidence that Jesus actually had brothers, much less brothers taking prominent roles in the church. And there is even less evidence of that in Paul (or any of the early Epistles). Because neither verse cited to the point (Galatians 1:19 or 1 Corinthians 9:5) can be established as referring to such a thing, rather than to simply rank-and-file Christians—as in, non-apostolic or 'mere' Christians.

Conclusion

Suppose we read a collection of letters from a traveling cult leader in America named Jones, written to his various congregations in the 1980s, and twice in those he mentions "going to McDonald's." With that information alone we would be right to conclude he means what most people mean when they say that: he visited a local affiliate of the fast food franchise McDonald's, perhaps to have a meal. But suppose in more than one of his letters he mentions having a mentor named McDonald, and that he often hangs out at his house; and furthermore, Jones makes clear to us that all his congregations were very familiar with this fact, indeed it is fundamental to their understanding of their movement that its leader

[32] The rate is actually higher: Carrier, *Probabilistic Argument*; see also: Carrier, *Historicity*, 569n73 and *Hitler Homer*, 370–71, reproducing "Prospect," 264–83 (265–66).

[33] 15,625 / (15,625 + 1) = 0.999936~ which is over 99.99%.

often spends time consulting at his mentor's home, and that their beliefs even extend in some way from this.

Then we could not say with confidence that a mere reference to Jones going to McDonald's means the restaurant—because now it could mean his mentor's home. We thus lose any access to the premise, for example, that Jones ate at McDonald's, because now we know that that is no more likely than that Jones actually meant he spent time at his mentor McDonald's *house*. Moreover, because we know Jones's congregations well knew the crucial importance of his visits to his mentor's house, it is actually not even *likely* that his other references to going to McDonald's mean the restaurant. Because Jones would never just say "I went to McDonald's" and mean the restaurant *without specifying that*—because *then* he would know he has to make clear that he means, this time, the restaurant and not his mentor's, given what he knows his congregations know and thus the confusion that could result. Which means that if Jones just casually says "I went to McDonald's" without further explanation, he almost certainly in fact means *his mentor's*.

The analogy holds here. The fact that Paul never says he knows biological brothers of Jesus exist, who thus could be confused for the fictive brothers of the cult everyone is routinely familiar with, removes from play any mere reference to 'Brothers of the Lord' as evidence for a historical Jesus. Because now we know Paul could mean fictive brothers; and he doesn't specify which kind of brothers he means. Moreover, Paul explicitly and repeatedly tells us he knows of those fictive brethren, and that all his congregations consider their being the adopted brothers of Jesus as fundamental to their entire faith. But he never seems aware of a different kind of brother he thus has to specify when referencing them. Again, Paul is aware he needs to make this distinction in Romans 9:3, where he refers to "my brothers" but knows he will confuse lest he specify that he means, in this case, "my fellow kin according to the flesh" (*tôn adelphôn mou tôn suggenôn mou kata sarka*), in order to indicate fellow Jews, not fellow Christians. Yet he does not think of doing that when referencing Brothers of the Lord (he does not say "James the brother of the Lord according to the flesh" and "the other apostles and the brothers of the Lord according to the flesh," or anything else comparable). Which means it is actually *more likely* that what Paul means whenever he says 'Brothers of the Lord' without qualification is *not* 'according to the flesh', but fellow Christians, and therefore that is what he must mean in Galatians 1:19 and 1 Corinthians 9:5. Because, there being no other kind of brother, it wouldn't occur to Paul that he had to make clear that he meant something other than he usually means; and he usually means *brother* (of the Lord) as in *Christian*. We can thus be confident he meant what he usually meant, and not some special extra different thing.

And yet, for all that, in *Historicity* I still allowed the possibility that these two passages remain strange unless real, and thus special, brothers are meant. So I still counted this as evidence Jesus existed—I simply counted it as weak, owing to its undeniable vagueness, and the readiness of other explanations for these passages that are not mere conjecture but empirically supported by the very context in which they appear. So, at a stretch, I concluded that these passages could yet be twice as expected to be written by Paul here if Jesus existed than if he didn't. Which is the farthest I could reasonably go. And even that was farther than logic should allow.

As I have just shown here, there is really no basis for seeing these lines as weird and thus unexpected *at all* if Jesus didn't exist. It is strange precisely in the opposite sense: their vagueness, their lack of qualification, their context, all suggest Paul is *not* talking about biological brethren, and therefore we *cannot* conclude he slipped into a reference to literal biology only in these two vague occasions, and just 'forgot' to make clear that he was—even to an audience he knows would readily take him to be referring to cultic and not literal brethren if he wasn't more specific. So counting these two passages together as twice as likely if Jesus existed than if he didn't is already stretching their weight too far. In context, both passages look pretty much entirely *expected* if Jesus didn't exist.

So even if you wish to count these two passages as still evidence for a historical Jesus, you can't count them as particularly weighty. Like the hypothetical Jones and his visits to McDonald's, Paul has given us information that calls that assumption into question. Indeed, personally, I think it's worse. We should read Paul at exactly what he said, and not try to invent implausible or unevidenced claims to get him to have said something else. So when Paul says 'Brothers of the Lord' he most likely means the fictive family of Jesus, the Christians themselves—just as he repeatedly informs us.

Either way, we cannot tell if Paul knew of any real, biological kin of

Jesus. And we therefore cannot use these two passages as evidence for a historical Jesus. They more stand as evidence against it, as the evidence *overall* signals that Paul was not aware of Jesus having *any* biological family one could speak to. That it would never occur to Paul to make clear that *biological* kin of Jesus are *not* what he meant on these occasions (or even that it *was* what he meant) is still explicable if Jesus existed; but it is not entirely *expected*, and thus not *entirely* probable. Therefore, on the lower margin of error, I think we must weigh these passages, in the peculiar form that we have them (lacking, as they do, all expected qualifications), the other way around: they are twice as likely to be written as we have them if Jesus *didn't* exist than if he did.

Either way, the evidence that Paul met any biological kin of Jesus is too weak to establish that Jesus existed. Our confidence in that should remain low. For Paul's ambiguous references to brothers, my original study's conclusion remains: at worst this evinces no one knew of the sort of Jesus who could have real brothers (counting weakly 2:1 against historicity) or it doesn't securely evince they did, and so at best it indicates only that they *might* have known of the sort of Jesus who had brothers (counting weakly 2:1 for historicity).

11

Where We Need to Go from Here

All the evidence of the previous ten chapters leans in one direction: Christianity began with revelations (just like Islam and Mormonism), and the Gospels are later literary mythologizations of their savior—which subsequent Christians historicized, expelling and condemning any remaining Christians who did not go along, even adding explicit assertions of historicity into the creed to ensure compliance. Christians who objected were explicitly shunned (as Ignatius and 2 Peter admit) and their teachings and writings not preserved (as is evident by their absence now, despite knowledge of them then). Which means our understanding of the origins of Christianity needs to be reconstructed from the ground up. And the content of the early Epistles needs to be reinterpreted in light of their authors' not knowing of a Gospel Jesus. And the content of the Gospels needs to be reinterpreted in light of their authors' inventing him.

The field of Jesus studies needs to reckon with these facts and address them. Continuing to ignore or evade them only leaves its collective head in the sand, pursuing the wrong avenues of inquiry for understanding how and why Christianity began and developed in its early generations, and the wrong avenues of inquiry for understanding the Gospels and the letters of Paul—and other literature as well.

The case for this was already made twice now under peer review, by myself in *On the Historicity of Jesus*, and by Raphael Lataster in *Questioning the Historicity of Jesus* (chapter one). Since then, none of our findings have been undermined, while many in fact have been reinforced by further scholarship from a wide array of experts (chapter two). Over ten years, all attempts at a critical response to our findings have uniformly evaded their actual contents, dismissing them unanswered or addressing them only with specious apologetics that won't even mention what our arguments and evidence actually were, much less answer them (chapter three). The historicity of Jesus has instead continued to be defended with bad arguments, so consistently now as to indicate that there are no good ones (chapter four).

Part of the problem has been a stubborn refusal by historians to even attempt to understand the logic of probability and evidence (and hence the *mathematics* of probability and evidence), which should no longer be given a pass (chapter five). Because all historical argumentation is inherently mathematical—even (and indeed especially) when it comes to ascertaining the historicity of ancient persons, whether they be mundane actors or mythologized heroes (chapter six). In ambiguous cases like Jesus, where the evidence is more scant, compromised, and problematic than for any other major figure believed to exist, an even closer attention is needed to fundamental questions of probability, such as whether any given fact even evinces one conclusion over the other—and how strong or weak that evidence is; and above all, *why*. Because historians need to start seriously asking themselves *why* they believe what they do—and rather than answer with a mere list of reasons (which at that level of analysis is always just a list of excuses), answer instead with an actual demonstration of *why that belief logically follows* from the facts as they are; or else acknowledge that the historicity of Jesus is just a field-wide dogma we are merely uncomfortable with questioning or discarding.

Which in turn requires seriously questioning why we should ever have thought Romans 1:3, Galatians 4:4, 1 Corinthians 9:5 and Galatians 1:19 attest a historical Jesus. They are in fact remarkably and suspiciously ambiguous. That historians don't see this is testament to how captured they are by the faith-born assumptions of the field. Paul explicitly says all baptized Christians were the 'brothers' of Jesus, and in neither 1 Corinthians 9:5 nor Galatians 1:19 is there any good reason to believe Paul meant any other kind of brother than that (chapter ten). Paul's only reference to Jesus having a mother was part of an extended allegorical argument about scripturally allegorical mothers that we all share with Jesus, and thus doesn't even remark on whether Paul knew Jesus had a real mother (chapter nine). And Paul's only reference to Jesus coming in some sense from the seed of David was scripturally required for him to say and believe regardless of what formality or metaphysics Paul imagined God employed to achieve it, and thus doesn't tell us whether Paul thought Jesus acquired that feature in an ordinary way (chapter eight).

Most significantly of all, our obsession with the dogma of historicity has blinded us to fruitful avenues of research and reconstruction. It led us to fabricate the entire concept of 'Docetism', for example, which misled us into mistaking what appear in fact to be references to Christians doubting the terrestrial historicity of Jesus as 'instead' reflecting some inconsistent dispute over the metaphysics of his body (chapter seven). But we have also been looking at the Gospels in the wrong way, implausibly attempting the impossible task of extracting history from mythology, when all along we should have been looking at what their authors were trying to say by their deliberate choices in constructing every single one of their scenes (chapter six). And we have been mistakenly trying to read those later myths into the letters of Paul, rather than reading Paul as meaning what he actually says: that Christianity began in private dreams or visions, just like other major world religions (from Mormonism to Islam), and the magical hero we know as Jesus of Nazareth was a contrivance of myth-making, in the same vein as many another mythical founder hero (from Moses to Dionysus, or from Ned Ludd to John Frum).

I think we should conclude that the real actual founder of Christianity was not Jesus, but more probably Cephas (Peter), and his small faction of cronies and followers, about whom we no longer have any real information (beyond the scant trivia preserved in early Epistles). In that case Christianity was built out of revelations (whether dreams or visions, or both; and whether purported or actual, or both) and a congeries of 'inspired' esoteric readings of scripture (whether spurious or plausible; either way, a pesher just like those we find at Qumran). And it then evolved as many an apocalyptic cult has throughout history, from an initial corps of charismatics or shamans to a full-blown mythology of an invented 'historical' superhero in aid of an institutional hierarchy.

Many a religion has had one of those. For the Jews, it was Moses; for the Bacchants, Dionysus; for the Luddites, Ned Ludd; for early Cargo Cults, John Frum or Tom Navy; for the Mormons, Moroni and his likewise 'historical' human father Mormon. Even Buddha and Confucius could be convenient fictions, under which to collect any text that needed the stamp of authority.[1] This conclusion leads to entirely different avenues for answering the question of what the first Christians thought they were doing, and why they did that.

But if you wish to resist this conclusion and continue pursuing the status quo in Jesus studies, you will have to actually defend the foundational assumption of your field—and not as a dogma, but as *in fact* the most probable reading of the evidence. And to do that, you will need to do much better than the only critics who have published in academic journals or monographs any attempt at a defense of the historicity of Jesus against the latest studies calling it into doubt. In chapter three I showed the defects they all share: (1) they are not truthfully representing the arguments of the studies they are supposed to be responding to; (2) they are simply repeating arguments those studies already rebutted as if they had not; (3) they are resting on provably false statements; and (4) they are making arguments with no logical relevance to the merits of the thesis being answered.

This is all non-responsive. It therefore leaves the only contemporary studies of the historicity of Jesus unchallenged. This does not bode well for the historicity position. To defend your foundational belief in a historical Jesus you need a capable and thorough reply to our studies and their actual findings and results, one that refrains from these four behaviors, and thus: (1) truthfully represents all the arguments in both studies questioning historicity (and this one); (2) actually responds to

---

[1] **Buddha:** Dhivan Thomas Jones, "Did the Buddha Exist? Contemporary Scholarly Debate about the Historical Buddha," *A Blue Chasm* (14 July 2019) at tinyurl.com/yerx-8u4m; David Drewes, "The Idea of the Historical Buddha," *Journal of the International Association of Buddhist Studies* 40 (2017), 1–25. See also John Kingsley, "A Bayesian Analysis of Early Śramaṇic Origin Stories," *LMU/LLS Theses and Dissertations* 1256 (2022). **Confucius:** Charlotte Allen, "Confucius and the Scholars," *The Atlantic Monthly* 283.4 (April 1999) at theatlantic.com/magazine/archive/1999/04/confucius-and-the-scholars/377530; Lionel Jense, *Manufacturing Confucianism: Chinese Traditions and Universal Civilization* (Duke University Press, 1998); Hongbing Yu, "Confucius the Untouchable: On the Semiotics of Historization," *Chinese Semiotic Studies* 18.3 (2022), 391–412.

their rebuttals of historicity apologetics (rather than merely gainsaying them), and thereby productively moving the argument forward; (3) does not rely on factually false statements; and (4) makes arguments that are logically relevant to the merits.

That is the only proper way to continue justifying a consensus favoring the historicity of Jesus rather than questioning it. Otherwise consensus is simply dogma, the crystallization of a stubborn disinterest in factual reality.[2] Whereas if a credible defense of the historicity of Jesus cannot be mounted *without* those four tactics of evasion, then in factual reality we are left with no valid reason to trust in the historicity of Jesus. And if that is the case, we need to embrace the corresponding paradigm shift in how we understand the origins and development of Christianity, and how we understand its early documents and literature.

---

[2] Richard Carrier, "On Evaluating Arguments from Consensus" (8 May 2014) at richardcarrier.info/archives/5553.

APPENDIX

In the concluding chapter of *On the Historicity of Jesus* (pp. 597–601) I ran the numbers based on a derived error margin for the prior probability (that Jesus existed) of roughly 6% to 33%. In chapter six here I argued a recent study suggests that that error margin may be closer to 21% to 26%. If we revised the original tables accordingly, the following would be our margin of error on the probability that Jesus existed altogether.

The consequent probabilities here are repeated from the original study, which are derived and explained there, but their corresponding tables will also be provided in one place now at the end of this appendix.[1] The hypothesis *h* is that Jesus historically existed—at least (and probably only) minimally, as a minor unremarkable preacher, as explained in chapter two of *Historicity* (meeting at least the conditions on p. 34). Its converse ($\neg h$) is the probability he didn't, in which case the best probability by far is that he was only *believed* to exist celestially at first (as explained in chapter three of *Historicity*, particularly on pp. 53–55).

In that model, Jesus began like Moroni and Gabriel, as a revelatory being, and was transferred into mythography (as every other mythical savior then was) a generation later, and was then preached to be historical (as happened to many savior figures throughout history, like Osiris and John Frum) a generation or two after that, and Christians hewing to the original doctrine were explicitly shut out and their literature and teachings discarded (per Ignatius and 2 Peter). The historicist church then won the propaganda war and captured the Empire. It thus would

[1] For mathematicians I provide a complete dependent-probability equation at richardcarrier.info/equation.pdf.

decide all dogma, doctrine, and literary preservation and production for the remainder of history. And *that* evolved into all the Christianities we know today.

The new concluding tables for the prior and consequent probabilities (i.e. the base rate and likelihood ratios) look as follows. As only the prior probability table is updated, it appears first, followed by the new calculation of the final odds on Jesus having existed, using the original study's consequent odds. The consequent probability tables (from which those consequent odds are derived) remain unchanged, and thus are reproduced only at the end here for reference.

The new best final odds on Jesus existing are:

PRIOR PROBABILITIES

	a fortiori (upper bound)		*a judicantiori* (lower bound)	
	ODDS	PROBABILITY	ODDS	PROBABILITY
P(h)	1 / 2.8	26% (1/4)	1 / 3.75	21% (1/5)
which entails…				
P(¬h)	2.8 / 1	74% (3/4)	3.75 / 1	79% (5/1)

[ODDS ON *H*] = [PRIOR ODDS] × [CONSEQUENT ODDS]

[BEST ODDS ON *H*] = [1 / 2.8] × [373248 / 390625]

= 373248 / 1093750

≈ 1 / 2.930357296 [odds]

≈ 0.2544297947 [probability]

≈ 25%

So with our new margins of error for the prior, at best there is only a 1 in 4 chance Jesus existed. I had previously estimated it was better than that, at 1 in 3. Which means it is still no better than 1 in 3. It's just that it's likely less than that now.

The new worst final odds on Jesus existing are:

$$[\text{Worst Odds on } H] = [\ 1 / 3.75\ ] \times [\ 3 / 2500\ ]$$

$$= 3 / 9375$$

$$= 1 / 3125 \text{ [odds]}$$

$$\approx 0.0003198976 \text{ [probability]}$$

So with our new margins of error for the prior, at worst there is near a 1 in 3000 chance Jesus existed. I had previously estimated it as near one in 12,000.

So the bottom margin has improved for Jesus, but the top margin has gotten worse. The odds on Jesus existing are now somewhere between 1 in 3000 and 1 in 4; or stated as probabilities, somewhere between a thirtieth of a percent and twenty-five percent—quite a wide margin of error, quantifying our cumulative uncertainty. We can still say it's "no better than 1 in 3," as that remains literally true (since 1 in 4 is no better than 1 in 3). But really we should be more skeptical than that. Which means my original study's conclusion is now even more confirmed than ten years ago.

As I also explained there, this means we do not know what the probability is *except that* it is somewhere in between those two values. So it is, for all we know, 1 in 4. It is also, for all we know, 1 in 3000. We cannot insist upon either—or anything else it could be, whether 1 in 20 or 1 in 5 or any odds in between the top and bottom margins. The best we can say is, "It's no better than 1 in 4." We can of course also say "It's no worse than 1 in 3000," but generally that's not the number people want to know. They are more interested to know the best odds (the maximum chance) not the worst odds (the minimum chance).

That margin can differ if you find different consequent odds on any of the evidence examined, as also explained in my original study. But, for example, if we added some new evidence that we agreed had to be three times more likely on historicity than on myth (reproducing the point in §12.2 of *Historicity*), the result would now be:

[ODDS ON *H*] =

[PRIOR ODDS] × [CONSEQUENT ODDS] **× [NEW CONSEQUENT ODDS]**

[BEST ODDS ON *H*] = [1 / 2.8] × [373248 / 390625] × [3 / 1]

= [373248 / 1093750] × [3 / 1]

= 1119744 / 1093750

≈ 1.02376594 / 1

The odds are then close to even—getting us to about a 49% chance Jesus existed. I had previously estimated the effect of such evidence would be to raise the probability Jesus existed to as much as 59%. The probability worsened here because of the newly reduced upper error margin. And then:

[WORST ODDS ON *H*] = [1 / 3.75] × [3 / 2500] × [3 / 1]

= [3 / 9375] × [3 / 1]

= 9 / 9375

≈ 1 / 1041.6667

The worst odds on Jesus existing with this hypothetical new evidence would be about 1 in 1000. I had previously estimated it would be about 1 in 4000. The odds improved here because of the newly increased lower error margin.

But without any such hypothetical evidence, the evidence as we have it leaves us with no better than a 1 in 4 chance (and no worse than a 1 in 3000 chance) that even a minimal historical Jesus existed.

* * *

The original §12.1 consequent odds tables remain unchanged as:

CONSEQUENT PROBABILITY ON MINIMAL HISTORICITY (*h*)

	a fortiori (upper bound)		*a judicantiori* (lower bound)	
	ODDS	PROBABILITY	ODDS	PROBABILITY
P(c|h) =				
P (EXTRA|h)	288 / 625	46.08%	1 / 10	10%
×				
P (ACTS|h)	18 / 25	72%	1 / 5	20%
×				
P (GOSPELS|h)	1 / 1	100%	1 / 1	100%
×				
P (EPISTLES|h)	72 / 25	100%	3 / 50	6%
P(e|h) / P(e|¬h) =	373248 / 390625		3 / 2500	
P(e|h) =		33.1776%		00.12%

CONSEQUENT PROBABILITY ON MINIMAL MYTHICISM (¬*h*)

	a fortiori (upper bound)		*a judicantiori* (lower bound)	
	ODDS	PROBABILITY	ODDS	PROBABILITY
P(e|¬h) =				
P (EXTRA|¬h)	625 / 288	100%	10 / 1	100%
×				
P (ACTS|¬h)	25 / 18	100%	5 / 1	100%
×				
P (GOSPELS|¬h)	1 / 1	100%	1 / 1	100%
×				
P (EPISTLES|¬h)	25 / 72	34.7222...%	50 / 3	100%
P(e|h) / P(e|¬h) =	390625 / 373248		2500 / 3	
P(e|h) =		34.7222...%		100%

The consequent odds shown for each of those four categories of evidence were derived from tables concluding each corresponding chapter. Those are now reproduced below for reference. How each line-item was calculated is explained in the original study.

The following tables calculate the consequent probability (the likelihood) of each category of evidence on *h* (rather than ¬*h*) because in nearly every case the consequent probability (the likelihood) of every subcategory of evidence on ¬*h* is simply 100% (it is entirely what we expect to have been produced and still survive if a real historical Jesus didn't exist but was invented). One exception (the Epistles, parts of which are allowed to count as evidence for historicity) is indicated.

EXTRABIBLICAL EVIDENCE

The original §8.13 consequent odds table for deriving P(EXTRA|h) and P (EXTRA|¬h) remains unchanged as:

	best	*worst*
TWIN TRADITIONS	4/5	1/2
DOCUMENTARY SILENCE	1/1	
1 CLEMENT	4/5	1/2
IGNATIUS & ASCENSION OF ISAIAH	4/5	1/2
PAPIAS	1/1	
HEGESIPPUS	9/10	4/5
JOSEPHUS	1/1	
PLINY	1/1	
TACITUS	1/1	
SUETONIUS	1/1	
THALLUS	1/1	
LACK OF GAINSAYING WITNESSES	1/1	

Totals:	576 / 1250	4 / 40
	288 / 625	1 / 10
	≈ 1 / 2.2	1 / 10
	= 0.4608	0.1000
	≈ 46%	10%
	vs.	
	100% | ¬*h*	100% | ¬*h*

ACTS

The original §9.7 consequent odds table for deriving P(ACTS|h) and P (ACTS|¬h) remains unchanged as:

	best	*worst*
VANISHING FAMILY ET AL.	4/5	2/5
OMISSIONS IN PAUL'S TRIALS	9/10	1/2
REMAINDER OF ACTS	1/1	
Totals:	36 / 50	2 / 10
	18 / 25	1 / 5
	≈ 1 / 1.39	1 / 5
	= 0.7200	0.2000
	= 72% | *h*	20% | *h*
	vs.	
	100% | ¬*h*	100% | ¬*h*

GOSPELS

The original §10.8 consequent odds for deriving P(GOSPELS|h) and P (GOSPELS|¬h) remains unchanged as simply 1/1. Because the effect of the Gospels (as mythologies) was already calculated in the prior odds; no other evidence in them was found to be any more or less likely on either *h* or ¬*h*.

EPISTLES

Finally, the original §11.11 consequent odds table for deriving P(EPISTLES|h) and P (EPISTLES|¬h) remains unchanged as:

		best	worst
OTHER CANONICAL EPISTLES		4/5	3/5
"GOSPELS" IN PAUL, HEBREWS, COLOSSIANS		3/5	2/5
THINGS JESUS SAID		1/1	
THE EUCHARIST (1 COR. 11:23-26)		1/1	
THINGS JESUS DID		3/4	1/2
MADE FROM SPERM		2/1	
MADE FROM A WOMAN		2/1	
BROTHERS OF THE LORD		2/1	1/2
Totals:		288 / 100	6 / 100
	=	72 / 25	3 / 50
	≈	2.88 / 1	1 / 16.67
	≈	[0.3472]	0.06
	≈	100% | *h*	6% | *h*
		vs.	
		34.7% | ¬*h*	100% | ¬*h*

BIBLIOGRAPHY*

Aasgaard, Reidar. *My Beloved Brothers and Sisters: Christian Siblingship in Paul* (T&T Clark 2004).

Adair, Aaron. "The Morning Star and the Womb of Dawn," *Biblica* 105 (2024), 420–43.

Adamczewski, Bartosz. *The Gospel of Mark: A Hypertextual Commentary* (Peter Lang, 2014).

Adler, Yonatan. *The Origins of Judaism: An Archaeological-Historical Reappraisal* (Yale University Press, 2022).

Ådna, Jostein. "The Servant of Isaiah 53 as Triumphant and Interceding Messiah: The Reception of Isaiah 52:13–53:12 in the Targum of Isaiah with Special Attention to the Concept of the Messiah," in Janowski and Stuhlmacher, *Suffering Servant*, 189–224.

Aitken, James, and James Paget (eds.), *The Jewish-Greek Tradition in Antiquity and the Byzantine Empire* (Cambridge University Press, 2014).

Alabi, Afetame. "'I Received from the Lord': Assessing the Arguments Against a Pauline Claim to Revelation in 1 Corinthians 11:23," *Neotestamentica* 56.1 (2022), 1–31.

Albertson, James. "An Application of Mathematical Probability to Manuscript Discoveries," *Journal of Biblical Literature* 78 (1959), 133-41.

Alexander, Philip. "The Rabbis and Their Rivals in the Second Century CE," in *Christianity in the Second Century: Themes and Developments* (ed. James Carleton Paget and Judith Lieu; Cambridge University Press, 2017), 57–70.

* In this volume I use the tinyURL protocol for lengthy URLs. They will automatically unpack when you use them in any web browser. But to unpack a tinyurl without going to the linked page, place the compression sequence (e.g., 36duh6fk) after tinyurl.com/preview/ (so, tinyurl.com/preview/36duh6fk).

Alexander-Frizer, Tamar. *The Heart Is a Mirror: The Sephardic Folktale* (Wayne State University Press, 2007), 171–72.

Allen, Charlotte. “Confucius and the Scholars,” *The Atlantic Monthly* 283.4 (April 1999) at tinyurl.com/c7wtpbj3.

Allen, David. “How Josephus Really Viewed Jesus,” *Revista bíblica* 85 (2023), 333–57.

———. “A Model Reconstruction of What Josephus Would Have Realistically Written about Jesus,” *Journal of Greco-Roman Christianity and Judaism* 18 (2022), 113–43.

———. “A Proposal: Three Redactional Layer Model for the Testimonium Flavianum,” *Revista bíblica* 85 (2023), 211–32.

Allen, James. *The Ancient Egyptian Pyramid Texts*, 2nd Edition (SBL Press, 2015).

Allen, Nicholas. “Josephus on James the Just? A Re-Evaluation of *Antiquitates Judaicae* 20.9.1,” *Journal of Early Christian History* 7.1 (2017), 1–27.

Allison, Dale. “The Pauline Epistles and the Synoptic Gospels: The Pattern of the Parallels,” *New Testament Studies* 28.1 (1982), 1–32.

———. “Acts 9:1–9, 22:6–11, 26:12–18: Paul and Ezekiel,” *Journal of Biblical Literature* 135.4 (2016), 807–26.

———. *The Resurrection of Jesus: Apologetics, Polemics, History* (T&T Clark, 2021).

Álvarez Cineira, David. “La Persecución Neroniana de los Cristianos Tras el Incendio de Roma (Tácito, *Anales* XV),” *Salmanticensis* 66.1 (2019), 7–50.

Angel, Joseph. “Enoch, Jesus, and the Priestly Tradition,” in *Enoch and the Synoptic Gospels: Reminiscences, Allusions, Intertextuality* (ed. L.T. Stuckenbruck and G. Boccaccini; SBL, 2016).

Applegate, Lloyd. “Zoroastrianism and Its Probable Influence on Judaism and Christianity,” *Journal of Religion and Psychical Research* 23.4 (2000), 184–96.

Archer, William. *The Paintings of the Casa Dei Vettii in Pompei* (University of Virginia, 1981).

Attridge, Harold. “Hebrews,” in *The Reception of Jesus in the First Three Centuries, Volume 1: From Paul to Josephus* (ed. Helen Bond; T&T Clark, 2019), 243–58.

———. *History, Theology, and Narrative Rhetoric in the Fourth Gospel* (Marquette University Press, 2019).

Ayali-Darshan, Noga. “The Death of Mot and His Resurrection (KYU^3 1.5 II, V) in the Light of Egyptian Sources,” *Ugarit Forschungen: Internationales Jahrbuch für die Altertumskunde Syrien-Palästinas* 48 (2017/2019), 1–20.

Baker, Coleman. "Peter and Paul in Acts and the Construction of Early Christian Identity: A Review of Historical and Literary Approaches," *Currents in Biblical Research* 11.3 (2013), 349–65.

Bale, Alan. *Genre and Narrative Coherence in the Acts of the Apostles* (T&T Clark, 2015).

Ballard, Andrew. *To Know All Mysteries: The Mystagogue Figure in Classical Antiquity and in Saint Paul's Letters to the Corinthians* (Fortress, 2022).

Barbu, Daniel, and Yaacov Deutsch (eds.), *Toledot Yeshu in Context: The Jewish "Life of Jesus" in Ancient, Medieval, and Modern History* (Mohr Siebeck, 2020).

Bar-Itzhak, Haya. "The Legend of the Jewish Holy Virgin of Ludmir: A Folkloristic Perspective," *Journal of Folklore Research* 46.3 (2009), 269–92.

Barker, Margaret. *The Great Angel: A Study of Israel's Second God* (Westminster/John Knox Press, 1992).

———. *The Great High Priest: The Temple Roots of Christian Liturgy* (T&T Clark, 2003).

———. "The Two Figures in Zechariah," *Heythrop Journal* 18.1 (1977), 38–46.

Barrett, Anthony. "The Great Fire," *The Emperor Nero: A Guide to the Ancient Sources* (ed. Anthony Barrett, Elaine Fantham, and John Yardley; Princeton University Press, 2016), 149–70.

Bates, Matthew. "A Christology of Incarnation and Enthronement: Romans 1:3–4 as as Unified, Nonadoptionist, and Nonconciliatory," *Catholic Biblical Quarterly* 77 (2015), 107–27.

Bauckham, Richard. *Jesus and the Eyewitnesses: The Gospels as Eyewitness Testimony* (Eerdmans, 2008; 2nd ed., 2017).

Becker, Adam. *Fear of God and the Beginning of Wisdom: The School of Nisibis and the Development of Scholastic Culture in Late Antique Mesopotamia* (University of Pennsylvania Press, 2013).

Becker, Eve-Marie. *The Birth of Christian History: Memory and Time from Mark to Luke-Acts* (Yale University Press, 2017).

Becker, Eve-Marie, Helen Bond, and Catrin Williams (eds.). *John's Transformation of Mark* (T&T Clark, 2021).

Becker, Eve-Marie, Troels Engberg-Pedersen, and Mogens Mueller (eds.), *Mark and Paul: For and Against Pauline Influence on Mark* (De Gruyter, 2014).

Beckwith, Roger. "Daniel 9 and the Date of the Messiah's Coming in Essene, Hellenistic, Pharisaic, Zealot, and Early Christian Computation," *Revue de Qumrân* 10.4 (1981), 521–42.

BeDuhn, Jason. *The First Edition of the New Testament: Marcion's Scriptural*

Canon (Polebridge, 2013).

Berger, Abraham. "Captive at the Gate of Rome: The Story of a Messianic Motif," *Proceedings of the American Academy of Jewish Research* 44 (1977), 1–17.

Berglund, Carl. *Origen's References to Heracleon: A Quotation-Analytical Study of the Earliest Known Commentary on the Gospel of John* (Mohr Siebek, 2020).

Bergsma, John. *The Jubilee from Leviticus to Qumran: A History of Interpretation* (Brill, 2007).

Berman, Jacob, and Robyn Faith Walsh, "Paul Did NOT Make up JESUS," *History Valley* (22 August 2023) at youtube.com/shorts/U4mN9X7giq8.

Bermejo-Rubio, Fernando. "Changing Methods, Disturbing Material: Should the Criterion of Embarrassment be Dismissed in Jesus Research?" *Revue des Études Juives* 175.1 (2016), 1–25.

———. *La invención de Jesús de Nazaret: Historia, ficción, historiografía* (Siglo XXI de España Editores, 2018; Akal, 2023).

———. *They Suffered under Pontius Pilate: Jewish Anti-Roman Resistance and the Crosses at Golgotha* (Lexington Books/Fortress Academic, 2023).

Bermejo-Rubio, Fernando, and Richard Carrier and Franco Tommasi, *Gesù resistente Gesù inesistente: Due visioni a confronto* (Manni, 2022).

———. *Jesus: Militant or Nonexistent? Two Views Compared* (Philosophy Press, 2025).

Bernier, Jonathan. *The Quest for the Historical Jesus after the Demise of Authenticity: Toward a Critical Realist Philosophy of History in Jesus Studies* (T&T Clark, 2016).

Berthelot, Katell. *Jews and Their Roman Rivals: Pagan Rome's Challenge to Israel* (Princeton University Press, 2021).

Betz, Hans Dieter. *Galatians: A Commentary on Paul's Letter to the Churches in Galatia* (Fortress Press, 1979).

Betz, Otto. "The Servant Tradition of Isaiah in the Dead Sea Scrolls," *Journal for Semitics* 7.1 (1995), 40–56.

Bilby, Mark, Margaret Froelich, and Michael Kochenash (eds.). *Classical Greek Models of the Gospels and Acts: Studies in Mimesis Criticism* (Claremont School of Theology Press, 2018).

Bilby, Mark, and Anna Lefteratou, "A Dramatic Heist of Epic Proportion: Iphigenia among the Taurians in the Acts of the Apostles," *Harvard Theological Review* 115.4 (2022), 496–518.

Bird, Michael, and Joel Willitts, *Paul and the Gospels: Christologies, Conflicts and Convergences* (T&T Clark, 2011).

Blom, Willem. "Why the Testimonium Taciteum Is Authentic: A Response to Carrier," *Vigiliae Christianae* 17.5 (2019), 564–81.

Blomberg, Craig. *The Historical Reliability of John's Gospel: Issues and Commentary* (IVP Academic, 2001).

———. "Quotations, Allusions, and Echoes of Jesus in Paul," in *Studies in the Pauline Epistles: Festschrift for Douglas J. Moo* (ed. Matt Harmon and Jay Smith; Zondervan, 2014), 129–43.

Blomberg, Craig, and Darlene Seal, "The Historical Jesus in Recent Evangelical Scholarship," in *Jesus, Skepticism, and the Problem of History: Criteria and Context in the Study of Christian Origins* (ed. Darrell Bock and J. Ed Komoszewski; Zondervan Academic, 2019).

Boccaccini, Gabriele. *Paul's Three Paths to Salvation* (Eerdmans, 2020).

Boda, Mark. *The Book of Zechariah* (Eerdmans, 2016).

Boman, Jobjorn. "Comments on Carrier: Is Thallus Actually Quoted by Eusebius?" *Liber Annuus* 62 (2012), 319–25.

Bond, Helen. *Caiaphas: Friend of Rome and Judge of Jesus?* (Westminster/John Knox Press, 2004).

———. "Gospel of John," in Bond, *Reception of Jesus*, 165–85.

——— (ed.). *The Reception of Jesus in the First Three Centuries, Volume 1: From Paul to Josephus* (T&T Clark, 2019).

Bonz, Marianne Palmer. *The Past as Legacy: Luke-Acts and Ancient Epic* (Fortress, 2000).

Boring, M. Eugene. "Structure," in *The New Interpreter's Bible, Volume 8: Matthew – Mark* (ed. Leander Keck; Abingdon, 1995), 110–18.

Bossman, D.M. "Paul's Fictive Kinship Movement," *Biblical Theology Bulletin* 26.4 (1996), 163–71.

Boyarin, Daniel. *The Jewish Gospels: The Story of the Jewish Christ* (The New Press, 2012).

Boyce, James Leonard. *Ixion: Origins and Meanings of a Myth* (PhD dissertation; University of North Carolina at Chapel Hill, 1976).

Boyce, Mary. *Zoroastrians: Their Religious Beliefs and Practices*, 2nd ed. (Routledge, 2000).

Boxill, Ian (ed.). *The Globalization of Rastafari* (Arawak, 2009).

Brady, Christian. "Talmudim," in Keith, *Reception of Jesus*, 89–101.

Brandon, S.G.F. "The Ritual Technique of Salvation in the Ancient Near East," *The Savior God: Comparative Studies in the Concept of Salvation Presented to Edwin Oliver James by Colleagues and Friends to Commemorate His 75th Birthday* (ed. S.G.F. Brandon; Manchester University Press, 1963), 17–36.

Brashler, James, and Roger Bullard. "The Coptic Apocalypse of Peter," in *Nag Hammadi Codex VII* (ed. Birger Pearson; Brill, 1996), 78–79.

Brent, Allen. "Can There Be Degrees of Docetism?," in Verheyden et al., *Docetism in the Early Church*, 5–26.

Brierley, Justin, Richard Carrier, and Mark Goodacre. "Did Jesus Exist? Richard Carrier vs Mark Goodacre—Unbelievable?" *Unbelievable?* (December 2012) at tinyurl.com/y2p7yc95.

Brodie, Thomas. *Beyond the Quest for the Historical Jesus: Memoir of a Discovery* (Sheffield Phoenix, 2012).

———. *The Birthing of the New Testament: The Intertextual Development of the New Testament Writings* (Sheffield Phoenix Press, 2004).

Brooke, George. *The Dead Sea Scrolls and the New Testament* (Fortress, 2005).

Brown, Daniel (ed.). *The Wiley Blackwell Concise Companion to the Hadith* (Wiley-Blackwell, 2020).

Brownlee, William. "The Servant of the Lord in the Qumran Scrolls," *Bulletin of the American Schools of Oriental Research* 132 (December 1953), 8–15.

Bühner, Ruben. *Messianic High Christology: New Testament Variants of Second Temple Judaism* (Baylor University Press, 2021).

Burke, T.J. *Adopted into God's Family: Exploring a Pauline Metaphor* (Apollos/IVC, 2006).

Burnett, Fred. "Characterization and Reader Construction of Characters in the Gospels," *Semeia* 63 (1993), 3–28.

Burridge, Richard. *What Are the Gospels? A Comparison with Graeco-Roman Biography*, 25th Anniversary Edition (Baylor University Press, 2018).

Busch, Austin. "New Testament Narrative and Greco-Roman Literature," in *The Oxford Handbook of Biblical Narrative* (ed. Danna Nolan Fewell; Oxford University Press, 2016), 61–72.

Bynum, Caroline. *The Resurrection of the Body in Western Christianity, 200–1336* (Columbia University Press, 1995).

Calhoun, Robert Matthew, David Moessner and Tobias Nicklas (eds.). *Modern and Ancient Literary Criticism of the Gospels: Continuing the Debate on Gospel Genre(s)* (Mohr Siebeck, 2020).

Callon, Callie. *Reading Bodies: Physiognomy as a Strategy of Persuasion in Early Christian Discourse* (New York: T&T Clark, 2019).

Cameron, Alan. *Greek Mythography in the Roman World* (Oxford University Press, 2004).

Campbell, William Sanger. *The We Passages in the Acts of the Apostles: The Narrator as Narrative Character* (Society of Biblical Literature, 2007).

Carrier, Richard. "Adam's Burial in Outer Space" (6 July 2020) at richardcarrier.info/archives/16930.

———. "Allen's New and Illogical Theory of the Testimonium Flavianum" (6 May 2024) at richardcarrier.info/archives/27782.

———. "All the Fantastical Things in the Gospel according to Mark" (30 July 2024) at richardcarrier.info/archives/29744.

———. "Are Paul and His Letters a Second Century Fabrication? A Critical Review of the Livesey Thesis" at richardcarrier.info/archives/3457.

———. "Blom on the Testimonium Taciteum" (29 September 2020) at richardcarrier.info/archives/17187.

———. "Book Review: *Varieties of Jesus Mythicism* Edited by John W. Loftus and Robert M. Price," *Socio-Historical Examination of Religion and Ministry* 4.1 (2022), 171–92.

———. "Critical Review of Maurice Casey's Defense of the Historicity of Jesus" (3 March 2014) at richardcarrier.info/archives/4282.

———. "Desperately Searching the Epistles for Anything That Attests a Historical Jesus" (20 March 2017) at richardcarrier.info/archives/12220.

———. "Did Any Pre-Christian Jews Expect a Dying-and-Rising Messiah?," *Canadian-American Theological Review* (forthcoming).

———. "Did Judas Exist?" (24 April 2025) at richardcarrier.info/archives/34055.

———. "Did Polycarp Meet John the Apostle?" (31 October 2019) at richardcarrier.info/archives/15999.

———. "Ehrman on Historicity Recap" (1 July 2021) at richardcarrier.info/archives/1794.

———. "Errata for *On the Historicity of Jesus*" (30 September 2015) at richardcarrier.info/archives/8551.

———. "Establishing the Biblical Literalism of Early Christians" (26 September 2020) at richardcarrier.info/archives/17150.

———. "Evidence in Philo of a Pre-Christian Archangel Named 'Jesus'" (forthcoming).

———. "Goldberg's Attempt to Rehabilitate the Testimonium Flavianum" (11 September 2023) at richardcarrier.info/archives/24794.

———. *Hitler Homer Bible Christ: The Historical Papers of Richard Carrier 1995–2013* (Philosophy Press, 2014).

———. "How To Fabricate History: The Example of Eusebius on Alexandrian Christianity" (20 November 2020) at richardcarrier.info/archives/17358.

———. "How We Know Acts Is a Fake History" (21 April 2023) at richardcarrier.info/archives/23447.

———. *Ιησούς: Τι Πραγματικά Πίστευαν Οι Πρώτοι Χριστιανοί Για Την Ιστορικότητα Του Ναζωραίου* (tr. Achilleas Fakatselis; Thessaloniki, Greece: Daedaleos, 2021).

———. "Interpreting 1 Clement's Supposed Descriptions of Fabulous Murders" (30 November 2023) at richardcarrier.info/archives/26310.

———. "Jesus and the Problem of the Fraudulent Reference Class" (20 August 2021) at richardcarrier.info/archives/18711.

———. *Jesus from Outer Space: What the Earliest Christians Really Believed about Christ* (Pitchstone, 2020).

———. *Jezus z kosmosu. Chrystys w wierze pierwszych chrześcijan* (tr. Magdalena Górska; Katowice: STAPIS, 2023).

———. "John Wick vs. Jesus and the Logical Significance of the Tragic Hero-King Genre: A Response to Gregor and Hansen" (forthcoming).

———. "Like, Can You Rebel Against Rome with Only Two Swords?" (31 January 2024) at richardcarrier.info/archives/27035.

———. "List of Historians Who Take Mythicism Seriously" (25 August 2022) at richardcarrier.info/archives/21420.

———. "List of Responses to Defenders of the Historicity of Jesus" (18 June 2014) at richardcarrier.info/archives/5730.

———. "Litwa's Confused Critique of Mythicism" (29 April 2020) at richardcarrier.info/archives/16658.

———. "Margaret Williams on Early Classical Authors on Jesus" (30 November 2023) at richardcarrier.info/archives/26243.

———. "Mark Goodacre on the Historicity of Jesus's Execution" (1 July 2021) at richardcarrier.info/archives/18498.

———. "Mark's Use of Paul's Epistles" (25 October 2019) at richardcarrier.info/archives/15934.

———. "Mason on Josephus on James" (17 May 2020) at richardcarrier.info/archives/16715.

———. *Not the Impossible Faith: Why Christianity Didn't Need a Miracle to Succeed* (Lulu, 2009).

———. "On Evaluating Arguments from Consensus" (8 May 2014) at richardcarrier.info/archives/5553.

———. "An Ongoing List of Updates to the Arguments and Evidence in *On the Historicity of Jesus*" (10 July 2023) at richardcarrier.info/archives/24341.

———. "On the Causal Irrelevance of Dramatic Date to the Likelihood of a Story's Historicity: A Reply to Gregor, Hansen, and Blais" (forthcoming).

———. "On the Historicity of Jesus and the Rhetoric of Justin's *Dialogue with Trypho*" (25 March 2023) at richardcarrier.info/archives/23326.

———. *On the Historicity of Jesus: Why We Might Have Reason for Doubt* (Sheffield-Phoenix, 2014; rev. ed. 2023).

———. "Origen, Eusebius, and the Accidental Interpolation in Josephus, *Jewish Antiquities* 20.200," *Journal of Early Christian Studies* 20.4 (2012), 489–514.

———. *The Probabilistic Argument for Interpolation in 1 Thessalonians 2:14–16* (forthcoming).

———. "The Problem with Varieties of Jesus Mythicism" (8 October 2022) at richardcarrier.info/archives/21352.

———. "The Prospect of a Christian Interpolation in Tacitus, *Annals* 15.44," *Vigiliae Christianae* 68 (2014), 264–83.

———. *Proving History: Bayes's Theorem and the Quest for the Historical Jesus* (Prometheus Books, 2012).

———. "The Rain Miracle of Marcus Aurelius: A Case Study in Christian Lies" (27 May 2017) at richardcarrier.info/archives/12480.

———. *Science Education in the Early Roman Empire* (Pitchstone, 2016).

———. *The Scientist in the Early Roman Empire* (Pitchstone, 2017).

———. "The Spiritual Body of Christ and the Legend of the Empty Tomb" in *The Empty Tomb: Jesus beyond the Grave* (ed. Robert M. Price and Jeffery Lowder; Prometheus Books, 2005), 105–232.

———. "Thallus and the Darkness at Christ's Death," *Journal of Greco-Roman Christianity and Judaism* 8 (2011/2012), 185–91.

———. "There's No Evidence for Trajan, Hadrian, or Pius?" (10 August 2019) at richardcarrier.info/archives/15665.

———. "A Thorough Fisk of the Arguments of Fernando Bermejo-Rubio and Marco Tommasi" (27 March 2025) at richardcarrier.info/archives/26700.

———. "Tucker's Review of *Proving History* in the Journal *History & Theory*" (3 February 2016) at richardcarrier.info/archives/9619.

———. "Was the Entire New Testament Forged in the Second Century?" (26 February 2024) at richardcarrier.info/archives/27161.

———. "What Is Now Needed to Defend the Historicity of Jesus" (forthcoming).

———. "Why the Resurrection is Unbelievable," *The Christian Delusion: Why Faith Fails* (ed. John Loftus; Prometheus, 2010), 291–315.

Case, Shirley Jackson. *The Historicity of Jesus: A Criticism of the Contention that Jesus Never Lived* (University of Chicago Press, 1912; 2nd ed. 1928).

Case, Stephen. "Inventing Heaven," *Aeon* (2 December 2022) at aeon.co/essays/how-heaven-became-a-place-among-the-stars.

Casey, Maurice. *Jesus: Evidence and Argument or Mythicist Myths?* (T&T Clark, 2014).

Chavez, William. "Richard Carrier. *Jesus from Outer Space*," *Review of Biblical Literature* (March 2024) at sblcentral.org/home/bookDetails/1000407.

Chilton, Bruce. *The Glory of Israel: The Theology and Provenience of the Isaiah Targum* (JSOT Press, 1982).

Chin, Catherine. "Rhetorical Practice in the Chreia Elaboration of Mara bar Serapion," *Hugoye: Journal of Syriac Studies* 9.2 (2006), 145–71.

Cho, Jae Hyung. *This Is My Flesh: John's Eucharist and the Dionysus Cult*

(Pickwick, 2022).

Church, Philip. *Hebrews and the Temple: Attitudes to the Temple in Second Temple Judaism and in Hebrews* (Brill, 2017).

Clifford, Richard. "Phoenician Religion," *Bulletin of the American Schools of Oriental Research* 279 (1990), 55-64.

Climenhaga, Nevin. "Papias's Prologue and the Probability of Parallels," *Journal of Biblical Literature* 139.3 (2020), 591–96.

Clouston, Eric. *How Ancient Narratives Persuade: Acts in Its Literary Context* (Fortress, 2020).

Cohen, Shaye. *The Beginnings of Jewishness: Boundaries, Varieties, Uncertainties* (University of California Press, 1999).

Collins, Adela Yarbro, and John Collins (eds.). *King and Messiah as Son of God: Divine, Human, and Angelic Messianic Figures in Biblical and Related Literature* (Eerdmans, 2008).

Collins, John. *The Scepter and the Star: Messianism in Light of the Dead Sea Scrolls*, 2nd ed. (Eerdmans, 2010).

Collins, John, and Adela Yarbro Collins. *King and Messiah as Son of God: Divine, Human, and Angelic Messianic Figures in Biblical and Related Literature* (Eerdmans, 2008).

Cook, John Granger. "*Chrestiani, Christiani*, Χριστιανοί: A Second Century Anachronism?" *Vigiliae Christianae* 74 (2020), 237–64.

———. *Empty Tomb, Resurrection, Apotheosis* (Mohr Siebeck, 2018).

Corrente, Paola. "Rethinking Frazer's Dying Gods: New Perspectives on the Death and Resurrection Pattern in Ancient Mediterranean Myths," *Annali di Scienze Religiose* 15 (2022), 345-363.

———. "The Gods Who Die and Come Back to Life: The Orphic Dionysus and His Parallels in the Near-East," *Tracing Orpheus: Studies of Orphic Fragments* (ed. Miguel Herrero de Jáuregui et al.; De Gruyter, 2012), 69–76.

Costley, Angela. *Creation and Christ: An Exploration of the Topic of Creation in the Epistle to the Hebrews* (Mohr Siebeck, 2020).

Counihan, Patrick. "Irish Priest Disciplined after Claims Jesus Never Existed in Controversial Book," *IrishCentral* (21 January 2013) at tinyurl.com/36duh6fk.

Crawford, Christopher S. (ed.). *Greco-Roman and Jewish Tributaries to the New Testament: Festschrift in Honor of Gregory J. Riley* (Claremont Press, 2019).

Crégheur, Eric, Louis Painchaud, and Tuomas Rasimus (eds.). *Nag Hammadi a 70 Ans. Qu'avons-Nous Appris? Nag Hammadi at 70: What Have We Learned?* (Peeters Publishers, 2019).

Cribiore, Raffaella. *Gymnastics of the Mind: Greek Education in Hellenistic and Roman Egypt* (Princeton University Press, 2005).

Crook, Zeba. "Matthew, Memory Theory and the New No Quest," *Theological Studies* 70.1 (2014), 1–11.

Crossan, John Dominic. *The Birth of Christianity* (Harper, 1998).

Crossley, James, and Chris Keith (eds.). *The Next Quest for the Historical Jesus* (Eerdmans, 2024).

Davies, Philip. "Did Jesus Exist?" *The Bible and Interpretation* (August 2012) at bibleinterp.arizona.edu/opeds/dav368029.

Dawson, Zachary. "The Books of Acts and Jubilees in Dialogue: A Literary-Intertextual Analysis of the Noahide Laws in Acts 15 and 21," *Journal of Greco-Roman Christianity and Judaism* 13 (2017), 9-40.

De Jong, Albert. *Traditions of the Magi: Zoroastrianism in Greek and Latin Literature* (Brill, 1997).

Delumeau, Jean. *History of Paradise: The Garden of Eden in Myth and Tradition* (University of Illinois Press, 2000).

Dettwiler, Andreas. "Colossians," in Schröter and Jabobi, *Reception of Jesus*, 3–9.

———. "Ephesians," in Schröter and Jabobi, *Reception of Jesus*, 10–17.

———. "Pastoral Epistles," in Schröter and Jabobi, *Reception of Jesus*, 19–26.

Díaz, Mar Pérez i. *Jesus in the Light of Paul's Theology* (Mohr Siebeck, 2020).

Dinkler, Michal Beth. "The Gospel of Luke," in Bond, *Reception of Jesus*, 139–64.

Doherty, Earl. *Jesus: Neither God Nor Man: The Case for a Mythical Jesus* (Age of Reason Publications, 2009).

———. *The Jesus Puzzle: Did Christianity Begin with a Mythical Christ* (Canadian Humanist Publications, 1999).

Drewes, David. "The Idea of the Historical Buddha," *Journal of the International Association of Buddhist Studies* 40 (2017), 1–25.

Drews, Robert. "Judaean *Christiani* in the Middle Decades of the First Century," *Journal of Early Christian History* 13.2 (2023), 1–20.

Droge, Arthur. "Whodunnit? Paul's Peculiar Passion and Its Implications," in *Recovering an Undomesticated Apostle: Essays on the Legacy of Paul* (ed. C.B. Zeichmann and J.A. Egger; McGill-Queen's University Press, 2023), 305–33.

Dubois, Jean-Daniel. "Le Docétisme des Christologies Gnostiques Revisité," *New Testament Studies* 63.2 (2017), 279–304.

Duff, David (ed). *Modern Genre Theory* (Routledge, 2000).

Duncan, Mike. *Rhetoric and the Synoptic Problem* (Fortress, 2022).

Dundes, Alan. *In Quest of the Hero* (Princeton University Press, 1990).

———. *Interpreting Folklore* (Indiana University Press, 1980).

Dykstra, Tom. "Ehrman and Brodie on Whether Jesus Existed: A Cautionary Tale about the State of Biblical Scholarship," *Journal of the Orthodox Center for the Advancement of Biblical Studies* 8.1 (2015), 1–32.

———. *Mark: Canonizer of Paul* (OCABS, 2012).

Dzielska, Maria. *Apollonius of Tyana in Legend and History* (L'Erma di Bretschneider, 1986).

Ehrman, Bart. *Did Jesus Exist? The Historical Argument for Jesus of Nazareth* (HarperOne, 2012).

———. *Forgery and Counterforgery: The Use of Literary Deceit in Early Christian Polemics* (Oxford University Press, 2012).

———. *Heaven and Hell: A History of the Afterlife* (Simon & Schuster, 2020).

———. *How Jesus Became God: The Exaltation of a Jewish Preacher from Galilee* (HarperOne, 2014).

———. *The Orthodox Corruption of Scripture: The Effect of Early Christological Controversies on the Text of the New Testament* (Oxford University Press, 1993).

Elior, Rachel. "The Garden of Eden Is the Holy of Holies and the Dwelling of the Lord," *Studies in Spirituality* 24 (2014), 63–118.

Endsjø, Dag Øistein. *Greek Resurrection Beliefs and the Success of Christianity* (Palgrave, 2009).

Eurell, John-Christian. "Paul and the Jesus Tradition: Reconsidering the Relationship Between Paul and the Synoptics," *Journal of Early Christian History* 12.2 (2022), 1–16.

Evans, Craig. "From Gospel to Gospel: The Function of Isaiah in the New Testament," in *Writing and Reading the Scroll of Isaiah*, vol. 2 (ed. Craig Broyles and Craig Evans; Brill, 1997), 651–91.

———. "The Recently Published Dead Sea Scrolls and the Historical Jesus," in *Studying the Historical Jesus: Evaluations of the State of Current Research* (ed. Bruce Chilton and Craig Evans; Brill, 1994), 563–65.

Eve, Eric. "Memory, Orality and the Synoptic Problem," *Early Christianity* 6.3 (2015), 311–33.

———. "Orality Is No Dead-End," *Journal for the Study of the Historical Jesus* 13.1 (2015), 3–23.

———. *Relating the Gospels: Memory, Imitation and the Farrer Hypothesis* (T&T Clark, 2021).

Evnine, Simon. "'But Is It Science Fiction?': Science Fiction and a Theory of Genre," *Midwest Studies in Philosophy* 39 (2015), 1-28.

Fales, Evan. *Reading Sacred Texts: Charity, Structure, Gospel* (GCRR Press, 2021).

Farrar, Thomas. "The Intimate and Ultimate Adversary: Satanology in Early

Second-Century Christian Literature," *Journal of Early Christian Studies* 26.4 (2018), 517–46.

Feldman, Louis. "Josephus' Portrait of Moses," *The Jewish Quarterly Review* 82.3/4 (1992), 285–328.

Ferguson, John. *Socrates: A Source Book* (Macmillan, 1970).

Festinger, Leon. *A Theory of Cognitive Dissonance* (Stanford University Press, 1957).

Festinger, Leon, Henry Riecken, and Stanley Schachter. *When Prophecy Fails: A Social and Psychological Study of a Modern Group That Predicted the Destruction of the World* (University of Minnesota Press, 1956).

Fischer, David Hackett. *Historians' Fallacies: Toward a Logic of Historical Thought* (Harper & Row, 1970).

Fitzgerald, David. *The Complete Heretic's Guide to Western Religion Book One: The Mormons* (CreateSpace, 2013).

Foster, Don. *Author Unknown: On the Trail of Anonymous* (Henry Holt, 2000).

Foster, Paul. "Ignatius," in Schröter and Jabobi, *Reception of Jesus*, 41–57.

———. "Memory, Orality, and the Fourth Gospel: An Ongoing Conversation with Stan Porter and Hughson T. Ong," *Journal for the Study of the Historical Jesus* 12.1–2 (2014), 165–83.

Fox, Michael. "From Folktale to Fantasy: A Recipe-Based Approach to Creative Writing," *Writing in Practice* 6 (2023), 131–43.

Frank, Russell. "Covering Captain Cool: The 'Miracle on the Hudson' as a Hero Tale," *Western Folklore* 72.1 (2013), 59–81.

Fredriksen, Paula. *Jesus of Nazareth, King of the Jews: A Jewish Life and the Emergence of Christianity* (Vintage, 2000).

Frey, Jörg. *Theology and History in the Fourth Gospel: Tradition and Narration* (Baylor University Press, 2018).

———. "Memory, Orality, and the Fourth Gospel: Three Dead-Ends in Historical Jesus Research," *Journal for the Study of the Historical Jesus* 10.3 (January 2012), 191–227.

Frisk, Kristian. "What Makes a Hero? Theorising the Social Structuring of Heroism," *Sociology* 53.1 (2018), 87–103.

Froelich, Margaret, Michael Kochenash, Thomas Phillips, and Ilseo Park (eds.). *Christian Origins and the New Testament in the Greco-Roman Context: Essays in Honor of Dennis R. MacDonald* (Claremont School of Theology Press, 2016).

Gager, John. "The Gospels and Jesus: Some Doubts about Method," *Journal of Religion* 54.3 (July 1974), 244–72.

García Martínez, Florentino. "Messianic Hopes in the Qumran Writings," in *The People of the Dead Sea Scrolls* (ed. Florentino García Martínez and

Julio Barrera; Brill, 1995), 159–90.

Gardner, Gregg. *Wealth, Poverty, and Charity in Jewish Antiquity* (University of California Press, 2022).

Garrett, Susan. *No Ordinary Angel: Celestial Spirits and Christian Claims about Jesus* (Yale University Press, 2008).

Garroway, Joshua. *The Beginning of the Gospel: Paul, Philippi and the Origins of Christianity* (Palgrave Macmillan, 2018).

Gathercole, Simon. "The Historical and Human Existence of Jesus in Paul's Letters," *Journal for the Study of the Historical Jesus* 16.2–3 (2018), 183–212.

Gaventa, Beverly Roberts. "Interpreting the Death of Jesus Apocalyptically: Reconsidering Romans 8:32," in *Jesus and Paul Reconnected: Fresh Pathways into an Old Debate* (ed. Todd Still; Eerdmans, 2007), 125–45.

Giacobbe, Mark. *Luke the Chronicler: The Narrative Arc of Samuel-Kings and Chronicles in Luke-Acts* (Brill, 2023).

Giannantoni, Gabriele. *Socratis et Socraticorum Reliquiae*, 4 vols. (Bibliopolis, 1990).

Gieschen, Charles. *Angelomorphic Christology: Antecedents and Early Evidence* (Brill, 1998).

Ginsberg, Harold Luis. "The Oldest Interpretation of the Suffering Servant," *Vetus Testamentum* 63 (1953), 25–28.

Girle, Rod. *Modal Logics and Philosophy*, 2nd ed. (Routledge, 2010).

Glazier-McDonald, Beth. "Malʾak habbərît: The Messenger of the Covenant in Mal 3:1," *Hebrew Annual Review* 11 (1987), 93–104.

Glover, Daniel. "'For That Is What His Name Means' (Acts 13:8): Luke's Etymology of Elymas the Magician," *The Catholic Biblical Quarterly* 84.4 (2022), 609–26.

Gmirkin, Russell. *Berossus and Genesis, Manetho and Exodus: Hellenistic History and the Date of the Pentateuch* (T&T Clark, 2006).

———. *Plato and the Creation of the Hebrew Bible* (Routledge, 2019).

———. *Plato's Timaeus and the Biblical Creation Accounts* (Routledge, 2022).

Godfrey, Neil. "Are the 'Rulers of the Age' in 1 Cor. 2:6–8 Human or Spiritual? – The Sea Change," *Vridar* (14 June 2018) at tinyurl.com/2ubm5ufv.

———. "Paul's 'Rulers of this Age'—Conclusion," *Vridar* (23 July 2018) at tinyurl.com/3csunnuw.

———. "Who Crucified Jesus – Men or Demons? Continuing Miller's Study of 1 Cor 2:6–8," *Vridar* (20 June 2018) at tinyurl.com/j33xy4my.

Goldberg, Gary. "The Coincidences of the Testimonium of Josephus and the Emmaus Narrative of Luke," *Journal for the Study of the Pseudepigra-*

pha 13 (1995), 59-77.

———. "Josephus's Paraphrase Style and the Testimonium Flavianum," *Journal for the Study of the Historical Jesus* 20 (2022), 1–32.

Goldingay, John. *Daniel* (World Biblical Commentary; Zondervan, 2019).

Goodacre, Mark. "Prophecy Historicized or Tradition Scripturalized? Reflections on the Origin of the Passion Narratives" in *New Testament and the Church: Essays in Honour of John Muddiman* (ed. John Barton and Peter Groves; T&T Clark, 2015), 37–51.

———. *The Fourth Synoptic Gospel: John's Knowledge of Matthew, Mark, and Luke* (Eerdmans, 2025).

Gooder, Paula. "Eden and Beyond: Images of Paradise in Biblical and extra-Biblical Literature," *New Blackfriars* 83.971 (January 2002), 3-15.

Gordon, Richard. "Osiris," in the *Oxford Classical Dictionary,* 4th ed. (Oxford University Press, 2012), 1051–52.

Görke, Andreas. "Muhammad," in Brown, *Companion to the Hadith*, 75–90.

Grabbe, Lester. "The Case of the Corrupting Consensus." *Between Evidence and Ideology: Essays on the History of Ancient Israel Read at the Joint Meeting of the Society for Old Testament Study and the Oud Testamentisch Werkgezelschap Lincoln, July 2009* (ed. Bob Becking and Lester Grabbe; Brill, 2010), 83–92.

Grant, Robert M. "Early Christian Geography," *Vigiliae Christianae* 46.2 (1992), 105–11.

Greenwood, David Neal. "The Alethes Logos of Celsus and the Historicity of Christ," *Anglican Theological Review* 96.4 (2014), 705-713.

Gregor, Kamil, and Brian Blais. "Is Name Popularity a Good Test of Historicity? A Statistical Evaluation of Richard Bauckham's Onomastic Argument," *Journal for the Study of the Historical Jesus* 21 (2023), 171–202.

———. "Re-Examining Richard Bauckham's Argument from Name Popularity in Light of Apocryphal and Talmudic Evidence," *Journal for the Study of the New Testament* 47 (2024), 271–96.

Gregor, Kamil, and Christopher Hansen. "Mytho-Historical Heroes: The Raglan Archetype in Application to Ancient Mediterranean Persons," *Literature & Aesthetics* (forthcoming).

Gregor, Kamil, Christopher Hansen, and Brian Blais. "The Prior Probability of Jesus Mythicism Re-evaluated in Light of the Gospels' Dramatic Date," *Journal of Early Christian History* (forthcoming).

Gregory, Andrew. "Disturbing Trajectories: 1 Clement, the Shepherd of Hermas and the Development of Early Roman Christianity," in *Rome, The Bible and the Early Church* (ed. Oakes; Paternoster, 2002), 142–66.

———. "I Clement: An Introduction," *The Expository Times* 117.6 (2006), 223–30.

Gruen, Erich. "Judaism in the Diaspora," in *Early Judaism and Its Modern Interpreters*, 2nd ed. (ed. Matthias Henze and Rodney Werline; SBL Press, 2020), 69–91.

Gullotta, Daniel. "On Richard Carrier's Doubts: A Response to Richard Carrier's *On the Historicity of Jesus: Why We Might Have Reason for Doubt*," *Journal for the Study of the Historical Jesus* 15.2–3 (2017), 310–46.

Habermas, Gary. *On the Resurrection* (B&H Academic, 2024).

Haensch, Rudolf. "The Contributions of Inscriptions to our Knowledge of the Herodian Dynasty," *Scripta Classica Israelica* 33 (2014), 99–116.

Hanel, Paul, Sarah Demmrich, and Uwe Wolfradt. "Centrality of Religiosity, Schizotypy, and Human Values: The Impact of Religious Affiliation," *Religions* 10.5 (2019), 1–17.

Hansen, Chris. "Book Review. Richard C. Carrier. *Jesus from Outer Space*," *McMaster Journal of Theology and Ministry* 22 (2020–2021), R1–6.

———. "Book Review. Raphael Lataster. *Questioning the Historicity of Jesus*," *McMaster Journal of Theology and Ministry* 21 (2019–2020), R75–79.

———. *The Empty Prison Cell: The Authenticity of Philemon Reconsidered* (Wipf & Stock, 2024).

———. "The Indisputable Fact of the Baptism: The Problematic Consensus on John's Baptism of Jesus," *Literature & Aesthetics* 33.1 (2023), 1–18.

———. "Jesus' Historicity and Sources: The Misuse of Extrabiblical Sources for Jesus and a Suggestion," *American Journal of Biblical Theology* 22.6 (2021), 1–21.

———. "Lord Raglan's Hero and Jesus: A Rebuttal to Methodologically Dubious Uses of the Raglan Archetype," *Journal of Greco-Roman Christianity and Judaism* 16 (2020), 129–49.

———. "The Number of the Myth: A Defence of the Ahistoricity of the Neronian Persecution," *Journal of Early Christian History* 13.2 (2023): 1–21.

———. "The Problem of *Annals* 15.44: On the Plinian Origin of Tacitus's Information on Christians," *Journal of Early Christian History* 13.1 (2023), 62–80.

———. "Reception of the Testimonium Flavianum: An Evaluation of the Independent Witnesses to Josephus' Testimonium Flavianum," *New England Classical Journal* 51.2 (2024), 50–75.

———. "Re-Examining the Pre-Christian Jesus," *Journal of Early Christian History* 12.2 (2022), 17–40.

———. "A Response to David Allen's 'A Model Reconstruction of What Josephus Would Have Realistically Written about Jesus'," *Journal of*

Greco-Roman Christianity and Judaism 19 (2023), 94-103.

———. "Romans 1:3 and the Celestial Jesus: A Rebuttal to Revisionist Interpretations of Jesus's Descendance from David in Paul," *McMaster Journal of Theology and Ministry* 22 (2020–2021), 31–60.

———. "You Invent for Yourselves a Trypho: Addressing Radical Reinterpretations of *Trypho* and Canonical and Non-Canonical Scriptures," *The American Journal of Biblical Theology* 23.4 (January 2020), 1–28.

Hansen, William. *Classical Mythology: A Guide to the Mythical World of the Greeks and Romans* (Oxford University Press, 2005).

Hardman, David, and Laura Macchi (eds.). *Thinking: Psychological Perspectives on Reasoning, Judgment and Decision Making* (Wiley, 2004).

Harmon-Jones, Eddie (ed.). *Cognitive Dissonance: Reexamining a Pivotal Theory in Psychology*, 2nd ed. (American Psychological Association, 2019).

Harris, Kylie, Adam Rock, and Gavin Clark. "Spiritual Emergence(y), Psychosis, and Personality: Investigating the Role of Schizotypy," *International Journal of Transpersonal Studies* 38.2 (2019), 1–30.

Harris, William. *Ancient Literacy* (Harvard University Press, 1991).

Hartog, Paul. "The Impact of the Christological Controversies: Comparing the Ignatian Kerygma and Romans 1," in Verheyden et al., *Docetism in the Early Church*, 175–95.

Hartog, Pieter, and Jetta Jokiranta, "The Dead Sea Scrolls in Their Hellenistic Context," *Dead Sea Discoveries* 24.3 (2017), 339–55.

Head, P. M. "On the Christology of the Gospel of Peter," *Vigiliae Christianae* 46.3 (1992), 209–24.

Heilig, Christoph. *Hidden Criticism? The Methodology and Plausibility of the Search for a Counter-Imperial Subtext in Paul* (Fortress, 2017).

Heilig, Theresa, and Christoph Heilig. "Historical Methodology," in *God and the Faithfulness of Paul: A Critical Examination of the Pauline Theology of N. T. Wright* (ed. Christoph Heilig, J. Thomas Hewitt, and Michael F. Bird; Fortress, 2014), 115–50.

Hengel, Martin, with Daniel Bailey. "The Effective History of Isaiah 53 in the Pre-Christian Period," in Janowski and Stuhlmacher, *Suffering Servant*, 75–146.

Herron, Thomas. *Clement and the Early Church of Rome: On the Dating of Clement's First Epistle to the Corinthians* (Saint Paul Center for Biblical Theology, 1989; Emmaus Road, 2010).

———. "The Most Probable Date of the First Epistle of Clement to the Corinthians," *Studia Patristica* 21 (1989), 106–21.

Hezser, Catherine. *Jewish Literacy in Roman Palestine* (Mohr Siebeck, 2001).

———. "Outer Space in Ancient Jewish and Christian Literature," *Re-*

ligion and Outer Space (ed. Eric Michael Mazur and Sarah McFarland Taylor; Routledge, 2023), 9–24.

Hilton, Andy. *Anthropology and Mysticism in the Making of Initiation: A History of Discourse and Ideas for Today* (Brill, 2019)

———. "Christian Mysteries," in Hilton, *Anthropology and Mysticism*, 111–25.

Hinnells, John. *Zoroastrian and Parsi Studies: Selected Works of John R. Hinnells* (Routledge, 2017; orig. 2000).

Hodge, Caroline Johnson. *If Sons, Then Heirs: A Study of Kinship and Ethnicity in the Letters of Paul* (Oxford University Press, 2007).

Hogeterp, Albert. *Expectations of the End: A Comparative Traditio-Historical Study of Eschatological, Apocalyptic and Messianic Ideas in the Dead Sea Scrolls and the New Testament* (Brill, 2009).

Hoklotubbe, T. Christopher. "What is Docetism?," in *Re-Making the World: Christianity and Categories: Essays in Honor of Karen L. King* (ed. Taylor Petrey: Siebeck 2019), 49–71.

Holbrook, Frank. "Christ's Inauguration as King-Priest," *Journal of the Adventist Theological Society* 5.2 (1994), 136–52.

Holladay, Carl. *Acts: A Commentary* (Westminster John Knox Press, 2016).

Hollander, Harm. "The Words of Jesus: From Oral Traditions to Written Record in Paul and Q," *Novum Testamentum* 42.4 (2000), 340–57.

Honigman, Sylvie. "In Search of a New Paradigm: Judean Literature as a Crucible of Appropriations from Multiple Imperial and Native Temple Cultures in Hellenistic Times," *Journal for the Study of Judaism* 53.4–5 (2022), 489–523.

Hopper, Paul. "A Narrative Anomaly in Josephus: *Jewish Antiquities* xviii:63," in *Linguistics and Literary Studies: Interfaces, Encounters, Transfers* (ed. Monika Fludernik and Daniel Jacob; de Gruyter, 2014), 147–69.

Horsley, Richard. "Can Study of the Historical Jesus Escape its Typographical Captivity?," *Journal for the Study of the Historical Jesus* 19 (2021), 265–329.

Howard, George. "Was James an Apostle? A Reflection on a New Proposal for Gal. I 19," *Novum Testamentum* 19 (January 1977).

Hoyos, Dexter. *Hannibal's Dynasty: Power and Politics in the Western Mediterranean, 247–183 B.C.* (Routledge, 2005).

Huebenthal, Sandra. "Gospel of Mark," in Bond, *Reception of Jesus*, 41–72.

Hurtado, Larry. *One God, One Lord: Early Christian Devotion and Ancient Jewish Monotheism* (Fortress, 1988).

Jacob, René. *L'Évangile de Marc: L'Évangile de la Foi* (L'Harmattan, 2020).

Jacobi, Christine. *Jesusüberlieferung bei Paulus? Analogien zwischen den echten Paulusbriefen und den synoptischen Evangelien* (De Gruyter, 2015).

———. "Pauline Epistles," in Bond, *Reception of Jesus*, 3–38.

Jacobson, David. *Agrippa II: The Last of the Herods* (Routledge, 2019).

James, Rob. *The Spiral Gospel: Intratextuality in Luke's Narrative* (Clarke 2022).

Janowski, Bernd, and Peter Stuhlmacher (eds.). *The Suffering Servant: Isaiah 53 in Jewish and Christian Sources* (William B. Eerdmans, 2004).

Jaynes, E.T. *Probability Theory: The Logic of Science* (Cambridge University Press, 2003).

Jefford, Clayton. *Apostolic Fathers and the New Testament* (Baker Academic, 2006).

Jenks, Gregory. "What Did Paul Know about Jesus?" *The Fourth R* 12.1 (2000), 1–8.

Jense, Lionel. *Manufacturing Confucianism: Chinese Traditions and Universal Civilization* (Duke University Press, 1998).

Jenset, Gard, and Barbara McGillivray. *Quantitative Historical Linguistics: A Corpus Framework* (Oxford University Press, 2017).

Jewett, Robert. *Romans: A Commentary* (Fortress 2006).

Jipp, Joshua. *Divine Visitations and Hospitality to Strangers in Luke-Acts: An Interpretation of the Malta Episode in Acts 28:1-10* (Brill, 2013).

Jobes, Karen. *1 Peter*, 2nd ed. (Baker Academic, 2022).

Johnson, Marshall. *The Purpose of the Biblical Genealogies: With Special Reference to the Setting of the Genealogies of Jesus* (Wipf and Stock, 2002).

Jones, C.P. "The Historicity of the Neronian Persecution: A Response to Brent Shaw," *New Testament Studies* 63 (2016), 146–52.

Jones, Dhivan Thomas. "Did the Buddha Exist? Contemporary Scholarly Debate about the Historical Buddha," *A Blue Chasm* (14 July 2019) at tinyurl.com/yerx8u4m.

Joosten, Jan. "The Date and Provenance of the 'Gospel of Barnabas'," *Journal of Theological Studies* 61.1 (2010), 200–15.

Jordan, Andrew. *Jesus the Nazarene: The Talmud and the Founder of Christianity* (Resource Publications, 2023).

Joseph, Simon. *A Social History of Christian Origins: The Rejected Jesus* (Routledge, 2022).

Kanavou, Nikoletta. *Philostratros' Life of Apollonios of Tyana and its Literary Context* (C.H. Beck, 2018) at books.openedition.org/chbeck/1688.

Keith, Chris (ed.). *The Reception of Jesus in the First Three Centuries, Volume 3: From Celsus to the Catacombs* (T&T Clark, 2019).

Keith, Chris, Helen Bond, Christine Jacobi, and Jens Schröter (eds.). *The Reception of Jesus in the First Three Centuries*, 3 vols. (T&T Clark, 2019).

Kim, Jintae. "The Concept of Atonement in the Fourth Servant Song in the LXX," *Journal of Greco-Roman Christianity and Judaism* 8 (2011-2012),

21–33.

———. "Targum Isaiah 53 and the New Testament Concept of Atonement," *Journal of Greco-Roman Christianity and Judaism* 5 (2008), 81–98.

Kim, Sook-Young. *The Warrior Messiah in Scripture and Intertestamental Writings* (Cambridge Scholars Publishing 2010).

King, Fergus J. "Hit or Myth? Methodological Considerations in Comparing Dionysos with the Johannine Jesus," *Biblical Theology Bulletin* 51.2 (2021), 88–100.

King, Karen. "Reconsidering Docetism," in Crégheur et al., *Nag Hammadi a 70*, 17–30.

Kingsley, John. "A Bayesian Analysis of Early Śramaṇic Origin Stories," *LMU/LLS Theses and Dissertations* 1256 (2022).

Kline, Meredeth. "The Structure of the Book of Zechariah," *Evangelical Theological Society* 34.2 (1991), 179–93.

Kloppenborg, John. "On Dispensing with Q? Goodacre on the Relation of Luke to Matthew," *New Testament Studies* 49 (2003), 210–36.

Knohl, Israel. *The Messiah Before Jesus: The Suffering Servant of the Dead Sea Scrolls* (University of California Press, 2000).

Kochenash, Michael. "Better Call Paul 'Saul': Literary Models and a Lukan Innovation," *Journal of Biblical Literature* 138.2 (2019), 433–49.

Kok, Michael J. "Does Mark Narrate the Pauline Kerygma of 'Christ Crucified'? Challenging an Emerging Consensus on Mark as a Pauline Gospel," *Journal for the Study of the New Testament* 37.2 (2014), 139–60.

———. *The Gospel on the Margins: The Reception of Mark in the Second Century* (Fortress, 2015).

Kolmogorov, A.N. *Foundations of the Theory of Probability*, 2nd English ed. (tr. Nathan Morrison; Dover, 2018; orig. German 1933).

Konradt, Matthias. "Gospel of Matthew," in Bond, *Reception of Jesus*, 107–38.

Kotrosits, Maia (ed.). "Reflections on the Category Gnosticism" = *Forum: Foundations and Facts* 5.1 (2016).

Krenkel, Max. *Josephus und Lucas: Der schriftstellerische Einfluss des jüdischen Geschichtschreibers auf den Christlichen* (H. Haessel, 1894).

Kugler, Chris. *Paul and the Image of God* (Fortress, 2020).

Lambert, Derek, and Bart Ehrman, "Jesus vs Paul: The Origins of a Religious Schism in Early Christianity," *MythVision Podcast* (9 June 2023) at youtube.com/watch?v=hJBb-zsgX-s.

Lambert, Derek, and Robyn Faith Walsh, "Everything You Thought You Knew About The Gospels Is Wrong!" *Mythvision Podcast* (20 December 2021) at youtube.com/watch?v=PLKMcIz8Vd0.

Lancel, Serge. *Hannibal* (Wiley-Blackwell, 1999).

Lange, Armin, Emmanuel Tov, and Matthias Weigold (eds.). *The Dead Sea Scrolls In Context* (Brill, 2011).

Lapinkivi, Pirjo. *The Neo-Assyrian Myth of Ištar's Descent and Resurrection* (Eisenbrauns, 2010).

Lataster, Raphael. "Bayesian Reasoning: Criticising the 'Criteria of Authenticity' and Calling for a Review of Biblical Criticism," *Journal of Alternative Perspectives in the Social Sciences* 5.2 (2012), 271–93.

———. "Book Review: Richard Carrier: *On the Historicity of Jesus*," *Journal of Religious History* 38.4 (2014), 614–16.

———. "The Fourth Quest: A Critical Analysis of the Recent Literature on Jesus' (a)Historicity," *Literature & Aesthetics* 24.1 (June 2014), 1–28.

———. *Questioning the Historicity of Jesus: Why a Philosophical Analysis Elucidates the Historical Discourse* (Brill, 2019).

———. "Questioning the Plausibility of Jesus Ahistoricity Theories—A Brief Pseudo-Bayesian Metacritique of the Sources," *Intermountain West Journal of Religious Studies* 6.1 (2015), 63–96.

Lavan, Myles. "Epistemic Uncertainty, Subjective Probability, and Ancient History," *The Journal of Interdisciplinary History* 50.1 (2019), 91–111.

Lazenby, J.F. *Hannibal's War: A Military History of the Second Punic War* (University of Oklahoma Press, 1998).

Leeming, David (ed.). *The Oxford Companion to World Mythology* (Oxford University Press, 2005).

Lemardelé, Christophe. "The Hebrew word [NAZIR] in Greek: From the Septuagint to the Christian Authors," *Semitica et Classica* 8 (2015), 1–6.

Lemche, Niels Peter. "How Does One Date an Expression of Mental History? The Old Testament and Hellenism," in *Did Moses Speak Attic? Jewish Historiography and Scripture in the Hellenistic Period* (ed. Lester Grabbe; Sheffield Academic, 2001), 220–24.

———. "On the Problems of Reconstructing Pre-Hellenistic Israelite (Palestinian) History," *The Journal of Hebrew Scriptures* 3.3 (2001), 1–14.

Levison, John. "Terrestrial Paradise in the Greek Life of Adam and Eve," *Journal for the Study of the Pseudepigrapha* 28.1 (2018), 25–44.

Lewis, Charlton, and Charles Short. *A Latin Dictionary* (Oxford University Press, 1995; orig. 1897).

Liddell, Henry George, and Robert Scott. *A Greek-English Lexicon*, 9th ed. w. revised supplement (ed. Roderick McKenzie and Henry Stuart Jones; Oxford University Press, 1996).

Lietzmann, Hans. *Mass and Lord's Supper: A Study in the History of the Liturgy*, vol. 1 (Brill, 1979), 204–07.

Linjamaa, Paul. *The Ethics of The Tripartite Tractate (NHC I, 5): A Study of Determinism and Early Christian Philosophy of Ethics* (Brill, 2019).

List, Nicholas. "The Death of James the Just Revisited," *Journal of Early Christian Studies* 32 (2024), 17–44.

Litwa, M. David. "Deification and Defecation: Valentinus Fragment 3 and the Physiology of Jesus's Digestion," *Journal of Early Christian Studies* 31 (2023), 1–18.

———. *Found Christianities: Remaking the World of the Second Century CE* (T&T Clark, 2022).

———. *How the Gospels Became History: Jesus and Mediterranean Myths* (Yale University Press, 2019).

Livesey, Nina. *The Letters of Paul in their Roman Literary Context: Reassessing Apostolic Authorship* (Cambridge University Press, 2024).

Loftus, John (ed.). *The Christian Delusion: Why Faith Fails* (Prometheus, 2010).

Loftus, John, and Robert Price (eds.). *Varieties of Jesus Mythicism* (Hypatia Press, 2022).

Luhrmann, T.M. *How God Becomes Real: Kindling the Presence of Invisible Others* (Princeton University Press, 2020).

Lüke, Nathanael. *Über die narrative Kohärenz zwischen Apostelgeschichte und Paulusbriefen* (Narr Francke Attempto Verlag, 2019).

Lyons, William John. "The Hermeneutics of Fictional Black and Factual Red: The Markan Simon of Cyrene and the Quest for the Historical Jesus," *Journal for the Study of the Historical Jesus* 4 (June 2006), 139–54.

MacDonald, Dennis. *The Dionysian Gospel: The Fourth Gospel and Euripides* (Fortress, 2017).

———. *From the Earliest Gospel (Q+) to the Gospel of Mark: Solving the Synoptic Problem with Mimesis Criticism* (Fortress, 2019).

———. *The Gospels and Homer: Imitations of Greek Epic in Mark and Luke-Acts* (Rowman & Littlefield, 2014).

———. *Luke and the Politics of Homeric Imitation: Luke–Acts as Rival to the Aeneid* (Fortress, 2018).

———. *Luke and Vergil: Imitations of Classical Greek Literature* (Rowman & Littlefield, 2014).

———. *Mythologizing Jesus: From Jewish Teacher to Epic Hero* (Rowman & Littlefield, 2015).

———. "Response to Karl Olav Sandnes," in *New Studies in Textual Interplay* (ed. Craig Evans, B.J. Oropeza, and Paul T. Sloan; T&T Clark, 2020), 69–72.

———. *Synopses of Epic, Tragedy, and the Gospels* (Mimesis Press, 2022).

Mack, Burton. *A Myth of Innocence: Mark and Christian Origins* (Fortress, 1988).

Mackay, Cameron. "Zechariah in Relation to Ezekiel 40–48," *Evangelical*

Quarterly 40.4 (1968), 197–210.

Malchow, Bruce. "The Messenger of the Covenant in Mal 3:1," *Journal of Biblical Literature* 103.2 (1984), 252–55.

Marcovich, Miroslav. "The Epigram on Apollonius of Tyana," *Zeitschrift für Papyrologie und Epigraphik* 45 (1982), 263–65.

———. *Refutatio omnium haeresium* (De Gruyter, 1986).

Marina, Marko. "Povijesni Isus i miticizam: kritička analiza teorije Richarda Carriera," *Diacovensia* 30 (2022), 215–35.

Martin, Dale. *The Corinthian Body* (Yale University Press, 1999).

Mason, Steve. "Did the Author of Luke-Acts Know the Works of Josephus?" in *Jews and Christians in the Roman World: From Historical Method to Cases* (Brill, 2023), 445–88.

———. "Jewish Sources: Flavius Josephus," in Schröter and Jacobi, *Jesus Handbook*, kindle loc. 3922–4054.

———. "Josephus and Luke–Acts," in *Josephus and the New Testament* (Hendrickson Publishers, 1992), 185–229.

———. *Josephus, Judea, and Christian Origins* (Hendrickson, 2009).

Massey, Brandon. "The Quest for the Historical Jesus, 2000–2023," *Journal for the Study of the Historical Jesus* 21 (2023), 75–161.

McAdon, Brad. *Rhetorical Mimesis and the Mitigation of Early Christian Conflicts: Examining the Influence that Greco-Roman Mimesis May Have in the Composition of Matthew, Luke, and Acts* (Pickwick, 2018).

McCant, Jerry. "The Gospel of Peter: Docetism Reconsidered," *New Testament Studies* 30.2 (1984), 258–73.

McDowell, Gavin. "The Alternative Chronology: Dating the Events of the Wagenseil Version of Toledot Yeshu," in Barbu and Deutsch, *Toledot Yeshu in Context*, 59–80.

McGillivray, Barbara, Jon Wilson, and Tobias Blanke. "Towards a Quantitative Research Framework for Historical Disciplines," in *Proceedings of the Workshop on Computational Methods in the Humanities 2018* (ed. Michael Piotrowski; Université de Lausanne, 2018), 53–58.

McKellar, Danica. *Math Doesn't Suck: How to Survive Middle School Math Without Losing Your Mind or Breaking a Nail* (Penguin, 2008).

McVann, Mark. "Conjectures About a Guilty Bystander: The Sword Slashing in Mark 14:47," *Listening* 21.2 (1986), 124–37.

McVey, Kathleen. "A Fresh Look at the Letter of Mara bar Serapion to His Son," *Orientalia Christiana Analecta* 236 (1990), 257–72.

———. "Mara bar Serapion," in Keith, *Reception of Jesus*, 71–88.

Meeks, Wayne. *The Prophet King: Moses Traditions and the Johannine Christology* (Brill, 1967).

Meggitt, Justin. "'More Ingenious than Learned'? Examining the Quest for the Non-Historical Jesus," *New Testament Studies* 65.4 (2019), 443–60.

———. "Putting the Apocalyptic Jesus to the Sword: Why Were Jesus's disciples Armed?," *Journal for the Study of the New Testament* 45.4 (2023), 371–404.

———. "The Resurrection and Comparative Microhistory," in Crossley and Keith, *Next Quest*, 507–27.

Menken, Maarten. "The Secessionists of the Jonannine Epistles and Docetism," in Verheyden et al., *Docetism in the Early Church*, 125–42.

Mercer, Samuel. *The Pyramid Texts* (Longmans & Green, 1952).

Merz, Annette. "Response to the Essays in Part 2," in *John, Jesus, and History, Volume 3: Glimpses of Jesus through the Johannine Lens* (ed. Paul Anderson, Felix Just, and Tom Thatcher; SBL Press, 2016), 299–317.

Metcalfe, Brent Lee. "Apologetic and Critical Assumptions about Book of Mormon Historicity," *Dialogue: A Journal of Mormon Thought* 26.3 (1993), 153–184.

Mettinger, Tryggve. "The Dying and Rising God: The Peregrinations of a Mytheme," in *Ethnicity in Ancient Mesopotamia* (ed. W.H. van Soldt; Nederlands Instituut voor het Nabije Oosten, 2005), 198-210.

———. *Reports from a Scholar's Life: Select Papers on the Hebrew Bible* (ed. Andrew Knapp; Penn State University Press, 2015).

———. *The Riddle of Resurrection: "Dying and Rising Gods" in the Ancient Near East* (Eisenbrauns, 2013).

Metzger, Bruce. "Names for the Nameless in the New Testament: A Study in the Growth of Christian Tradition," *New Testament Studies: Philological, Versional, and Patristic* (Brill, 1980), 23–45.

Meynet, Roland. "La composition de l'évangile de Marc," *Gregorianum* 96.2 (2015), 231–52.

Milani, Milad. "Raphael Lataster: *Questioning the Historicity of Jesus*," *Journal of Religious History* 45.2 (2021), 354–55.

Miller, Richard. "Foreword." *Varieties of Jesus Mythicism* (ed. John Loftus and Robert Price; Hypatia Press, 2022).

———. "Mark's Empty Tomb and Other Translation Fables in Classical Antiquity," *Journal of Biblical Literature* 129 (2010).

———. *Resurrection and Reception in Early Christianity* (Routledge, 2014).

Milstead, Zachary. "Religion and Arguments from Silence," *European Journal for Philosophy of Religion* 10.3 (2018), 155–69.

Miner, Alan. "A Chronological Setting for the Epistles of Mormon to Moroni," *Journal of Book of Mormon Studies* 3.2 (1994), 94–113.

Mitchell, David. *Messiah ben Joseph* (Campbell Publishers, 2016).

———. "Rabbi Dosa and the Rabbis Differ: Messiah ben Joseph in the Babylonian Talmud," *The Review of Rabbinic Judaism* 8.4 (January

2005), 77–90.

Mittmann, Ulrike. "11QMelch im Spiegel der Weisheit," in Lange et al., *Dead Sea Scrolls In Context*, 413–35.

Mojsov, Bojana. *Osiris: Death and Afterlife of a God* (Blackwell, 2005).

Moore, Kevin. *Why Two Swords Were Enough: Israelite Tradition History Behind Luke 22:35–38* (University of Denver, 2009).

Mosbo, Thomas. *Luke the Composer: Exploring the Evangelist's Use of Matthew* (Fortress, 2017).

Moscicke, Hans. *Goat for Yahweh, Goat for Azazel: The Impact of Yom Kippur on the Gospels* (Fortress, 2023).

———. *The New Day of Atonement: A Matthean Typology* (Mohr Siebeck, 2020).

Moses, Robert. *Practices of Power: Revisiting the Principalities and Powers in the Pauline Letters* (Minneapolis: Fortress, 2014).

Muesse, Mark. *The Age of the Sages: The Axial Age in Asia and the Near East* (Fortress, 2013).

Müller, Mogens, and Heike Omerzu (eds.). *Gospel Interpretation and the Q-Hypothesis* (T&T Clark, 2018).

Munro, Winsome. "Interpolation in the Epistles: Weighing Probability," *New Testament Studies* 36.3 (1990), 431–43.

Murray, Evan, et al. "The Role of Psychotic Disorders in Religious History Considered," *Neuropsychiatry* 24.4 (2012), 410–26.

Myers, Elizabeth. *Intertextual Borrowing between 1 Peter and Hebrews: Probability of Literary Dependence and the Most Likely Direction of Borrowing* (Pistos Ktistes, 2020).

Nadeau, Nathan. "The First Pauline Chronologist? Probably Not: A Review Essay of Ryan Schellenberg's 'The First Pauline Chronologist' from a Bayesian Perspective," *Journal of Greco-Roman Christianity and Judaism* 16 (2020), 150–82.

———. "Greek Resurrection Beliefs and the Resurrection of Jesus in the Gospel of Luke: Contexts for Consideration," *McMaster Journal of Theology and Ministry* 22 (2020–2021), 120–67.

———. "The Philosophy of History and New Testament History: A Survey of the Former with Some Implications for the Latter," *Biblical Interpretation* 30 (2022), 374–97.

Nelligan, Thomas. *The Quest for Mark's Sources: An Exploration of the Case for Mark's Use of First Corinthians* (Pickwick, 2015).

Neusner, Jacob (ed.). *The Christian and Judaic Invention of History* (Oxford University 1990).

Newcombe, Suzanne, and Sarah Harvey (eds.). *Prophecy in the New Millennium: When Prophecies Persist* (Routledge, 2013).

Nickell, Joe. *Detecting Forgery: Forensic Investigation of Documents* (Rowman & Littlefield 1996).

Nieminen, Petteri, and Juuso Loikkanen, Esko Ryökäs, and Anne-Mari Mustonen, "Nature of Evidence in Religion and Natural Science," *Theology and Science* 18.3 (2020), 448–74.

Nodet, Etienne. *Le fils de dieu: procès de Jésus et évangiles* (Cerf, 2002).

Nongbri, Brent. *God's Library: The Archaeology of the Earliest Christian Manuscripts* (Yale University Press, 2018).

———. "Palaeography, Precision and Publicity: Further Thoughts on *P.Ryl.*iii.457 (P52)," *New Testament Studies* 66.4 (2020), 471–99.

———. "The Use and Abuse of P52: Papyrological Pitfalls in the Dating of the Fourth Gospel," *Harvard Theological Review* 98.1 (2005), 23–48.

Oaksford, Mike, Nick Chater, and Ulrike Hahn. "Human Reasoning and Argumentation: The Probabilistic Approach," in *Reasoning: Studies of Human Inference and Its Foundations* (ed. Jonathan Adler and Lance Rips; Cambridge University Press, 2008), 383–413.

O'Connor, J.P. "'Spiritual Blindness' in the Bartimaeus Pericope (Mark 10:46–52): Toward Decentering Ableist Readings," *Biblical Interpretation* 20 (2023), 1–19.

Oegema, Gerbern. *The Anointed and his People: Messianic Expectations from the Maccabees to Bar Kochba* (T&T Clark 1998).

Olson, Ken. "A Eusebian Reading of the Testimonium Flavianum," in *Eusebius of Caesarea: Tradition and Innovations* (ed. Aaron Johnson and Jeremy Schott: Harvard University Press, 2013), 97-114.

———. "Eusebius and the Testimonium Flavianum," *Catholic Biblical Quarterly* 61.2 (1999), 305-22.

———. "The Testimonium Flavianum, Eusebius, and Consensus," *Historical Jesus Research* (13 August 2013) at tinyurl.com/mr2uehpc.

Omerzu, Heike. "'My Power, Power, You Have Left Me': Christology in the Gospel of Peter," in *Connecting Gospels: Beyond the Canonical/Non-Canonical Divide* (ed. Francis Watson and Sarah Parkhouse; Oxford University Press, 2018), 163–88.

Orlinsky, Harry, and Norman Snaith. *Studies on the Second Part of the Book of Isaiah* (Brill, 1967).

Orlov, Andrei. *The Glory of the Invisible God: Two Powers in Heaven Traditions and Early Christology* (T&T Clark, 2019).

Osborne, Grant. *Romans* (InterVarsity, 2004).

Pagé, Anna June. "Deirdriu and Heroic Biography," *Studia Celtica Fennica* 15 (2018), 102–19.

Page, Sydney. "The Suffering Servant between the Testaments," *New Testament Studies* 31.4 (1985), 481–497.

Patmore, Hector, and Josef Lössl (eds.), *Demons in Early Judaism and Christianity: Characters and Characteristics* (Brill, 2022).

Patrick, James. "Matthew's Pesher Gospel Structured around Ten Messianic Citations of Isaiah," *Journal of Theological Studies* 61.1 (2010), 43–81.

Pearce, Jonathan M.S. *The Resurrection: A Critical Examination of the Easter Story* (Onus, 2021).

Pearson, Birger. "Mystery and Secrecy in Paul," in *Mystery and Secrecy in the Nag Hammadi Collection and Other Ancient Literature: Ideas and Practices (Studies for Einar Thomassen at Sixty)* (ed. Christian Bull, Liv Lied, and John Turner; Brill, 2011), 287–302.

Peeler, Amy. *You Are My Son: The Family of God in the Epistle to the Hebrews* (T&T Clark 2014).

Penner, Ken. "The Tree of Life in Enochic Literature," in *The Tree of Life* (ed. Douglas Estes; Leiden: Brill, 2020), 166–82.

Peppard, Michael. "Adopted and Begotten Sons of God: Paul and John on Divine Sonship," *The Catholic Biblical Quarterly* 73.1 (January 2011), 92-110.

Persuitte, David. *Joseph Smith and the Origins of The Book of Mormon*, 2d ed. (McFarland, 2000).

Pervo, Richard. *Dating Acts: Between the Evangelists and the Apologists* (Polebridge, 2006).

Peterson, Brian Neil. *John's Use of Ezekiel: Understanding the Unique Perspective of the Fourth Gospel* (Fortress, 2015).

Petterson, Anthony Robert. *Behold Your King: The Hope For the House of David in the Book of Zechariah* (T&T Clark, 2009).

Petterson, Christina. "*On the Historicity of Jesus*," *Relegere* 5.2 (2015), 253–58.

Pfiffig, A.J. "Eine Nennung Hannibals," *Studi Etruschi* 35 (1967), 659–63.

Poirier, John, and Jeffrey Peterson (eds.). *Marcan Priority Without Q: Explorations in the Farrer Hypothesis* (T&T Clark, 2015).

Porter, Stanley, and Hughson Ong, "Memory, Orality, and the Fourth Gospel," *Journal for the Study of the Historical Jesus* 12.1–2 (2014), 143–64.

Portier-Young, Anathea. *Apocalypse against Empire: Theologies of Resistance in Early Judaism* (Eerdmans, 2014).

Prchlík, Ivan. "Tacitus's Knowledge of the Origins of Christianity," *Acta Universitatis Carolinae: Philologica* (2017), 95–110.

Prevas, John. *Hannibal Crosses the Alps: The Invasion of Italy and the Second Punic War* (Da Capo, 2001).

Proctor, Travis. *Demonic Bodies and the Dark Ecologies of Early Christian Culture* (Oxford University Press, 2022).

Puech, Émile. "Fragments d'un apocryphe de Levi et le personnage christologique. 4QTestLevi$^{c–d(?)}$ et 4QAJa," in *The Madrid Qumran Congress* (ed.

Julio Trebolle Barrera and Luis Vegas Montaner; Brill, 1992), 449–501.

Punt, Jeremy. "He Is Heavy...He's My Brother: Unravelling Fraternity in Paul (Galatians)," *Neotestamentica* 46.1 (2012), 153–171.

Puskas, Charles, and C. Michael Robbins. *The Conceptual Worlds of the Fourth Gospel* (Cascade, 2021).

Reeves, John. *Trajectories in Near Eastern Apocalyptic: A Postrabbinic Jewish Apocalypse Reader* (Society of Biblical Literature, 2005).

Rendell, Kenneth. *Forging History: The Detection of Fake Letters and Documents* (University of Oklahoma Press, 1994).

Riley, Gregory. "Second Treatise of the Great Seth," in Pearson (ed.), *Nag Hammadi Codex VII*, 129–99.

Robertson, Donald, "Was Socrates a Real Person?" (29 April 2018) at tinyurl.com/yrrpfh38.

Rogan, Wil. "Review of Peterson, Brian Neil. *John's Use of Ezekiel: Understanding the Unique Perspective of the Fourth Gospel*," *Review of Biblical Literature* (December 2017) at sblcentral.org/home/bookDetails/11199.

Rosenberg, Roy. "The Slain Messiah in the Old Testament," *Zeitschrift für die alttestamentliche Wissenschaft* 99 (1987), 259–61.

Roth, Dieter. *The Text of Marcion's Gospel* (Brill, 2015).

Rothman, Joel. *The Cosmic Journey in the Book of Revelation: Apocalyptic Cosmology and the Experience of Story-Space* (T&T Clark, 2023).

Rovang, Paul. *The Archetype of the Dying and Rising God in World Mythology* (Lexington, 2023).

Rowland, Christopher. *'By an Immediate Revelation': Studies in Apocalypticism, Its Origins and Effects* (Mohr Siebeck, 2022).

Rüggemeier, Jan, and Elizabeth Shively (eds.). *Cognitive Linguistics and New Testament Narrative: Investigating Methodology through Characterization*, special issue of *Biblical Interpretation* 29.4–5 (2021).

Rutgers, Leonard Victor. "Roman Policy towards the Jews: Expulsions from the City of Rome during the First Century C.E.," *Classical Antiquity* 13.1 (1994), 56–74.

Sadananda, Daniel. *The Johannine Exegesis of God* (de Gruyter 2004).

Sandnes, Karl Olav. "Mimesis and Criticism," in *New Studies in Textual Interplay* (ed. Craig Evans, B.J. Oropeza, and Paul T. Sloan; T&T Clark, 2020), 55–68.

Schäfer, Peter. *Two Gods in Heaven: Jewish Concepts of God in Antiquity* (Princeton University Press, 2020).

Schattner-Rieser, Ursula. "Levi in the Third Sky: On the 'Ascent to Heaven' Legends within Their Near Eastern Context and J.T. Milik's Unpublished Version of the Aramaic Levi Document," in Lange et al., *Scrolls In Context*, 801–19.

Schellenberg, Ryan. "τὸ ἐν λόγῳ ἰδιωτικὸν τοῦ Ἀποστόλου: Revisiting Patristic Testimony on Paul's Rhetorical Education," *Novum Testamentum* 54.4 (2012), 354–68.

Schiavone, Aldo. *Spartacus* (tr. Jeremy Carden; Harvard University Press, 2013).

Schmidt, T.C. *Josephus and Jesus: New Evidence for the One Called Christ* (Oxford University Press, 2025).

Schoedel, William. *Ignatius of Antioch: A Commentary on the Letters of Ignatius of Antioch* (Fortress, 1985).

Schreckenberg, Heinz. "Flavius Josephus und die lukanischen Schriften," in *Wort in der Zeit: Neutestamentliche Studien* (ed. Karl Rengstorf and Wilfrid Haubeck; Brill, 1980), 179-209.

Schreiner, Thomas. *Romans* (Baker, 2018).

Schröter, Jens, and Christine Jabobi (eds.). *The Jesus Handbook* (Eerdmans, 2022; orig. German edition: Mohr Siebeck, 2017).

———. *The Reception of Jesus in the First Three Centuries, Volume 2: From Thomas to Tertullian* (T&T Clark, 2019).

Scott, James. *Adoption as Sons of God: An Exegetical Investigation into the Background of υἱοθεσία in the Pauline Corpus* (Mohr Siebeck, 1992).

Segal, Alan. "Iranian Views of the Afterlife and Ascent to the Heavens," *Life after Death: A History of the Afterlife in Western Religion* (Doubleday, 2004), 173–203.

———. *Two Powers in Heaven: Early Rabbinic Reports about Christianity and Gnosticism* (Brill, 1977).

Shaw, Brent. "The Myth of the Neronian Persecution," *Journal of Roman Studies* 105 (2015), 73–100.

———. "Response to Christopher Jones: The Historicity of the Neronian Persecution," *New Testament Studies* 64 (2018), 231–42.

———. *Spartacus and the Slave Wars: A Brief History with Documents* (St. Martin's, 2001).

Shellard, Barbara. *New Light on Luke: Its Purpose, Sources, and Literary Context* (Sheffield Academic, 2002).

Siegel, Michal Bar-Asher. *Early Christian Monastic Literature and the Babylonian Talmud* (Cambridge University Press, 2013).

Sivertsev, Alexei. *Judaism and Imperial Ideology in Late Antiquity* (Cambridge University Press, 2011).

Smith, David Oliver. *Matthew, Mark, Luke, and Paul: The Influence of the Epistles on the Synoptic Gospels* (Resource, 2011).

Smith, Dennis, and Joseph Tyson (eds.). *Acts and Christian Beginnings: The Acts Seminar Report* (Polebridge, 2013).

Smith, Jonathan Z. *Drudgery Divine* (University of Chicago Press, 1994).

Smith, Mark. "Osiris and the Deceased," in *UCLA Encyclopedia of Egyptology* (ed. Jacco Dieleman and Willeke Wendrich; University of California, 2020; article, 2008) at escholarship.org/uc/item/29r70244.

———. "Resurrection and the Body in Graeco-Roman Egypt," *Deuterocanonical and Cognate Literature Yearbook* (2009), 27–42.

———. *The Ugaritic Baal Cycle* (Brill, 1994).

Smyth, Herbert Weir. *A Greek Grammar for Colleges*, revised ed. (Harvard University Press, 1984).

Soal, Alexander, and Desmond Henry, "The Reversal of Babel: Questioning the Early Church's Understanding of the Gift of the Holy Spirit in Acts as a Reversal of the Curse of Babel," *Verbum et Ecclesia* 39.1 (2018), 1–10.

Sorenson, John. "Mormon's Sources," *Journal of the Book of Mormon and Other Restoration Scripture* 20.2 (2011), 2–15.

Staples, Jason. *The Idea of Israel in Second Temple Judaism: A New Theory of People, Exile, and Israelite Identity* (Cambridge University Press, 2021).

Starcky, Jean. "Les quatres étapes du messianisme à Qumrân," *Revue Biblique* 70 (1963), 492.

Staszkow, Ronald. *The Mathematical Palette*, 3rd ed. (Brooks/Cole, 2004).

Stecher, Carl, Craig Blomberg, Richard Carrier, and Peter Williams. *Resurrection: Faith or Fact? A Scholars' Debate Between a Skeptic and a Christian* (Pitchstone, 2019).

Sterling, Gregory. *Historiography and Self-Definition: Josephos, Luke–Acts and Apologetic Historiography* (Brill, 1992).

Stevens, Anne, and Molly O'Donnell (eds). *The Microgenre: A Quick Look at Small Culture* (Bloomsbury Academic, 2020).

Stibbe, Mark. *John as Storyteller: Narrative Criticism and the Fourth Gospel* (Cambridge University Press, 1992).

Streett, Daniel. *They Went Out From Us: The Identity of the Opponents in First John* (De Gruyter, 2011).

Stuhlmueller, Carroll. *Rebuilding with Hope: A Commentary on the Books of Haggai and Zechariah* (Eerdmans, 1988).

Sundermann, Werner. "Zoroastrian Motifs in Non-Zoroastrian Traditions," *Journal of the Royal Asiatic Society* 18.2 (2008), 155–65.

Swanson, Reuben. *New Testament Greek Manuscripts: Variant Readings Arranged in Horizontal Lines against Codex Vaticanus: 1 Corinthians* (Sheffield Academic Press, 2003).

Tabor, James. *Paul and Jesus: How the Apostle Transformed Christianity* (Simon & Schuster, 2012).

Taussig, Hal. "Christianity Seminar: A Report on the 2014 Fall Meeting," *The Fourth R* 28.2 (2015), 21–24.

Taylor, Joan. "Pontius Pilate and the Imperial Cult in Roman Judaea," *New Testament Studies* 52.4 (2006), 555–82.

Thatcher, Tom. "Johannine Epistles," in Bond, *Reception of Jesus*, 297–307.

———. *Why John Wrote a Gospel: Jesus—Memory—History* (Westminster John Knox, 2006).

Theophilos, Michael. "The Roman Connection: Paul and Mark," in *Paul and Mark, Comparative Essays, Part I: Two Authors at the Beginnings of Christianity* (ed. Oda Wischmeyer, David Sim, and Ian Elmer; De Gruyter, 2014), 45–71.

Thomassen, Einar. "There Is No Such Thing as Gnosticism: But What Have We Got Instead?" in Crégheur et al., *Nag Hammadi a 70*, 3–16.

Thompson, Stephen. *Ancient Egypt: Facts and Fiction* (Santa Barbara: ABC-CLIO, 2020).

Thompson, Thomas, and Philippe Wajdenbaum (eds.), *The Bible and Hellenism: Greek Influence on Jewish and Early Christian Literature* (Acumen Publishing, 2014).

Titelbaum, Michael. *Fundamentals of Bayesian Epistemology 1: Introducing Credences* (Oxford University Press, 2022).

Trebilco, Paul. *Self-designations and Group Identity in the New Testament* (Cambridge University Press, 2012).

Trendall, A.D. *The Red-Figured Vases of Lucania, Campania and Sicily* (Clarendon Press, 1967).

Trobisch, David. *On the Origin of Christian Scripture: The Evolution of the New Testament Canon in the Second Century* (Fortress, 2023).

Trudinger, L. Paul. "[*Heteron de tōn apostolōn ouk eidon, ei mē iakōbon*]: A Note on Galatians I 19," *Novum Testamentum* 17 (July 1975), 200–02.

Tucker, Aviezer. *Historiographic Reasoning* (Cambridge University Press, 2025).

———. *Our Knowledge of the Past: A Philosophy of Historiography* (Cambridge University Press, 2004).

———. "The Reverend Bayes v. Jesus Christ," *History and Theory* 55 (2016), 129–40.

Ulrich, Dean. "How Early Judaism Read Daniel 9:24-27," *Old Testament Essays* 27.3 (January 2014), 1062–83.

Uytanlet, Samson. *Luke-Acts and Jewish Historiography: A Study on the Theology, Literature, and Ideology of Luke-Acts* (Mohr Siebeck, 2014).

Van de Water, Rick. "Michael or Yhwh? Toward Identifying Melchizedek in 11Q13," *Journal for the Study of the Pseudepigrapha* 16.1 (2006), 75–86.

Van der Kam, James. *From Joshua to Caiaphas: High Priests after the Exile* (Fortress, 2004).

Van der Lans, Birgit. "The Politics of Exclusion: Expulsions of Jews and

Others from Rome," in *People under Power: Early Jewish and Christian Responses to the Roman Empire* (ed. M. Labahn and O. Lehtipuu; Amsterdam University Press, 2015), 33–77.

Van der Lans, Birgit, and Jan Bremmer. "Tacitus and the Persecution of the Christians: An Invention of Tradition?" *Eirene: Studia graeca et latina* 53.1–2 (2017), 299–321.

Van de Weghe, Luuk, and Jason Wilson. "Why Name Popularity is a Good Test of Historicity: A Goodness-of-Fit Test Analysis on Names in the Gospels and Acts," *Journal for the Study of the Historical Jesus* 22 (2024), 184–214.

Van Henten, Jan Willem. "Testimonium Flavianum," in Bond, *Reception of Jesus*, 365–70.

Van Ruiten, Jacobus. "Garden of Eden—Paradise," in *The Eerdmans Dictionary of Early Judaism* (ed. John Collins and Daniel Harlow; Eerdmans, 2010), 658–61.

Van Voorst, Robert. *Jesus Outside the New Testament: An Introduction to the Ancient Evidence* (Eerdmans, 2000).

Vearncombe, Erin, Brandon Scott, and Hal Taussig. *After Jesus Before Christianity: A Historical Exploration of the First Two Centuries of Jesus Movements* (HarperOne, 2021).

Verheyden, Joseph, Reimund Bieringer, Jens Schröter, and Ines Jäger (eds.). *Docetism in the Early Church: The Quest for an Elusive Phenomenon* (Mohr Siebeck, 2018).

Verman, Mark. "Jesus as 'Rabbi/Rabbouni' and Mark's Use of Aramaic as Messianic Code Language," *Journal for the Study of the Historical Jesus* 21 (2023): pp. 1–34.

Vermes, Geza, with Timothy Lim. "The Oxford Forum for Qumran Research Seminar on the Rule of War from Cave 4 (4Q285)," *Journal of Jewish Studies* 43 (1992), 90–92.

Vette, Nathanael. *Writing with Scripture: Scripturalized Narrative in the Gospel of Mark* (T&T Clark, 2022).

Vinzent, Markus. *Resetting the Origins of Christianity: A New Theory of Sources and Beginnings* (Cambridge University Press, 2023).

Viviano, Benedict. "The High Priest's Servant's Ear: Mark 14:47," *Revue Biblique* 96.1 (1989), 71–80.

Von Wahlde, Urban. *Gnosticism, Docetism, and the Judaisms of the First Century: The Search for the Wider Context of the Johannine Literature and Why It Matters* (T&T Clark, 2015).

———. *The Johannine Commandments: 1 John and the Struggle for the Johannine Tradition* (Paulist, 1990).

Wajdenbaum, Philippe. *Argonauts of the Desert: Structural Analysis of the He-*

brew Bible (Routledge, 2011).

Wallach, Efraim. "Bayesian Representation of a Prolonged Archaeological Debate," *Synthese* 195.1 (2018), 401–31.

Walsh, Matthew. *Angels Associated with Israel in the Dead Sea Scrolls: Angelology and Sectarian Identity at Qumran* (Mohr Siebeck, 2019).

Walsh, Robyn Faith. "*Argumentum ad Lunam*: Pauline Discourse, 'Double Death', and Competition on the Moon," *Harvard Theological Review* 117.4 (2024), 720-743.

———. *The Origins of Early Christian Literature: Contextualizing the New Testament within Greco-Roman Literary Culture* (Cambridge University Press, 2021).

Walters, J.C. "Paul, Adoption, and Inheritance," in *Paul in the Greco-Roman World. A Handbook* (ed. J. P. Sampley; T&T Clark, 2003), 42–76.

Watson, Francis. "'I received from the Lord…': Paul, Jesus, and the Last Supper," in *Jesus and Paul Reconnected: Fresh Pathways into an Old Debate* (ed. Todd Still; Eerdmans, 2007), 103–34.

———. "Pauline Reception and the Problem of Docetism," in Verheyden et al., *Docetism*, 51–66.

Watts, Joel. *Jesus as Divine Suicide: The Death of the Messiah in Galatians* (Pickwick, 2019).

Whealey, Alice. "The Testimonium Flavianum in Syriac and Arabic," *New Testament Studies* 54 (2008), 573-90.

Whitsett, Christopher. "Son of God, Seed of David: Paul's Messianic Exegesis in Romans 2:3-4," *Journal of Biblical Literature* 119.4 (Winter 2000), 661–81.

Wilhite, David. "Was Marcion a Docetist? The Body of Evidence vs. Tertullian's Argument," *Vigiliae Christianae* 71.1 (2017), 1–36.

Willard, Aiyana, and Ara Norenzayan. "'Spiritual but not religious': Cognition, Schizotypy, and Conversion in Alternative Beliefs," *Cognition* 165 (2017), 137–46.

Williams, Margaret. *Early Classical Authors on Jesus* (T&T Clark, 2022).

Wischmeyer, Oda, and David Sim (eds.), *Paul and Mark: Two Authors at the Beginnings of Christianity* (De Gruyter, 2014).

Wise, Michael. *The First Messiah: Investigating the Savior Before Jesus* (Harper- One, 1999).

Wlodarski, Rafael, and Eiluned Pearce. "The God Allusion: Individual Variation in Agency Detection, Mentalizing and Schizotypy and Their Association with Religious Beliefs and Behaviors," *Human Nature* 27 (2016), 160–72.

Wright, Benjamin. "Were the Jews of Qumran Hellenistic Jews?" *Dead Sea Discoveries* 24.3 (2017), 356–77.

Yamauchi, Edwin. "Religions: Persia," in *The International Standard Bible Encyclopedia*, vol. 4 (ed. Geoffrey Bromiley; Eerdmans, 1979).

Yu, Hongbing. "Confucius the Untouchable: On the Semiotics of Historization," *Chinese Semiotic Studies* 18.3 (2022), 391–412.

Zeichmann, Christopher. "Herodian Kings and Their Soldiers in the Acts of the Apostles: A Response to Craig Keener," *Journal of Greco-Roman Christianity and Judaism* 11 (2015), 178–90.

Zumwalt, Rosemary. *American Folklore Scholarship: A Dialogue of Dissent* (Indiana University Press, 1988).

Xeravits, Géza. *King, Priest, Prophet: Positive Eschatological Protagonists of the Qumran Library* (Brill, 2003).

Scripture Index

Subject Index

About the Author

Richard Carrier, PhD, is a world-renowned author and speaker. As a professional historian, published philosopher, and prominent defender of the American freethought movement, he has appeared across the United States, Canada, the United Kingdom, and Puerto Rico, and on American television and Canadian and London radio, defending sound historical methods and the ethical worldview of secular naturalism. With a doctorate from Columbia University in ancient history, he specializes in the intellectual history of Greece and Rome, particularly ancient philosophy, religion, and science, with an emphasis on the origins of Christianity and the use and progress of science under the Roman Empire. He is also a published expert in the modern philosophy of naturalism as a worldview. He is the author of *On the Historicity of Jesus, Proving History*, *Sense and Goodness without God*, *The Scientist in the Early Roman Empire*, *Science Education in the Early Roman Empire*, *Not the Impossible Faith*, *Why I Am Not a Christian*, *Jesus from Outer Space*, and *Hitler Homer Bible Christ*. To learn more about Dr. Carrier and his work, please visit richardcarrier.info.